NEW GUIDE TO
DISTANCE RUNNING

NEW GUIDE TO

DISTANCE RUNNING

by the editors of

Runner's World

Library of Congress Cataloging in Publication Data

New guide to distance running.

   1. Running--Addresses, essays, lectures.
I. Runner's world.
GV1062.N48   796.4'26   78-55786
ISBN 0-89037-133-4

©1978 by
World Publications
Mountain View, CA 94042

CONTENTS

Preface

Running has grown vigorously in recent years; that is the whole reason for this book. There is a new element of interest in running that past volumes on the subject have not taken into account. This book is concerned with not merely the routine of exercise, but also with the *possibilities* of exercise. Included is an entire section on the effects of running on the mind, as well as some of the most comprehensive articles yet published on mountain running, the aging process, vegetarianism, and the future of running. There are new interpretations of such familiar subjects as Arthur Lydiard's training program, fasting, and the Zen of running.

It's always difficult to have ideas of substance accepted on a popular and critical level by society. Social critic H. L. Mencken pointed out this difficulty back in 1920: "Obviously, it is out of reason to look for any hospitality to ideas in a class so extravagantly fearful of even the most palpably absurd of them."

Yet running has broken through the barrier—via Kenneth Cooper's *Aerobics, Runner's World*, and others. The idea that running has considerable untapped potential has been successfully spread, not only on an individual basis, but within society as well. For this reason, the book ends with a section entitled "The Possibilities."

Running isn't the sort of idea that catches on and then fades, like hula hoops or Pet Rocks. The distinction is between a mere idea and a possibility, between a fad and a contribution. Like running, this book doesn't offer a traditional beginning and end. It is rather a presentation of ideas.

The articles cover the spectrum of running. Some are from the original *Guide to Distance Running*; others are from *Runner's World*; many are published here for the first time. The intention in compiling this book is to present the latest information on a variety of topics. The book is for the liberated runner: the runner who goes to his run each day, not out of a sense of obligation, but with hope for discovery. We believe this book will further help you discover running, and through running, discover your own possibilities.

Jim Lilliefors

Foreword

With the December 1977 issue of *Runner's World,* I closed out the longest, hardest, most productive, and most satisfying chapter of my working life so far. I stepped aside as editor of the magazine after sitting in that position through eight years and seventy-eight issues.

Now that that period is over, I can see it better than when I lived through it. It is now a finished whole—with a start, a middle, and an end—not separate days coming so fast that I can't see far ahead or back. Now I can talk about what that period meant to me, to *Runner's World,* and, most of all, to running.

I saw in late 1977 that I needed a change, and there was only one I could make: back to being the runner and writer I'd been when I took the job of editor in late 1969. But I couldn't return all the way, because running wasn't the same as it had been then—and neither was I.

I was just getting started as a writer when Bob Anderson hired me as his editor; I'd just published my first book. Bob's magazine was starting as a professional journal; he was moving it from Kansas to California and changing its name from *Distance Running News.* And both the running-as-exercise and road racing movements were just gathering momentum, the sport was filling with new faces and new ideas. Hardly anyone knew the names of Frank Shorter and Lasse Viren then, let alone Alberto Juantorena and Tatyana Kazankina. Now, Shorter has two Olympic marathon medals; Viren has won four times in the Games; and Juantorena and Kazankina twice each.

In 1969, there were fewer than forty marathons in the United States, and probably fewer than 2,000 marathoners. Boston was already big, but it had less than half as many runners as now—and this was without entry limits. Without entry limits, the race would be overrun now, with 200 races now producing 20,000 marathoners a year.

Women couldn't officially run long-distance races at that time. A few of them tried anyway, but they weren't too successful at it. No U.S. woman had broken 3:10 for a marathon when the decade began. Now, women are welcome to compete. Women marathoners now total about 1,000, and the U.S. record is under 2:38. The record women's marathon time from the early 1970s wouldn't even make the top 100 today.

As the sixties became the seventies, older runners were just beginning to realize that they too could run hard and fast. They began to approach Masters running from two directions: fitness joggers graduated to running and racing, and longtime runner/racers avoided retiring. Now older runners are not merely "good for their age." They're good for *any* age, as Jack Foster showed when he ran a 2:11 marathon at age forty-one, and Miki Gorman proved with her 2:39 at the same age. While older runners improved, the young, too, became involved. Kids in their teens ran as well in the 1970s as the Olympians of the fifties had.

Back in 1970, no one except the doctors themselves had heard much about exercise physiology and podiatry. Now, these specialists are accepted—even revered—members of the team that tests and treats runners.

Things have changed a lot in a rather short time—more in the last eight years than in any other similar period. Long-distance runners were formerly the stepchildren of track and field. Their situation was much the same as race walkers today. When distance runners weren't being viewed as inferior creatures who were a little weird, they were ignored. Road runners made do with shoestring budgets and slipshod organization. Races were ragtag collections of characters. As often as not the course distances and finish times were so far off that runners didn't trust them even when they were accurate.

Now, road racing is outgrowing track. Top runners choose road runs ahead of track meets, since road races offer more money and attention. Lower level runners race on the roads, because this is the place they're invited to run. Corporations sponsor events, computers score them, and runners complain loud and long if arrangements aren't just right. They've become a little spoiled by their good fortune.

At the turn of the decade, long-distance running was a combination of things: a cult activity, and underground movement, and part of the counterculture. It moved with the same stream that carried the Beatles, Bob Dylan, and the hell-no-we-won't-go, tune-in-turn-on-drop-out, get-back-to-nature, and flowers-in-your-hair. Running then was a rejection of conformity. People who conformed looked down their noses at scruffy runners just as they did scruffy hippies. Running was a badge of individualism that runners wore proudly.

Now, running has moved into the mainstream, just as stylishly long hair has reached the executives, and Dylan and the Beatles are now sung in Las Vegas and played on Muzak. You can't open a magazine or turn on the television without seeing running in the columns and ads. You can't go into the supermarket without seeing running warm-ups on the legs of shoppers and running shoes on the feet of their children. Running is "in," and the running look even more so.

Runner's World has done much to generate and accelerate these changes. Not only has the magazine reported this sudden, dramatic trail of events; it has caused some and made others happen faster than they otherwise would have. It has been a catalytic force for the sport at a time when it needed it most. I can say without exaggerating that *Runner's World* has been a major mover in several directions: the growth of the marathon; the acceptance of women in long-distance running and their interest in it; age-group competition for both the young and old; preventive medical advice to make the sport safer; and the popularity of fun-running.

As I was living through all these changes one month at a time, I hardly noticed them. But looking back now, over a period of nearly a hundred months, I see the differences clearly. The clearest evidence of that change stands out when I compare two books. The first is the original *Guide to Distance Running*. Bob Anderson and I put it together near the start of my career with the magazine, and it was the company's first full-sized book. It reflected the state of running knowledge through 1970, and showed how far we'd come as runners and as a publication by then. This *New Guide* shows how much further we've progressed in the years since. Because the years between the first two guides mark the boundaries of my stay on the magazine, I'll always think of this book as a history of all that happened in running during my stay as editor.

Joe Henderson

PART ONE

BEGINNING

1

Guidelines for Beginners

by Jim Lilliefors

Running is such an individualized sport that rules are almost irrelevant. Advice is helpful, but often only superficially. Common sense experimentation is generally the best approach.

- *Clothing:* Run in what's most comfortable.
- *Shoes: Runner's World* annually ranks the top shoes, but individual fits differ. Thus, it is advisable to try on several of the top-rated brands before making a decision.
- *Medical checkups:* In the past, it has always been advised that anyone about to embark on an exercise program first get a full checkup from his doctor. This is still a good idea, but if a person is in good shape and starts cautiously, it may not be essential. As Joe Henderson wrote in his book *Jog, Run, Race* (World Publications, 1977), "Don't think about it any longer. Do it. Don't check with your doctor to see if it's okay. By the time you do, it may be too late."
- *Starting:* Many start too quickly and later lose interest. It's best to begin gradually. Find what feels most comfortable. At first, it may be advisable to mix running with walking.

Unfortunately, many more people buy expensive running shoes each year than wear them out on the roads. Therefore, more important than guidelines for clothing and shoes is advice that may help a runner stick with the sport. Stereotypically, running has been viewed as an activity to be endured. More recently, though, it has been promoted as an enjoyable activity. This should be the most important criterion: "Is it enjoyable?" Are you running only because it feels good afterward, or because the activity itself is enjoyable?

The following ten pointers will help all runners—particularly beginners—in continuing with the sport.

1. *Slow down:* Perhaps slowing down one's thoughts is more important than slowing down one's pace. If thoughts are racing too

fast while running, much is missed. Take time to notice the trees, the grass, and the scenery around you.

2. *Don't force yourself:* If a run isn't enjoyable, don't force yourself beyond what is comfortable. This will quickly lead to a weariness with running.

3. *Test:* For building confidence, "test" yourself—whether in a race or just an extra fast or long training run. This should take place naturally, and only when the runner feels the inclination.

4. *Vary:* Vary pace, course, terrain, and thoughts, so that running regularly offers unique surprises.

5. *Use it:* Take advantage of the antidepressant qualities of running. Its benefits are free and simple.

6. *Understand it:* Running has a more profound meaning if the runner considers why he is doing it, beyond the mere physical benefits.

7. *Set reasonable goals:* Goals that are too strict may induce disinterest; keep your goals flexible and you will progress.

8. *Bestow importance:* If you accept running as important, it will mean more than if it is viewed as a novelty that others ridicule.

9. *Tabulate:* Keep track of what running has done for you, perhaps in the form of a journal. Record how it has improved your health, lowered your weight, and improved your well-being.

10. *Run for life:* Accept running on a long-term basis, and run to enjoy. If you accept it as a partnership, not an annoyance, you'll enjoy getting to know it.

2

The Basics of Jogging

by George Sheehan, M.D.

Our fancy often turns to dreams of past glories, to those years when our bodies did our will. The morning air, the bright sun, the green trees recall days when only darkness could end our play. We were giants—if not in strength, at least in endurance. We knew what it was like to be a good animal. And we wonder if we could ever be that way again.

The answer, of course, is yes. We can walk or jog or run our way back to those days, those joys, that level of fitness. All we need to know is the fitness equation, the answers to the questions: How fast? How far? How often?

HOW FAST?

Few people know how fast to train. Most assume they must punish themselves to become fit. They think that becoming an athlete is hard work. It just isn't so. Fitness must be fun. The rule is "train, don't strain." So the pace for fitness should be comfortable and enjoyable. Effort—not speed—should be the measure; and your body should tell you your proper pace, not the stopwatch.

I use the word *pace* deliberately. It is a better word than *speed*. Speed has to do with numbers, statistics, minutes-per-mile. Pace has to do with feelings and is not a matter of precise mathematics. It has to do with adjectives like *easy, rash, breathless,* and *headlong.* But the adjective we are looking for is *comfortable,* and we find it by asking our bodies.

This seemingly unscientific idea has a solid scientific basis in the theory of perceived exertion. Proposed by Gunnar Borg in 1960, it states that the effort perceived by the body is almost identical to that recorded by a machine. Borg discovered that body perception is, in fact, superior to any single physiological determination.

The Borg scale starts at 6 (very, very light) and ends at 20 (very, very hard). Adding a zero to the rating gives the usual pulse rate for that level of activity. The walker, jogger, or runner therefore aims at the midrange between light and hard—the area we perceive as comfortable. This is a pace at which we could hold a conversation with a companion—Bill Bowerman's "talk test."

TABLE 1		The Borg Scale: Perceived Exertion			
Rating		**Pulse**	**Rating**		**Pulse**
6-7	very,very light	60-70	14-15	hard	140-150
8-9	very light	80-90	16-17	very hard	160-170
10-11	fairly light	100-110	18-20	very, very hard	180-200
12-13	somewhat hard	120-130			

Now, you might say that you couldn't run across the room without being short of breath. Then don't. Begin by walking and then work up to "scout pace" (alternating 50 steps walking and 50 running). Eventually you will be able to jog continually in comfort. You will be able to put yourself on "automatic pilot" and enjoy your thoughts and the countryside.

Listen to your body. Do not be a blind and deaf tenant. Hear what your muscles and heart and lungs are telling you. Above all, get in union with your body. Ride yourself as a jockey does a horse, finally becoming one with it. There will come times when the sheer joy of this mysterious fusion—the wholeness—will drive you to see just what you can do. But this is unnecessary, for you now have the pace. Do not push. You have found the groove. Stay in it.

Even when you have become proficient and the comfortable pace becomes faster and faster, you must still run the first six to ten minutes very slowly. You must allow the juices to flow, the temperature to rise, and the circulation to adapt. You must give the body time to make all those marvelous, intricate adjustments that happen when you finally set yourself in motion. When you do, you will experience that warm sweat that accompanies the onset of the second wind, feel that you just might spend the rest of the day running.

When I reach that second wind, I settle into my comfortable pace and let the body do the thinking. My ground speed varies with the time of day (early morning runs take me one minute a mile longer) or with heat and humidity, but the effort does not. The identical thing happens when I run against a headwind, up hills, or on those days when I am upset psychologically. But whether the stopwatch says eight minutes a mile or ten, the pace is the same. It is comfortable, and because my perceived exertion is always the same, the effort and the physiological benefits remain the same, too.

Once you have begun this way, success is assured. There is no need to rush, no need to hurry. "Only the sick and the ambitious," said Ortega, "are in a hurry." Nor is there any need to worry. When you run at a comfortable pace, you stay well within your physical limits. "I have never been harmed," said Montaigne, "by anything that was a real pleasure." Find the comfortable pace and enjoy it. Fitness is bound to follow.

HOW FAR?

Again, we must consult the body. The jogger/runner, whether in his first day or his twentieth year, is concerned with minutes, not miles—time not distance. The goal is to work up to thirty minutes at a comfortable pace. The rule is to run at that comfortable pace to a point this side of fatigue. Do not bother with distance. It is effort and time that do those good things to our bodies. This perspective frees us from the tyranny of speed and distance. There is no need, then, to count laps or measure miles, no need for the stopwatch and the agonized groans that go with it. Simply set the body on comfortable and go on automatic pilot. Then continue running to fatigue or thirty minutes, whichever comes first. It is even better not to reach fatigue, but instead to reach the kitchen door or the gym still eager to do more, ready to resume on that note the next time out.

Our aim, as I said, is thirty minutes. In the beginning, five minutes may be all you can handle. But quite soon—sooner than you expect—you will be able to run continuously for thirty minutes. I have seen a thirty-year-old woman get up to thirty-minute runs with one month of training, and run a five-mile race within ten weeks of buying her running shoes.

That thirty minutes is as far as we need go. It is the endpoint for fitness. That thirty minutes will get us fit and put us in the 95th percentile for cardiopulmonary endurance. At twelve calories per minute, it will eventually bring our weight down to desired levels. It also will slow the pulse and drop the blood pressure. It will make us good animals.

That first thirty minutes is for my body. During that half-hour, I take joy in my physical ability, the endurance and power of my running. It is a time when I feel competent and in control of my body, when I can think about my problems, and plan my day-to-day world. In many ways, that thirty minutes is all ego, all the self. It has to do with me, the individual.

What lies beyond this fitness of muscle? I can only answer for myself. The next thirty minutes is for my soul. In it, I come upon the third wind, which is psychological (unlike the second wind, which is physiological). And then I see myself not as an individual, but as part of the universe. In it, I can happen on anything I ever read, saw, or experienced. Every fact, instinct, and emotion is unlocked, and becomes available to me through some mysterious operation in my brain.

Recently, I came upon that feeling about thirty-five minutes out. I had just attacked a long hill on the river road and had been reduced to a slow trot. Then it happened. The feeling of wholeness and peace and contentment came over me. I loved myself and the world and everyone in it. I no longer had to will what I was doing. The road seemed to be running me. I was in a place and time I never wanted to leave.

To achieve fitness, there is no need to do more than thirty minutes at a comfortable pace. Past that, you must proceed with caution. Fitness can change your body. But the third wind can change your life.

HOW OFTEN?

How often must we run this thirty minutes at a comfortable pace? The answer the exercise physiologists give us is four times a week, a figure they've arrived at by testing innumerable individuals of both sexes at all ages. Running four times a week, they assure us, will make us fit and keep us that way. Looked at another way, this is just two hours of exercise a week. Does it need to be done at least one day apart; as it is usually prescribed? Could we do all our exercise on one day and then rest the other six? Or would it be okay to run an hour every third day and thereby satisfy the requirements?

The experts, as expected, are divided on this question. They have not adequately explored the subject of detraining. They do not know how soon we lose the benefits of prolonged exertion. There is some reason to suspect that weekend running may be enough. I have a colleague who for personal reasons has limited his running to two hours or more on Saturday and a race on Sunday. On this unscientific regimen, he has broken three hours in the marathon and more often than not beats me at lesser distances. His is just one way to train. Training is after all simply a matter of applying stress, allowing the body to recover, and then applying stress again. For each of us, the appropriate stresses and recovery times are different.

This is not a real problem in the minimum program for fitness. Almost everyone can handle an easy thirty minutes four times a week, or one hour twice a week, or even two hours once a week. But we are not minimizers, we are maximizers; and our difficulties involve doing too much rather than too little. The runner frequently gets caught up. He finds that running must be done daily, and longer and longer. The question then becomes not how much is enough but how much is too much. The problem becomes not fitness but exhaustion.

All this occurs, it seems to me, because we seek not only physical fitness, but psychological fitness as well. I need the minimum program for fitness because, like 95 percent of Americans, I have an occupation that isn't physical enough to make me fit. The thirty minutes four times a week is enough positive input to balance my negative physical output. It is not enough, however, to counteract the minuses in my day-to-day psychological life. To achieve a psychological balance, I need much more.

How many minutes of running do I need, then, to keep in a happy frame of mind? How many times a week must I run to have a capacity for work and the ability to enjoy life?

All too often, there are days when I don't feel like running. Then I am not sure whether I am tired or just lazy, whether I am physically exhausted or merely bored and lack the willpower to do what I should do. On those days when I lack zest and enthusiasm, I use the second wind to tell me whether what I'm experiencing is physical or psychological. When the second wind comes—as it does for me at the six-minute mark—I know.

If the usual good feelings are there, the warm sweat, and that feeling of strength and energy, I know my aversion is largely mental. I need a new route or pace or companion on the run. If, however, I feel a cold, clammy sweat and weakness, I pack it in and go home. I have even at such times had to walk or accept a ride home, having gone less than a mile, even though a few weeks before I may have run a very good marathon. Such physical exhaustion, however, is usually preceded by an elevated pulse in the morning. When mine is 10 beats above my usual basal pulse of 48, I know that I have once more overtrained. I need a nap instead of a workout.

So you see, your body is the ultimate arbiter in your fitness program. The body tells you how fast to run. Dial to "comfortable," and run at a pace that would permit you to talk to a companion. The body tells you how long to keep it up. Run just this side of fatigue. The body will tell you how often. Feel zest; respond to the second wind; note any changes in your morning pulse rate.

Follow these rules. Then somewhere between the minimum suggested and the maximum you can handle, you will find the fitness beyond muscle we all need to live the good life.

3

The Physiological Function of Running

by Lee Rodin

Everyone knows the heart quickens when someone yells "boo," when you're going to see someone you love, and when you're about to run a race. During a run, the heart deals with the stress of exercise by increasing the pulse rate. This pumps the blood faster, circulates it better, and lets you take in and use more air.

Before you run, you consume only 0.3 liters of oxygen per minute (0.28 quarts). But during exercise you need up to three liters (2.82 quarts), or ten times more. It takes the body two to three minutes to adjust, and those minutes can be pretty uncomfortable. You are likely to become breathless, have muscle or chest pain, get a headache, become fatigued, or feel vaguely distressed. Many doctors and researchers think this two- to three-minute time lag could explain the second wind: when your body adjusts to the increased oxygen demand, you feel better. That is, you feel better unless you're running too fast. According to Dr. Harley Feldick, athletic team physician at the University of Iowa, "A beginner shouldn't push himself; he should be able to jog and carry on a conversation—stress without strain."

If you can't run and talk at the same time, it means your body can't consume oxygen fast enough. The muscles compensate by producing lactic acid, which can cause muscular fatigue when it builds up in large doses. There's a difference between being tired and being fatigued. You get tired after a satisfying run; you get fatigued when you place excessive stress on your body.

According to Dr. Carl V. Gisolfi, exercise physiologist in men's physical education at the University of Iowa, "When you begin to exercise you've created an oxygen demand within the muscles. Cardiac output (how much blood the heart can pump with each beat and how fast it beats) will increase, blood flow to the lungs and ventilation will increase—these changes are precisely geared to the rate at which work is being performed."

Not only does the heart have to pump more blood per stroke during exercise, but the blood must go to the right places. You have more than 400 voluntary body muscles, which make up 40 percent of your total weight. To get the body in motion may require as much as one hundred times more blood during exercise than when the body is not moving. At rest, the kidney receives about 22 percent of the blood flow, while the skeletal muscles receive 15 percent. During exercise, blood to the kidneys drops to 0.2 percent and the muscles get an overwhelming 90 percent.

This is one good reason not to run for four to five hours after you've eaten. During digestion most of the blood goes to the stomach, not the muscle. As you run, the muscles first contract, then relax. During contraction the blood vessels are squeezed. This pumping action speeds up blood flow to the heart, increasing the amount of blood sent back to the muscles. This cycle continues until the runner stops and rests.

The good effects of running will continue to snowball, but only if you keep it up. But this means more than just running the same distance every day. To get lasting benefits you have to keep increasing the level. This is because running increases your capacity to run.

"To achieve a training effect," Gisolfi explains, "the organism must be stressed beyond the level of activity regularly encountered. The intensity of the load required to produce an effect will increase as performance improves." In other words, if you want to get better, you must either increase distance or speed.

According to Gisolfi, a good beginning pace is thirty minutes, three times a week. As early as one month after starting, you'll notice a decrease in your resting heart rate. The average untrained heart, which beats at least 70 times a minute, will beat only about 60 times with training—16,500 less times a day. According to Dr. Feldick, "The heart works for 70 odd years, and the only rest it gets is between beats. A slower pulse increases the rest time—the less strain your heart is under, the more efficient it is."

You'll also notice a decrease in body fat and an increase in lean body weight, which simply means you're firming up. And, if you don't compensate for the extra exercise by eating too much, you might lose weight, too—10 to 20 pounds within a year. (To find out how many calories you're burning, multiply the number of minutes you run by 10 (assuming you're running at a moderate pace).)

Other changes occur more slowly, some taking years. Due to the stress of exercise muscle fibers grow, enlarging the left side of the heart. An enlarged heart has more pumping strength, increasing circulation to the whole body and reducing the possibility of a heart attack. Blood volume can increase by 30 percent—almost a quart— and *stroke volume* can also increase.*

Exercise lowers cholesterol levels, which in turn helps lower blood pressure. The lungs take in more air. A beginning runner can consume, at most, 3 liters (2.82 quarts) of oxygen a minute, while a trained runner can consume 6 to 8 liters (5.64 to 7.52 quarts).

Exercise also has secondary influences. For instance, better blood circulation causes new capillaries to form in muscle fibers and induces the ones you already have to open up. Not only do these additional, enlarged capillaries provide increased surface area for the blood supply, but they increase muscular endurance and may even increase the size of your leg muscles.

Besides all this—or because of it—running can improve your feeling about yourself and even your attitude toward life. Feldick said it can give a general feeling of improved well-being. According to him, "People who don't run complain of fatigue, but it's inactivity that breeds fatigue. If they'd go out and get physically tired, their lethargy would disappear."

Gisolfi agrees, saying postcoronary patients on training programs had a better outlook on life even when they weren't running. "The burden of life just wasn't there anymore," he said. Asked if running could extend life span, Gisolfi added, "Running may not add years to life, but it certainly adds life to years."

---

* *Stroke volume* is the amount of blood pumped by the heart each beat.

4

To Run or to Race?

by Jean Colvin

Should every box of Adidas, New Balance, or Nike shoes bear the warning: "Running or racing can be dangerous to your health"? Some people would have the shoeboxes read: "Welcome to the greatest sport in the world." Probably the best compromise would be something like "Running or racing can change your life."

Interviews with a dedicated fun-runner, a doctor who treats injured runners, an injured runner, and a veteran marathoner indicate that running and racing are whatever you make of them. It doesn't have to be an either/or proposition. You can run and race, or just run. But there are some things to consider in doing either.

The joys and health benefits of aerobic running are well documented. Roger Eischens, a veteran runner of "fifteen years or more" is one of the strongest promoters of the sport. "Racing is a corruption of running," said Eischens in an interview at the athletic store where he works. "If you concentrate so much on preparing for a race, you lose the beauty of the daily run."

Eischens admitted to entering a number of road races annually, but said he races "going almost all out" only about twice a year. "Road runs are great social events," he said. "I go there to see my friends. Occasionally I like to run fast."

Besides racing for social reasons, Eischens believes some people race to test themselves on a measured course. But he adds, "You can do everything on a daily run that you can do in a race."

Eischens, who teaches Hatha yoga for runners, holds beginning running clinics, and coauthored the book *Run to Reality*, has what he calls a "Zen approach" to running. "I run today, for today," he said. But he adds that if people are interested in racing they should give it a try, since they won't know how they feel about competition until they do.

But, according to Dr. Peter G. Hanson, Clinical Assistant Professor of Medicine at the University of Wisconsin Medical School, racing can be a risky proposition. "Because of the injury rate and the disappointment being so high, I would be strongly on the side of running as opposed to racing."

Hanson speaks from experience. At the Biodynamics Lab at the University of Wisconsin he treats many runners, and their hurts aren't all physical ones. "They come here with downers," he said. "They have no alternatives to running. For them the daily run is not fun, it's training. It's a high stress situation." Some runners train too hard for goals they set too high. Others worry about getting older. In addition to their physical problems, which Hanson says "start from the foot and come up," many are depressed.

To avoid both injuries and the depression that can accompany racing disappointments, Hanson urges people who want to try racing to first "categorize themselves. Decide whether you're an elite runner, a fit runner, or an underfit runner," he says. "Decide whether you want to undertake competitive running seriously; [decide] if you want to win."

Hanson recommends using physical fitness guidelines and tests, outlined in the many running books now on the market. "See where you're at. Estimate your oxygen consumption. Test yourself," he says.

For those people interested in getting involved in fun-runs, Hanson sees no reason not to. According to him, "Anyone can run long distances to compete with himself."

Hanson has been running "seriously" for about five years, and enters competitions. "It would be difficult to give advice about it if I didn't do it," he explains.

Jody Alexander, twenty-three, hasn't run for the past seven months. But before a back injury forced her to stop running, she consistently placed first or second in local races. The year she was injured, she ran three marathons, a 20-mile race, and a number of 10- to 15-milers. At that time, she was training about 70 miles a week. Her problem became worse when she continued to train and do stretching exercises after she was injured.

"Once you're winning races and you're up there," she says, "you get the fever and you have to go."

But she soon discovered something about running and racing. "I enjoyed running so much more when I wasn't training," said Alexander. "I looked forward more to my runs. I got to run with others, which I like. I let my mind go free, creative, instead of constantly pounding."

Alexander said she felt guilty missing a day of running at the time she was training. She added that she had "better peace of mind" when she was just running. "It was more a meditation."

Alexander suggests that runners who want to race "start slow and do everything right—diet, nutrition—and it won't necessarily lead to injury."

"I see other young runners pushing themselves and I just want to tell them, 'Slow down!'" she says.

One experienced runner who's not slowing down is Bill Kohrs, who is fifty-two. In 1978, Kohrs ran his fifth Boston Marathon. He began running after a heart attack in 1971. "It was almost like a joke," recalls Kohrs. "I was running three miles a day and I said 'one of these days I should run in the Boston Marathon.'" Kohrs's wife overheard the remark and "held me to my word." The Boston Marathon was the second race he ever entered.

"I had gotten eighth place in a 10 kilometer race—my first—because there were nine entrants and the ninth guy was late for the gun," Kohrs laughs.

Now he qualifies respectably for Boston every year. (If you're over forty you must have run a 3:30 marathon the previous year.)

"I look forward to testing myself," says Kohrs. "It's nice to have the different age-groups so you're not competing with the young guys."

Meeting people is another reason for Kohrs's interest in racing, especially at Boston. "Boston is unique. I just enjoy the day to the point where I don't concentrate on running. I talk with the racers and the crowd," he says. "With 800,000 people there it's like a Fourth of July parade."

Kohrs tries not to race more than 5 to 10 percent of his total mileage. "You're mostly running against yourself," he says. "I would still run if I didn't race, but I probably wouldn't enjoy it as much."

His enjoyment of running has spread to his family. His three sons have all been state champions in the mile, his two daughters compete, and his wife bikes along with him while he trains.

"I guess I got hooked," he says. "I started entering road races and I just didn't want to stop."

I've been running a year now, two to three miles a day, every day—ever since I got caught in the rain and found that a three-block sprint home from the library left me gasping and with sharp pains in my side. I suddenly discovered that although I was twenty-eight, slender, a non-smoker, and swam twice a week, I wasn't necessarily fit.

I've participated in two races, fun-runs really. I got a kick out of the T-shirt I received, felt a modest thrill at all the pageantry, felt pride that I didn't finish dead last, and was happy to be with my friends. For those reasons, I'll probably enter more fun-runs.

But I run for other reasons. I run alone, usually in the morning, on silent, empty, country back roads. Dogs chase me. Sometimes a hawk wheels overhead. But always it's just me, the sound of my breathing, the pad of my shoes on the tarmac. I'm alone, unencumbered with bills, telephones, cars, television, or commitments. It's the purest kind of freedom; I could never give it up.

The runners I spoke with for this article were an easy-going group. All seemed soft-spoken and self-assured. The glint of competition didn't burn in their eyes, yet all of them compete in varying degrees.

There are rewards to running and racing. There are also frustrations and hurts. Dr. Hanson said he treats both recreational runners and racers for injuries. The difference is only in degree; racers' injuries are usually more severe.

So it would seem then that the choice isn't really whether to run or to race, but whether or not to run. If you do race, do it sensibly, within your limits, as Hanson suggests. If you run, it's what you make it. If you're not a runner, what are you waiting for?

5

Converting the Nonrunner

by Jane Underhill

Runners have lots of characteristics in common. One of these is the evangelistic zeal with which we endorse our sport. No one is exempt from our enthusiasm: mothers-in-law, flabby brothers, sophisticated sweethearts, or aged grandfathers. To runners, all types of people—even the unlikeliest—are candidates for conversion to the world of running.

Winning converts to such a strenuous and apparently masochistic sport, however, is not the world's faintest challenge. Picture the boss: too comfortable, overweight, cigarette-smoking, the classic heart attack candidate. Does he give you an "I'd better humor the poor boy" look when you casually ask the man if he's ever gotten into a "little jogging"?

Or picture your lady: maybe a little pudgy or phlegmatic, but she's scrupulously groomed, cosmetically, and intends to stay that way. Unfortunately, she's seen what you look like when you run and that's enough to cramp anyone's style.

Or, your gentleman? Ambitious and busy, he rushes through the pressures of his day. Could you be suggesting that he has nothing better to do with his time—or worse, that his body needs improvement?

What obstacles! Nevertheless, runners themselves are usually totally convinced about the benefits of running. Trying to express the benefits of running is a favorite topic among the "elect." These benefits are often very personal and subjective. Regardless of how articulate we are, communicating such subjective, vague benefits can be self-defeating.

Therefore, we have to develop a different strategy. We must convince ourselves that running *can* appeal to others, in spite of its apparent masochism. We must emphasize not only the intangible joys of running, but also its practical side. For although making running partners of lovers, friends, parents, spouses, and other normal out-of-shape mortals is almost impossible, there are ways. This is where running salesmanship comes in.

STEP 1: CONVINCE OURSELVES

Think first of the practical side. No doubt one appealing thing about running is that it is cheap. All one really needs is a good pair of running shoes. In addition, running doesn't require a trip to the "Y," to the public pool, or a day-long trip to the mountains. All you need to do is step out the front door.

Running doesn't require the skill of skiing, judo, or swimming. There are few opportunities to be disappointed in running. When no one else shows up, it's as good to go alone. How many sports can boast that advantage?

Running is incredibly independent of other things—other people, the seasons, or the hour. Under such circumstances, it's hard to find excuses for not running. Therefore, you should emphasize the conveniences of minimum investments of time, training, and money.

Continue to think positively. Assume that you probably have health, glow, and enthusiasm, and probably an attractive, energetic body going for you. If you lack these, you may have to talk faster to convince yourself you can sell others! If you happen to be an accurate judge of others' needs and personalities, you have another thing going for you. If you are also kindly disposed toward others, and patient and sensitive, you will find these qualities advantageous. A large part of success in winning converts to running will depend on your intuitive talents.

In a coarser vein, we all know that we have others' fears, guilts, and phobias about cholesterol, pollution, coronaries, food preservatives, obesity, and stagnancy going for us. Running offers a way of coping with some of these fears. Since I don't believe enjoyment in running is based on fear, I feel it is unethical to challenge others to run solely on the basis of their fear. We all have fears that enter somewhere into our running rationales, so use them but don't abuse them.

One last point here: I'm a self-made runner. No one had to convince me of anything. Before I became a runner, I felt guilty about physical decadence and threatened by all those guys "out there running." Though I was not a tremendous athlete, I thought even I could run.

I think many potential converts are like that. They are ripe for being convinced. They will sell themselves. Such people know they should do something. But is it necessary to do something as frantic, sweaty, and suspiciously exhibitionist as running? From the outside, remember, running does seem blatant and extreme. Runners just don't seem to be nice, easy-going Joes.

STEP 2: CONVINCE OTHERS

Once we're convinced that people can be convinced, we're ready for the next step: convincing others. Here we actually approach our target person. This is a subtle step involving all our intuitive resources.

How do we stimulate interest? Since everyone is different, a pat answer here would be shallow. We must rely on our intuition to determine what another individual will find appealing about running. Running may appeal to people for: weight control or reduction, sheer physical fitness, slowing down aging, insurance against heart disease, the aesthetic exhilaration of being outdoors and close to nature, the sociability of a road runner club, the individuality of running, or a challenge.

We must determine which of these will appeal to whom and emphasize those. The prospect's physical condition and age will usually determine our tactics. Common sense will do the rest. After all, can you imagine bragging about how running retards aging and keeps your weight down to an emaciated sixteen-year-old scarecrow? Can you imagine stressing the sociable side of running to a celebrated hermit?

The things that convinced us that running was appealing will also convince others. In terms of money, time, and training, the convenience and economy of running are impressive. Its ability to subdue certain fears is impressive, as well. Sparkling eyes, energy, *joie de vivre*, and other side effects of running must appeal to others.

If we've been around our prospect for long, there is no doubt that he will know you are a runner. Our dedication will show. This is the subtle stage at which another person may begin to suspect what we know: that, like fishing, there is more to running than meets the eye. Possibly our prospect will begin or size us up positively, or (alas!) run from us in fear that whatever we have may be contagious.

This is also the stage at which to volunteer casually unsolicited information about running. Volunteer that last weekend you entered a five-mile road race and cranked out a few more miles between meals. You may even go so far as to say, "Man, you know, lately I don't know if it's that extra mileage or what, but I never felt better in my life!" You may also want to pack around a few copies of *Runner's World* as conversation pieces, or to "forget" at strategic locations.

I personally recall one successful tactic used at this stage of conversion. This is rather high pressure for this strictly low-pressure phase, but some may be ripe for it. Invest a buck or two for a copy of *Aerobics* by Kenneth Cooper. One evening, I passed a copy to a likely prospect. If that approach doesn't appeal to you, you might leave a copy on your desk at work. One convert tried it and before long got a nibble: "Uh...can I borrow this?" Often, *Aerobics* will speak for itself and your coaching will end there.

If someone complains to you about the price of gas, doctor bills, headache, sore back, runny nose, weariness, "exhaustion," or any other ailment, this is your clue to offer running as a potential panacea. In short, in this stage we try to initiate enthusiasm or discussion about running. We volunteer information about our sport, tailor its appeals to the person we wish to convert, get in some scientific data via *Runner's World* or *Aerobics*, and baby any spark of interest we can conjure. We urge cooperation in a "trial" run.

STEP 3: TWELVE-MINUTE TEST

If your would-be convert is ready for this step, he is ready for the twelve-minute test on the track. At this stage, all powers of nurturing, love, and patience are called to the fore. You will have to intuit how much and what kind of encouragement to offer, and how much coaching. You will have to know what you're doing in order to proceed safely.

But most of all, if you get to this stage, you will experience a sense of pride in your accomplishment. Your would-be convert is now your protégé. Congratulate yourself and feel confident that he may eventually become a bonafide jogger or runner.

Regarding safety, in *Aerobics*, Cooper admonishes those over thirty and any individual with physical problems to seek a physician's approval before starting any strenuous activity. But since the rest of our protégés didn't seek their physicians' approval to gain weight and get out-of-condition in the first place, they don't need it to reverse that now.

Depending on the individual, a little coaching goes a long way, particularly in such an individual sport as running. In other words, don't jump the gun or talk about any feat or challenge but the immediate one: getting around the track for twelve minutes in any manner. Based on the person's accomplishment during the twelve-minute test, you will know how to proceed safely using the guidelines in *Aerobics*.

You must determine whether your protégé needs your presence, your moral support, or privacy. Some will require a mother's indulgence, others will spurn it and forge their own, independent trail.

If your protégé needs support, supply it. Send notes of congratulations. Comment affirmatively on the performance, how it impressed you, how phenomenal the progress was, how the person can be sure of accomplishing a goal (conditioning, weight reduction, etc.), and how you've already noticed changes.

If your protégé is independent, don't be surprised. This is the individual for whom a little coaching goes a long way. He is the kind who has already accomplished the run you have just suggested. He may go his own way entirely, feeling no obligation to keep you informed and showing no interest in doing so. Imagine—no gratitude! Nevertheless, this person is proud of progress. Reinforce it. Show your respect. I've found that this type of person is likely to surpass one's own dedication to running.

I remember handing a copy of *Aerobics* to an independent sort and in a few weeks hearing, "Guess how far I went last night?" It was ten miles. I took this to mean that I had just become the proud "parent" of a running partner.

Along the general track of offering encouragement, there is nothing wrong with offering material encouragement. If your protégé is not too shy, take a picture of a workout and present him with a copy. Once my protégé broke five miles, we scheduled a seven-mile run. Neither of us was sure about the wisdom of that, but it turned out to be a solidifying run, a pleasant surprise to both of us. To celebrate, I gave my new partner a T-shirt with his nickname initials on it. This must be proof of being "one of us"—initiated!

For certain persons, seeing a local road race may be encouraging. Your intuition will have to determine that. Sometimes an unassuming road race will look "slick and professional," and alienate the beginner. But some protégés may dazzle you by entering!

Once your protégé has completed the twelve-minute test and the first five-mile run, start looking for symptoms that running is becoming addictive. If it is becoming no longer merely the means to an end, but rather the end in itself, you're already at the last step in the conversion process.

STEP 4: BEYOND FITNESS

Unfortunately, this does not mean that you are at last free to get careless with the word *marathon*. For now, constrain yourself and keep in mind that runners are never happy without trying to make themselves even better. But even though your protégé is beginning to look like a fanatic and you're beside yourself with joy, now is not the time to blow it. Though you may be inclined to push your protégé, divert the impulse toward things like running clothing and diet.

Up to this time, we have been unconditionally supportive, encouraging everything and restraining most advice until asked for it. This lessens the chances of making your protégé any more self-conscious than he may already be. But if your protégé is out there running in sneakers, what can you do? I mentioned that I'm a self-made runner. In ignorance, I started running in street shoes. When the heels wore out, I advanced to boys' sneakers and ran in those for six months. I was happy. I hardly knew I was hurting. But my ankles were swollen.

One day I met a friend out running. For some reason, what we wear running is understood to be a very "personal" matter, and my new friend barely dared venture to say anything about my tennis shoes. Eventually, my friend showed me four or five battered, frayed pairs of "running" shoes. I didn't like them but my ankles were swollen and I made the connection.

Moving from tennies to Tigers or Nikes, Adidas or Pumas shows real commitment on the part of your protégé. Some sensitive individuals will resent the implication that they are being pressured to conform, or to be instantly "professional," or to buy equipment. Therefore, fall back on the characteristics we emphasized before—sensitivity and a sense of timing.

Moreover, what about that Arrow dress shirt and those tight Wranglers? Is there any way to nudge someone over to something more comfortable, like T-shirts, shorts, and sweats? I suffocated in blue slacks and a blue shirt before I had the faintest idea that there was clothing designed for the activity of running. The point of running gear is safety and comfort. If your protege has both of these and is happy, say nothing. If neither, tactfully suggest something looser, lighter, and safer. The variety of running clothes is a tribute to individuality, and I would encourage such individuality rather than conformity.

Once sloth starts giving way to fitness, there is increased motivation. At this point, you might start stressing further habits companionable with running—like excellent diet. For starters I usually refer to Adelle Davis's *Let's Eat Right to Keep Fit.*

If you detect that your runner is beyond jogging for fitness (do we fanatics unquestioningly assume that this is desirable?) and that your own obsessions are visible, you may have broken the barrier around the word *marathon.* The marathon is the ultimate long-distance experience, and if you have arrived here the conversion is complete.

6

The Relevance
of Running

by Carolyn W. Clarke

What are you going to do when you grow up?" Bob Lipsyte, *New York Times* sports columnist and author of *Assignment Sports*, feels that anyone who chides him with this question can't be too smart. "The world of sports is no sanctuary from reality," he responds.

Lipsyte, in his remarks, speaks of the world of long-distance running. For running is not only a sport; it is also a way of life. And the process of becoming a runner is relevant to our modern-day world.

Entering the ranks of the distance runner demands aspiration, determination, and self-motivation. It also involves defying three widely held premises of the day:

The other directed man. Writer David Riesman states members of today's society are unduly attentive to and influenced by peer-group pressure. But then emerges the runner. Has he ever curtailed a workout for fear of what people will think? The answer, of course, is "no." Oblivious to the opinions of others, he is in his ultimate glory as he lopes across the land.

Why does he run? According to author George Sheehan, "The runner does not run because he is too slight for football or hasn't the ability to put a ball through a hoop or can't hit a curveball. He doesn't run primarily to lose weight or become fit or to prevent heart attacks. He runs because he has to."

And during his period of fantasy and flight what does the runner get? "Joy and pain," replies former Boston Marathon winner Amby Burfoot. "Good health and injuries. Exhilaration and despair. A feeling of accomplishment and a feeling of waste. The sunrise and the sunset."

"A sensation of movement," replies British marathon champion Ian Thompson. "You lose a sense of identity in yourself. You become running itself." Perhaps Thompson speaks for all runners as he continues, "I only have to think of putting on my running shoes, and the kinesthetic pleasure of floating along, the pleasure of movement starts to come. I get a feeling of euphoria, almost real happiness." Thompson concludes, "It's the platonic ideas of knowing thyself. Running is getting to know yourself to an extreme degree."

Limiting worldly possessions. Philip Slater, like Riesman, is a theorist—and a pessimistic one at that. In his book *The Pursuit of Loneliness* he sees a society obsessed with the acquisition of material goods. But this study surely excluded the runner who heeds the words of Marcus Cicero: "Beware of ambition for wealth. . . . There is nothing more honorable or noble than indifference to money."

Now don't be misled. It is not that the runner lacks an appreciation for fine furniture or cars. It's simply that by running daily and stretching properly, he doesn't have time to acquire them. The runner's needs are basic: gallons of fluid, pounds of chocolate, and an absence of the number one enemy—pain. His affinity? It is not with those who have equal rank or wealth, but rather with fellow sufferers of sore knees, shin splints, and Achilles tendonitis.

And what about the runner's clothes? Writer George Sheehan states that before he began running he was a card-carrying member of the fashion conspiracy. But his running changed all that. He replaced his stylish clothes with long-johns, large-size turtlenecks, skin-tight Levi's, and over-the-calf hose. After experiencing the comfort and practicality of such attire, Dr. Sheehan vowed never again to buy another dress outfit.

And finally the runner's feet. These marvels of engineering surely deserve the best of care. With the increased mileage comes blackened toenails, raw blisters, and fallen arches. Therefore, the runner's tendency is to match dress outfits, not with fashionable slingbacks or platform shoes, but rather with a good, solid, multi-colored pair of training shoes. And if, heaven forbid, the runner suffers from that dreaded affliction known as Morton's foot, you just may see him wearing his Adidas SL 76s at all times. As a runner, function—not fashion—is the ultimate consideration.

A different kind of hero. Today's Super Bowl and all-star greats rival national leaders in media exposure. They command high salaries, unequaled prestige, and have adoring fans. Conversely, their sports careers may be curtailed by bad knees, contract disputes, and inflated egos. They often give credence to Ralph Waldo Emerson's remark: "Every hero, becomes at last, a bore."

However, from within the ranks of the runner comes that familiar theme: "Nobody knows my name." And the runner is probably right. For he may variously win gold medals, finish the course, or never run races at all. And what does he get for his efforts? T-shirts, not contracts; blisters, not endorsements. He must contend with scorching lungs, dry heaves, and winter ice that refuses to thaw.

But his days as a runner are never numbered. With passing years he comes to accept decreased mileage, faltering times, and extended days off as part of the game. But he also experiences a satisfaction that few people ever know. It's this special satisfaction, so hard to define, that will ensure his return to the roads.

But make no mistake. Although overflowing with these virtuous qualities, the runner is by no means universally loved. Consider the neighborhood dogs that look after the runner's jaunting with ire and wrath; or the family cook who views the runner's nutritional needs as a source of despair. And then there are the podiatry bills. Some years they may rival the national debt!

There are also those critics who view the runner as a loner who will never contribute to the common good. Perhaps they are right. For the runner, unlike many athletes, has no ultimate goal. He is in the process of becoming.

But the runner can show that the good life is not one of ease but of challenge: that approval need only be sought from within; and that perpetual wealth can be found on the roads. Then he has contributed to a nobler, happier world.

PART TWO

TRAINING

1

The Fundamentals of Training

by Jim Lilliefors

Training for distance running has advanced from a strict emphasis on track intervals in the thirties and forties to the more natural training, introduced by Percy Cerutty in the fifties. Eventually the trend moved toward long-distance road running, as espoused by Arthur Lydiard. But even by the late seventies, the evolution of training had not reached a stable acceptance. While individual programs, such as the Lydiard system and the Bill Bowerman/Oregon philosophy, gained a general respect and acceptance, there remained no single accepted approach to training. Even runners of near-equal ability had very different training ideas.

Frank Shorter, for instance, was notorious for his Herculean interval sessions as he prepared for the 1972 Olympics. Bill Rodgers, by contrast, said, "I have never done much interval or fartlek training. I train at 6:00 to 6:40 pace on most runs."

Even though there is no single "best" training program, most runners draw upon one of the following approaches.

Beginning. Novice runners, who take up the activity to improve their physical condition, have less reason to follow any set programs than competitive runners. But if they desire to anyway, there are two guides that can help them along: *Aerobics* by Kenneth Cooper (New York: M. Evans & Co., Inc., 1968) and *Jog, Run, Race* by Joe Henderson (Mountain View, Calif.: World Publications, 1977). Each presents a program: Cooper's based on "aerobic points," Henderson's on practical advice.

Once the runner progresses to the stage where he is only interested in physical fitness, his interest may turn to racing—to running a marathon. The following is Joe Henderson's schedule for a first-time marathoner:

SCHEDULE FOR RUNNERS

NOTES ON USING THE SCHEDULE

1. Choose the marathon you want to run, then begin the program exactly three months earlier.

2. The schedule presumes that you're starting from a base of about a half-hour of running a day. If you're significantly below that, don't begin this program until you've reached that basic level.

3. If you're running more than 35 minutes a day, start later and at the appropriate place in the schedule. There is, of course, no reason to back down.

4. Typically, the weeks will run from Monday (day 1) through Sunday (day 7), with the longest run on Saturday. But weeks can start and end anywhere you want.

5. One day a week—labeled "optional"—is left open for rest or as a makeup day if you've come up short for the week.

6. The entire schedule has alternating long and short days to allow cycles of work and recovery. They're planned on about a 1-2-3 ratio: a short run is one part, a medium-long run two parts, and the longest run three parts.

7. The program calls for a 5-week buildup, leveling off at an average of an hour a day for 7 weeks and then a 1-week easing off before the marathon.

8. In the next-to-last (11th) week of full training, you're asked to go at least a half-hour longer than ever before. This is a confidence-builder.

9. You are trying to accumulate an average of an hour a day for an 8-week period (all averages are figured on full 7-day weeks). This theoretically gives you the ability to *run* for 4 hours or to *race* for 3 hours.

10. Three months includes 13 weeks, and I give only 12 here. We hope you aren't superstitious, because the 13th is race week. "Taper" all week with runs averaging about half of normal—30 minutes a day.

11. Do all your training at about the pace you expect to maintain for the full marathon at the end of the program.

12. You may run a race of 5-10 miles in the first month and one of 10-15 miles in the second month instead of one of the long runs. But this is not a requirement.

Day	Week 1	Week 2	Week 3	Week 4
1	25 min.	30 min.	35 min.	35 min.
2	50 min.	55 min.	1:00	1:10
3	25 min.	30 min.	35 min.	35 min.
4	50 min.	55 min.	1:00	1:10
5	25 min.	30 min.	35 min.	35 min.
6	1:10	1:20	1:30	1:45
7	optional	optional	optional	optional
Ave.	35 min.	40 min.	45 min.	50 min.

continued on next page

SCHEDULE FOR RUNNERS *(continued)*			
Day	Week 5	Week 6	Week 7	Week 8
1	40 min.	40 min.	40 min.	40 min.
2	1:20	1:30	1:30	1:30
3	40 min.	40 min.	40 min.	40 min.
4	1:20	1:30	1:30	1:30
5	40 min.	40 min.	40 min.	40 min.
6	1:45	2:00	2:00	2:00
7	optional	optional	optional	optional
Ave.	55 min.	1:00	1:00	1:00
Day	Week 9	Week 10	Week 11	Week 12
1	40 min.	40 min.	40 min.	40 min.
2	1:30	1:30	1:30	1:30
3	40 min.	40 min.	40 min.	40 min.
4	1:30	1:30	1:30	1:30
5	40 min.	40 min.	40 min.	40 min.
6	2:00	2:00	2:30	2:00
7	optional	optional	optional	optional
Ave.	1:00	1:00	1:05	1:00

Speed play (fartlek). Fartlek, or speed play (the English translation), became universally recognized in the 1940s through the efforts of Swedish mile greats Gunder Hagg and Arne Andersson. It is a free-form type of running, in which the runner leaves the track, and runs on roads, in the woods, over golf courses, surging when he feels like it, constantly varying the pace. When done properly, fartlek training can produce the same benefits as interval workouts, without the tedium of going in circles around a track.

For those whose temperament requires a more structured program fartlek may not be suitable. As was pointed out in the *Runner's Training Guide* (Mountain View, Calif.: World Publications, 1973), "The disadvantage of fartlek is that it lacks the specific goals some runners need. They want to see progress: in distances run, in times recorded, in carrying out set tasks."

For others, though, it can be a refreshing and valuable approach to running.

Interval training. Even top marathoners and ultramarathoners include interval work in their training. Dan Cloeter, a 2:19 marathoner, regularly does one-mile intervals on the track, seven of them in 4:50, with a ¼- to ½-mile rest in between. Former Boston Marathon winner Jon Anderson runs three to four miles of intervals each week, the longest three-quarters of a mile, the shortest a series of

110s. Bob Varsha, a 2:15 marathoner, often runs a series of sixteen 440s. Other runners, such as Jim Bowles, who competed in the 1976 Olympic Trials marathon, regularly use shorter races for interval work.

Through Paavo Nurmi, Emil Zatopek, and Hungarian coach Mihaly Igloi, intervals became the accepted means of training for distance runners. With Arthur Lydiard's emphasis on longer roadwork, intervals are no longer stressed as much as they once were. But interval work—whether on the road or on the track—is important for several reasons. It not only trains an athlete to handle the stress of a race, but it also helps ingrain in the runner a feel for pace. Tom Fleming, a 2:12 marathoner, said, "I think of learning pace through track reps; in training this way I become aware of my capabilities and limitations."

Though specific workouts vary with each runner, there are certain principal goals to be accomplished through interval training. Woldemar Gerschler and Hans Reindell, the two German doctors who formalized interval training in the 1930s, set this rule: "The running effort in interval training should send the heart to around 180 beats per minute. From this point, the heart is allowed 90 seconds to return to 120-125 beats per minute. If it takes longer, the effort demanded has either been too violent or too long."

Long slow distance. This type of training is a product of Arthur Lydiard's training philosophy and the general interest in fun-running. The name was popularized by Joe Henderson in his booklet *Long Slow Distance: The Humane Way to Train* (Los Altos, Calif.: Tafnews, 1969).

Many top runners, such as Bill Rodgers, train mostly using long slow distance (LSD), and are still able to race marathons at a sub-five-minute pace. Tom Fleming said, "At this stage, I never really think about the pace of my training. I could never run 5:00 or under in practice anyway." Gayle Barron, a world-class woman marathoner, even lists LSD as a suitable means for learning pace, contrary to the advocates of interval training.

Lydiard. Arthur Lydiard, whose ideas are discussed in an article in this section, pioneered a then-revolutionary program of long endurance running with sharpening work, even for middle-distance runners. The success of his approach was demonstrated by the performance of his protégé Peter Snell at the 1960 Olympics.

The following is his schedule for a marathon:

For the first 8 weeks:

Monday	30- to 45-minute jog
Tuesday	45- to 60-minute jog
Wednesday	30- to 45-minute jog
Thursday	45- to 60-minute jog
Friday	rest or 30-minute jog
Saturday	30- to 45-minute jog
Sunday	60- to 90-minute jog

For the next 6 weeks:

Monday	6-8 x 200 at relaxed stride
Tuesday	45- to 60-minute jog
Wednesday	5000-meter time trial
Thursday	45- to 60-minute jog
Friday	rest or 30-minute jog
Saturday	5,000-meter time trial
Sunday	60- to 90-minute jog

For the next 6 weeks:

Monday	8-10 x 100 at fast, relaxed pace
Tuesday	45- to 60-minute jog
Wednesday	30- to 45-minute easy fartlek run
Thursday	30- to 45-minute jog
Friday	rest or 30-minute jog
Saturday	10,000-meter time trial
Sunday	60- to 90-minute jog

For the next week:

Monday	8-10 x 100 wind sprints every 200 meters
Tuesday	45-minute jog
Wednesday	3,000-meter time trial
Thursday	4 x 200 at a relaxed stride
Friday	rest or 30-minute jog
Saturday	3,000-meter time trial
Sunday	60-minute jog

During the last week:

Monday	6-8 x 100 at a fast, relaxed pace
Tuesday	1,500-meter time trial
Wednesday	45-minute jog
Thursday	30-minute jog
Friday	rest or 30-minute jog
Saturday	fun-run
Sunday	60-minute jog

Cerutty. Percy Cerutty's ideas on running, though still controversial, produced a number of world-record runners, most notably the 1960 Olympic champion Herb Elliott. More than just instigating a training program, Cerutty preached a whole new philosophy about the sport. Even in the mid-fifties, his athletes lived a communal existence by the sea, reading poetry, eating a completely natural diet, and deriving inspiration from Cerutty's philosophical discourses.

Perhaps the most controversial aspect of Cerutty's approach was his idea about breathing. He theorized that athletics was stagnating because athletes did not use their lungs properly. He advocated the "Five Basic Movements" as the optimal means of filling one's lungs. The final movement involved galloping like a horse.

Though Elliott practiced a portion of what Cerutty preached, the coach maintained, until his death in 1975, that no one had really given his theories a fair chance. He felt that athletics would be forever revolutionized when his ideas were finally understood and adopted.

Bowerman. Of the training ideas that drew attention in the late sixties and early seventies, probably the one that gained the most respect from top competitive athletes was the "hard-easy" training program espoused by Bill Bowerman, track coach at the University of Oregon (and 1972 Olympic coach).

Bowerman was opposed to the frantic high-mileage trend that flourished early in the seventies. He lectured frequently on the hazards of spreading oneself too thin, of trying to do too much. "In every case, I would prefer to undertrain a runner rather than overtrain him," he said in 1972. "Young runners tend to think the farther they run and the faster they run in training, the better it's going to be for them. A runner can have just as much success if not more success by finding what his limit is in relation to his progress."

2

Evolution of Training

by O. Karikosk

The first information available on training for distance running dates back to British professionals in the nineteenth century. Training in those days was dominated by running at even speed, but not daily nor year-round. Further details are unfortunately rather vague.

At the beginning of this century, the early British methods were adopted by Americans, who added shorter repetitions to the even-speed runs. Well-known runners, such as Murphy, Robertson, Cromwell, and others, used this type of training, which was later used by the Finns. Kolehmainen dominated distance events in the Stockholm Olympic Games, giving Finland's distance running a great boost. Lauri Pihkala wrote in 1916 that for the development of endurance fast, short repetitions with suitable recoveries, combined with steady-speed cross-country runs, was superior to even-speed running around the track. This type of training produced many outstanding athletes, including the great Paavo Nurmi, Ritola, Stenroos, Larva, Purje, and later Lehtinen, Iso-Hollo, Salminen, Maki, and Heino.

In 1932, Poland's Olympic gold medalist Kusocinski, coached by Estonian decathlete Kolmpere, further developed the Finnish technique by reducing the number of repetitions in his training program. These were replaced by repetitions over dramatically shorter distances (200, 300, and 400 meters) at faster than competitive speed.

A little later, Gerschler became one of the leading middle-distance coaches in Germany. His approach to training became famous through the many world records set by Rudolf Harbig. Harbig trained three to four days a week nearly all year round, in winter using forest trails and snow-cleaned running tracks. On the track he concentrated on 500- to 1,200-meter repetitions, with recovery walks of five to twenty-five minutes. He also included resistance exercises in this program, and made *speed-endurance* an accepted term in middle-distance running.

During World War II, the record-breaking performances of Haegg, Andersson, and Strand drew attention to the Swedish running school. This was based on two new approaches in training as well as a trend toward avoiding monotonous track workouts. The Swedish methods were introduced by Olander and Holmer. Olander came out with the revolutionary idea of training in summer on soft forest surfaces, sand, mud, and clay, and in winter in deep snow. Holmer introduced the well-known Swedish *speed-play* or *fartlek*, but also recommended track workouts to develop the necessary feel for pace. Despite their contrasts—Olander's based on short but very intensive daily training and Holmer's avoiding frequent hard efforts in short time periods—both systems were used simultaneously by Swedish athletes.

According to the information available, it was Emil Zatopek who first employed interval training, a method copied by runners the world over. Zatopek started using 100- and 200-meter repetitions with recovery jogs over the same distance. In 1944, for example, his day's workout included 10 x 100 and 10 x 200 meters, or 10 x 400 meters, in intervals of 13, 26-28, and 60 seconds. He later increased the number of repetitions, but decreased the speed. In 1948-49, for example, he covered 20-30 x 400 meters in 67-70 seconds. Later he did 60-100 x 400 meters, but slower (75-80 seconds) and with shorter recovery jogs (100-200 m.). At the same time, Zatopek began to include 200-meter repetitions in his workouts, and by 1954 was using repetitions of slow interval runs to build the cardiorespiratory system and fast repetitions to improve metabolism.

Reindell and Gerschler introduced a different type of interval training method in the 1950s. They were convinced that the recovery phase is decisive in heart development. So, using 100- and 200-meter distances, they increased the number of repetitions and therefore also recoveries. Middle-distance runners used 50 x 100- or 30 x 200-meter repetitions, usually in 14-16 seconds and in 30-33 seconds, respectively. The recoveries were as short as Zatopek's, but were taken lying down to speed up the pulse recovery. As soon as the pulse rate had dropped to 120-140 a minute, the next phase was started. Pirie and Wiggs were among those who used this type of training.

Zatopek's interval training methods were also developed by Soviet Union, Hungarian, Polish, and East German coaches. Most famous among them was Igloi, whose well-known athletes included Rozsa-volgyi, Iharos, Tabori, and Czaplar in Hungary, and, later, Beatty, Grelle, Seaman, and Schul in the United States. According to Polish coach Mulak, Igloi was not influenced by Zatopek's successes. He employed different distances, varying from 100 to 1,200 meters, as well as intensive training runs to create oxygen debts. Igloi improvised his training and did not make long-range plans, but decided each day's workout according to how the athlete felt, weather conditions, training targets, and so on. He regards himself mainly as an educator and has never made known, in detail, his training principles. His dictatorial approach, failure of his athletes in major competitions, and the monotony of his training system have been criticized by many. But the positive side of Igloi's approach is the consideration and development of individual ability.

Soviet coaches developed Zatopek's system by increasing intensity, while decreasing the training load. Nikiforov, the coach of Vladimir Kuts, added more variations in distance (100 to 2,000 meters) as well as further changes in pace. In one training session in 1956, Kuts went through a 35-minute warm-up run, 5 x 100 meters with increasing speed, 5 x 400 meters (61-64 seconds) with 100-meter jog recoveries, 2 x 1200 meters (3:12), 3 x 400 meters (65 seconds), and exercises. To Kuts's program, Bolotnikov added long cross-country runs.

Fresh winds entered running training again when Percy Cerutty, inspired by his visit to Olander after the Helsinki Games, reintroduced in part Olander's methods through Herb Elliott. Cerutty's system included long hikes with a heavy rucksack, running in sand and water, and carrying heavy loads up sand hills with a steep grade. Cerutty claimed that Gerschler, Igloi, Stampfl, and other interval training theorists lacked an understanding of human nature.

Arthur Lydiard, who followed Cerutty as a leading distance coach, based his training approach on a solid base of general endurance. According to his method, middle-distance runners covered over 100 miles a week in long, steady runs. His system is divided into four cycles: cross-country training, marathon training, hill training, and track training. Marathon training lasted fourteen weeks, and included long runs every day, and fartlek once a week. Hill training took six weeks, and emphasized creating oxygen debt tolerance using interval work six days a week. One day was set aside for a long run (up to twenty-two miles). On the track, Lydiard's method is based on two four-week cycles. The emphasis is on repetition runs over 100 to 1,200 meters and interval sprints (50 meters fast, 50 meters slow, etc.).

Multi-world record-holder Ron Clarke, who had no coach and

worked according to his own experience, trained all year round and every day. His training changed little and did not aim for a culminating point each season. Clarke, who expected to be in form all the time, increased his training load year after year. He used mainly long endurance runs on grass surfaces or roads and covered them fast. Clarke, who seldom used a track and never a stopwatch, trained twice or three times a day. His occasional track workouts included 10 x 200 meters (26-28 seconds) or 10 x 400 (60 seconds) with recovery jogs for equivalent periods of time.

Summing up, it appears that distance running training methods have developed through endurance runs, mixed endurance and repetition runs, Holmer's fartlek, Olander's system, interval training (Zatopek, Gerschler, Igloi, Nikiforov, etc.), and the methods of Cerutty, Lydiard, and Clarke. Cerutty and Lydiard were responsible for major changes in training in the 1960s by increasing training loads, making training more natural, using mainly long endurance runs and fartlek for preparation, and including specific endurance training with emphasis on uphill work. Only Igloi stuck to his interval principles.

3

The Importance of Pacing

by Jim Lilliefors

For years, coaches, runners, and joggers have accepted the importance of pacing. Arthur Lydiard listed it among the eleven essential factors needed for a runner to reach his racing potential. Vladimir Kuts, former Olympic champion, called it one of the four qualities responsible for racing success. Joe Henderson wrote, in a 1970 *Runner's World* article, "Generally, it's pace that kills, not distance." In a 1978 survey of the nation's fastest distance runners, 81 percent agreed that in a race with runners of near-equal ability, pacing is a prime factor in determining who wins or loses.

Yet even though runners and coaches acknowledge the importance of pacing, it remains a confusing subject. Consider the inconsistency that showed up in our survey of forty of the nation's top distance runners. Even pacing, 96 percent said, is the most efficient means of running a marathon. Yet in the poll's next question, 76 percent of the runners admitted they generally ran the first half of the race faster than the second half. There is a clear discrepancy between understanding pacing and its actual application.

The trend in long-distance running has been toward more even-paced racing. Runners now pace themselves more evenly than they did in the mid-sixties. Also, the top runners generally pace themselves more evenly than the slower ones. Yet this area is still open to many questions.

Certainly uneven pacing has been the trademark of several extremely successful runners. Former mile record-holders Jim Ryun and Filbert Bayi often ran unevenly paced races. Ryun sometimes covered the last lap of a mile in 53 seconds, while Bayi might run that fast for the first lap. There is a tactical basis for each runner's

38

technique, even if they are not the most physiologically sound methods of racing.

"I'm pretty sure one's best times in races (from marathons down to six-milers) are achieved as a result of even pacing," said Bill Rodgers, America's fastest marathoner. "If I've had any success in racing, this is one of the major reasons why. In my training and in my racing, I've tried to run at a steady, rhythmic pace."

The importance of even pacing is also emphasized by Manfred Steffny, a West German marathon expert. According to him, "A factor in marathon racing that is of supreme importance is the even pace. In no other sport will you gain so much from an ability to apportion your energy carefully. Poor pacing is disastrous; usually it takes the form of going out too fast."

The common problem of starting too quickly is a natural result of anticipation and crowd excitement. Generally, though, the top runners are able to avoid this temptation to go with the flow, and instead run at their own pace.

Jon Anderson, 1973 Boston Marathon winner, said, "If one is to race effectively, he must realize what pace to begin the race at—this is the key to being able to finish the race effectively."

Although more people run a faster first half of a marathon than second, the fastest races (such as Derek Clayton's and Christa Vahlensieck's records) have been accomplished on fairly even pacing. Manfred Steffny has pointed out that proper pacing is especially crucial in the first half of a marathon, citing the example that Olympic marathon champions very rarely lead at the halfway point (Frank Shorter being an exception). Proper pacing in the first half may alleviate, or totally eliminate, the infamous "wall" that runners are prone to discover in the closing miles.

Chris Berka, a 2:19 marathoner, lent support to the idea that the "wall" may simply be a product of improper pacing: "My best races in the marathon have been when I have started slow, at an even 5:45-6:00 pace for the first 5-10 miles, then finished strong, at 5:00-5:15 pace. I think this is a good strategy because the runner who goes out slowly and spends the remainder of the race passing people stays confident and excited throughout the entire race, whereas the ones who go out fast become discouraged at 15-20 miles. Maintaining enthusiasm for the race is the single most important factor in race pacing."

Although even pacing is accepted as preferable, it is not always practical. Joe Henderson wrote, "The trouble with most marathon pacing guides is that they're too perfect.... They give a mathematical tidiness. Unfortunately, they don't take into account the effects of early race excitement and late-race fatigue. The fact is very few marathoners hold this steady a pace, and it may not even be right for them to try."

Sixty percent of the runners polled agreed running one's own pace is more crucial than varying it to match that of the competition. Most of the other 40 percent indicated that the two should be closely entwined. "Your pace should account for your competition," said Bob Varsha.

The beginner, though, should probably first work on learning even pacing and not worry about the competition. As Tony Sandoval, who missed the 1976 Olympic marathon team by one spot, said, "Beginning runners, who don't have pace ingrained, should be more cautious and run their own pace. Very good runners can play the odds a bit more because they will have a good idea of what they're up to pacewise and probably will be in good enough shape to survive a pace that is erratic or adjusted to the competition."

The difficulty in even-paced running is perhaps best summed up by Chuck Smead, a 2:14 marathoner: "I agree that, ideally, even pacing is the best way to run your fastest time. However, it is very difficult to pace yourself evenly when you are in a large marathon, due to terrain and fellow competitors."

There is no simple key to learning pacing. Seventy-two percent of the runners said that pacing is something that must become ingrained through disciplined training. Eighty percent claimed that they are able to tell if the pace they are running in a race is too fast or too slow.

But how does a runner reach this state where pacing is ingrained? Opinions varied widely, from Gayle Barron's comment, "I feel you are born with the ability to pace," to John A. Kelley's, "Learn pacing? Years and years of practice." Most agree, though, that practice runs at race pace or faster are crucial. Bill Rodgers said, "I do believe simulated race-pace training (periodically, once or twice a week) and heavy mileage are a good mixture, which will ingrain in the runner the ability to go on 'automatic pilot' for a good part of his race."

Pace practice doesn't necessarily have to be done exclusively on the training track; many runners use unimportant races for this purpose. Tom Fleming, the 2:12 marathoner from New Jersey, believes that once race pace is learned, regular interval work is not absolutely necessary, since a runner can derive the same benefits from racing. This idea obviously favors the runner who races frequently. "At the stage I'm at now," Fleming said, "I never really think about the pace in training. I could never run 5:00 pace or under in practice anyway."

This still leaves the question unanswered: How can race pace be ingrained in a runner? Lydiard believes it happens through a combination of track training and racing or running time trials: "If careful speed control is maintained, ten weeks of track training before the important competition for which you are training should not be too long a period."

The only consensus on training from the survey was that once or twice a week the racer should train at race pace or faster. There were as many sets of specifics as there were runners queried.

Advice from the experts on how to develop pace:

Frank Shorter: "I consciously train myself to run at a specific pace. It's done through interval training."

Jon Anderson: "A runner should learn pacing through timed efforts over specific distances—these can be races or workouts. I suppose it would take a long time for a runner to develop a feel for pace just through races—also it would likely result in some disappointing race results. Timed efforts in workouts over short or long distances will speed the process of developing a sense of pace. I would add that the timed efforts need not be any more frequent than once a week."

Amby Burfoot: "A runner can learn pace only by racing. Specific training will of course affect the pace a runner can maintain during a race (the hard, fast trainer can run at a hard, fast pace) but I doubt that any particular kind of training prepares the runner for even pacing. Racing experience alone will provide this."

Jeff Galloway: "I run intervals at set paces—many intervals at the same pace."

Bill Rodgers: "I always try to train at an even pace and don't do much interval or fartlek running. I train at 6:00 to 6:40 pace on most runs. I believe even running on a daily basis can help in developing a sense of pace, as does working with a watch when one is doing intervals on a track. One comes to be able to estimate distance and know his approximate pace at the end of a run."

Walt Stack: "Check your watch, compare times at key checkpoints."

Nina Kuscsik: "By being aware of how her body feels at certain paces. Breathing, leg movement, foot strike, push off, leg lift, strides per minute, concentration—all factors that change according to pace. I think running alone is the best way to learn these variances."

Brian Maxwell: "It's best to learn by timing oneself on courses of known measurement or on the track."

Gayle Barron: "Pacing can be developed through practicing long, steady distances, or by running with someone who knows how to pace evenly."

Chuck Smead: "I try to train faster than I want to race. Then, when I get in a race, the pace seems slow. This can really help when running a marathon."

All of the runners surveyed have raced at distances ranging from the half-mile to the marathon and beyond, though in most cases their specialty is the marathon.

When asked what they believed to be the crossover point in terms of even pacing versus uneven pacing, the runners' answers varied from "one-mile or less" to "15-18 miles." Most, though, indicated that there is no crossover point, that even pacing is just as important in a 440-yard race as in a 50-miler.

"I don't think that there is or ever should be a crossover point at which faster times might be achieved if uneven pacing were utilized," said Bill Rodgers. "Even 200- or 400-meter races would benefit from even, rhythmic pacing."

Jon Anderson added to this concept: "There is no crossover point. Just take a look at the statistics of most world-record races. These will show even or near-even pacing in all races from 800 on up."

Said Frank Shorter, "I think even pacing is the most economical means for every event from one mile up."

In gauging pace for shorter races, Lydiard has recommended keeping within a safety zone, generally no more than five seconds per mile faster than even pace. He warned, "The payment for a one-second speed-up in the early laps is a two-second slowdown in the late ones."

Considering some of the fast times achieved through uneven pacing, one wonders what, say, Jim Ryun could have run had he been on an even pace. But then we're ignoring the individual psyche that made Ryun run the way he did. In answer to the question, "In a race with runners of equal ability, is pacing often a factor in who wins or loses?" Don Kardong's reply was, "There are no runners of equal ability."

The skeptics of strict pace training said, "Between competitive people, pride often wins out over patience" (Bob Varsha), and "Pace, pace, pace. Whatever happened to inspiration, magic, and poetry?" (Don Kardong).

Those who feel that pacing is not the telling factor in racing prefer to believe emotional factors are more important, that strict pace training is simply "mathematical tidiness," as Joe Henderson wrote.

Yet emotional qualities, too, depend on pacing. Runners who let inspiration take over too early have trouble later. Kardong has said, "I let inspiration take over when perspiration has done its job." So pacing is more than just speed. A runner must learn to pace his enthusiasm as well.

Kenny Moore said, "An intense, highly competitive frame of mind over the early part of the run seems to evaporate after twenty miles. So I prefer to begin in a low-key sort of yawning-sleepy state of semi-consciousness. I watch the scenery and the other runners with appreciation rather than any sort of competitive response. Later, entering the last six miles, I try to get enthusiastic about racing."

Perhaps this, pacing of enthusiasm, is the most important pacing of all.

4

Less Is More

by Doug Rennie

The American way of life teaches us from childhood that bigger is always better. The axiom has therefore dictated that we attempt to buy big cars, carry big bankrolls, eat big meals, and, as runners, use big mileage figures to boost performance. The theory that big mileage makes a big-name racer has been reinforced by veteran racers who've made good.

As a result of all the publicity that "big mileage: the key to success" gets, thirty- to forty-year-old runners who decide to make the transition from fitness running to racing often see this as the "roadwork to success." "If Frank Shorter runs 140 miles per week and I want to be as good as Frank Shorter, I must run 140 miles per week" seems to be the prevailing training philosophy. If a racer enjoys moderate success at 40 miles per week, he'll logically enjoy twice the success at 80 miles per week, and will theoretically *become* Frank Shorter at 140 miles per week.

Imposing such rigid limitations on a runner's life-style is not necessarily desirable—or even necessary—if the racer's goal is to run close to his potential and be competitive in his age-group at the local or regional level. If a racer is harboring Olympic hopes, perhaps total commitment to endless 100-mile-plus weeks is mandatory. For most runners-turned-racers in their thirties, such prohibitive training schedules can sometimes do more harm than good to race times. Too many Masters—or those even younger—frantically chase the miles, often experiencing little or no improvement, subjecting themselves to chronic physical and psychological staleness.

Consider, for instance, the syndrome of "mileage mania." You call a runner friend and make a date for a six-mile run. It's set for 6 p.m. He arrives at 5 p.m. and puts in eight miles before you ever arrive. He then drags himself through the scheduled six miles with you and happily rushes home to record 14 miles in his logbook. When the weekend comes, you trounce him in the 8-mile race by a healthy two minutes, as he has trouble, late in the race, putting one foot in front of the other. His response? More mileage! He'll surely get revenge at the next race. After all, he's doing twice your mileage, and that has to make him faster, doesn't it? This raises the question that is so often applied to art: Is less really more?

There are many successful racers in their thirties and forties who race at or near the top of their age-groups at distances up to the marathon by training for only about 50 miles a week. Recent discussion with racers on the various levels indicates that racing success is not so much dictated by the quantity of mileage, but rather by the quality of those miles. Less, for them, is definitely more.

KENT GUTHRIE

Kent Guthrie of Pleasant Hill, California, recently turned forty and immediately proceeded to obliterate Masters records in virtually every important northern California race from five through twenty miles. As of this writing, he has twenty-two consecutive victories.

Guthrie's impressive feats include such enviable times as 53:51 for 10 miles and 32:52 for 10,000 meters—times that make him competitive with top runners barely half his age. It is not uncommon for Guthrie to finish in the overall top ten in races with more than 400 competitors. Guthrie's accomplishments are so awesome that his rivals are convinced that he is a fanatic who runs 150 miles a week.

Guthrie's training is not based on staggering mileage, however. Instead, he runs "about 40 or 50 miles a week, a good deal of it over hills with maybe a weekly long run of about 11 miles." He sometimes logs as few as 25 miles a week if he's tired, although about 50 is his regular distance. His only deviation from that schedule came in September 1976, when he trained at 70 miles per week for four weeks, after which he returned quickly to his regular 50-mile regimen. Two months later he ran the Pepsi 20-mile race in 1:51:07, a blistering pace of 20 back-to-back 5:33-minute miles! It was the fastest 20-mile time in 1976 by a U.S. Master, and placed Guthrie thirteenth overall in a field of nearly 1,100 runners from northern California. More remarkable than his race-day accomplishment was his admission that during those two months prior to the Pepsi, he had averaged 45 miles per week, with a high week of 56 miles and a low week of 30 miles.

It should not be assumed, however, that Guthrie jogs his 45-50 weekly miles. Much of it is intensive, high-quality mileage done on the track and over hills. One of his favorite workouts consists of running up a 300-yard hill ten to twenty times. Although this workout takes only about forty minutes to an hour and totals about 6 to 8 miles, the training effect is profound. Another regular workout course is an 11-mile run from Guthrie's home to neighboring Moraga, a demanding course with hills of all lengths and gradients. That is his most frequent workout session, and he runs it once or twice a week. In between, he does slow 3- to 5-mile runs, and often takes a day off each week. To further complement his rough terrain workouts, he occasionally trains at the Diablo Valley Junior College track, where he runs six to twelve 440s, with about a 220 jog in between. Running hills exclusively tends to make the legs heavy and slow, so the sprints seem to keep his legs lively.

One of Guthrie's training partners, the late, legendary Jim Shettler, trained along similar lines—with comparable results. In 1976 Shettler related that he alternated 40- and 60-mile weeks, and incorporated hills in his training as often as possible. This approach made it possible for him to dominate the northern California Masters scene for many years.

BOB BOURBEAU

Bob Bourbeau, a 41-year-old runner from Reno, Nevada, is hardly the typical ectomorphic distance man. At 5'11" and 178 pounds, he seems too bulky to travel any great distances in times approaching those of his emaciated rivals. In spite of this, Bourbeau has translated his 50-58 weekly miles into such impressive times as 26:44 for 5 miles and 1:55:21 for 20 miles.

He reports having experimented with extended periods of longer training, having run 70 to 85 miles a week during the summer of 1975. To his consternation, though, he found that "when I began racing in September, my times were much slower than the previous year. Also, I felt worse while racing. Late in October I contracted mononucleosis and didn't run for eight weeks." Upon recovering and returning to his 50+ miles per week, Bourbeau turned tiger once again, helping his West Valley Joggers and Striders teammates win the 1976 National Masters AAU cross-country title.

His usual training pattern consists of a few runs of 8 to 10 miles over hills or "rolling terrain" early in the week, followed by a track workout of four hard half-milers, usually on Wednesday. Then comes what Bourbeau considers the most important part of his training: an all-out race or 5-mile trial each weekend.

His conclusions about his training methods are twofold: "The best way for me to get in shape for racing is to race regularly"; and

"Running more than 60 miles a week makes me tired and does not improve my performance."

ABE UNDERWOOD

Abe Underwood of Sacramento took up long-distance running six years ago when he was nearly fifty pounds overweight—"a grotesque caricature of the Hindenberg," Abe says. Since then he has propelled his forty-year-old body (now a slinky 137 pounds) to a 2:45 marathon, a 1:56 20-miler, and a third-place finish in the Pacific Association AAU 50-mile championship race. Underwood runs equally well at shorter distances. Yet his 1976 average weekly mileage was a modest 49.

His training diary reveals some startling facts, seemingly incompatible with his ultra-distance achievements. The two-month period prior to his 50-miler included weeks of 15, 36, 38, and 45 miles, with a high week of 72 miles. During the month of February, when he ran his 50-miler, he totaled only 219 miles for the month—and that total included the 50-miler itself.

In preparing for his 72-mile trek around Lake Tahoe last September, he confessed that he threw in a few weeks of 70 miles or more in the two months leading up to the race. From training that barely totaled 2,500 miles for the year, he finished third in the grueling Tahoe test of endurance, beating many good runners whose training mileage was nearly double his.

"I suppose you could call me a low-mileage runner," Underwood admits, "and I'm sure my training violates some of distance running's sacred cows. But I'm just not the kind of person who can constantly log high-mileage weeks. I get tired and dull and the next thing I know my body takes over and slows me down. I used to have mileage goals (3,500 for 1976, for example) but have since given them up because these goals force you to run when your body says you should rest. So now I just run how I feel and this produces both low and fairly high mileage weeks, although I virtually never go more than 70 or so." Underwood's log bears this out: nearly every month has one week of around 30 miles, one week in the 60-70 range, and two others in the 40-55 range. His approach apparently keeps him fresh, eager, and able to race well year round.

He also subscribes to Bourbeau's theory of "racing often to race well." Underwood ran thirty-three races in 1976 of 6 miles or longer, and feels that such high-volume racing precludes the necessity of a lot of speed work. He therefore does little speed work during the week. Underwood operates on a three-day cycle of two 12- to 13-mile days (two workouts: 5 a.m. and 7 p.m.) at a steady pace, followed by an easy 5-mile run on the third day. On weekends he races and, whenever possible, does long runs of 12 miles or more, often in the hills. Another of Underwood's training secrets is to run a sub-three-hour marathon every six to eight weeks as a means of maintaining endurance, as well as the psychological perspective required for ultra-distance running.

DAN GREENWALD

Dan Greenwald, the 37-year-old track and cross-country coach at Bella Vista High School in Fair Oaks, California, also exemplifies the "less is more" principle. Full-time coaching, a demanding class-room schedule, graduate studies, and an active family life preclude long training sessions. Greenwald rarely runs more than 25 to 35 miles a week ("most of them over a hilly four-mile course") and yet he is able to maintain a sub-six-minute-per-mile pace in 8- to 10-mile runs. He insists that he is rarely tired and is usually able to run fast whenever he chooses.

THE AUTHOR'S EXPERIENCE

My own experiences have parallelled those of the athletes dis-cussed. Following my thirty-sixth birthday, I set personal records in every race I ran, including a 26:47 5-miler, a 32:40 6-miler, and a 55:50 10-miler. These were achieved with a training mileage that ranged from 48 to 57 miles a week over a ten-week period. Adding three weeks of 70 to 85 miles in April, I was able to run a 2:38 at the Avenue of the Giants Marathon after reducing my training to weeks of 48 and 39 miles two weeks prior to the race. Like Bourbeau and Underwood, I have tried training at 70 to 80 miles a week for extended periods on several occasions (building up gradually), but have found that I am burdened with chronic fatigue, a sour dispo-sition, aching legs, a diminished zest for running, and poor racing performance.

CONCLUSIONS

What conclusions, then, can be drawn from studying a sampling of the training programs of runners in their thirties and forties? Careful scrutiny of the runners' training diaries reveals striking similarities. There are a half-dozen ingredients that are common to all the "aging" runners who have achieved good race results.

1. Quality racing is attainable on 60 miles or less training per week. If the miles are properly organized and varied, the runner is kept fit, as well as fresh and eager for racing. Physical and psychological readiness for fast, hard running should accompany moderate training volume. Furthermore, such training is conducive to a well-rounded life-style that allows time and energy for other (non-running) interests, family activities, and, in most cases, an eight-hour-per-day job. On the other hand, carefully controlled periodic increases to 70- to 80-mile weeks for brief periods are good for increasing strength gradually, especially in preparation for races of 20 miles or more.

2. Hill running cannot be too strongly emphasized. Every runner surveyed ran hard two or three times a week, and much of this hard training included running up and down hills. This is a universal component in the training systems of all the respondents. Many felt that this was the single most important element in their training. The muscular strength and psychological toughness generated by hill training are difficult to duplicate through any other method. (Hills amount to push-ups for the legs.) Some (such as Guthrie) are fortunate enough to be surrounded by hills, but others (such as those in the Sacramento Valley) must find any hill they can and run repeats up and down it. This is not the most enjoyable kind of running, but it does produce superior racing. A runner just beginning hill training should expect to feel more than usual fatigue for two to three weeks after starting this program. But after that period, the increase in strength for races should be apparent. Hill training also builds strength for late-race kicks, something every runner should have in his running arsenal. Those who swear by hill training suggest running 3 miles at a steady pace, then doing a challenging hill six to ten times, followed by 3 more miles at a steady pace as a warm-down.

3. In your weekly schedule, include at least one longer run of 10 to 12 miles, usually over the weekend so there is no pressure to finish it before work. All runners surveyed indicated they did one long run a week. The pace is not important; but the regularity of a long run per week is.

4. Speed work (hard, fast running for brief periods) was another universal. Most of the racers use it as a supplement to hill work, not as a substitute for it. With the exception of Kent Guthrie, the runners reported that they preferred to run their speed work on trails, grass, or on the roads, rather than on a track. All ran for

• sustained periods as fast as they could *without straining*. The objective is to achieve a fast, but comfortable and relaxed, tempo. Some racers reported running fast and relaxed until they began to strain, whereupon they slowed down to recover. Others preferred to run timed repeats of one to four minutes with slower running in between. Speed work of this sort was done twice a week as part of a hard fartlek workout that also included some hill running. Combining the hill work with speed work helps assure that the legs will become less tight and will have more vitality than they would if only hill running were used.

5. Rest is an important, but all too often overlooked, part of wise training. It is no surprise, therefore, that all the surveyed racers stressed the need for at least two days a week of easy, steady recreational running, often as slow as 7:30- to 8:00-minute miles. This is often done in the company of friends, with the emphasis on relaxation and good conversation. As Bob Bourbeau puts it: "I certainly don't think that it is necessary to train hard every day." Abe Underwood credits not only easy days, but entire easy weeks of as little as 15 or 20 miles as the key to his ability to race well year-round.

6. The final principle of the "less is more" guidelines is the need for regular racing. The majority of the racers took part in competition at least every other weekend. And when races became less frequent, they often substituted hard, sustained (but not maximal) runs of 5-8 miles.

TRAINING SCHEDULE

Based on the above principles, a sample training schedule (created from a composite of those submitted) might look something like this:

Sunday: A long, steady (but not exhausting) run of 10-13 miles, including a few long hills, if possible.

Monday: Eight miles of hard fartlek, including some hard hill running combined with some fast, but relaxed tempo running on the flat. This workout should leave the runner tired, but not exhausted. He should feel that he has accomplished something substantial.

Tuesday: 6-10 miles at a pace that feels comfortable over flat terrain.

Wednesday: Repeat of Monday, although the workout might be limited exclusively to either hill work or fast repeats on flatter terrain. Again, try to maintain the workout at 8 miles.

Thursday: 6-10 miles at a pace that feels comfortable.

Friday: 3-5 miles of easy running, possibly including four or five runs through a 110- to 150-yard distance at half-effort. This could also be a rest day. Most racers questioned took off at least one day per week.
Saturday: Race or fast time trial of 5-6 miles.

This sample schedule produces 47 to 60 miles of balanced, quality training per week and is similar to the schedules of the runners surveyed. Thus, 50 miles or so a week can provide a substantial training effect if it includes a judicious blend of aerobic and anaerobic running. The tendency of those who pursue high mileage is to run everything at the same, steady pace in order to avoid exhaustion and injury. The result is that the body and mind are never forced to adapt to the oxygen debt and physical discomfort incurred during a fast race. Nor are the leg muscles or neurological responses adapted to the greater stress of racing. Conversely, running hard *every* day tears down the body, and allows no opportunity for the longer, easier runs that promote aerobic fitness.

If you are one of the many racers happy training at 80-100 miles per week and you have performances you are proud of with that program, by all means stick to it. The information presented here is not a panacea. There are obviously many different roads to enjoyable running and successful racing.

Still, many of us have neither the time nor the energy to consistently log titanic mileage. So it is comforting to know that we can race as well or even better than some of our high-mileage rivals. It is encouraging to see runners like Guthrie, Bourbeau, and Underwood validate the premise that, even in running, often less is more.

5

Lydiard's Training System

by John Hamburger

The place is Auckland, New Zealand. It's March 12, 1977, and 20,000 competitors are crowding toward the starting line of the race that fields more runners than any other. The 11.27-kilometer "Round the Bays" run exemplifies the enthusiasm for running that has captured people far from this port city. One of the people primarily responsible for inspiring New Zealanders to take to the roads is Arthur Lydiard. His training approach, perfected over the past thirty-five years, has altered the training of nearly all distance runners.

Lydiard has coached runners in Finland, Mexico, Venezuela, and Denmark, as well as in his native New Zealand. His training system has been responsible for numerous records in middle- and long-distance events. The successes of Peter Snell, Murray Halberg, and Barry Magee at the 1960 Rome Olympics were largely the result of Lydiard's pioneering training methods.

Before Lydiard's influence was felt on training techniques, most distance runners trained using interval work. This training involved running a series of 400-meter sprints. Both the sprints and the rest intervals between them were carefully regulated.

Lydiard changed all this with his radical departure from earlier training methods. The Lydiard approach involves a base of long-duration, even-paced running with strong speed. Even Peter Snell, for instance, whose event was the 800 meters, ran twenty-mile workouts in practice. But once the runner has achieved a solid base of long-distance running, the skills must be sharpened on the track. Lydiard has made a science of pinpointing the precise moment to begin the various stages of training. He has assembled training schedules for runners of different ages for specific events. These appear in detail in his book *Running the Lydiard Way.**

THE PHYSIOLOGY OF EXERCISE

Lydiard's training system involves a balanced combination of *aerobic* and *anaerobic* running.* * Lydiard stresses the importance of concentrating first on aerobic running. Researchers Laurence Morehouse and Augustus Miller have demonstrated that aerobic exercise is nineteen times more economical than anaerobic exercise.* * *

Aerobic training enlarges the heart and improves its efficiency in pumping blood throughout the body. The lungs, too, become more efficient, enabling the blood to absorb oxygen more rapidly. For best results, aerobic running should be faster than long slow distance (LSD) work. This type of training should be performed at a level above 70 percent of your best aerobic effort.

Anaerobic training, on the other hand, pushes your body beyond its ability to use oxygen. This helps develop anaerobic capacity, which improves the body's ability to withstand maximum oxygen debts. In anaerobic running, oxygen debts are built up, accompanied by the accumulation of lactic acid and other waste products. Lactic acid upsets the *blood pH*, the measure of the blood's acidity or alkalinity. Since this can lead to neuromuscular breakdown, it is important to gauge carefully the amount of anaerobic work you are doing.

Four weeks of anaerobic running is usually sufficient. During this time, train hard for about three days to lower the blood pH (making it more acidic); train lightly for a day to allow blood pH to return to normal; then pull it down again with anaerobic work the following day. The main thing is to keep the blood pH fluctuating.

Lydiard stresses that interval training is the least important aspect of training. The object of anaerobic training is to lower the blood pH, and this can be accomplished in various ways. According to Lydiard, "There is no coach in the world who can say exactly what an athlete should do as far as number of repetitions, distances, and

---

* Arthur Lydiard with Garth Gilmour, *Running the Lydiard Way* (Mountain View, Calif.: World Publications, 1978).

** *Aerobic* running involves running within your capacity to use oxygen. If you run beyond this limit, you move into *anaerobic* running. Anaerobic running creates what is known as *oxygen debt.*

*** Laurence Morehouse and Augustus T. Miller, *The Physiology of Exercise* (St. Louis: The C. V. Mosby Co., 1967).

intervals are concerned. Not even physiologists can tell an athlete that. The important thing is that the athlete knows what he's trying to achieve and goes out and works at it until he does."

Lydiard's training program is organized into several phases: marathon training, anaerobic training, track training, and cross-country training. In this article, each area will be dealt with separately. However, when you put together your own training program, realize that these various types of training must be balanced if you expect to achieve good results.

MARATHON TRAINING

This part of the program is the same whether you plan to run 800 or 10,000 meters. The main goal at this stage is to develop enough stamina to maintain necessary speed over the entire distance you are running. This involves training until your body does not create oxygen debts quickly, thus ensuring your ability to recover rapidly.

Begin by training on a time basis, rather than by mileage. Determine your pace by running an out-and-back course for a total of thirty minutes (fifteen minutes each way). Run at a pace that is your best aerobic speed. Increase your training time until you can follow the following schedule (for adults):

Monday	1 hour
Tuesday	1½ hours
Wednesday	1 hour
Thursday	2 hours
Friday	1 hour
Saturday	2-3 hours
Sunday	1½ hours

Once you have mastered that schedule, you can turn to one that is concerned more with distance than time. At this point, you should run about 160 kilometers a week at about your best aerobic level. Do supplementary jogging if you wish, as that benefits the cardiac system and aids recovery. A weekly schedule for this stage would be:

Monday	15 kilometers at one-half effort over an undulating course
Tuesday	25 kilometers at one-fourth effort over a reasonably flat course
Wednesday	20 kilometers at one-half effort over a hilly course
Thursday	30 kilometers at one-fourth effort over a reasonably flat course

Friday	15 kilometers at three-fourths effort over a flat course
Saturday	35 kilometers at one-fourth effort over a reasonably flat course
Sunday	25 kilometers at one-fourth effort over any type of terrain

Relax as much as possible, particularly the upper body. Keep your arm action low, and avoid clenching your fists, as tense muscles waste energy. Don't run on your toes. Foot-fall should be nearly flat, with the heel hitting first, and a slight roll in from the outside edge of the foot. Lydiard recommends training on roads rather than cross-country, since traction is better, and thus more economical. Just be sure to use well-made shoes with good rubber soles. It doesn't matter how you take in oxygen; breathe through your mouth if necessary. To improve your running posture, keep your eyes fixed on a point about sixty meters ahead of you.

ANAEROBIC TRAINING

This phase of training follows the marathon training period. Now you should begin to emphasize muscle development of the upper legs by running on steep hills. It is also essential to do suppling and loosening exercises regularly, with particular attention to ankle flexibility.

For the hill training, find a hill 300 meters long, with 400 to 800 meters of reasonably flat ground at the top and bottom. Starting at the base of the hill, spring up it on your toes, not running but bouncing. Strive for high leg action. Run with your head up, looking straight ahead. Keep your arms, shoulders, neck, and facial muscles relaxed. Do only as much hill springing as your condition allows, and only increase the work load as your muscles become acclimated. At the top of the hill don't stop running, but slow to an easy jog. When you reach the downward side, run faster, with relaxed, slightly longer strides. At the base of the hill, practice sprint repetitions on the flat over distances from 50 to 400 meters. These repetitions begin development of anaerobic capacity. At this stage, confine your anaerobic workout to what you can do in 600 to 800 meters.

Spend an hour on the hill circuit just described, as well as fifteen minutes each warming up and cooling down. Continue this program for six weeks. During this stage, spend three days a week on hill training, alternating these with three days of leg-speed running and

Arthur Lydiard's coaching methods revolutionize long-distance running
(Photo by Dave Drennan)

one of long-distance running. Run about 150 kilometers a week, with an additional thirty minutes of easy running each day.

Leg-speed training requires a flat area of 100 to 120 meters. Warm up for fifteen minutes, and then run over the course ten times, moving your legs as fast as possible. Allow three-minute intervals between runs, and cool down afterward for fifteen minutes.

TRACK TRAINING

By the time you reach this stage, you have already completed the most important part of the training—preparing the body for anaerobic work. "Without that preparation," says Lydiard, "track schedules are not worth the paper they are written on." By this point, you should have developed good endurance. Now, speed training becomes the primary focus.

Practice fast, relaxed speed running for 100 to 150 meters, with recovery intervals of at least three minutes between each run. A typical workout at this stage includes: warm-up; suppling and loosening exercises; running 80 to 100 meters, with shoulders and arms relaxed, on the toes, with high knee-lift and fast leg action; jogging or walking three minutes; and repeating the sequence. This should be followed by fast, relaxed running.

Initially, according to Lydiard, track training should be at less than full speed. Otherwise you will sharpen to racing condition before reaching the best coordination of stamina and speed. As long as you maintain careful speed control, ten weeks of track training prior to competition should not be excessive.

Lydiard recommends a balanced program of the following training exercises:

1. *Fartlek* involves running at various speeds over forest trails, in parks, and through the countryside. It incorporates both aerobic and anaerobic running. Fartlek running is ideal for aiding recovery from hard training and racing.
2. *Paarlauf training* is a form of relay racing over predetermined track distances, with an overlap of one runner. The runners continue to race other teams until stopped by a signal. This exercise is recommended for anaerobic training and speed development.
3. *Time trials* are timed runs at distances slightly less than you are training to race. Concentrate on strong, even-paced running to develop coordination of stamina and speed.
4. *Starting practice* helps improve reflexes.
5. *Repetitions* develop anaerobic capacity. But you must vary the

number of repetitions, the distance, the time each run takes, and the intervals. However, the times of the repetitions and intervals, the number of repetitions, and the distances are *not* important. (That's what makes this different from interval work.) Run until the oxygen debt makes you tired, indicating you have developed a low blood pH.

6. *Sharpeners* put the knife-edge on anaerobic training capacity. This is a type of anaerobic training, with less volume and intensity. Run five laps on the track, sprinting 50 in every 100 meters, and jogging the other 50 (twenty sprints in all). Do these about once a week.

7. *Sprint training* is used for development of speed. Allow adequate recovery intervals between fast runs.

During the first four weeks of track training, alternate the above types of training daily. Do two or three days of anaerobic training, two or three days of speed or sprint training, and others of jogging or fartlek. Daily training should depend on your reactions to the previous day's training. Track training should continue for 4½ weeks.

Lydiard recommends the following typical schedule for this period:

Monday	Sharpeners
Tuesday	Sprint training or easy fartlek
Wednesday	Race, time trials, sprint, and middle distance
Thursday	Use for coordinating, depending on previous time trials (fartlek, sharpeners, or sprint training)
Friday	Jogging
Saturday	Race near your racing distance
Sunday	Long, easy run

During the final ten days of track training, Lydiard recommends lightening training to build mental and physical reserves. Continue to train every day, but do so well within your capacity.

When the main competitions begin, you do not need to train hard, but do time trials at least twice a week. A typical training schedule during competition is:

Saturday	Race
Sunday	Easy, longish run
Monday	Sharpeners or easy fartlek
Tuesday	Light sprint training
Wednesday	Race sprints and middle or short distances

Thursday	Jog
Friday	Stride-outs

Every day during this time, do some supplementary long aerobic running.

CROSS-COUNTRY TRAINING

Cross-country training helps those with tight upper body muscles to use more relaxed, economical running techniques. Hilly cross-country terrains also help develop power and ankle flexibility for a more driving, natural stride. Running up hills improves knee-lift. This is beneficial, since knee-lift governs stride length and speed. There is also psychological value to cross-country training.

"You find that you'll run over these terrains in a nonpressured way," says Lydiard, "speeding up or slowing down according to the lay of the land, the conditions, and your personal reactions."

Since accurate timing is impossible, cross-country running is conducive to a pace that makes you pleasantly tired, but not exhausted. There's no need to time your runs during cross-country training and racing, as courses and weather conditions vary daily and affect performances.

If you are training for a cross-country race, you should follow a schedule for ten weeks preceding the race.* This schedule should include a combination of anaerobic running (including sharpeners and longer repetitions), time trials, and races. But these ten weeks should be preceded by two to three months of aerobic cross-country running.

TRAINING SUMMARY

According to Lydiard, the more often you train, the better. If time allows, it is advisable to train two or three times a day. This improves cardiac efficiency and assists in recovery from low blood pH.

Vary the terrains you train on, as changes in scenery will stimulate you to train more consistently. For conditioning training, it is best to choose terrain that offers good traction. Then you can run at a high aerobic effort without tiring your leg muscles too rapidly.

If you train in extremely low temperatures, it is vital that the humidity be low. Otherwise your lungs may ice up. If, on the other

---

* *See* Arthur Lydiard with Garth Gilmour, *Running the Lydiard Way* (Mountain View, Calif.: World Publications, 1978), pp. 205-28.

hand, you are training in high temperatures, the humidity should be high. High humidity will keep your skin wet with perspiration and help cool your body temperature.

After the competitive season ends, you should do light jogging for at least fifteen minutes a day. Continue to train as much as possible, preferably daily.

As you put together your training program, keep in mind Lydiard's advice: "Attempt to understand why you are doing your training, and what physiological and mechanical improvement each phase will bring you.... An athlete should know why a certain exercise is being used and how it will affect him."

6

A Practical Approach to Training

by Ron Hill

Most of today's top cross-country, road, and middle-distance track runners are putting in long distances (around 100 miles per week) in training. There are some exceptions, but these "low-mileage" people are probably not realizing their full potential.

For working people, especially those who are married, it is not easy to fit in 100 miles a week without conflicting with social and family life. But with careful planning it can be done. The easiest way of accomplishing this is by training twice a day—once before breakfast and once in the evening, preferably before the evening meal.

The best way to train twice a day is by running to work and back. Using myself as an example, I run 7 miles to work each morning and between 8½ and 12 miles home again in the evening.

The morning run must always be easy—mine takes around 50 minutes—and the hard work can be done in the evening. At 6:10 p.m. I am completely finished with my day's running. To complete the picture, on Saturdays I usually do an easy 4 miles before breakfast and on Sundays, 20 miles. The main beauty of training this way is that it becomes a habit; if long distances are to be covered, this is how it must develop.

Naturally, working out a schedule to fit one's own requirements usually entails training alone. This is a good thing. If you are going to push yourself in a race you must learn to push yourself alone in training. If you ever get to the top, remember you are on your own when leading a race. Training alone avoids wasted time waiting for training companions. It means you can do exactly what you want, depending on how you feel, without trying to accommodate someone else's training requirements.

Having discussed my own training, let me add that I am not suggesting that everyone should run 7 miles in the morning. This

61

became necessary by force of circumstances, representing the shortest route between home and work. I started off at 18 by doing 3 miles before breakfast. This gradually developed through 4½, 5, 5½, and now finally to 7 miles, as I adapted myself to the increased mileage, and as circumstances changed.

Training need not be a drag, and I regard it as a quiet period when I can be alone between work and my family life—a kind of mental rest. Rather than causing work or social life to suffer, running can actually benefit them.

As I mentioned, it is an accepted fact that most top runners train long mileages and twice a day. But I can say with certainty that anyone who decides to follow these principles will improve over athletes of similar capabilities. This is because 99 out of 100 people will find excuses not to do any more training than they are now doing; it is the exceptional runner who will train and improve.

Let me warn anyone who works out a schedule or routine along the lines of my own not to expect results too soon. I've found in my own experience that improvement is slow, but steady.

The figure of 100 miles per week is not a magic one. It is a useful guideline for mature athletes, those over twenty-one. For those who are younger, I suggest something like 70 miles at age eighteen, 80 miles at ages nineteen and twenty, working up to 100 or more miles over the next two or three years. This could be easily accommodated, but much depends on the individual.

England's Ron Hill held the Boston Marathon record for five years. He's shown here winning the Maryland Marathon. (Photo by Yankee Runner)

7

Ron Clarke on Training

by Ron Clarke

In thinking about training, I find few if any trends, but rather a myriad of ideas. In distance running, there is no single path to success. Every distance runner lives in his own environment, and has his own characteristics, physically and psychologically. These must be adapted to his individual training.

In any type of training consistency in effort is essential. Training cannot be too easy, definitely not too hard, but above all it must be consistent.

CONSISTENCY IN TRAINING

Over the past twenty years—since Franz Stampfl used highly systematic interval training, followed by Percy Cerutty's unsystematic approach, and Lydiard's combination of both types—everybody has been trying to work out the formula. The answer appears to be consistency. If I was to lean toward any trend, it would be Lydiard's training approach. His preseason training, characterized by at least one long run a week of over 22 miles in a hilly environment, and his emphasis on competition and track work during the season appeal to me.

One essential workout, which even Lydiard is unsure about, is a 50-yard repetition series. I altered this to a 100-yard repetition series, but the distance doesn't matter as long as it is not over 150 yards.

The type of training chosen depends on your approach. The English are succeeding with one, and the Americans with another. Besides individual psychology, physical characteristics, and environmental differences, all approaches are based on one essential—consistency. The type I think best is naturally the one that works best for me. It is based mainly on long-distance work, with one or two track workouts a week to sharpen up. Run for at least 10 miles in your major session every day, interspersed with two long runs a week, one 22 miles and one 15 miles. The others can be easy 10- or 12-mile workouts.

In track training, I run four or five lanes wide for 10 laps, sprinting 100 yards, followed by tempo jog recoveries. The jog around the bend has improved my running rhythm considerably and convinced me of the importance of rhythm in distance running. Times are not important, but the sprints should be flat out and the jog should be at a pace that allows for physical and mental recovery without upsetting the rhythm. It is a very tough workout; during a visit to South Africa I discovered that their best runner could only last a few laps on this type of training.

Doctors and physiologists can argue the benefit of this type of training, but I feel that—despite all the medical research—they have not yet distinguished between the superfit and the very fit. Physiologists are not capable of telling which type of training will produce great times, because if they could the Russians would be far in front of the world. Russian research is excellent, but they have yet to produce the runners to match their research achievements.

To summarize, consistency is the key to training, provided it is not too hard nor too easy. Training should include at least one long run a week and possibly some track work. The shorter the race the more track work is required. But since track training can be tough, it is advisable to follow it with an easy recovery session.

The type of training that helps you is usually the training that you don't like. Psychologically, we are all lazy and tend to do the things we enjoy most. Most people like to practice what they can do well and avoid what they are not so good at. This is why it is a good idea to do training that you do not like a bit more often.

TRAINING QUESTIONS AND ANSWERS

Question: What do you regard as the role of a coach in distance running?

Answer: To keep the athlete training consistently and to discuss tactics with him. Tactics in racing can be important. A person whose opinion you respect and in whom you have confidence can clarify a plan for you far better than you can for yourself. I feel, looking back, that if I had had someone in whom I had more confidence, I would not have come in second or third in the Tokyo Olympics and Kingston (Commonwealth) Games. My main problem was that I changed my plans too quickly. Instead of having confidence in the way I thought I should run the race, I panicked, altered my tactics, and failed.

Question: Do you think track training is as important during the cross-country season as it is in track season?

Answer: It is hard to say, but I have found that one session of track training a week is always important. I don't see why you should vary your training pattern during summer and winter. If you get fit on preseason work by the time the competition season starts, long work [steady-paced road work] should be eased off. Personally, I don't like to change my training pattern too much, and never worry about pre-season and postseason training.

Question: How many days a week do you train?

Answer: Every day, but I don't think it is really necessary to train twice a day. The evening session is the most important one. If the morning session does not affect your evening workout, continue twice-a-day training.

Question: Why is the evening training better?

Answer: You perform better physically when you have eaten four or five hours before.

Question: Do you advocate easing up training at all before competition?

Answer: Ease up before big competitions for two or three days, because you are not going to gain any more fitness. You can run the risk of making yourself tired.

Question: Should you train on the day of competition?

Answer: It depends on what you're doing. If there is nothing else to do, it's better than lying around. But it's not real training, just easy running.

Question: What do you feel are the maximum number of competitions that you can allow yourself, say, in a week?

Answer: My definition of fitness is that the fitter you are the faster you race. If you break a world record, you are the fittest you have ever been. And the fitter you are the quicker you recover. Three or four days of racing in a week is not too hard if you are running that well. However, if you are not running well there is no way you can do it.

Question: When you run many races within a limited period—say three a week—are you still training between these races?

Ron Clarke, shown here leading Dick Tayler and Lache Stewart in the Commonwealth Games 10,000 meters, is still considered by many as the greatest distance runner in history. (Photo by Tony Duffy)

Answer: Yes, I am still training every day because if you are not fit your form goes down.

Question: When starting to get fit, is it better to preserve it with a slow 10 miles or a fast 5 miles?

Answer: I think you should run any distance as hard as you can.

Question: Do you place much emphasis on weight training?

Answer: I do a little weight training, but it is only supplementary to running. The best training for running is running.

8

Igloi, Man and Method

by Arnd Kruger

One of the most successful and often-discussed coaching person-alities is sixty-six-year-old Mihaly Ignacz Igloi. Admired, some-times criticized, but no doubt successful, Igloi is among the best-known coaching personalities today. Formerly of Hungary, he moved to the United States in 1956. He was coach of the Santa Monica Athletic Association until moving to Greece, where he now coaches the Greek military team. His impact on Hungarian distance runners at the Honved Club in Budapest made world headlines and history. He also had great success with American distance runners.

Igloi's training is based on the Freiburg interval principle, which is now regarded as outdated. Although it differs from the Freiburg method in quantity and distribution of work, it still might not be accepted by the majority of distance coaches. Nevertheless, even now that complex endurance training is used by most coaches, it is inter-esting that Igloi's methods still produce outstanding results. Perhaps we have not yet heard the last word on endurance training and interval principles.

Igloi had his first contact with track at the age of seventeen. At nineteen, he was the junior pole vault champion of Hungary, and from 1929 to 1933 he studied physical education at the University of Budapest. It was during his studies that Igloi became interested in middle-distance running and clocked 2:01.0 for 800 meters and 4:18.0 for 1,500 meters.

In 1933, he had an opportunity to watch the training of Polish distance champion Janis Kusocinski, who used a type of interval training based on 200-meter repetition runs. This gave Igloi incentive to use the same method in his own workouts, and he made remark-able progress. He became an Olympian in 1936 and reduced his 800-meter time to 1:53.9, the 1,500 meters to 3:52.0, and clocked 5:29.0 and 8:28.8 over 2,000 and 3,000 meters, respectively. During a training camp at Vieromaki, Finland, he also gained first-hand experience in fartlek, which he later used in his training method.

68

However, it was Dr. Misangi, under whom Igloi studied at the University of Budapest, who had the strongest influence on the development of his training system. From Misangi, he learned the importance of the long and slow progression required to adapt the athlete to his new tasks. He also learned that a coach has to be more than just a computer calculating the daily training loads for the athletes.

After the war, Igloi continued his job as a physical education teacher until finally, in 1951, he became a professional coach at a Budapest athletic club. Although he was coaching all events, Igloi made his name in working with distance runners. His athletes set forty-nine Hungarian, twenty-five European, and twenty-one world records. His athletes, Andras Cseplar, Sandor Iharos, Istvan Rozsa-volgyi, and Laszlo Tabori dominated distance running for many years.

After the 1956 Olympics in Melbourne, Igloi came to the U.S. with Tabori and became an American citizen. Assisted by *Life* magazine, he established the Santa Clara Valley Youth Village and with Jim Beatty and Tabori began another era of records. In 1961, his group moved south and formed the Los Angeles Track Club. They won 25 AAU titles and set 19 U.S. records.

How does Igloi's training differ from other distance runners? Igloi sets an individual training regimen for each athlete. The athlete trains under the observant eye of his coach, who makes necessary adjustments according to his observations. For this reason, the training is carried out only on the track (cinders or grass).

The training is based on the interval principle, which differs from the Freiburg method on two major points—quantity and distribution. To allow for a constantly increased training intensity and load, the repetitions are conducted in series and different distances are used for active recoveries.

In principle, all athletes train alone. This rule is bypassed only for time-trials and on especially hard training days when stronger runners assist the weaker.

It is impossible to describe a typical Igloi training plan, since he has over 40,000 different ones. However, I watched some of Igloi's track students at Santa Monica City College in action and left wondering how the human body could stand it.

A normal workout lasts about three hours, and starts with a 5-mile warm-up run, followed by 15 long accelerations with jog-back recoveries before the real work begins. A thirteen-year-old girl, for example, performed after the warm-up four series of 6 x 400 meters with 200-meter recovery jogs, and 10 fast 100-meter sprints between each series. In one workout she covered over 13 miles. One of the male athletes followed the same warm-up with five series of 12 x 400 meters with 200-meter recovery jogs. Between each series, the athlete executed one rather brisk 1,200-meter run. He covered about 28 miles during this session, and trains in addition 1½ to 2 hours in the mornings every day of the week. A 30-hour training week is regarded as normal.

Igloi compares his athletes with violin players preparing for an important concert. They repeat the same piece thousands of times, repeat parts of it, and occupy themselves for hours with their task. A runner preparing for an important meet cannot get bored running around a circular track. Like an artist, he has an important aim—to play the first violin in the concert of the world's best trackmen.

One of Igloi's exrunners compares him with Attila, who requested obedience from the Mongols. He assured them he would lead them to the promised land thousands of miles away. Those who believed in him covered the distance in many hard stretches (the interval principle) and reached the land Attila had promised. But there is a need for enormous will-power and belief to avoid being left on the road. Igloi, the short man with sparkling eyes, does the same. He promises success, but the records of his best athletes give him the right to make such promises.

Igloi's methods have often been discussed, but his training plans have never been published with explanations. Igloi himself is usually silent. The only published work covering his training principles was part of the book *Atletika*, and came out in 1956. To my knowledge, it has never been translated.

When asking about his method, one is met with silence because the "system" can't be separated from Igloi, the person. Igloi knows how to use it, he improves it constantly, and understands how it leads to success.

9

Mountain Running

by Ray Hosler

There are three routes to the top of Colorado's Pikes Peak: by Cog Railway (making a beeline to the 14,110-foot summit), by a precarious, winding dirt road, or the hard way—up Barr trail.

Each year in August, hundreds of runners gather at the base of the mountain in Manitou Springs. Pikes Peak is the "Boston Marathon" of mountain racing. Invariably, the runners decide to take the long way up, though some of the leaders have been known to march virtually straight up the side of the mountain, oblivious to the terrain. Some even take the cog railway up.

With six months running and one marathon behind me, I received my initiation to mountain running on "the Peak." It was a rude awakening. Almost five hours into the run, I found myself belly up, spread-eagled on a carpet of not-so-soft pine needles, with a great view of the deep blue sky, asking myself why I got involved in such a crazy race. I had already hit the "wall" halfway into the run, at the summit. The Pike's Peak race was dubbed "the world's highest marathon" by the *Guinness Book of World Records*. But the motivation of accomplishment didn't seem to be enough to get me up and running. I did struggle to the finish line later, where three extra large Icees were waiting to be slurped.

To this day flashbacks, like nightmares, haunt me. There are the sixteen Golden Stairsteps, the last switchbacks to the summit with the pink granite shimmering in the sun. And there is the small metal plaque at the fourteenth switchback with a name etched on a granite tombstone paying tribute to one whose journey was cut short—death by heart attack. Fortunately, most runners never even noticed the memorial, nor would I if not for a friend who jokingly mentioned it just before the race started.

Of course, I'll never forget the awesome view of the Kansas plains from the top. But mountains just weren't made to be raced up by most people. I'm the type who prefers savoring nature at my leisure.

But for the challenge of the mountain, I would never have done it.

I came back to Pikes Peak five years later, not to race, but run up and take the time to enjoy it. Racing up a mountain is like rushing through a fifteen-course meal. But unlike my previous experience when I quit running for five months, this time I was walking the next day. It was fun.

In the words of one great mountain runner, "You have to maintain your equilibrium." I discovered the second time around that mountain races are more tests of survival than tests of speed.

Mountain training and racing has become a phenomenon. Certainly, Frank Shorter's settling down in Boulder had much to do with it. But the phenomenon goes back much further than that. The official Pikes Peak Marathon began in 1956, although there were many unofficial races dating back to the 1930s. In 1971, when I ran, more than 150 runners scaled the peak. In 1977, the trail became a traffic jam of more than 600, and some 220 made the round trip, a fourfold increase in six years.

Almost all of the thirteen states with peaks over 9,000 feet high have mountain races, either on trails or roads. Two of the most popular are in Colorado—Mount Evans (on road) and Pikes Peak. Most of the notorious mountain races are linked to the high altitudes, although there are some popular low-level races that are just as tough. Two of these are the Double Dipsea in northern California and Mount Washington in New Hampshire.

It seems like every time I go for a mountain run, bittersweet memories result. You take in the scenery, but get sore muscles in the process. One workout I'll never forget was on a beautiful fall day in the Colorado Rockies. Imagine an eight-mile run up a pass outside Aspen to 11,100 feet, followed by a jump into a natural hot spring with 100-degree water for a half-hour. Then imagine running back down the backpacker's trail, all your energy having bubbled away back at the hot spring. The trip down was harder than the run up.

MOUNTAIN MEN

Today's mountain runners should not be confused with those who run in the mountains. Olympian Frank Shorter does most of his training on trails outside Boulder, Colorado, but he is not a mountain man. True mountain men are ones who race up and down mountains. The mountains are their lives.

The Indians of North America and the Incas of South America were known for mountain running. It was a way of life, but their accomplishments are history. The Tarahumara Indians of northern

Mexico have a kickball-type game they play in their mountain setting. The games go for days or until exhaustion sets in. Though their endurance is well documented, they make poor competitors outside this environment, mainly because of cultural barriers.

One of the greatest mountain runners is a Pueblo Indian, Steve Gachupin, who from 1966-71 was undisputed "king of the mountain" at Pikes Peak. A coin to commemorate the race and the man was struck with his figure and record time engraved on one side. It is the highest tribute ever paid an American mountain runner. But Gachupin is older now, and although he runs Pikes Peak every year, age has caught up with him.

In his place are two who can be called the contemporary "mountain men." They are Chuck Smead, 1972 round-trip winner at Pikes Peak, and Rick Trujillo, five-time round-trip champ and course record-holder.

Chuck and Rick are runners in contrast, both in ability and attitude. Chuck is the competitor, who thrives on racing. He excels at uphill racing. Trujillo, four years older, races infrequently and takes his running as though it were religion. He's best at downhill racing. Rick lives in isolation in the Colorado Rockies, while Chuck makes his home in California, the center of road racing. The common bond is their mountain training grounds. Their views on racing technique and training, which often clash, are the most authoritative today.

Chuck Smead

At twenty-six, Chuck Smead holds four Pikes Peak ascent titles and has won the rugged Mount Baldy race in California six times. A 2:14:39 marathon ranks him as one of the top fifteen marathoners in American history. He is the American 50-kilometer record-holder and finished second in the Pan American Games marathon in 1975.

How competitive is Chuck? His philosophy about mountain racing tells us. "I will never walk in a mountain race, no matter how tough the course, if I can help it." His definition of a mountain race explains the sport. "A race has to be completely uphill and downhill on some sort of dirt road or trail and with a dramatic elevation change. You should be up against the altitude."

His racing technique is documented in a *Runner's World* profile.* For the uphill "I use a quick, short stride, always on my toes—leaning into the hill. The steeper the hill, the more I lean into it. Don't

---

* David Hill, "Profile of a Mountain Man," *Runner's World*, September 1974, pp. 18-19.

use excessive arm motion. It wastes energy." Going downhill, Chuck puts on the brakes if he is not racing. He keeps his eyes glued to the trail, with his knees up to avoid tripping. "The most common injury I see in races," says Chuck, "is scrapes from falls going downhill."

He is adamant about running a course before racing on it, both for psychological reasons and to scout the turns. "Imagine the impression you would get seeing a course level out, then looking up and finding a dozen switchbacks reach to infinity. It can be devastating."

For Smead, mountain running requires no special clothing, other than wearing good shoes and a sweat top at higher elevations. He wears the lightest possible shoes, even to the extent of making his own racing shoes. If the race course is extremely rocky, particularly on the downhill, he wears thick-soled shoes. "Training for mountain races I also go with a thick sole."

Running at high altitude the first time can be a depressing experience. The lungs burn, movement comes with effort, and headaches and nose bleeds are not unknown. Smead comments on making the transition from low altitude. "Cut the mileage the first week and give yourself as much time as possible to adjust. Also, don't go to the extreme altitude right away; go to maybe 5,000-6,000 feet for a week. It eliminates a lot of body shock."

The physiological benefits of high altitude may be illusory, although research shows an athlete with this kind of training maintains a higher red blood cell count—meaning increased oxygen carrying capacity. Certainly, though, high altitude running gives a psychological edge in competitive situations. Chuck feels that mountain running and high altitude training do more than that, and help running at all distances. His only warning is: "If you train in the mountains all the time, you gain endurance but lose leg speed."

In 1977, Chuck made a European tour to run mountain races. He came back impressed by the organization and recognition given to mountain runners. Based on the trip, Smead says the sport in this country has plenty of room for improvement. "Most races here are poorly organized and offer useless awards," says Chuck.

In Europe, where participation is greater, an organization— Champion International of Mountain Racing in Europe (CIME)— devotes itself entirely to the sport. Smead explains races are graded A, B, or C, the A races being international caliber and C races local events. Runners earn points for placing in each race (more for A races), and a champion is named at the end of the year. Stefan Soler of Switzerland was the 1976 champion.

Smead was more than a match for the Europeans. He won two of the three races in which he competed.

Rick Trujillo

Rick Trujillo lives and trains for one race—the Pikes Peak Marathon, which he has run since 1973. It is his mountain. He has the race down to a fine art, knowing the switchbacks by heart. Rick is just one win shy of the six-victory all-time record by Gachupin, and he hopes to break it. He holds the time record for both the old short course (26.8 miles) of 3:31:05, and for the present 28.2-mile race in 3:34:15, set in 1976.

But Rick is more than a mountain runner. He climbs them. In 1977, he scaled Alaska's 20,000-foot Mount McKinley.

Rick has adapted to the harsh ways of the mountains. He lives in Ouray, Colorado, a sleepy mining town in the heart of the San Juan Mountains (at 7,800 feet), and works as a geologist. His longest time away from home was to attend the University of Colorado, where he posted a 4:11 mile and did some cross-country racing. Even with this speed, he avoids flatland races—partly because there are few within hundreds of miles, but mainly because he fears injury. "The two times I tried to run a marathon I was hurt," Rick says.

His training is divided by the seasons into winter and summer running. Winter running includes an occasional road workout, when the roads are plowed. This lasts until late April, when the snows begin to melt. His summer running is almost exclusively in the mountains.

Rick's training method allows him to approach top shape in four very intense weeks. A race four or even two months away is just too far in the future for him to consider.

"I work on the 'push-recover' system, five days a week," Rick says. "I will have one to three very demanding runs during my week, with one to three days of recovery runs between them. The system holds true whether I am in good shape after a long period of training, or just beginning to train seriously after a long layoff."

Unconventional is the best description of Rick's running. Typically, he holds to a highly unstructured training plan. "I rely on experience and inspiration to determine the course of training, within limits." He considers mileage the least important gauge of performance. If you do measure it, it's extremely variable, usually between 15 and 45 miles a week, with perhaps 25 to 30 being average. "Many laugh at this low mileage, but it suits me well."

Nobody who sees the kind of terrain Rick runs on should laugh.

Rick Trujillo, like the mountain goat, is shy. He strides among the boulders near the top of Pikes Peak. (Photo by Andy Cox)

It's either straight up or straight down. The average trail in the Ouray area climbs with a gradient of 700 feet per mile. The footing is more suited to mountain sheep.

He has names for his most bizarre workouts: "Here, There, and Everywhere" (H, T, and E). "It is cross-country in the raw," says Rick. On the H, T, and E workout, Rick avoids trails and instead bashes through talus, rock fall, scree, undergrowth, grassy meadow, swamps, and anything else that gets in the way. He'll even run through creek beds. H, T, and Es happen about once a week and aren't based on mileage, just time. They can be up to four hours, at altitudes ranging from 7,000 to 13,000 feet. He says of H, T, and Es, "They are soul inspiring."

Here is where Rick polishes his rough terrain skills for racing. By the time he's ready for Pikes Peak's trails, they'll seem like super-highways with no speed limit.

Ken Young, no slouch at mountain running himself (he finished one minute behind Rick at Pikes Peak in 1977), is one of the few who has run with Rick and lived to tell about it. He calls the experience "frightening." He gives this account:

> We went out on an easy run through Sutton Forest. It was easy enough getting there, ignoring the bushes of stinging nettles and overgrown trail. Running through the forest consisted of trying to hurdle fallen aspen, which reduced us to jumping up on one log, down again and back up on another.
>
> When we reached a beaver dam the only way across was over the dam. We went across—through more stinging nettles. Next, we came to an open space and a cliff. Rick proceeded to jump from rock to rock like a mountain goat. I crawled down. Finally, we reached the bottom where the Uncompahgre River flows. Rick ate a few berries and then dashed out onto a waterpipe over the river. It was barely three feet wide, and *not* designed for foot traffic. I ran alongside, on the road.

Offhandedly, Rick says of Ken, "He has acrophobia, you know."

Rick's training preparation for Pikes Peak climaxes with an 18-22 mile run over several mountain passes, including a 5,200-foot vertical climb, one week before Pikes Peak. "Once I pushed beyond that invisible line and found myself hypoglycemic with a thousand feet or so of ascent to go and miles of descent to go. Like it or not, I had to finish. There are no nearby roads." He rests three days before the race.

Rick reveals his downhill racing technique here for the first time. The bounding technique evolved from practice and watching deer and elk run.

> I usually trade off constantly between two different kinds of strides. The first and most familiar to runners is the "more or less even stride." I use this only when the trail is relatively flat or smooth.
>
> The other downhill stride I use is the "Lope," and I use it for rough or

extremely steep ground. The only thing I can compare it to is how a deer covers ground after being spooked. It bounces, coming in contact with the ground for only an instant before bounding into the air again. I land on my toes, one foot hitting just before the other one. The first foot stabilizes me somewhat and begins to slow me down. The second planting completely stabilizes me and completes the braking. I immediately push off with the second leg for the next landing spot to complete the sequence again.

It's somewhat like hopping or skipping, one stride two feet long, the next anywhere from two to six feet, depending on the ground.

Like Chuck, Rick wears no special clothing. He is concerned about a certain brand of shoe no longer made in the original style. "The pair I used had a leather upper and had the herringbone sole with a thick, durable sole. I'll rip through the new nylon shoes after a few runs." He considers flare-heeled shoes a liability in the mountains because they are more apt to trip him.

Rick's approach to running is refreshingly simple. "For me running is the best way to get into the mountains I love. Some of the most pleasant moments of my life have been when I was completely alone miles from nowhere on a high mountain trail. I let the challenge of the mountains be my inspiration for running." For this reason, Rick looks at the growth of mountain racing with mixed emotions.

Chuck once encountered a bear during a workout on Topatopa Mountain in California. "We both jumped two feet into the air and the bear took off running." On the same run he casually leapt over a prairie rattler. Where man is the intruder, such encounters aren't uncommon.

The story Rick tells sounds like something from a Walt Disney movie. "In May I went on a run with a herd of about twelve elk. At first all I could do was chase them. Gradually, they slowed down and after about three hours we were running together. They stopped and finally seemed to accept me, even though they wouldn't let me approach closer than about twenty-five feet. Since then, I often see the same herd on my spring running route and they usually allow me to pass very near without spooking."

THE RACES

You should be warned about the most popular mountain races. They are often crowded with runners on narrow trails. After experiencing a larger one, you might be better off sticking to the local mountain runs that attract less media attention. There are many such runs. The following are the most demanding:

1. Pikes Peak Marathon: 28.2 miles; August. An out-and-back run

on Barr trail from downtown Manitou Springs to the summit. The trail is well maintained, with good footing except near the top where all but a few walk. Altitude: 7,000 to 14,110 feet. Vertical climb: 7,110 ft./500 ft. per mile.

2. Mount Evans Run: 14.2 miles; July. A point-to-point race from Echo Lake, Colorado, to the summit, on paved road. Traffic congestion is becoming a problem. Altitude: 10,650 to 14,200 feet. Vertical climb: 3,550 ft./250 ft. per mile.

3. Crested Butte Run: 6-9 miles; July. Begin in the town of Crested Butte, Colorado, and run for 1.5 miles on level ground to the base of a mountain. An open course. Altitude: 8,909 to 12,162 feet. Vertical climb: 3,253 ft./433 ft. per mile.

4. La Luz Trail Run: 7.5 miles; August. An out-and-back course on a well-maintained trail outside Albuquerque, New Mexico, that is more of a challenge due to the heat than the gradient. Altitude: 7,000 to 10,678 feet. Vertical climb: 3,680 ft./490 ft. per mile.

5. Baer Gutsman: 10 miles; August. A point-to-point race on rough trail, changing to a dirt road on ascent. Very steep, through swamps and creeks. Spectacular views of Salt Lake City. Race begins near Kaysville, Utah. Altitude: 4,700 to 9,400 feet. Vertical climb: 4,700 ft./470 ft. per mile.

6. Mount Marathon Run: 3.4 miles; July. Ascent and descent on a steep open course near Seward, Alaska. Run since 1909. Extremely steep, with a descent involving slides down snow slopes. Altitude: 50 to 3,060 feet. Vertical climb: 3,000 ft./882 ft. per mile.

7. Imogene Pass Mountain Run: 18 miles; September. A point-to-point race with a little of everything—trails, jeep trails, and road. From Ouray to Telluride, Colorado, over passes. Altitude: 7,812 to 13,114 feet and down to 8,640 feet. Average vertical climb: 600 feet per mile.

8. Double Dipsea: 13.4 miles; September. From Stinson Beach to Mill Valley, California, and back. Run through the Muir Woods on a rough, steep trail. Low altitude race.

9. Mount Baldy: 8 miles; September. Mostly dirt road from the Mount Baldy Ski Area east of Los Angeles to the top of the lift. Extremely steep the last mile over loose rock on the point-to-point course. Altitude: 6,500 to 10,060 feet. Vertical climb: 3,560 feet/ 445 ft. per mile.

10. Western States Endurance Run: 100 miles; June. More of a mountain survival test than a race. Run from Squaw Valley to Auburn,

California, following the historic Western States trail. Altitude: 9,000 to 1,500 feet. Altitude gain 17,040 feet; loss 21,970 feet. Net altitude loss: 4,930 feet.

ALTITUDE

Mountains and altitude, together, impair the runner so that walking is almost the rule on most long training runs. The 1968 Mexico City Olympics mirrored the effects of altitude, when the world's best distance runners were left gasping for air in the 7,500-foot setting. The African athletes, the only ones who seemed unaffected, live and train at high altitudes. Living year-round at high altitudes may thus be the runner's first line of defense against altitude.

M. H. M. Arnold, a British scientist who conducted extensive studies of athletes in the high Andes Mountains of South America, reached the same conclusion.* According to him, "What runners are coming to realize is that a sudden shift in altitude is a major shock to the system. It takes time and careful planning to adjust to these shocks." Arnold speculates runners should train around 10,000 feet, instead of at the generally accepted 7,000-foot level. But he concedes there are few readily available athletic facilities for this purpose in the United States or elsewhere.

The general rule is that the higher you go into the mountains, the more respect altitude deserves. Perhaps the greatest thrill of mountain running results from its proximity to nature. It affirms the realization that it is possible to come and go without disturbing the delicate balance between man and the environment.

TRAINING TIPS

- Gauge your training efforts carefully. Figure that 1 mile of vertical climb is equivalent to 10 miles of flat mileage.
- Build up gradually to trail running.
- Use different types of trails for training: rolling, long steady, short, and steep climbs.
- Do plenty of stretching before and after running, especially of the Achilles tendons.
- Forget about pace and stride. An even stride on rough ground is a

---

* M. H. M. Arnold, "Benefits of Altitude Training," *Runner's World*, November 1972, pp. 34-35.

sure way of breaking your neck. Every step should be different, based on the terrain ahead.

- Don't be afraid to run downhill occasionally at a hard pace, but don't overdo it.
- Train at the altitude of your race, and higher if possible.
- Don't walk in a race if you can help it.
- Dress warmly when running at high altitude. Storms and foul weather develop quickly there. Above all, know the trail and terrain you are running on. It's easy to get lost in the mountains.

10

Balancing the
Oxygen Budget

by Joe Henderson

The key limiting factor in distance-running performance is the ability to take in and utilize oxygen. The shorter and faster the race, the more severe the oxygen demands. In the sprints, the runner goes into a state of *oxygen debt*, where nearly all the "debt" is repaid after the race ends. As the distance of the race increases, a progressively larger amount of required oxygen is utilized during the exertion.

Anaerobic exercise occurs when the oxygen supply is inadequate, and the runner goes into a state of heavy-breathing oxygen debt. *Aerobic* activity allows immediate replacement of consumed oxygen, so that breathing is normal. No form of running is purely anaerobic or aerobic. Pace determines the level of each. All-out sprints are almost completely anaerobic in nature, while long, slow distance is primarily aerobic.

Fred Wilt, perhaps the leading American authority on distance training, has theorized that a runner's training must conform to the oxygen demands of his race. Table 2 indicates the approximate requirements for various distances, the amounts supplied while running, and the "debts" that must be repaid later.

Wilt identifies three factors that are developed in training:

1. *Pure speed:* all-out sprinting ability
2. *Anaerobic endurance:* the ability to withstand an oxygen debt over an extended distance
3. *Aerobic endurance:* the ability to run long distances with normal breathing

Table 3 lists the contributions of various forms of training to these factors, according to Wilt's empirical evidence.

TABLE 2

EVENT	TOTAL OXYGEN REQUIREMENT	OXYGEN UPTAKE	OXYGEN DEBT
Marathon in 2:15	763.0 liters	745 liters (97.5%)	18 liters (2.5%)
10,000 m in 29:00	178.0 liters	160 liters (90%)	18 liters (10%)
5000 m	90.0 liters	72 liters (80%)	18 liters (20%)
2 miles in 9:00	40.0 liters	22 liters (55%)	18 liters (45%)
1500 m in 3:40	38.0 liters	20 liters (52.5%)	18 liters (47.5%)
800 m in 1:45	27.6 liters	9.6 liters (35%)	18 liters (65%)
800 m in 2:00	27.0 liters	9 liters (33.3%)	18 liters (66.7%)
400 m in 45.0	22.1 liters	4.1 liters (18.5%)	18 liters (81.5%)
200 m	20.0 liters	1 to 2 liters (5-10%)	18-19 liters (90-95%)
100 m	8 to 9 liters	0.0 liters (0.0%)	8-9 liters (100%)

TABLE 3

TYPE OF TRAINING	SPEED	AEROBIC ENDURANCE	ANAEROBIC ENDURANCE
Repetitions of sprints	90%	4%	6%
Continuous slow running	2%	93%	5%
Continuous fast running	2%	90%	8%
Slow interval	10%	60%	30%
Fast interval	30%	20%	50%
Repetition running	10%	40%	50%
Speed play	20%	40%	40%
Interval sprinting	20%	70%	10%
Acceleration sprinting	90%	5%	5%

Finally, table 4 indicates what Wilt considers to be optimum training for the various distances.

The 1974 Sunkist 500-yard run, with Maurice Peoples leading. (Photo by M. J. Baum)

TABLE 4

EVENT	SPEED	AEROBIC ENDURANCE	ANAEROBIC ENDURANCE
Marathon (26+ miles)	5%	90%	5%
6 miles/10,000 m	5%	80%	15%
3 miles/5000 m	10%	70%	20%
2 miles/3000 m	20%	40%	40%
1 mile/1500 m	20%	25%	55%
880 yards/800 m	30%	5%	65%
440 yards/400 m	80%	5%	15%
220 yards/200 m	95%	3%	2%
100 yards/100 m	95%	2%	3%

PART THREE

THE BODY

1

Physiology of Distance Running

by Henry T. Uhrig, M.D.

This article is a synopsis of current research on the physiology of distance running. We will be concerned mainly with distances from 3 miles to the marathon. We will present the scientific basis for certain aspects of distance running, as well as methods of preparing for a distance run.

GENERAL ADAPTATION SYNDROME

The famous researcher Hans Selye has done extensive studies on the reactions of animals, including humans, to stress. Certain of his concepts may help us understand certain phenomena in athletic training. Selye describes the *general adaptation syndrome*, the way an organism reacts to stress. The general adaptation syndrome is divided into three stages: (1) alarm reaction, (2) resistance, and (3) exhaustion. By adaptation, he means the organism's increased resistance to stress as a result of previous exposure to stress. He holds that chronic exposure to a particular stress not only increases resistance to that stress, but reduces nonspecific resistance to other stresses. Selye believes that the body has a finite quantity of adaptation energy, so stresses should be considered when analyzing their effect on the body.

This should help us understand the approach to physical training, where a stress is applied that is within the organism's capacity to adapt. Suitable recovery periods must be allowed for the adaptation to take place. This must be followed by further stress and recovery, gradually increasing the stress as the organism's adaptation increases. If the individual goes beyond his capacity to adapt, he begins to break down, resulting in exhaustion.

But with properly applied and individualized programs, the human organism shows remarkable adaptive powers. These concepts support the idea of alternating hard and easy training days, depending on the stress of a workout and not necessarily on the overall mileage. They also help us realize why it is important for an athlete involved in a strenuous training program to avoid other stresses, such as insufficient rest, intercurrent infection (colds, sore throats, etc.), and various minor injuries. Other fundamental health requirements should be followed as to sleep, nutrition (including hydration), avoidance of overindulgences, and observation of health habits.

Experience has shown that the training of champion long-distance runners is a year-round job, requiring the utmost dedication for years if the individual is to reach top performance.

There are as many training systems as there are runners and coaches. Systems have been developed empirically, copied from champion runners, or derived and distilled from theories of both coaches and runners. Since the combination of physical and physiological factors that comprises the individual runner are so varied, there is probably no single ideal program for all runners. However, it is possible to determine certain training procedures, based on physiological research, which should produce improved performance.

OXYGEN CONSUMPTION

Energy is required to run a race. This energy is derived from potential energy stored in foodstuffs. Through a series of chemical reactions, the potential energy in food is converted to free energy in the cells. This energy accomplishes work, or can be converted to heat energy, which cannot do work and is a measure of inefficiency of the body. In our area of interest, this free energy results in contraction of muscle systems, which ultimately move the individual from the starting line to the finish line.

The living processes involved are described by the term *metabolism*. In discussing energy metabolism, two general forms are described—*aerobic* and *anaerobic*. In aerobic metabolism, the final electron acceptor in the chemical reaction is oxygen, while in anaerobic metabolism the final electron acceptor is a molecule other than oxygen. For the purposes of our discussion, anaerobic metabolism refers to a condition in which the individual cannot supply sufficient oxygen to the tissues for the degree and duration of exertion. A condition known as *oxygen debt* ensues. After the exertion has ended, the "debt" is paid off during the recovery period. Aerobic metabolism may be viewed as a condition whereby the individual supplies his tissues with sufficient oxygen to meet the demands of the active muscles. For less than two minutes, anaerobic power is more important. For a two-minute maximal effort, the aerobic and anaerobic processes are equally important. But with longer work time, aerobic power becomes more dominating. Dr. Nocker calculates that a 100-meter sprinter assumes a 95 percent oxygen debt, while an 800-meter runner assumes about 66⅔ percent.

The proportions change for the long-distance runner. Here, too, the runner first accumulates an oxygen debt. However, he must govern his pace so that, looking ahead, his expenditure of effort is within his capacity to supply oxygen to his tissues. His energy output is largely balanced by his oxygen supply. In a final sprint, a long-distance runner may again make use of his remaining capacity for oxygen debt. Although long-distance running is thought to place greatest stress on aerobic mechanisms, some researchers have recently reported that the reserves for anaerobic work may play an important role in prolonged aerobic running. For the distance runner, the anaerobic source is a limited store of energy, which must be called on only when the individual is unable to meet the oxygen demand via his oxygen uptake. As a consequence of anaerobic metabolism, lactic acid and other metabolites are formed in the muscle cells. These will eventually cause cessation of the exercise. If two runners perform similar amounts of work, the one who is able to delay utilization of these limited energy reserves will be able to work longer.

The major energy requirements for a long-distance run must come from aerobic metabolism. Therefore, the ability of the individual to supply oxygen to the tissues is fundamental. The terms *aerobic capacity* or *maximum oxygen consumption capacity* are used to describe this ability. Maximum oxygen uptake is a quantitative measure of this capacity, and can be measured in laboratory experiments.

The physiological capacity of the body to consume oxygen during exhausting exercise depends on pulmonary ventilation, pulmonary diffusion, the oxygen-carrying capacity of the blood, cardiac output, and the arteriovenous difference in oxygen saturation. Research studies indicate that trained distance runners have superior circulatory and respiratory systems. An individual's *vital capacity* is the maximum volume of gas that can be expelled from the lungs by a forced effort after maximal inspiration. This can be significantly enlarged as a result of years of training. Distance runners are notably above average in this respect. When computed on the basis of comparative body size, the difference for distance runners is even more marked.

Distance runners have tremendous respiratory muscle stamina and strength. The *maximal breathing capacity* (MBC) is the maximum volume of air that can be breathed per minute. One study showed that the normal young adult male had an MBC of 125-70 liters per minute, while a group of ten college cross-country men had a mean MBC or 207.51 liters per minute.

Another study showed that highly trained distance runners during an exhaustive running test maintained a breathing rate of 120 liters per minute for over 20 minutes. In the average untrained individual and in many trained men, such a large minute volume is attained only in the final minutes of exercise and for only a few minutes. This suggests that the distance runner has a superior respiratory musculature, as well as reduced respiratory resistance. A distance runner's oxygen transport system is a highly developed and efficient system. The main driving force behind all of this is, of course, the distance runner's superior cardiac function.

The maximal oxygen uptake of distance runners, calculated in milliliters per kilogram of body weight per minute, is higher than most other athletes. David Costill, Ph.D., of Ball State University, reports a correlation of 0.82 between maximal oxygen uptake (ml/kl/min) and distance running performance. One remarkable ability of distance runners is their capacity to function at a high level of oxygen consumption for a protracted period of time. Development of this capacity is a key part of their training. World-class marathoners are able to sustain this activity at 75-80 percent of maximum for the duration of the race. Various physiological studies indicate that maximum oxygen uptake is the best single predictor for achievement in long-distance running.

Let's recap what we know at this point. Aerobic capacity is fundamental to distance running. Maximal oxygen uptake, a measure of aerobic capacity, gauges the efficiency of the individual's oxygen transport system. The heart is the driving force of the oxygen transport system. We need to determine what is necessary to bring the oxygen transport system to its highest capacity. For minimal improvement in cardiorespiratory endurance, a runner must run at a speed that will elicit a heart rate of 130 beats per minute, or about 50 percent of his maximal oxygen uptake capacity. Research indicates that to improve endurance to a maximal level, a person must run at a speed requiring near-maximum heart rate or a maximum oxygen uptake.

Karlson and others have shown that when building up the oxygen transport system, the stress or load put on it should be maximum. Herbst showed that if intensity of work (pace) is increased to a certain point, oxygen uptake also increases to a maximum level of oxygen uptake. However, it was found that increasing stress beyond this level does not produce further increases in maximal oxygen uptake. A plateau is reached. The important point is that there is a speed below an individual's top speed that produces maximal oxygen uptake. This speed is an adequate stimulus for building up the oxygen transport system. This submaximal speed implies less fatigue and makes it possible to increase the volume of training.

DIET

It appears that glycogen stored in muscle is utilized by the muscle as a primary source of energy. Exhaustive exercise can empty these glycogen stores. Little information is available about replenishing muscle glycogen after exhaustive exercise. But some interesting studies of the response of muscle glycogen stores have a bearing on training, and postexercise and precompetition nutrition for the distance runner. Muscle biopsy techniques have been used in these studies.

Studies by Bergstrom and Hultman show that the muscle glycogen stores can be considerably increased by first emptying the store through strenuous work and then administering a carbohydrate-rich diet. Only the muscles that have been exercised are affected. A fat-protein diet following exercise produces only slow, incomplete glycogen replacement. Carbohydrate given without previous exercise increases only slightly the muscle glycogen. By ingesting a carbohydrate-rich diet after exhaustive exercise, working capacity decreases by more than 100 percent.

It would appear then that the runner should be given a carbohydrate-rich diet following the final hard training session before competition. This might also lead one to question the concept of tying the long-distance runner to a program of daily training. Since research to date has not dealt with the effects of various levels of exercise along with the high-carbohydrate diet following glycogen depletion, it is not clear just what the optimum schedule might be. It is also not clearly understood just how high glycogen muscle stores can be raised with such training. However, distance runners' training programs should make use of this method of increasing muscle glycogen stores.

TRAINING

In training for long-distance running, the use of continuous running and interval training gives rise to considerable debate. Both have their staunch disciples. Let us look at what's involved in each, and what physiological changes are produced. Interval training refers to running repetitions of comparatively short distances, with a recovery interval between runs. Zatopek's great success in the 1952 Olympics, where he won gold medals in the 5,000, 10,000, and marathon, gave this method great impetus.

Downs has a good series of articles in *Track Technique* called "A Review of Interval Training." Toni Nett, Professor Smit, Dr. Gerschler, and others have some interesting comments on interval training in the book *Run, Run, Run.* I'll try to sort out some features that are of importance to training.

The researchers hold that the important concept in interval training is that the major adaptation takes place during the recovery phase. During this phase, it is believed that the heart adapts by increasing its stroke volume. Some researchers believe this interval should be no more than 90 seconds or when the heartbeat returns to 120 beats per minute, whichever is first (but not less than 30 seconds). This interval is felt to be connected to the permeability of the capillary bed of the muscles of the lower extremities. Certain exercise physiologists hold that the interval may be extended to 2-4 minutes or longer to permit recovery. This will permit a greater quality training load, and as a result a greater response to stress than continuous training for the same time but at a necessarily reduced rate. In other words, interval training should assume a pace somewhat faster than race pace. The first group feels that the pace and distance of the run should be adjusted so that the pulse does return to less than 120 in 90 seconds or less. The duration of the stress should be 30 seconds to 90 seconds, with longer exposure for long-distance running.

Interval training may be summarized:

- distance run: 30-90 seconds
- recovery interval: 90 seconds or 120 beats per minute
- repetitions: start with 4 and work upward gradually
- pace: 5 seconds faster than race pace per quarter-mile

The stress should be such that it brings the pulse equal to or slightly less than 180 beats per minute, but so that it returns to 120 beats per minute in 90 seconds or less.

European observers emphasize that the interval is the time when the beneficial results take place. Activity during recovery can be anything from a walk to an easy jog. However, some recent work supports anything from complete rest to more than a jog. Toni Nett describes another form of discontinuous running training, which is characterized by repetitions of shorter distances run at higher relative speeds. This emphasizes development of anaerobic conditions. This he calls *tempo training*. This training also conditions the reflexes of the musculoskeletal system to become accustomed to performing rapid movements smoothly under anaerobic conditions. Since the emphasis here is on speed and anaerobic adaptation, Nett believes this sort of training is more appropriate for 1,500-meter and shorter races. He feels interval training is for longer distance races, rather than shorter ones.

Problems arise with interval training when the individual without a coach does not really understand how he is supposed to go about it. A common pitfall is to select a pace faster than race pace, but which cannot be maintained for more than a few repetitions (reps) and maybe not even for more than one. Another pitfall involves shortening the interval so that the appropriate recovery can't take place, so that a proper workout is precluded. Injuries usually occur when relaxation and running form are lost, and "the whole thing falls apart."

One group suggests the following as an introduction to interval training for someone who is just beginning. Take the person's best average time for the 440 and add 20 seconds. His pulse is checked after each 440 for recovery, as above. Pace is increased by reducing two seconds per quarter each month. The number of reps may be increased as the individual responds, and the duration of the interval may be shortened. Properly applied interval training improves the cardiorespiratory response—i.e., the oxygen transport system—and improves the individual's maximum oxygen uptake. Interval training provides multiple, repeated stress stimuli for short duration but of a quality that could not be sustained in a continuous run. Dr. Dill believes interval training improves a person's ability to carry an oxygen debt; this develops and gradually increases during the workout. However, the emphasis in interval training is on the development of maximal aerobic capacity.

Continuous running training generally refers to steady pace running at distances longer than the intended race. The pace is below race pace. There are various approaches to pace. It would appear, however, that to get full effect on the oxygen transport system, the pace should be one that will produce maximum oxygen uptake for the individual. Some observers believe there is improvement in the capillarization of the muscles from continuous work. It seems plausible, but I haven't seen it proved experimentally. Other important benefits of continuous training include conditioning the individual to continue as fatigue sets, and demonstrated to the runner that he can go the distance. Lydiard's marathon preparation for all runners suggests that his system first produces a minimal effect on the oxygen transport system and possibly capillarization effects, before going on to complex training with more emphasis on interval and speed work.

Fartlek or speed play is a combination of interval and continuous running, with an emphasis on experimentation and relaxation. Europeans have used it to advantage. Since it doesn't lend itself well to objective research because of the emphasis on variety, there is not much physiological literature on it.

OTHER INFLUENCES

Various things affect performance.

Altitude. The effects of altitude seen at the 1968 Olympics in the distance events demonstrate the problem. Although acclimatization to reduced ambient oxygen can be accomplished in a relatively short time, individuals who live and train at higher altitudes have an advantage.

Cold. Not much needs to be said here for most temperature ranges encountered during the running season. In the Washington, D.C., area, cold does not present great problems. Usually keeping head, ears, and hands warm takes care of it.

Heat. Heat presents a real hardship for the distance runner. Heat accumulation from the running as well as that superimposed by ambient temperature, humidity, and solar radiation must be reckoned with. Bud Demar has said that it could easily make the difference of half an hour in a marathon winner's time. Although experiments show that acclimatization to heat can be recognized by slower heart beat, increased sweating, and lower rectal temperature in less than a week, in the heat it's probably better to allow 10-14 days of gradually increased effort for adaptation. Even for the heat-acclimatized individual, conditions may reach a level where pace reduction is necessary in order to complete the race—especially the marathon. No one has been able to achieve complete acclimatization for running a marathon at top speed under all possible heat conditions. Some things that aid in heat dissipation are: wearing a porous shirt outside of the shorts; using a light, ventilated head covering in sunlight; wetting the head and shoulders with cool water before starting; cool sponging of head and shoulders during the race; and periodic ingestion of fluids throughout the race. Costill found improved results when his subjects took cool fluids containing salt during protracted exercise in heat. Periodic fluid intake is recommended in any marathon.

Warm-up. This is important for loosening and stretching the muscles. For a marathon in the heat, any prerace action that tends to raise the body temperature is of questionable value, and some feel it should be avoided. The temperature will rise fast enough.

Warm-down. Warm-down assists recovery by the muscles, by massaging veins and helping venous blood return to the heart, and avoiding pooling in the lower extremities. Some recent research questions this. However, it's rather an individual thing, and many feel better with a light jog, especially after a speed workout.

Clothing. Here is another note on clothing of special interest to the distance runner. A study was made on the effects of the weight of footgear on performance. It was reported that the decrement on performance of footgear weighing one kilogram was equivalent to more than a 4-kilogram load in a backpack. This emphasizes the importance of lightness of footgear. However, this idea must be balanced against conditioning the feet, ankles, and legs to light footgear. Some compromises may have to be made depending on the individual.

CONCLUSION

There is no unanimity as to the ideal system of training. An individual's maximal oxygen uptake capacity is fundamental to performance. Champion distance runners have high capacities for maximal oxygen uptake and can sustain an exertion using 75-80 percent of their maximal oxygen uptake for a protracted period. Training of the oxygen transport system (i.e., the cardiorespiratory system) to its top level is necessary to attain the utmost in maximal oxygen uptake for an individual. For maximal effect, the training stress must be such that an individual reaches his maximal oxygen uptake. This can be reached at a point below his absolute top speed. It is with interval training that such a level can be reached many times during a training session. With continuous long duration running, maximal oxygen uptake is sustained only for a relatively short time, and usually only for one period. However, since attainment of 50 percent of an individual's maximum oxygen uptake is the minimum for cardiorespiratory training, some benefit can accrue from such work besides others already mentioned.

There are various views or interpretations of interval training, and the concept of tempo training is an important distinction. The most rational approach is a system using combinations of the various forms of training under a long-range plan (a year or more), with the program tailored to the particular athlete. Glycogen muscle stores can be increased by periodic workouts to produce glycogen depletion, followed by three days of carbohydrate-loading. Application of this technique prior to competition should be considered.

2

Running and the Aging Process

by Thomas Bassler, M.D.

One of my favorite television shows involves a pathologist who drives around in his coroner's station wagon and solves puzzles involving illness and death. He uses his scientific tools to track down evil-doers, be they animal, vegetable, or mineral. This TV super-pathologist has been known to reconstruct an entire body from a single bone—learning the age, sex, height, weight, and occupation of the former owner of the bone!

Since I have had experience with the coroner's office, I often get a phone call when a local runner dies. Several years ago, a jogger wearing a blue sweat suit was struck from behind by a passing automobile. (The driver was not held, since the jogger was essentially invisible in the predawn darkness.) However, since the jogger did not regain consciousness before he died, and since he carried no I.D., his identity was not known. In cases like this, the coroner assigns a "John Doe" number to the file. An autopsy was done, and the age was estimated at fifty-five years. With the information from the coroner's pathologist, a search through the "missing persons" was started. After a week, the identity had not been learned. We began to search through the local track clubs for a missing runner in his mid-fifties.

Ten miles from the death scene, the police had impounded an abandoned auto. The driver was missing. But he couldn't be our missing fifty-five-year-old; he was in his seventies. You can guess the rest. The widow, also in her seventies, was called down to claim her car and identify the body of her husband. The pathologist had estimated the age 33 percent too low. My favorite TV super-pathologist would never make that mistake; or would he? I began to look for signs of "old age" in the reports of deaths of marathon runners. I found none.

First I looked for arteriosclerosis, the fatty degeneration of our blood vessels. It usually starts in teenage Americans and gets worse as we approach forty. Beyond forty, about half the male Americans have one coronary artery narrowed by 50 percent or more. But the marathoners had nice looking vessels beyond age seventy. I could show pathologists slides of these older runners, and they might guess they came from a teenager.

Then I looked at the lungs. With age, lung tissue loses its elastic quality. In nonsmokers, lungs should last over a hundred years. But a heavy smoker can die from emphysema before age sixty, at half the age he could expect to live. Marathoners who used to smoke have some damage, but their lungs are pretty good if they can run the 42 kilometers.

Senile changes in the brain are related to the arteries. If the arteries are healthy, there are no senile changes. Senile bones get soft, but running a marathon gives you a young-looking, tough skeleton.

So, it appears that my TV super-pathologist would have to make some allowances for his estimates on aging if he were dealing with a marathon running population. I think the black toenails would tip him off that he was working on a runner. He would give the audience some new formula for calculating age by adding a "fitness allowance"—perhaps ten years for each black toenail? I can imagine him saying, "This fellow looks twenty-nine, but he has three black toenails, so he must really be fifty-nine. Have Missing Persons search their files for a man about sixty years old."

AUTOPSY RESEARCH

When you have your librarian make a search of the literature for reports on aging, you soon find yourself deep into molecular biology and biochemistry. *Parallel aging* studies show that all of the body tissues seem to age together. Young tendons are found with young arteries, but are not necessarily related to the actual age in years. That is because we all age at different rates. To estimate the age of the arteries, we can biopsy the skin, and estimate the age with a microscope, using special stains for fat. If we biopsy the Achilles tendon, we can estimate the age of the coronary artery. A young Achilles indicates a young coronary artery; an old Achilles means an old artery. The marathon run is a good test of the integrity of the Achilles. Above the marathon "threshold," all tendons and arteries must be young.

The parallel aging theory supports the concept that all marathoners have the physical attributes of teenagers, since the marathoner has passed the minimum "tendon test" when he covered the 42 kilometers. (Don't worry about injuring your Achilles *after* finishing a marathon. Even teenagers have breaking points if you overload them. But you should worry if you are disabled with an injured Achilles *before* you run a marathon.)

SILICON THEORY

Is there anything you can do to keep your tendon young and strong? That is a very important question, because the age of all your body parts rests on the answer.

The tendon is made of collagen. Klaus Schwarz has published his "silicon theory," which states that *silicon* helps prevent the aging of collagen by forming oxygen/silicon bridges that cross-link with the hydrocarbon chains. He cites human autopsy studies that show an inverse relationship between the tissue levels of silicon and the degenerative diseases of arthritis and arteriosclerosis.

Schwarz found high levels of silicon in alfalfa (about 12,000 ppm). The use of alfalfa tea, alfalfa tablets, and alfalfa sprouts begins to make good sense. Bran and whole-meal flour are also rich in silicon. How many successful marathoners talk about "real bread" and "raw, unprocessed, miller's bran"? It begins to appear that the proper diet for a young marathoner is high in silicon.

In support of his silicon theory, Schwarz and Schroeder studied hair-silicon levels of runners. Normal levels (over 20 ppm) were found in champion marathoners and 50-milers. Some "very low levels" (under 4 ppm) were found in cardiac patients disabled during marathon training. A variety of joint and tendon problems appeared in the low-silicon runners when they tried to train. Patients who began to consume added food fiber (bran, pectin, and alfalfa) had high levels of hair-silicon (up to 100 ppm).

It is interesting to speculate that Americans age more rapidly because the silicon was taken out of their diet when food fiber was removed. Think of all the calories that are highly refined: white flour, white sugar, and shortening. None of these foods have enough silicon to prevent tissue aging. Schwarz even tested some bran products and found that they also had been milled in such a way that the silicon was removed. But the marathoner need not worry about his diet. If he *can* run the 42 kilometers, then he is getting adequate silicon.

FAT IN THE DIET

What about fat? We read that a high-fat diet is the cause of all our problems. But is it the total fat, or the quality of the fat? Animal autopsy studies have shown that small amounts of burned fat (cholesterol oxide) can cause early lesions in arteries. When studied with electron microscopes, small amounts—just a few calories—caused early arteriosclerosis in a few hours.

I am sure we all have had a few steaks in our lives. Cholesterol oxides are formed when we burn the fat on the steak. But why doesn't this cause arteriosclerosis in marathoners?

I searched for a good study on monkey autopsies to see if arteriosclerosis can be removed. The best one came from India, published in the journal *Atherosclerosis* [28 (1977):405-16]. First, the monkeys were given "bad bread," which had been filled with hydrogenated vegetable oil until the fat in the diet reached 40 percent of the calories. Hard peanut oil was used. (The monkeys also received adrenaline and half a gram of cholesterol.) The presence of arteriosclerosis was documented by checking blood levels of fat and doing autopsies on several of the animals. When the monkeys were given "good bread" with liquid vegetable oil, their blood tests returned to normal. At autopsy, the arteriosclerosis improved significantly, after only five months on the good diet. It is exciting that the "good bread" also brought the fat level up to 40 percent of the calories at the same time it removed the arteriosclerosis. The "good fat" used was high in linoleic acid, an essential fatty acid found in peanuts, seeds, whole grains, and other unprocessed vegetarian items. It appears, then, that a marathoner can eat an occasional steak, since he naturally has a high intake of seeds and nuts.

The marathoner's ability to burn fat enables him to run through the 30-kilometer checkpoint and pick up the pace. Don Kalmar showed that the marathoner's maximum oxygen uptake increases as he begins to burn fat. Don checked some of our local runners, marathoners, and middle-distance men. He determined their volume of oxygen uptake the usual way, and then repeated it after a 14-hour fast and a 14-mile run, when they were operating on fat for fuel. Marathoners showed an increase in maximum oxygen uptake as they switched to fatty fuel, while the other runners showed the expected decrease. I suspect that the marathoner's fat-burning ability is a result of both diet (which contains a more favorable mix of liquid vegetable fats) and training (which contains more of the long, slow distance runs).

Many studies show that autopsy evidence of atherosclerosis is inversely related to the tissue levels of linoleic acid. The high levels of linoleic acid in the marathoner's diet probably protect his blood vessels from aging at the same time they help him run long distance. It is significant that runners crave this diet. It is nature's way of helping him run and stay young at the same time.

Now our TV super-pathologist can run tests for silicon and linoleic acid. I can imagine him telling his partner or girlfriend, "The reason this fellow looks so young is his diet. He ate like a marathon runner." That's my kind of television show!

3

Why Take a Stress Test?

by Jack Galub

There is a mystique to *stress testing*. What do doctors actually "see" when they wire you up to an electrocardiograph machine as you exercise? Can they help the mature, would-be fitness runner, who is especially vulnerable to medical and physical problems? Are the tests really worth the time, effort and money involved?

To get the facts, I interviewed Abner Delman, cardiologist and medical director, and William S. Gualtiere and Kerry J. Stewart, exercise physiologists, at Cardio-Metrics, Inc. (C-M). C-M, located in New York City, is the only private facility in New York state licensed to administer stress or exercise tests and to write the follow-up exercise programs. C-M's exercise programs apply the principles of interval training. Its staff believes this is the safest and most effective means of conditioning mature women or men who have spent too many years in front of the television set or the dinner table.

The following is the transcript of our conversation.

Question: Doctors are sending patients for stress or exercise testing before they start training. Why not be satisfied with the resting electrocardiogram (ECG)?

Delman: Let's take the analogy of a car that has been used primarily around the neighborhood or on an occasional run into the country. Under normal conditions it sounds well, performs well. But take it out at highway speeds for several hundreds of miles, and you may start hearing pings and noises you never suspected existed.

It's often the same with the heart. It may look good during an at-rest ECG, but when you make it really work for a period of time you may discover severe arrhythmias and other cardiac problems you did not know existed. Arrhythmias are variations from the normal rhythm of the heart. There is now evidence they can be forerunners of cardiac arrest.

Question: If an individual is of healthy stock and has no history of cardiac problems, shouldn't a good, routine examination be enough to give him a clean bill of health?

Gualtiere: In general, I would say yes, particularly if the person shows a good cardiac profile, normal blood pressure and blood lipids (fats), and so on. That reduces the risk of anything happening. But stress testing reduces that risk even further, particularly if the individual has been inactive over a period of years.

Question: Is stress testing new?

Gualtiere: About fifty years ago, it was called *performance testing*. Over the years, considerable work was done in the laboratories, dealing with the body processes and the body's response to physical stress. The data we accumulated helped us place exercise programming on a rational, or objective, basis. In track, that work has also contributed to many of the better times we have seen in the mile, cross-country, and marathon.

Question: When did testing leave the laboratory and become accepted for general use?

Delman: Sometime in the mid-fifties with the use of exercise in the management of suspected or known cardiac patients. Since then, it has gained in popularity, as do many new medical and health developments. But I think that is all to the good.

Question: There has been some questioning of the entire procedure though. For example, the mere suggestion a would-be runner take a test is enough to scare him off.

Gualtiere: You can build a case for that point of view, I am sure. But you can also make a case for gaining as much cardiovascular data about an individual as possible before you let him start training. Our experience is that most people tend to overdo. They overstress and come down with all kinds of muscular and skeletal problems. Sometimes they come down with cardiac problems.

Let's face it, people sometimes die because they embark on a training program they shouldn't have undertaken. They thought they were all right. Most people who feel healthy usually don't see a physician—at least not until they've shown symptoms. The stress test, on the other hand, is capable of detecting early evidence of heart problems.

Question—What does a typical stress test include?

Gualtiere: We start by taking a comprehensive medical history of the individual, with emphasis on cardiac incidents. We also check his report with his own physician if he is a walk-in subject. Most of those we test are referred by their physicians, so that step usually isn't necessary. Then, if we believe we can safely test a person, we start with a resting ECG. We're looking for anything new that might have developed since his last visit to a doctor.

Delman: Some people have silent heart attacks and don't know it. Assuming everything is in order after the initial workup—blood pressure reading, ECG, and so on—we move on to the testing area. (By the way, we will not test anyone with recent angina pains or cardiac irregularities.)

During the stress test, we take a continuous ECG and monitor the person's heart action at the same time on oscilloscopes. We also do a series of blood pressure readings and measure the body's oxygen-handling ability. This is all done while the individual is exercising under increasing stress. We believe we're able to detect any available evidence of heart strain this way. The test also gives us the data we need to develop a personalized exercise prescription for cardiac enhancement.

Stewart: We use electrically driven treadmills for our tests. This lets us control the belt's speed and also lets us tilt it at regular intervals. This makes the individual "climb a hill," causing his heart to work harder. His body also consumes more oxygen even though we keep the belt's speed constant. The more deconditioned the person is, the more quickly he'll peak out during the test. With those in better shape, the heart takes longer to reach the maximum beat rate we are targeting for during the stress period.

This way, we're able to quite accurately predict a person's maximum aerobic capacity. We don't have to continue the test to exhaustion, even though we have done so for some competitive runners. For the average person, we'll test up to 85 percent of his maximum heart beat rate. At that point, we slow the belt and start lowering it. We keep monitoring the runner's heart action and blood pressure, and continue to even when we get him off the belt and into a chair. We want to detect any suspicious changes in his ECG that might appear only during the cool-down period. An abnormal response, for instance, might be an upsurge in blood pressure.

Question: What happens after the test?

Gualtiere: After we have had a chance to analyze the test, we bring the person back for a group session with others to explain our training philosophy. Then we review each person's personalized exercise prescription individually so he can start training on a controlled basis.

Question: What is your training philosophy?

Gualtiere: Given an individual over thirty years of age who has been sedentary, our feeling is that of all the components associated with physical fitness, cardiovascular is most important. That is the cornerstone, the base from which a fitness runner can go on if he wants to build muscle bulk, improve flexibility, extensibility.

We also believe that interval training offers the best approach to beginning involvement with running. There are a number of reasons for this. Most important is that the older person's body will not allow him to exercise continuously at the necessary intensity, frequency, and duration to do him good. Interval training eases him into running and builds him up to where he can phase into continuous training if he wants it.

Stewart: Even with younger people who might be able to skip the interval training phase, there is enough of a risk of coming down with muscular and skeletal problems to make it advisable to start with interval training. This lets the runner gradually condition his body. He isn't wasting time; he is playing it safe.

Gualtiere: Our sessions are divided into three stages: warm-up, stimulus, and cool-down. It's in the stimulus stage that the runner makes his heart work, builds up his fitness. We have him working at 75-85 percent of his maximum heart beat. (See table 5.) That's when the workout stimulates an improvement in his aerobic capacity.

Question: A number of concepts have been advanced for conditioning the beginning runner. One is built on a point system. Another calls for a minimum run of six miles. The doctor who takes that approach says that any distance under six miles does little good.

Delman: It's not a matter of distance or of running against the clock. Our studies show that approximately 75-85 percent of an individual's age-related maximum heart rate must be attained for a length of time if he is to benefit. Our objective is to help him enhance his cardiovascular fitness. This calls for training 15-20 minutes at the target heart rate level 3-4 times a week over a 6-9-month period.

The training prescription we write for the runner tells him when and how often he should count his pulse beat. That tells him if he is under- or over-stressing. We actually have him count his pulse for five seconds and then multiply by 12—not a particularly difficult task.

Question: What about the mature individual who lives in an area without testing facilities. What can he do?

Gualtiere: He should seek the guidance of a physician. If that is impossible, he should become aware of the cardiac risk factors and should assess his own history against those factors. Then, if he has a good cardiac profile, he should start slowly. He must practice moderation from the very beginning. Should he at any time develop any unusual symptoms—chest pains, undue muscular soreness—he should stop.

If all goes well for the first three weeks to a month, he might limit himself to walking—first at a slow or moderate pace. Depending on his age, brisk walking is all he may have to do to start rounding into shape. When he feels he has reached a peak in his walking, he might start jogging, using an interval approach. But he must remember to make it easy. He is out to enhance his cardiovascular system and to become a fitness runner. He's not out there preparing for competition. If he wants to go in that direction, that kind of training can come later.

Stewart: He should learn to keep his inner ear tuned to his body. If he's beginning to push too hard, his body and pulse count will tell him. He should be willing, too, to train consistently. We recommend at least one-half hour three times a week. Later on, if he wants, he can increase the frequency of his training periods. But he must remember he's no longer a kid and must practice moderation.

TABLE 5

AGES AND PULSE RATES

As the individual grows older, his maximal pulse rate decreases (by about one beat per year after age 20). To enhance cardiovascular fitness, the doctors at Cardio-Metrics say the training program should call for sufficient stress to make the heart work at 75-85% of maximum. These are the estimated ranges.

Age	Maximal Pulse Rate	75-85% Pulse Rate	Age	Maximal Pulse Rate	75-85% Pulse Rate
20	200	150-170	50	175	131-149
25	195	146-166	55	171	128-145
30	190	142-161	60	168	126-143
35	186	139-158	65	164	123-139
40	182	136-155	70	160	120-136
45	179	134-152			

4

Getting to the Heart

by Paul Milvy, M.D.

I f appearance and reality were identical, there would be no need
for science. The task of science, then, is to discern what really is,
not just to accept the obvious as necessarily representing the truth of
a phenomenon.

Less than fifty years ago, conventional wisdom held that too much
exercise would result in an "athlete's heart," and that this was bad.
We know today that, although activity may indeed create a heart
somewhat larger than average, the term "athlete's heart" is no
longer used in a pejorative sense, and we recognize that "average" is
not necessarily healthy. (Paul Dudley White, the great cardiologist
and advocate of exercise, referred to this as the "porpoise syndrome"—a large heart, and a slow pulse rate.)

The average American male is, for example, considerably overweight by all indices of good health, and the average American
smokes. We also know that at the time of his death at seventy, the
great marathoner Clarence DeMar (Boston's "Mr. Marathon") had
coronary arteries two or three times the cross-sectional area of men
his age. DeMar was hardly average.

Men and women who run footraces—be they Olympians or joggers—usually look in the peak of health, and they feel so as well.
Thus, the conventional wisdom of today is that physical activity is
good for you—good for your mood, good for your health, and good
for you in terms of life expectancy.

STUDY OF BUS EMPLOYEES

What does the scientific and medical evidence tell us about this
matter of mortality? In 1953, British doctor J. N. Morris presented
the results of an ingenious study. He had monitored men who
worked for the London transport system for a number of years, long
enough for some of the workers to die from coronary heart disease
(CHD).

CHD may be loosely defined as: disease of the heart resulting from the deposition of a fatty substance on the inside walls of the coronary arteries, so that the vessels become constricted and are unable to supply portions of the heart muscle with adequate supplies of oxygen (*ischemia*).

Two classifications of workers are involved in the operations of London buses. One is the driver, who is pretty much sedentary. He sits and drives. The other man on the bus is the conductor or ticket-taker. Since the London buses are double-deckers, he's considerably more active. He must run up and down the steep stairs collecting tickets. He's also a bit of a showman. He jumps off the bus at its frequent stops, and only jumps on again after it has picked up speed.

We all can guess the results of this study. The conductors had lower overall mortality and lower mortality from CHD than the sedentary drivers.

THE COLLEGE OARSMEN

Another study is perhaps more to the point. In 1972, an article appeared by Dr. C. Prout on the life expectancy of college oarsmen. Prout had studied the mortality of Harvard and Yale oarsmen, classes of 1882 through 1902. One problem in epidemiological research results from the fact that many aspects of existence may vary in the group that the scientist studies, not just the single factor in which he is most interested. For example, the oarsmen are, above all, college men. And college graduates, as a rule, live considerably longer than noncollege graduates. This is primarily so because college graduates come from a privileged socioeconomic group, which has a lower risk of mortality.

Thus, if we use the device that the British use, and divide the population into five social classes from highest to lowest, we find that mortality in the lowest social class in the U.S. is more than 200 percent higher than in the highest social class. More simply, at each age interval more than twice as many people will die per year in the lower than in the higher social classes.

College oarsmen, just by virtue of being college men, can be expected to live longer. So how do we separate this effect from any effect that crewing might exert? The solution to this is to make every variable in life circumstances the same for two groups, except for the one variable in which you are interested (in this case intense exercise). One group is the one you are interested in, while the other is the control group. As a control group, Dr. Prout used those college classmates of these oarsmen who did not exercise to any exceptional degree. He found that the oarsmen lived 6.3 years longer, on average.

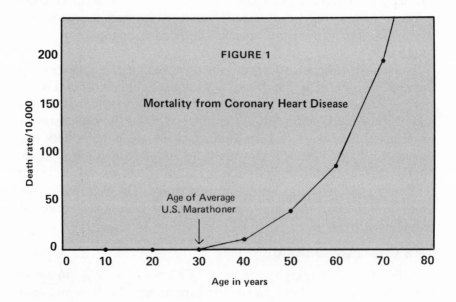

THE MASAI

The Masai Steppe extends from Nairobi, Kenya, 300 miles south to northern Tanzania. In southern Kenya and northern Tanzania a somewhat nomadic tribe, the Masai, was studied by George Mann and his colleagues in 1962 and again in 1963. Two hundred thirty-six Masai men, aged thirty or older, were examined. (Only three men were over fifty-five, the age at which CHD begins to appear clinically in large numbers of Americans.)

The Masai were found to be equivalent in height to the average American male, but weighed generally less than 135 pounds. The serum cholesterol levels averaged about 55 percent of that in comparable U.S. men, a phenomenally low value. Their general physical condition, measured by treadmill, was remarkable, not infrequently surpassing the performance of Olympic caliber athletes.

Mann found almost no electrocardiographic or other clinical manifestations of atherosclerosis or of CHD. Yet the Masai diet contains plentiful supplies of whole milk and fatty beef, although they consume almost no salt. Since the diet consists of high levels of cholesterol (from the milk) and saturated fatty acids (from the animal meat), the authors suggest that the long, brisk walks required of these men in tending their herds explains their freedom from heart disease. The authors state, "All of these facts indicate that CHD, obesity and diabetes, the prevalent chronic diseases of Western society, are a consequence not of diet but of indolence and inactivity."

THE H.I.P. STUDY

A population study was made by the Health Insurance Plan of Greater New York (HIP), which for many years has kept careful medical records of all its participants. One of the questions, asked on a detailed questionnaire sent to patients or their families after diagnosis of a heart attack or death, sought to assess the patient's level of physical activity. The data appear impressive. The least active men had an increase of heart attacks and deaths from heart attacks 71 percent higher than the incidence among the general membership.

But it's not quite so straightforward. Let's examine the incidence of *angina pectoris*, the term for a recurrent pain in the center, left of the chest, which often radiates down the left arm. It frequently develops during exercise and is a sign of CHD. The HIP study showed that angina was 23 percent less frequent in sedentary men than in the active men.

Furthermore, it seems that intermediate levels of activity are better than being in the most active category, since the incidence of CHD is even lower in the intermediate category.

FURTHER STUDIES

Several hundred studies have dealt with the relationship of physical activity to CHD or mortality from all diseases. These studies show that those people who are physically active tend to have a lower incidence of disease at any particular age than those who are not.

The scientific and medical field involved in these studies is *epidemiology*. Epidemiologists seek to discover through statistical studies of man and his environment the causes of pathology and disease. Whether the problem is cholera in nineteenth century England (solved), the Legionnaires' disease in Philadelphia in 1977 (solved), the primary cause of lung cancer (solved), bladder cancer (unsolved), or CHD (unsolved), epidemiologists seek to demonstrate cause-and-effect relationships. The criteria for demonstrating these relationships are quite specific and difficult to satisfy. Sophisticated mathematical techniques are often employed so the epidemiologist can achieve valid conclusions. It's a difficult discipline because, while it's very easy to prove "association," it is infinitely more difficult to demonstrate cause-and-effect.

For example, in the 1960s Yudkin studied the relationship between dietary sugar, CHD, and its final manifestation, the heart attack. He took very careful dietary histories of three groups of hospital patients: (1) patients hospitalized for any one of a large variety of reasons (broken legs to appendectomies); (2) patients suffering from CHD; and (3) patients who had had *myocardial infarcts* (heart attacks). The amount of sugar each group consumed prior to hospitalization was shown to be least for the "control" patients in the first group, intermediate for the CHD patients, and highest for the heart attack patients. This study strongly suggests that sugar consumption was a contributing factor in the development of CHD and in its final manifestation, the heart attack. However, several investigators have questioned this.

In the 1970s, two groups working independently showed that there was a better correlation between the development of this disease and the amount of smoking. And there was an even better correlation between smoking and sugar consumption. (Those who smoked more also consumed more sugar.)

From a scientific and medical viewpoint, there is no obvious reason why sugar and CHD should have a causal relationship. Fats, especially saturated fats, are probably causally related to CHD, but sugar is not. But one can suggest any of a number of good, medically sound explanations why smoking might cause CHD. And there is statistical evidence for this. So we were fooled for a number of years by the earlier study showing a correlation between CHD and sugar consumption, when in fact no causal relationship existed.

In this case, the epidemiologist refers to sugar as a *confounding variable*, which goes along with the causal variable. It's absent when the real cause is absent, and it's there when the real cause is there, and it's a damned confusing problem to handle in all epidemiological studies.

We can only speculate why sugar and smoking consumption are correlated. We do know that the lower socioeconomic groups in our country generally eat more sugar than higher socioeconomic classes. Although I haven't checked it out, they almost certainly smoke more as well. So both smoking and sugar consumption may, in this light, be viewed as related to one's socioeconomic status.

We also know that CHD is higher in the less affluent classes. So perhaps the cause of CHD should be looked for in some common aspect of the environment or the life-style of the less-advantaged socioeconomic classes. Do they go for checkups less frequently? Do they smoke and consume fats or salt in larger amounts?

It's very difficult for the epidemiologist to pinpoint the environmental needle in the haystack of potential causes. Let me cite an additional problem that plagues the researcher. The two hypothetical models for the development of CHD shown in figure 2 may be suggested as reasonable schemes.

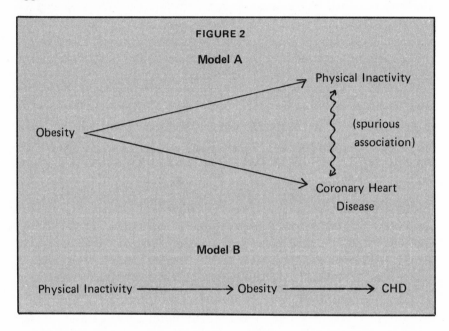

In model *A*, obesity leads directly to CHD and to physical inactivity. But looked at from another point of view, it appears that physical inactivity causes CHD. This is what is referred to as a *spurious association*. Model *B* proposes that physical inactivity leads to obesity and obesity in turn leads to CHD. In this model, obesity is referred to as an *intervening variable*.

Each model can, to an extent, be supported by medical evidence. For instance, research shows that if you overfeed babies just a few months old, their fat cells (which are constant in number but can vary in size) become large, so the baby becomes fat, and becomes accustomed to that state of affairs. For the rest of that baby's life, his mind craves food whenever these fat cells feel a little depleted, and there is little he can do about it. The other model can also be supported with medical facts. (There are other models for obesity as well.)

The moral is, I suppose, that things are not as simple as they sometimes seem. Just because things are connected (obesity, CHD, and physical inactivity) doesn't mean that any one of them necessarily causes any of the others.

ANALYZING THE RESULTS

Now that the complexities of the epidemiological study of the relationship between CHD and its proposed "causes" are a little more apparent, let's reexamine the studies summarized earlier in this article. For instance, what is the story behind Clarence DeMar—his great running prowess and his large coronary arteries? If we are not careful, we might draw the fallacious conclusion that his large arteries were a consequence of his years of long-distance running. Yet, how do we know DeMar did not become the fine runner because he was born with the genetic inclination towards the development of large coronary arteries? If we had access to autopsy reports on DeMar's mother and father, and we discovered that each had normal arterial dimensions, this might be helpful in deciding between the two alternative hypotheses. But we do not. So the report is anecdotal in nature and, although true, it really tells us nothing definite about the relationship of exercise and CHD.

What about Morris's study of London bus drivers and conductors? Several years after Morris's study, a paper appeared that showed that these same drivers and conductors differed not only in their physical activity, but also in another important way. The drivers were less physically active than the conductors, but as a group they also were fatter (greater "girth," as the report put it) than the active ticket-takers.

Perhaps there should be nothing surprising about this. After all, the drivers had quite sedentary occupations. The surprising part of the study (formally subtitled "epidemiology of uniforms," because the data was obtained from the size of uniforms issued to both groups) was that, from the moment the two groups of men first obtained employment, the fatter men chose or took the drivers' jobs while the thinner men took the job of conductors. The two groups differed in body fat even before their moment of employment!

Thus, the first study had not randomized all the variables save one—level of physical activity—which it sought to study in its relationship to CHD. Another significant difference might be present. The drivers have responsibility for the safety of all the passengers. With a small driving error, a fatal accident might occur. Would this psychological burden lead to a continuous, albeit small, level of anxiety? Some studies indicate that anxiety and CHD may be related. This is another example of a confounding variable.

I think it is a tribute to the honesty and integrity of Morris that he published this second study, devoted to the weights of the two groups of London transport workers, although it invalidated his first study to some extent.

Prout's article on the mortality of college oarsmen compared to the mortality of their college classmates has serious flaws as well. The facts cannot be disputed: the oarsmen lived considerably longer than their classmates. But Prout says in his paper: "Obviously, the oarsmen were in good condition to begin with. Otherwise, they would not have been chosen (for the team)."

At least some of the students who were not on the crew obviously had an increased risk of CHD, since some smoked, some were overweight, and some had various medical conditions that would have kept them off the team. The oarsmen were in better physical condition before they ever got on the team, so they would have been expected to live longer, irrespective of any benefits that crewing conferred on them.

Unfortunately, since this study is circular and self-fulfilling, it cannot be cited as proof that physical activity can lower mortality. Unfortunately, it is often cited for just this purpose.

The study of the Masai tribe can also be critically evaluated. First of all, Mann studied Masai who had volunteered, not those chosen at random. And random sampling is the essence of statistical studies. Study after study shows that those who volunteer are never a random sample of anything. They simply have different characteristics than nonvolunteers.

Ancel Keys, an epidemiologist who has studied the role of diet and physical exercise in the development of CHD, has shown that the main weakness of Mann's study is that inadequate numbers of Masai were available for medical evaluation. Although electrocardiograms showed no clinical signs of CHD, Keys shows that this result could not be considered statistically significant unless four times as many Masai had been examined. The same result could occur from pure chance.

Keys shows, too, that the Masai's level of physical activity—much walking, but very little intense activity—cannot explain the physical findings. Mann himself notes that the village elders, who also were free of CHD, "seemed sedentary." So for Mann and his colleagues to zero in on exercise appears to me quite capricious. Other variables— the Masai's extraordinary leanness, their unique genetic endowment, their extraordinarily low serum cholesterol levels, and their negligible consumption of salt—are dismissed as explanations for their

apparent freedom from CHD. To opt for exercise as the key explanation for their good health does not strike me as a conclusion that is
warranted.

Finally, let's examine the New York HIP study. Here, inadequate
numbers are no problem. As mentioned, the incidence of heart
attacks and death from heart attacks is greatest for the least active
HIP members. The incidence of CHD (usually an accurate leading
indicator of an approaching heart attack) is also lower among the
physically active than the inactive. But at intermediate levels of
activity, CHD is significantly lower than in the most active category.

Some men who had medical exams to determine the status of their
cardiovascular systems never had medical histories taken of their
levels of physical activity. Although the incidence of CHD for these
men was known, their activity levels were classified as unknown. This
"unknown" category had an incidence of CHD more than five times
lower than the incidence of CHD in the most active category.

Examining the data base for this study a little more carefully, we
find that the men studied did not include any who previously had
suffered a myocardial infarct (heart attack). Yet many of the men
studied were already suffering from incipient CHD, although it had
not been diagnosed medically. Such men probably would tend (1) to
be physically inactive, and (2) to suffer a heart attack eventually.

Thus, we might anticipate that the inactive group would have a
high incidence of men who eventually suffer heart attacks—not
because of their physical inactivity but perhaps because they self-
selected themselves into this classification after having subtle hints of
lowered endurance. Therefore, physical inactivity and heart attacks
become statistically associated, but no causal relationship can be
demonstrated. So once again the old devil self-selection makes its
appearance, and louses up the statistical significance of the study. It
unduly loads the least active category with men who are prime candidates for a heart attack.

A common weak link runs through each of these studies. In fact, it
runs through just about all of the studies that tackle the problem of
clarifying the relationship among CHD, mortality, and level of
physical exercise. This common link has been expressed succinctly
and eloquently by Hermann Hellerstein, a well-known cardiologist
from Case Western Reserve University School of Medicine, and a
recent convert to jogging.

According to him, "There are no data worth a damn to snow
that exercising middle-aged, sloppy, overweight, cigarette-smoking,
paunchy men, 20 percent of whom are hypertensive and 7 percent of

whom are diabetic, will make a bit of difference in survivorship. I say this despite the fact that I have had 454 such people in exercise training programs since 1960. There are no data because there's self-selection!"

Self-selection means leaving the choice of the level of physical activity to the individual. If the individual is vigorous and active, he may well be chosen for a physically demanding job. As Morris says, "The fit will thus preserve and enhance their fitness." But if he is weak and sedentary, no similar freedom of choice is present.

We may ask how many nonrunning American men might be expected to die during a one-year period, compared to a group of men equal in number, in age, and in several other attributes to American men who ran a marathon during the same year. Once we have an answer to this problem, we are in a position to ask how many similar men—different only in that they run—might be expected to die of an infarct. The results might give insights on the hypothesis that running marathons provides some protection from CHD—or, as Dr. Tom Bassler asserts, provides absolute protection.

Ken Young, head of the National Running Data Center, informs me that 9,958 men completed a marathon in 1975. (Almost exactly 20 percent more ran one in 1976, Young adds.) It is not difficult to estimate from available mortality tables, smoking and weight risk factor tables, and so on the number of men expected to die from CHD in one year. These figures are for men who have characteristics similar to the marathoners, except that their level of physical activity matches that of the general population. Out of a random sampling of 9,958 men, the number who may be expected to die is about 1.5. The main reason for this low value is that the group of men is very young, since 80 percent of American marathoners are thirty-nine years or younger and 55 percent are under thirty. If we were to try to prove statistically that marathoning, and the life-style that is said to go with it, offer protection from heart disease, then we must be able to demonstrate that fewer than this number of marathoners die yearly from heart disease.

Even if marathoning offered 100 percent protection (and we don't know this), and consequently no man who ran a marathon would die from CHD, this could not be demonstrated statistically. The statistical error associated with 1.5 deaths on the one hand and zero deaths on the other is so small from a statistical point of view that the two numbers must be viewed as equivalent. Thus, a pathologist who autopsies every marathoner who dies, and never sees a death from CHD, may only have the statistics on his side. Any statement that marathoning provides protection is absolutely unjustified if based on the meager evidence provided by an informal study of 10,000 U.S. marathoners.

Finally, rest assured that there is simply no evidence that intensive or prolonged exercise is in any way bad for you. It's just that there is no hard scientific or medical evidence that, from the point of view of mortality, it is in any way good for you.

But although it's neither here nor there, I wouldn't give up running marathons if all the ornery dogs in the local pound ran with me!

I suspect that this long-running debate will continue, with no need for these personal testimonials or anecdotal "proofs."

REFERENCES

Bassler, T. J. 1977. Marathon running and immunity to atherosclerosis. In *The marathon: physiological, medical, epidemiological, and psychological studies*, ed. Paul Milvy, pp. 579-92. New York: Annals of the New York Academy of Sciences.

Currens, J. H., and White, P. F. 1961. Half a century of running: clinical, physiologic, and autopsy findings in the case of Clarence DeMar (Mr. Marathon). *N. Eng. J. Med.* 265:988-93.

Fox, S. M., III. 1976. Physical activity and coronary heart disease. *Controversy in cardiology*, ed. E. K. Chang, pp. 201-19.

Hellerstein, H. K. 1976. Exercise tests inadequate for cardiac patients. *The physician and sports medicine.* 4:68.

Keys, A. 1970. Physical activity and epidemiology of coronary heart disease. In *Physical activity and aging, medicine, and sport*, ed. D. Brunner. Baltimore: University Park Press. 250-60.

Mann, G. V.; Shaffer, R. D.; and Rich, A. 1965. Physical fitness and immunity to heart disease in Masai. *Lancet* 1308-10.

Milvy, P. 1977. Statistical analysis of deaths from coronary heart disease anticipated in a cohort of marathon runners. In *The marathon: physiological, medical, epidemiological, and psychological studies*, ed. Paul Milvy, pp. 620-26. New York: Annals of the New York Academy of Sciences.

Milvy, P.; Forbes, W. F.; and Brown, K. S. 1977. A critical review of epidemiological studies of physical activity. In *The marathon: physiological, medical, epidemiological, and psychological studies*, ed. Paul Milvy, pp. 519-49. New York: Annals of the New York Academy of Sciences.

Morris, J. N.; Heady, J. A.; and Raffle, P. A. 1956. Physique of London busmen. *Lancet* 566-70.

Morris, J. N.; Heady, J. A.; Raffle, P. A.; Roberts, C. G.; and Parks, J. W. 1953. Coronary heart disease and physical activity of work. *Lancet* ii, 1053-57, 1111-20.

Paffenberger, R. S. 1972. Factors predisposing to fatal stroke in longshoremen. *Prev. Med.* 522-27.

Paffenberger, R. S., and Hale, W. E. 1975. Work activity and coronary heart mortality. *N. Eng. J. Med.* 292:545-50.

Prout, C. 1972. Life expectancy of college oarsmen. *JAMA* 220:1709-10.

Shapiro, S.; Weinblatt, E.; Frank, C. W.; and Sager, R. V. 1965. The H.I.P. study of incidence and prognosis of coronary heart disease. *J. Chronic Dis.* 18:527-58.

5

What Went Wrong?

by Jim Lilliefors

Most safety rules are so simple they are taken for granted. Running safety, too, is not something that is always subscribed to religiously. Nine times out of ten it may be unnecessary, but that one time in ten, the runner will be glad he took the precautions.

When racing on the road, runners should abide by some of the same rules an automobile follows, but blatantly disregard some others. For example, runners should not try to run a red or even a yellow light. Drivers are not always as alert as they should be, and are seldom on the lookout for runners.

Runners are better off to run against the traffic, rather than with it. This way you can see what's coming before it arrives. This is especially important after a race has thinned out; a single runner is less noticeable than a pack of runners. Always approach road racing with caution. No matter how you feel about automobiles, when you're on the road, you're on their turf and must follow most of their rules.

To avoid possible injuries, it is important to preface each race with a thorough warm-up. The amount of time spent and the type of exercises will vary with each person and the distance of the race. A good warm-up not only acts as partial insurance against racing injuries, but also helps a person run faster and race easier.

Sometimes, trouble signs can be detected before the runner has even taken his first step. If the previous day's workout has been a pounding road run or a series of grinding intervals, his body may be imploring him to take it easy. If he tries to run an all-out race anyway, he might encounter undue fatigue and possible danger.

After a race, the runner should put on his sweat clothes as soon as possible, so as not to become sick when his body temperature drops. It usually becomes clear after the race whether the signs of normal and abnormal running have been read properly. If the runner has to be carried off in a stretcher, they obviously haven't. If he faints, vomits, or feels an exhaustion that lingers for days, he has probably pushed too hard, and may not be far from being the runner on the stretcher. If he walks around afterward and feels like doing another hard run, he's been taking it too easy.

Maintaining a safe body temperature is probably the most important physical safety measure, and one that is often overlooked. On a hot day, in particular, loss of body weight is something that has to be dealt with.

"Loss of more than 3% of body weight...puts the athlete in danger of heat exhaustion," says Dr. George Sheehan. With a 140-pound individual, this is just over 4 pounds, not an uncommon amount to lose in a distance race on a hot day.

If a runner experiences excessive wheezing or has trouble breathing in hot weather, this can be a serious danger sign, even for top competitive runners. At an Amateur Athletic Union (AAU) championship in the mid-fifties, the 10,000 meters was run in near 100-degree heat. Hal Higdon was running in that race and remembers the tragedy of Austin Scott, a New York runner who beat him, but was gasping abnormally in the heat: "He seemed to be wheezing badly, but he pulled away in the last few laps to finish ahead of me—then collapsed.... A week later, I learned he died in the hospital, never having gained consciousness."

Before something this drastic happens, there are usually reliable clues about what is happening. One of the most common is the feeling that the body is becoming overheated, that it is encased in a cocoon of heat. Often, a throbbing head on hot days is a trouble sign. Another danger sign is a feeling of sand in your eyes—a sign of dehydration. Whenever the runner begins to see everything with a yellowish tint and seems to lose conscious control of his running, he is in trouble and should stop. Derek Clayton, history's fastest marathoner, once lost control of his running and ran full speed into a tree. When any of these danger signs appear, the best advice is to proceed with caution, or not at all. It's more important to be alive than it is to finish a race.

If a runner does collapse, it's important to get him to a hospital as soon as possible. Don't accept the statement of a collapsed runner who says, "I'll be okay." Before reaching the hospital, it is helpful to pour cold water on him to help cool his system.

Evaporation is the process of cooling the body, in which secretions from the sweat glands are changed to vapor. If the runner is wearing constrictive clothing, this evaporation may be inhibited. In warm weather, it is best to wear light clothing, such as nylon mesh tops.

For winter running, the best dress is several layers of loose, relatively light, clothing. Frank Shorter once won a national cross-country title wearing pantyhose. If a runner is overdressed, with clothing that is too thick, he becomes susceptible to some of the same problems as in summer running: overheating and dehydration.

One of the greatest safety hazards—and the most tempting to disregard—is running too hard too soon, particularly after an injury or illness. Many runners have only worsened their condition by doing this, and some runners have even died. If a person has been seriously ill, or away from the sport for a length of time, physically he's a beginner again, even though he may think like a veteran. In the case of a serious sickness, a severe cold, or flu, he can train, but should not race.

There are several commonsense rules for avoiding injury and for preventing minor injury from becoming major. The most basic—and this holds true with temperature, traffic, and terrain—is to watch where you run. Uneven terrain, such as the edge of a road, should be avoided as much as possible in races. This can be the source of blisters and sprained ankles. If blisters do develop, they should be cleaned and bandaged immediately so they don't become infected. Keeping the feet dry and clean, and the toenails clipped, helps in avoiding foot injuries.

Ideally, a racing situation should be a challenge, a safe and rewarding struggle. The runner's body and mind should reflect this after the race. He should be tested beyond what he does in training, and should feel a sense of accomplishment from the results. But three days later, the runner should be thinking about what his next race will be and when he will run it.

6

Steps Toward Painless Running

by George Sheehan, M.D.

f you want to run a marathon, you must train the "Magic Six" (miles a day). If you are looking for that natural high distance runners talk about, you must do the same. And if you would prefer to die of something other than a heart attack, the daily 6 miles is the physiological magic.

But know this: disaster will pursue you to the very gates of this heaven unless you do another "Magic Six." These are the "Magic Six" exercises designed to counteract the bad effects of daily training—the muscle imbalance that contributes to overuse syndromes of the foot, leg, knee, and lower back. Without this "Magic Six," you will soon become an ex-runner, no longer able to accept 5,000 foot-strikes an hour on a hard, flat surface with a foot constructed for sand or dirt.

Training overdevelops the prime movers, those muscles along the back of the leg, thigh, and lower back become short and inflexible. The *antagonists*—the muscles on the front of the leg, thigh, and abdomen—become relatively weak. The "Magic Six" are necessary to correct this strength/flexibility imbalance: 3 to stretch and 3 to strengthen.

Wall pushup. This first stretching exercise is for the calf muscles. Stand flat-footed about 3 feet from the wall. Lean in until it hurts, keeping the knees locked, the legs straight, and the feet flat. Count "one elephant, two elephants," and so on. Hold for 10 "elephants." Relax. Repeat for 1 minute.

Hamstring stretch. Put your straight leg with knee locked on a footstool, later a chair, and finally a table as you improve. Keep the other leg straight with the knee locked. Bring your head toward the

Wall Pushup

Hamstring Stretch

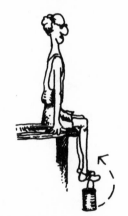

Shin Strengthener

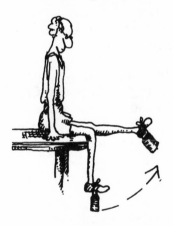

Quads Strengthener

Backover

Bent-leg Sit-up

Drawings by Nora Sheehan

knee of the extended leg until it hurts. Hold for 10 "elephants." Relax. Repeat for 1 minute, and then do the same exercise with the other leg.

Backover. This is the final stretching exercise for the hamstrings and lower back. Lie on the floor. Bring straight legs over your head and try to touch the floor with your toes until it hurts. Hold for 10 "elephants." Relax by bringing your knees to your ears for 10 "elephants." Repeat stretch and relax periods for 1 minute each.

Shin strengthener. This exercise strengthens the shin muscles. Sit on a table with the legs hanging down. Put a 3- to 5-pound weight over the toes. Flex foot at ankle. Hold for 6 "elephants." Relax. Repeat for 1 minute with each leg.

Quads strengthener. This exercise is for the *quadriceps*, or thigh muscles. Assume the same position with the weight as in the previous exercise. This time, straighten the leg, locking the knee. Hold for 6 "elephants." Relax. Repeat for 1 minute, and then do the same with the other leg.

Bent-leg sit-up. Lie on the floor with your knees bent and your feet close to your buttocks. Come to a sitting position. Lie back. Repeat until you can't do any more or have reached 20.

It takes a little over 6 minutes to do the "Magic Six." Done before and after running, this means just 12 minutes a day to keep you in muscle balance.

7

First Aid for the Injured

by Joe Henderson

K **nee.** The knee, the body's shock-absorber, takes an awful beating during running. One in four of the runners surveyed by *Runner's World* reports knee injuries as the main complaint. Dr. Richard Schuster says three in four of those patients he sees have some knee pain, although they may be in his office for another reason.

Among distance runners, the most common complaint is irritation at the bottom edge of the kneecap. This ailment, called *chondromalacia*, is thought to result from excessive rotation of the knee at foot-strike.

Preventive measures: Stabilize the foot with heel or arch supports: emphasize the quads strengthener exercise from the "Magic Six."

Achilles. This thin cord connects the heel bone with the calf muscle, and it takes its name from Greek mythology. Achilles, like about one in five runners, was vulnerable only in this spot.

Many people are born with short, thin Achilles tendons that don't stand up well to the stresses of running. Nearly all runners acquire additional tightness here because of the action of running. At push-off, the tendon may not have enough "give" to stretch properly. Irritation and inflammation set in, usually at a point about two inches above the top of the heel bone.

Preventive measures: Take stress off the heel with a well-heeled shoe or a heel lift about a quarter-inch thick; stretch the calf muscles with the wall pushup from the "Magic Six."

Shin. *Shin splints* are any of a number of injuries with common symptoms—namely, sharp pain radiating along the front of the leg from the knee down. The source of the pain may be a tearing away of the muscle from the bone, an inflammation of the bone lining, a stress fracture of the shin bone or tibial tendonitis.

Other than sudden changes in routine—the "getting-in-shape syndrome"—major causes of shin problems are thought to be inflexibility at the ankles and imbalance of the front-and-back-leg muscles. The ankles don't provide a full range of motion, either because the calf muscles are tight or because the shoes are too stiff up front. The shin muscles are weak in comparison to the calf.

Preventive measures: Find shoes that bend easily at the forefoot; use higher-heeled shoes or heel lifts; give special attention to the wall pushup from the "Magic Six" and shin strengthening.

Ankle. Ankles take more of a beating in contact sports and so-called mixed motion sports than in running, where the only contact is with the ground and the main motion is straight ahead. Ankle twists and sprains are relatively rare in this sport, and usually have obvious causes (stepping the wrong way on a rough spot) and cures (temporary limitation of activity).

Chronic ankle problems may relate to shoe wear and shoe type. Badly worn heels on shoes may throw the foot too much to the outside, straining the tendons of the outer ankle. Some runners also report being bothered by shoes with widely flared heels. These may cause the foot to flatten too much or too quickly, and lead to inner-ankle strain.

Preventive measures: Choose shoes with adequate, but not excessive, heel width; don't allow the heels to wear down more than a quarter-inch; practice the shin strengthener from the "Magic Six."

Heel. The heels absorb approximately three "G's" of force at contact. In other words, if you weigh 150 pounds, an area smaller than your fist is accepting more than 450 pounds of shock. It's surprising the heels hold up as well as they do.

Heels have "spurs"—sharp points at the top-rear portion, at the insert of the Achilles tendon, and on the bottom-front, where the fleshy band of the arch connects with the heel bone. (The bottom problem is discussed in the "Arch" section.)

Many runners display prominent bumps—redness, blistering, swelling of the bursa, and actual bony growth—on their heels. The major cause is suspected to be heel instability, complicated by irritation from the shoe back.

Preventive measures—Wear shoes with a wide heel base, good heel lift, and a solid, well-padded, nonirritating heel counter; use the wall pushup and shin strengthener from the "Magic Six."

Arch. One of the most distressing and hard-to-treat running injuries is concentrated in a spot no bigger than a dime. This is the point where the arch's bowstring or *plantar fascia* meets the base of the heel bone. Though this problem affects only about one runner in twelve, this ailment causes more and longer suffering than the more "popular" ailments, because a runner's sore heel takes the full force of impact with each step.

These heel spur injuries, which are often mistaken for bruises, apparently are related to excessive tugging on the plantar fascia. This, in turn, has to do with abnormal motion of the heel and forefoot.

Preventive measures: Take pressure off the sore spot with pads, and control motion with well-supported shoes and additional arch supports; emphasize the shin strengthener exercise from the "Magic Six."

Calf. Sprinters pull their upper-leg muscles most often (see "Hamstring"), but distance runners seem more prone to calf tears. Calf muscles grow quite strong with hundreds of training miles, but they also grow tight and out of balance relative to the front-of-leg muscles.

The "pull" comes suddenly and sharply, like a knife plunging into the muscle. It often happens when the runner is well into a run or race. Unlike in sprinting, the injury may not be associated with violent activity.

While true muscle tears in the calf are common, the injury may also have an origin in a tendon or nerve. Both the tibial tendon and sciatic nerve pass through the calf.

Preventive measures: Find shoes with a high heel (or add a heel lift), and with a flexible forefoot; employ all three stretching exercises, plus the shin and quad strengtheners.

Hip. Hip injuries usually are messengers carrying news of trouble from above or below. From above come the results of lower back miseries, most often sciatic nerve irritation. That nerve, rooted at the base of the spine, travels all the way down the back of the legs to the feet. Sciatica manifests itself in many ways, one of them being pain through the hips and buttocks. Strengthening the stomach muscles helps relieve irritation to the nerve by improving posture.

Most people are shorter in one leg than the other, either because they were born that way, or because they have acquired a postural difference. Hips may take the strain of this difference. Pads under the heels offer compensation.

Preventive measures: Place a heel lift in one shoe (experiment to find which one and how high); use bent-leg sit-ups and the three stretching exercises from the "Magic Six."

Hamstring. Muscle pulls at the back of the upper leg most commonly occur during sprinting and speed-work. They are caused by tight hamstring muscles and relatively weak thighs. Distance runners have different problems, but they can be just as disturbing, both to running rhythm and peace of mind.

The main bugaboo is sciatica—an irritation of the long nerve that travels the length of the lower body. Sciatica appears as a dull, hot throb, something like a "headache" in the hamstring area. It is worse during inactivity than when running, but it eventually interferes with motion. It is aggravated by hills and rough terrain.

Preventive measures: Do all of the "Magic Six" exercises, with special attention to the bent-leg sit-up, hamstring stretch, and the quad strengthener.

Forefoot. Considering the fact that there are about two dozen small bones in the forefoot, plus numerous ligaments, tendons, cartilages, and nails, we might expect more trouble than we get here.

The most frequent problems are rather minor—blisters, bruised toenails, and the like. They only become disabling when complications, such as infections, set in.

The most serious forefoot injury is a stress fracture of the metatarsals, the bones connected to the toes. These are more often caused by abnormal motions in the foot than by the simple pounding of running. These can be controlled with well-constructed shoes and added supports.

Preventive measures—Consider using shoes with limited forefoot flexibility if you can wear them without other injuries developing; add arch supports and pads under the balls of the feet.

8

The Curse of Achilles Pain

by Denis Wright

It would appear that injuries involving the Achilles tendon are on the increase. This fact would be of little consequence if this injury could be classified along with other athletic inconveniences. Unfortunately, this is not the case, and neither doctor, physiotherapist, nor athlete can afford to ignore the slightest sign of trouble.

I find it rather distressing to meet so many athletes who have pursued "run it off" advice. One can excuse this advice in the lower realms of the athletic world, but when one encounters it at top levels, involving people who should know better, the situation becomes serious.

Far be it from me to minimize the difficulty facing those whose task it is to diagnose, treat, and advise about problems of the Achilles tendon. In fact, of all athletic injuries, I consider this to be the most serious and most difficult to manage. Consequently, I would be amply rewarded if this article influenced athletes and their advisers to think more seriously about the factors likely to endanger this vital part of the propulsive mechanism.

There are three distinct tendon injuries: (1) tendonitis—an inflammation of the tendon; (2) partial rupture—when a varying number of tendon fibers are torn; and (3) complete rupture—a complete severance of the tendon.

CAUSES

The following list is by no means complete. It merely covers my experience with this type of injury, as sustained in sport.

Tendonitis:
1. Caused by a sudden change in routine (e.g., a change in footwear—flats to spikes; a change in surface—grass to cinder; a change in training—endurance to speed)

129

2. Caused by ignoring the reaction from a heavy training session, or a competitive effort

Partial rupture:
1. Results from a weakness due to longstanding tendonitis
2. A sudden stretching influence applied while the calf muscles are contracting vigorously

Complete rupture:
1. Caused by a direct blow to the tense tendon
2. Result of a logical sequence following tendonitis and partial rupture
3. Similar cause to that of a partial rupture

DIAGNOSIS

Although there should be little difficulty in recognizing a complete rupture—particularly if one witnesses the incident—the differentiation between tendonitis and partial rupture is often difficult to make. Severe tendonitis may resemble a minor rupture, and vice versa. However, the main factors for aiding diagnosis are (in order of importance):

The history of the injury. The history of any injury is often relevant, but there can be few injuries where it is of greater importance.

The limitations imposed by the injury. Achilles tendon injuries, no matter how serious, always impose some limitations on the athletes ability. The limiting factor is usually pain, which may vary in severity. Pain may only be initiated while attempting to sprint, but it may even be present on simple movements of the ankle joint.

The appearance of the tendon. The appearance of the tendon often helps in diagnosing the severity, since its shape is often altered or disguised by swelling or thickening.

The effect of previous treatment. This is worth noting because any improvement or other effect gives an indication of severity, as well as treatment method.

My diagnosis for each ailment would be based on the following clinical data:

Tendonitis:
1. No previous history of tendon trouble
2. Whether it is bilateral
3. Awareness of pain and stiffness an hour or so following activity, particularly after rest

4. Variable swelling, often only detectable by the experienced eye. if present, obvious the following morning
5. Pain on contraction and stretching of the calf muscles; more severe when stretching, with knee extended
6. Tenderness to squeezing pressure, applied at the tendon's narrowest point
7. Walking possible; running difficult; sprinting impossible

Partial Rupture:
1. A history of tendonitis
2. Unilateral
3. Onset of pain—sudden, and during activity
4. An obvious swelling, sometimes severe enough to disguise the contour of the tendon, and apparent within an hour
5. Pain on contraction, much more severe when stretching
6. Hypersensitive to squeezing pressure
7. Walking is difficult; running, other than perhaps a jog-trot, is impossible

One is not always fortunate enough to be able to diagnose and treat the initial occurrence, and a time lag often clouds the issue. The most disconcerting factor involves alternating periods of improvement and deterioration.

Chronic Tendonitis:
1. A residual tenderness to squeezing pressure, as compared with the unaffected tendon
2. Pain always experienced during the warm-up session, or in the initial stages of the race
3. A reaction the following day, which gradually diminishes over the next two days

Chronic Partial Rupture:
1. A tendon thickened to sometimes double normal size, and much less pliable in side-to-side movement when it is relaxed
2. A slight increase in the range of dorsi-flexion, especially when the knee is flexed
3. A very tender localized area when deep pressure is applied
4. Pain on attempts to sprint, with a feeling that a recurrence would result if the athlete did so
5. A history of two or three acute recurrences

TREATMENT

My approach to treatment is essentially a practical one. The aim is
to be of some help to the unfortunate sufferers, as well as to those
who become frustrated by the lack of interest shown by medical professionals. To those intimately involved in sport, it is difficult to
appreciate that most athletic injuries are regarded as orthopedic
minutiae. Obviously, knowledge and surgical skill abound in medical
circles. The problems arise in trying to find these qualities combined
with sufficient interest in sport, and an appreciation of the fact that
to prevent certain athletes from running is to remove all the pleasure
from their lives. We need only discuss the treatment of tendonitis
and partial rupture, because if the tendon is completely torn it
requires a surgical repair as soon as possible, and therefore becomes
a hospital problem.

The natural response of body tissues to injury involves inflammation. The cardinal signs and symptoms of inflammation are: redness, heat, swelling, pain, and limitation of function. These basic
pathological changes occur as the body attempts to heal the
damaged tissues. In the treatment of tendon injuries (or any other
injury) we must never lose sight of the fact that the signs and symptoms are normal reactions. The healing begins as soon as the
damage occurs. These changes take place according to an expected
time schedule. Experience gives one a time table of improvement,
with diminishing symptoms and a return to normal.

By judicious treatment, nature can be assisted and the processes
speeded up slightly. Similarly, nature can be impeded and the
healing processes delayed by interference. Unfortunately, athletes
generally fail to observe the most important aspect of treatment,
which, without doubt, is that of rest. The mechanism of pain is a
complex problem, but for our purposes it is sufficient to say that
pain experienced in Achilles tendon injuries arises from two sources.
One is the pressure from swelling, and the other is from damaged
tendon fibers that have nerve endings sensitive to pain stimuli.

Therefore, two factors will prolong the pain—namely, swelling and
movement. If you can prevent these, the pain will be minimized. This
is why rest is so obvious and so necessary. There are of course
degrees of rest: complete bed-rest; local rest in the form of a plaster
cast; or modification of daily activity, such as eliminating unnecessary walking.

Another major consideration is the prevention of excessive swelling
in the initial stage. This excess of tissue fluid contains an important

substance called *fibrinogen*, which is normally carried in the blood. Fibrinogen is important in the production of fibrous tissue, which the body produces in its attempt to repair damage. Unfortunately, in bringing about this repair, the fibrous tissue often implicates other surrounding structures and forms fibrous adhesions between them. These adhesions are frequently a source of trouble, particularly if they are formed with the structures in a shortened position. Often nothing other than a manipulation will overcome these inelastic adhesions. If swelling is not allowed to occur, these adhesions will obviously not need removing. Therefore, what happens to the injury within the first 48 hours is of paramount importance. Heat, in any shape or form, is inadvisable during this period. Prevention or control of swelling can be achieved by applying cold compresses and packing areas where it tends to accumulate. After two days, heat in its many forms, plus skilled massage, should reduce swelling to a minimum.

We now reach the next important aspect of treatment—namely, the restoration of function. Unless this is organized most carefully, in a progressive manner, all previous care means nothing. The athlete must have great patience. Whatever the stage of progress, both physiotherapist and athlete are constantly tempted to test the injury under greater conditions of stress. For this reason, in one's initial assessment of damage, one must observe and record the factors that initiate pain. These facts provide a yardstick against which progress can be judged. They also determine the severity of the exercise to which the tendon can be subjected. Realize, however, that within reasonable limits the tendon will benefit from increasing demands on it. With these major considerations in mind, let us consider exercise in relation to tendonitis and partial rupture.

Tendonitis. It is necessary to reduce normal, everyday activities to a minimum. There should be no unnecessary walking for 48 hours, and no attempt to run for 10 days. During this time a sorbo-rubber raise inside the heel of the shoe will prevent undue stretch of the muscles while walking.

In the vital first 48-hour period, control of swelling can be achieved by cold water dressings around the ankle and the lower third of the leg. The ideal means of creating compression locally involves two *L*-shaped pads placed on either side of the tendon and behind the malleoli of the ankle. Cotton-wool could be used for this, but adhesive felt is most ideal. Cover the complete lower leg, from toe to knee, with Tubagrip bandage. The dressing should be kept damp for 48 hours. There should be no heat applied, and the usual postrace bath should be modified to a shower or a sponge-down. After 48 hours, apply gentle heat to the back of the lower leg, followed by gentle massage to assist drainage from the area. After 7 days, deeper forms of heat and a more localized massage of the tendon can be instituted. Following this sedative-type treatment, active movements of the foot and ankle should be encouraged. At 10 days, the athlete should be ready to begin easy exercises using the body-weight, such as raising and lowering the heels. By 14 days, easy jogging on a yielding surface, in flat shoes, should be possible. From here, progress is made by increasing distance, and then pace.

Particular care is necessary in considering the change to a firmer surface. Any reaction to the previous training session must be approached with common sense. At this stage, a day's rest from running may be all that is required. At one month following injury, the athlete should be ready for full training schedules. This may seem rather timid and overcautious. My answer to criticisms on this score would be to relate numerous case histories and show some interesting slides where caution has been thrown to the wind—and with it a useful athletic career.

Partial Rupture. The minor degrees of this injury may be approached in a similar way to tendonitis, with a slightly slower progression and much more organization of the actual return to running. Distances must be measured, reactions observed, and modifications made accordingly. The ultimate objective of any athlete would be the need to run at speed, in spikes, and on a firm surface. All three of these variables must be considered. To indulge in a combination of all three without a detailed progressive schedule would be sheer folly. The result undoubtedly would be a recurrence of the injury. For more severe ruptures, there are two alternatives. One is the immobilization of the foot and ankle in a plaster splint for about six weeks. The other is surgical repair of the defect.

From observation and experience, I have no hesitation at all in saying that for an athlete of international standard who wishes to continue at this level, the only course is to undergo surgery. The plaster method will most certainly bring about a good, sound repair by scar tissue, but it will only be strong enough to withstand the strains of moderate athletic standards. A factor of great importance, when deciding, is the type of event involved. The shorter track events, demanding real speed, make greater demands on Achilles tendons, and consequently increase the need for surgery. Whatever the method chosen, there is still a lot of hard work to follow. This will involve mobilization of the ankle joint and strengthening of the leg muscles. The lengthy resting period will have resulted in atrophy of muscle, consequent loss of strength and adaptive shortening of fibrous structures, particularly on the back of the lower leg. Any slight impairment of ankle movement will be apparent in the athlete's gait. For this reason, immobilization of an athlete's joints is a major decision—a decision to be made when all else has failed, or as a result of experience in similar circumstances.

I have deliberately omitted another common method of treatment because of the controversial opinions surrounding its efficacy. This is the use of hydrocortisone injections. I feel that to condemn it out of hand is grossly unfair. But at the same time, it has effects that would suggest greater care should be exercised than is currently the practice in sports medicine. As with most new drugs, their development is greeted with loud acclaim, and hydrocortisone is no exception.

To use this injection, one must be discriminating on four main counts: the type of injury, the stages of the inflammation process, the precise localization of the structure involved, and the length of the resting period following injection.

In conclusion, I should like to underline my theme throughout this article. When the all-important Achilles tendon is involved in an injury, the athlete is risking everything by following well-meaning, but ill-informed, advice. "Run it off" and "go through the pain barrier" are phrases of folly and ignorance. The word *rest* has, unfortunately, become a dirty word in modern athletics. But rest offers some hidden benefits. I always consider that the mental benefit from rest far outweighs any physical loss.

9

The Trouble with Blisters

by Bob Carman

CAUSE AND EFFECT

Foot blisters in runners are caused by heat; they are essentially burns. The heat may come from running in thin-soled shoes on hot, paved surfaces, or more often from the abrasive action of shoes or socks on skin. Ill-fitting shoes, shoes with improperly placed stitching and worn insoles may be the source of the irritation.

Ill-fitting socks, holes in socks, seams or folds in socks, may produce blisters. Tape worn as protection for previous blisters is a prime source of the "hot spots" that quickly become new blisters. The effect of any of these is to produce a minor hot spot, where a water-filled bubble of skin appears. Continued friction may enlarge the blister, break it, and expose the tender lower layers of skin to further blistering. If one continues to run, there is an unconscious tendency to adjust the posture and action of the blistered foot to minimize pain. The resulting action may lead to other, more serious, leg injuries, as well as reduced running efficiency. For succeeding days, the injury may cause you to reduce the quantity and intensity of training. Taping may result in more blisters, and lack of proper attention may lead to infection.

PREVENTION

By far the best way of dealing with blisters is to be sure that one never appears. Super-marathoners race up to 50 and even 100 miles on paved roads, and many put in 100 to 200 miles per week of running, and never get a blister. These runners suggest the following for preventing blisters:

Don't wear socks. Few super-marathoners wear socks. They sacrifice the small comfort of the sock for the reduction of potential trouble socks represent. If you insist on wearing socks, wear clean, properly fitting ones and be prepared to suffer.

Get comfortable, properly fitting shoes. Break them in gradually, identifying, and removing or adjusting the potential blister-causing agents.

Never wear a new pair of shoes in a race. Be certain you check your shoes thoroughly for potential trouble before using them in a race. In practice, when breaking in new shoes, be sure to bring an older pair for a quick change if trouble appears.

Don't get blisters. The best prevention is to be extremely careful at all times. Remember, blisters lead to trouble and probably more blisters. Don't stubbornly push on in a training run when you know your feet are being chewed up. However, if you are 20 miles from home and the only way back is on foot, keep going. Think of the future; stop and pay attention to the trouble. Don't be a stubborn, dull-witted stoic. Stoics make great racers, but it also takes brains.

Buy good shoes. Adidas, Puma, and Tiger shoes are designed for foot comfort and minimum blister troubles, when running without socks. The New Balance shoe, one of a few good American-made shoes, is also used by knowledgeable runners. Not all of these shoes are suitable for all runners, and one must experiment a great deal to find the best shoe. All feet are different in shape, and shoes from different manufacturers have their own characteristics.

When you locate a friction spot in a shoe, use Vaseline liberally on the foot at this point. This has two useful purposes: (1) the friction between foot and shoe is reduced for awhile; and (2) the Vaseline soaks into the shoe at the point of friction, causing the shoe to soften, so that continued wear reshapes the shoe and may remove the difficulty.

Avoid using so-called skin-tougheners, advertised as the solution to the blister problems of baseball, football, and basketball players. In general, they do not help distance runners. A runner in a 10-mile race takes something more than 10,000 steps, each one in almost exactly the same manner and direction as every other. This is true in no other sport, so it is unreasonable to expect that these remedies will solve your problems.

Avoid those physical education teachers, baseball coaches, general practitioner M.D.s, and others who know nothing about the specialized problems of the distance runner. If you need advice on prevention, go to an M.D. or podiatrist (foot specialist) who is a sports medicine expert; to a successful college cross-country coach; or, best of all, to a marathon runner who has been solving these problems successfully for many years.

TREATMENT

Despite all your efforts at prevention, you will acquire an occasional blister if you run long distances. The important goals of treatment are to: (1) prevent infection, (2) keep running without impairment, and (3) prevent the initial blister from becoming a major problem. The following suggestions should help:

- Keep it clean, especially if the blister has broken.
- Do not puncture small blisters immediately. Ideally, one would prefer the skin to reheal itself. Twenty-four hours after acquiring the blister, it may disappear. In this case, protect the tender spot with a fit of form rubber and tape, and try to find the cause of the blister.
- If after 24 hours the blister has not disappeared, it is probably best if it is punctured and the fluid pressure released. Clean the blister and surrounding area with an antiseptic solution, puncture the blister with a sterile needle, and squeeze the fluid out gently with sterile gauze. Use a sterile gauze pad over the blister, as well as foam rubber and tape. Do not remove the skin that formed the blister. Removing it might be a sensible procedure for a baseball or football player, but it is not reasonable for a long-distance runner, who is trying to maintain his regular, arduous daily training schedule. Let it remain to protect the tender skin beneath during healing.
- When taping a blister, tape carefully, avoiding any bulges, wrinkles, or turned edges that may cause further blisters. Tape on a clean, dry foot, with one- or two-inch-wide tape. After taping, wax the tape by rubbing with a block of paraffin or candle wax to prevent the tape from sticking to the shoe and causing a hot spot.
- If any sign of infection or serious complication appears, hustle to a competent M.D. or a podiatrist immediately. If you can find an M.D. interested in distance running or sports medicine, you are indeed fortunate.

In summary, the key to treatment of blisters is not to get any. The key to avoiding them lies in meticulous attention to the details of suitable shoes and foot care.

10

The Burden of
Heat on Runners

by David Costill, Ph.D.

To the average spectator, a sunny day with the temperature at 75-80 degrees must seem a near-perfect day for distance runners to compete. The veteran road runner, however, is well aware of the toll that must be paid for running on a day like the one described. The runner's time will be slower, he will lose more weight, and he must be careful that he does not overheat. We have been able to make these observations on national- and world-class distance runners in research in our laboratory, at the 1968 Boston marathon, and during the 1968 Olympic marathon trial. Despite these experiences, many distance runners do not understand why these limitations impair their performance.

Road runners must overcome four major physical limitations if they hope to perform well on a warm day. First, man is only capable of partial adjustment (acclimatization) to the heat. A runner can make specific physiological adjustments to hot environments only by training under comparable conditions. Despite the extent of acclimatization, racing on a hot day will never produce as fine a performance as might be achieved on a cool, cloudless day.

This leads us to a second limitation: the runner has only a confined volume of blood to accomplish three major tasks. During any phase of running the circulating blood has the primary job of (1) delivering nutrients (oxygen, glucose, etc.) to the working muscles; (2) removing waste materials; and (3) transporting heat produced in the muscles to the surface of the body, where it can be dissipated to the environment. During a marathon race, a runner's muscles will produce about 11 times as much internal heat as they would at rest. The muscles and skin must, therefore, share the limited amount of circulating blood. On a hot day, more blood is demanded by the skin, so the muscles must take what they can get.

The runner involuntarily reduces his running speed to accommodate the impairing capacity of the circulatory system.

If a runner ignores the restrictions placed on his circulation and insists on running at his usual pace, he is faced with the third physical limitation: that under any heat stress condition the skin can only eliminate body heat at a limited rate. If the heat produced by the muscles is greater than the rate of heat being removed from the skin, then the runner will accumulate heat internally.

The final physical limitation experienced while working in the heat is the runner's critical tolerance to a high body temperature. If a runner forces himself to accumulate internal heat, he may well reach a critical temperature that will produce extreme weakness and unconsciousness. Through our research, we have found that several nationally ranked marathon runners experienced significant distress when their temperatures exceeded 104.5 degrees (F). However, Amby Burfoot, winner of the 1968 Boston marathon, was able to tolerate a rectal temperature of 105.3 degrees with no noticeable ill-effects. We have concluded that each person has his own tolerance limits. However, it is safe to assume that any runner whose temperature exceeds 106 degrees is unlikely to finish a race. Even more serious is the possibility that such a runner may affect his nervous system to the extent that he ceases to sweat, causing his rectal temperature to jump to 110 degrees. This condition is commonly known as heat stroke, and the chances of survival after one's temperature reaches 110 or 111 degrees are one in a thousand.

ENVIRONMENTAL HEAT STRESS

One of the most deceiving indicators of heat stress from the environment is the air temperature. A temperature of 60 degrees can be just as deadly as 90 degrees if the humidity is 95-100 percent. We have recorded data on one runner during a 10-mile run who developed a rectal temperature of 106.1 degrees under the exact conditions mentioned above (60 degrees air temperature and 95 percent relative humidity).

During a distance race, about 80-90 percent of the heat removed from the body is accomplished by sweat evaporation. Under extremely humid conditions, very little sweat can vaporize, making it difficult for the body to lose heat. Runners often think that they sweat more on humid days. This is quite possible if the runner's rectal temperature is very high, but we have noted very little difference in the sweat rates of runners under varied heat stress conditions when the air temperature exceeds 70 degrees.

At the 1968 Boston Marathon, the air temperature was 73 degrees, and the humidity 68 percent. Our subjects lost an average of 7.4 pounds by sweating. At the Olympic trial in Alamosa, Colorado (air temperature 74 degrees, humidity 23 percent), the average sweat loss was 7.6 pounds. In our laboratory, where we are able to offer greater heat stress (83 degrees and 73 percent humidity) we found the runners lost 7.53 pounds in the same period of time while running at their usual marathon pace on the treadmill. This would seem to indicate that these men are sweating at a maximal rate. The important point to remember is that such sweat loss is of little value unless it can be vaporized. If your skin becomes dry, it is important that you pour on water to help remove heat by continued evaporation.

While most runners dread a head wind because of the added resistance (a head wind of 10 miles per hour can increase your final time by about 5 percent), the additional flow of air provides greater evaporation. On the other hand, running with the wind can eliminate most of the air flow over the skin and, therefore, reduce sweat evaporation and heat loss. While a 10 mile per hour tail wind can reduce your running time by about 3 percent, it will substantially increase the heat stress.

TRAINING FOR THE HEAT

As was mentioned earlier, it is possible to acclimatize or gain greater tolerance to the heat, by training under similar conditions. If an unacclimatized person is suddenly exposed to work in a hot environment, he begins to adjust with the first exposure, progresses rapidly, and is well acclimatized within seven days. The ability to perform maximally in the heat is attained quickly by progressively increasing the intensity of the daily training. A maximal effort on the first daily exposure in the heat may disable a runner for several days.

If a runner does not receive adequate water and salt, his rate of acclimatization may be retarded. One of the subjects of our recent research was Tom Osler, 1967 U.S. 50-mile champion, who claims to tolerate the hot weather because of his nonsalt diet. Tom states that, "I never use salt in the race, on my food, or in its preparation." Our laboratory findings reveal that Tom's body fluids (blood and urine) contain the same amount of sodium chloride (salt) as the other runners. However, he comments that, "Before I went on my low-salt diet, I noticed a ring of salt formed around the ankle area of my shoes as the sweat dried following a hard run. I have not seen such salt rings since my low-salt diet." It is quite possible that his sodium chloride, sweat loss is lower than the other runners. That is, his heart rate, sweat loss, and rectal temperature was quite similar to such runners as Ted Corbitt, Amby Burfoot, Lou Castagnola, Ed Winrow, and Hal Higdon. We are, therefore, led to conclude that Osler is probably obtaining sufficient amounts of salt from the natural contents of the foods he eats. His ability to perform well in the heat is probably the result of his pacing and use of water to keep his skin cool during a race.

Runners who tend to train in the early morning or evening during the summer months do not appear to be acclimatized to the heat. One runner demonstrated very little tolerance to the heat after such training. While running at 6 minutes per mile for two hours (air temperature 80 degrees, and humidity 63 percent), his rectal temperature reached 105.0 degrees. After he had trained extensively in midday heat, we observed that his temperature leveled off at 102.4 degrees under the same working conditions.

Ed Winrow attempts to stay acclimatized to the heat for as much of the year as possible. To accomplish this task, he trains during the winter by wearing a double set of sweat clothing. As a result, Ed's tolerance to work in the heat is exceptional. On one occasion he rode a stationary bicycle for an hour in a heat chamber where the temperature was 171 degrees (humidity 15 percent). Most men are incapable of working for more than a few minutes in these conditions, yet Winrow's rectal temperature at the end of 60 minutes was only 100.6 degrees.

Acclimatization to heat is well retained during periods of non-exposure for about two weeks. Repeated training in the heat may not be tolerable for many runners. It would, therefore, be possible to train during the cool part of the day after gaining acclimatization, and when preparing for competition. Most people lose a major portion of their acclimatization in two months.

HINTS FOR RUNNING IN THE HEAT

Every runner should try to promote sweat evaporation as much as possible by wearing a lightweight shirt and shorts. The shirt should be as brief as possible and never tucked into the shorts. If the skin tends to be dry, cold water should be poured over the head and dry areas of the body.

While most runners concern themselves with drinking fluids only to satisfy their thirst, we have found that by ingesting cold fluids a runner can keep his internal temperature nearly two degrees lower. Not only does ingesting liquids provide more fluids for the body to sweat, but the cold nature of the fluid absorbs part of the internal heat. We have found no cases of stomach cramps or upset stomachs caused by drinking frequent volumes of cold fluids until the midpoint of the race. However, Billy Mills was reported to experience some stomach distress at the 1968 Olympic marathon trial, where he refrained from taking fluids until the mid-portion of the race. At that time, he ingested a large volume, which produced a negative response from his stomach. To gain maximum benefits, marathon runners should ingest cold fluids frequently throughout a race.

Finally, runners and race directors must be alerted to the problems of heat stress in distance running, and should make special considerations for marathon competition. Summer competition should be conducted during the coolest part of the day. The Heart of America Marathon, run in Columbia, Mo., on Labor Day, begins at 6 a.m. Efforts should be made to schedule long-distance races at times and places that will not expose the competitors to the stress of extreme heat. Such conditions exist at the Holyoke Marathon, where the temperatures are usually in excess of 90 degrees. For the health and safety of the athletes, definite governing limits should be placed on the environmental conditions of distance running competition.

11

While an Injury Is Mending

by Paul Kiell, M.D.

They both arrived the same day: the *Exercises for Runners* book at my home and a five-pound weight from shoulder height on the big toe of my right foot. The book I recommend highly, but I am less enthusiastic about the X ray. The latter showed a fracture of the right toe, through the thickness as if sliced by a knife. (Moral: make sure your locking collars on the barbells are on tight!)

The large toe is most important in supporting your weight and in providing a good push-off. Though this area has an abundant blood supply, there is little an unhappy runner can do except rest assured the fracture is in good alignment, splint the fractured toe to the second toe (optional, and only for a few days), and use a cane for the first seven to ten days. A steel shank inside a walking shoe, or a metatarsal crest added to another shoe, does help, but the main ingredient is time. The usual healing period is six weeks.

"Worst thing that could happen to me," this depressed psychiatrist muttered to the orthopedist. I was instantly ashamed at such self-indulgent utterances and simultaneously aware that self-pity and depression are destructive and alien to any type of rehabilitation. At that moment I crystallized the positive essentials and goals for the next six weeks:

- an optimistic mood free of the doldrums
- some type of general cardiopulmonary conditioning compatible with the injury
- later, a gradual return to running as healing permits

The following course followed for the six weeks immediately following the injury.

First week. Less than twenty-four hours after the accident, I was

144

pedaling a stationary bicycle (rented at a local drug-surgical store). This required use of the heel and ball of the foot, but not the toe. I would pedal for about an hour a day, or ten miles, using increasing resistance. This should be enough for a cardiopulmonary workout. It is most boring, so the bike is best set up in front of a television or where music can be heard.

I did bike work daily for the first two weeks. Every second or third day I did weight training, with no particular emphasis on progression, only an attempt to keep certain muscle groups active. Bike activity develops the quadriceps, creating a strength imbalance over the antagonist muscles. Leg curls with a weighted boot were done while standing to strengthen the hamstrings, and dorsiflexion of the feet was done while seated. To this, I added upper body weight work, as well as stretching and yoga-type exercises.

There was considerable pain at first, along with significant swelling and discoloration. Gradually both subsided, but I was never completely free of the soreness and swelling. Pain should give us pause. Runners are a particular breed—often in a type of trance, oblivious to various stimuli and stoic in tolerating pain. My orthopedist was impressed that I registered little or no pain. Yet pain is a protective warning sign, inhibiting movement that would cause further damage. So runners must be wary of their enthusiasm and their high pain threshold.

Second week. I continued the program with bike, yoga, and weights. On the tenth day I attempted a 4-mile hill run. Swelling was still very much present, and I was unable to put any weight on the foot. What had begun as a brisk walk merged into an awkward jog. It was a beautiful day and I could not resist the temptation. Running on hilly terrain seemed optimal. Uphill running minimized leg shock and the downhill angle provided a natural push-off. Two days later, I did another slow 4-mile run, and the next day, I ran 10 miles.

Prior to the fracture, I had recorded four 60-mile weeks, so this 10-mile run was relatively easy and little conditioning seemed lost. But my euphoria masked acknowledgment of pain in the sole pad of my right foot. While I ran, I had rolled over the broken toe, with the metatarsal head absorbing all the shock. The next day, after a difficult 4-mile run, there was considerable discomfort in that area.

The orthopedist termed my misery *metatarsalgia*, and reminded me that healing of the fracture would be a good six-week process. Inability to place any significant weight on the toe, plus the new pain, made me a believer. Bright elation yielded to dark clouds of despair.

Third week. At this stage, I did two more days of bicycling, exercises, and weights, but no running. All this was done under the shadow of a blue mood, probably the precursor of severe throat pain and obvious signs of the flu. The stress of the fracture experience, augmented by my lowered mood, was enough to allow the flu virus to take hold. Weakness and malaise permitted no real exertion, and the whole program ground to a temporary halt.

Fourth week. At midweek, I felt well enough to attempt a 6-mile hill run. Afterward, the leg pains were reminiscent of runs years before when 6 miles was quite a distance. My left thigh was considerably more stiff than the right, indicating it was compensating. Obviously, I was getting much less push-off from my right toe, which was functioning at about 50 percent efficiency.

The next day I recovered readily from a 7-mile run. Before this run, I had tried straight-leg raising with the weighted foot. In this run, I had none of my chronic knee pains, which lately had been accentuated by the imbalanced running style.

The vigorous weight warm-up and the subsequent increase in blood flow apparently helped protect the area. I have repeated this procedure since with equally good results. Therefore, I suggest occasional prerun work with weights.

By the end of the fourth week, I could apply full pressure when walking. The toe seemed at about 75 percent strength.

In the four weeks—three of which included general cardiopulmonary conditioning and the equivalent of one week actual running—I had lost much of my training base. This did not occur after the first 10 days of abstaining from running, but was apparent 3½ weeks after the injury.

Fifth week. I put in thirty-two miles of running. Thigh imbalance was slightly corrected. The toe was still moderately stiff, sore, and somewhat swollen, but I was obtaining a push-off at 90 percent strength.

Sixth week. I logged 50 miles, including one 13-mile run. The toe was stronger, though a degree of swelling, stiffness, and soreness persisted. An X ray showed fine healing.

I easily resumed 60-mile per week running during the seventh and eighth weeks, the latter including a 19-mile run. Slight stiffness and swelling was still present. (A "cuff" of hard tissue surrounded the old fracture site, but it did not present any functional impairment.)

Resumption of competition produced times comparable to previous tests.

I learned things from this episode that can be valuable to anyone recovering from a serious foot or leg disorder. My advice is to:

- Set goals well below the threshold of further injury. Keep a positive attitude. Noninjurious cardiopulmonary work, supplemented by stretching and weight training, is essential.

- Don't run until pain and tenderness is diminished and some degree of push-off is possible. Start with frequent short runs emphasizing proper form. Don't attempt any long runs for a while. (Running on the tenth day was too soon for me. The onset of illness was the result of unrealistic planning, yet perhaps it was a lucky interlude.)

- If you are optimistic and realistic and run within the limits of pain, relatively little time and conditioning will be lost.

PART FOUR

THE MIND

1

The Running High

by Jim Lilliefors

Once, not long ago, running was thought of as merely physical exercise. Running books from the 1960s and early 1970s detailed the physical benefits and offered specific training schedules. In the mid-1970s, when running participation quadrupled in the U.S., the underlying reason seemed to be the discovery of benefits that weren't solely physical. Magazines, such as *Newsweek, People,* and *Time,* ran major feature stories on running, centering on what was being termed "the running high." By 1978, not only was running considered among the plethora of methods available for self-actualization, it was possibly the most popular.

One of the pioneers in this crusade was Thaddeus Kostrubala, M.D., a San Diego psychiatrist who began prescribing jogging to his patients. In his groundbreaking book *The Joy of Running* Kostrubala wrote of the changes the mind goes through during a one-hour jog: "At about 45 minutes into the run, the first of the possible alterations in consciousness begins. It is from 45-60 minutes that visions may occur."

A number of celebrities, such as Alice Cooper, Brian Wilson, and Linda Ronstadt, have credited jogging with keeping them from vices and drug habits. James Allen, at the Sunflower Mental Health Center in Concordia, Kansas, conducted a study on the effects of athletics on mental health. According to him, "Individuals who sought mental health services inevitably lacked both regular exercise programs and the motivation to initiate them."

The running high occurs in varying degrees, and is often dependent on the runner's frame of mind immediately before the run. There are three basic physiological reasons behind it: (1) a general increase in blood circulation; (2) increased oxygen flow to the brain; and (3) *epinephrine*, a hormone connected with feelings of happiness, doubles in the body after 10 minutes of sustained exercise.

In a poll of *Runner's World* readers, it was determined that 88 percent occasionally experienced a euphoric effect while running, but 73 percent were unable to tell beforehand if it would occur on that particular run.

One effect of the running high is a heightened appreciation of nature. Iowa psychiatrist Peter Whitis says that running puts him almost uniformly in a state in which "the sky is bluer and the trees greener."

In a sense, the sensations of the running high are uncannily similar to those experienced during childhood. Dr. William Glasser, a Los Angeles psychiatrist, believes that running simply reactivates an ancient neural pattern. He believes "this need to run has been genetically programmed into our brains."

Entertainer Shirley MacLaine lent support to this idea recently when she said, "Psychologically, I've been a long-distance runner all my life." She runs 35 miles per week.

Several theories have emerged about the specific causes of the running high, beyond merely increased blood flow to the brain.

Dr. Herbert DeVries, at the University of Southern California, found that running significantly lowers muscular electrical activity in the brain. Another researcher discovered a correlation between emotional depression and changing biomechanical levels in the serum catecholamine produced by exercise. But the inconsistency of the high indicates it is probably more intricate, and interesting, than mere alterations in serum levels. Some researchers have recently suggested that running may be some key to uncharted areas of the mind.

The search that drives us, the ultimate motive behind our actions, is to approach a better understanding of the mystery of our existence.

As Marie Benyon Ray wrote in her book *Doctors of the Mind*, "Something still rises up in us that says, 'There is more to man than his chemistry. Calcium is not a man, nor is oxygen or carbon or electricity. Yes, he is all these and many other chemicals.... There is something missing, an unknown quantity, an X that exists in man alone. If you possessed all possible knowledge of him on these physical levels, you still wouldn't begin to know or understand this extraordinary creature."

Nobel prize-winning author-researcher Albert Szent-Gyoergyi reports that physical exercise promotes *syntropy*—the tendency to reach higher levels of organization, harmony, and order.

One reason why the effects of running on the mind have taken so long to be considered—and will still take a long while to be understood—is because our definitions aren't as sophisticated as our perceptions. We sometimes find things in our lives that answer our needs, although we cannot verbally convey it. Perhaps we have already solved the mystery, but just haven't a vocabulary proficient enough to explain it. For instance, we now accept what Dr. George Sheehan called a "third wind." Five years ago, we only knew about second wind. Is there subtler territory ahead? A fourth or fifth wind? This mystery may be at the core of the tremendous interest in the running high, and of running in general.

As Paul Reese, an age-group record-holder in his fifties, has said, "Someone who asks 'What is love?' has never been in love; someone who asks 'Why do you run?' has never run. Only runners and lovers know."

2

Can Running Cure Mental Illness?

by Hal Higdon

A tale, undoubtedly apocryphal, is told about the executive who came home one night, nervous, depressed, and unable to face the rigors of modern society any longer. He decided to kill himself. But aware of the stigma this would place on his family, he planned a most subtle form of suicide. He would run himself to death; he would jog. Because he was middle-aged, overweight, and a three-pack-a-day smoker, this would naturally kill him. He would die honorably of a heart attack.

So the executive donned an old pair of sneakers and sprinted out the door at top speed (which was not very fast) until exhaustion finally brought him to a halt one block from his home. He stood gasping on the sidewalk, waiting for the inevitable. But the heart attack never came. He sheepishly returned home.

The executive decided his suicide attempt failed because of improper preparation, so he went to bed early, and ate a lighter lunch. When he began his suicide run the next evening, he started slower, figuring he would have to go a greater distance to have a quality heart attack. This time he got two blocks before chugging to a stop, too exhausted to continue. The executive waited, but death ran one step ahead. He headed home once more, but this time noticed a strange sensation: he felt pretty good after the run. For the first time in months, he did not seem depressed. Aha, thought the executive. If running can't kill me, maybe it can cure me.

So the next day he went out a bought a pair of jogging shoes for $37.95; a double-knit sweat suit with rolled collar and zippers on the side for $63.50; and a split-second, luminous, continuous-display, chronograph for $95.28 to time himself in case he broke any world records. That evening, as the executive crossed the street after having covered his third block of running, he was hit by a truck and killed.

THE RUNNING CRAZE

Whether motivated by a suicidal impulse, or by the desire for immortality, more and more people who never before believed in exercise have begun to run. In so doing, they are discovering running's therapeutic effect on the scars caused by the stresses of modern society—including depression, nervousness, insomnia, and inability to cope with the environment. Running is good for people's mental health. This is a lesson that many psychiatrists, psychologists, and physiologists have also begun to discover, albeit belatedly and somewhat reluctantly. "Runners supply the answers," insists George Sheehan, M.D. "It's up to doctors to supply the questions."

Several physicians have begun to ask questions as to why running improves the mental, as well as the physical, health of those who engage in it. They have begun to explore the uncharted regions of running and the mind, and have come to the conclusion that jogging—and even running marathons—may prove to be a superior form of therapy than that practiced, traditionally, by psychiatrists seated beside a couch.

One such pioneer is Thaddeus Kostrubala, M.D., a San Diego psychiatrist, who claims to have moved from the couch to the track. In his recent book *The Joy of Running* Dr. Kostrubala writes: "I have talked to many runners—runners who run long, medium, and short distances—and I have come to the conclusion that running done in a particular way is a form of natural psychotherapy. It stimulates the unconscious and is a powerful catalyst to the individual psyche."

At the University of Virginia, psychiatrist Robert S. Brown, M.D., describes his analysis of psychological tests given to participants in that university's athletic programs: "We showed that there is some anti-depressant effect with a sport that is not too vigorous, such as girls' softball. There is much *more* therapeutic value in something more active, like girls' basketball or tennis. But as for maximum results, jogging seems to offer the most sustained improvements. Jogging shows very measurable changes in depression levels before and after. Even people who score normal on the depression scale become even more normal as they become physically fit."

Meanwhile, William P. Morgan, Ed.D., a psychologist at the University of Arizona, cites the results of studies at the University of Missouri involving 100 professors who engaged in various exercise programs, such as jogging, swimming, cycling, and weight lifting.

"All of those who showed depression in psychological testing before the six-week program," he states, "had a reduction in the level of depression by exercising." Other studies made by Dr. Morgan, involving prisoners in Wisconsin and police officers in Texas, showed similar reductions in anxiety levels.

Yet not everybody in the scientific community, Dr. Morgan included, was ready to trumpet running as a panacea for mental illness. Writing in *The Physician and Sportsmedicine*, managing editor Jack Martin says: "So far, only a few psychiatrists and psychologists have investigated running for mental health, so its benefits and potential are far from documented."

When Dr. Brown approached two prestigious psychiatric journals to publish the results of his running research, he encountered a stone wall. "They didn't believe in it," remarks Dr. Brown, who admits there are only about a half-dozen people in the United States seriously researching (as opposed to "armchairing") the effects of running on the mind.

Nevertheless, the academic world has begun to take notice of this promising area for both research and accomplishment. This is evident from a research seminar on physical fitness and mental health organized September 7 and 8, 1977, by the University of Nebraska. Its prospectus claimed: "The purpose of the research seminar is to review the present status of knowledge in regards to the subject of physical fitness and mental health with emphasis on correlations of mental health to levels of physical fitness. The objective is to establish guidelines, including suggested mental health parameters for research, to document objectively mental health implications with levels of physical fitness."

Among the key participants at the seminar was William P. Morgan, who, at various times during the two-day event, showed both great skepticism and great enthusiasm about the idea that exercise—and specifically running—might benefit mental health. "We've been told about the benefits of running by *Newsweek* and *Time*, and everybody knows about it now," stated Dr. Morgan. "You could stop the first person you meet on the street and he would tell you that running is good for you. The link between exercise and tension reduction is so clear it is no longer even questioned by most researchers. It's a dead issue."

Yet, he continued: "We should stop asking those questions. But *why* is it good for you? If it's good because of some time-out factor, that's one matter. If it's good because of cell adaption, that's another." In referring to "time-out," Dr. Morgan annunciated one of his pet theories: that any measurable psychological benefits from running may come not from the act itself, but from the opportunity that act gives the runner to get away from the stresses and pressures of modern civilization. You cannot answer a jangling telephone or pay bills while circling a running track. Long runs in the woods or on backcountry roads may permit otherwise harassed business executives, or housewives, to let their minds "spin free." That may encourage the form of conscious daydreaming and relaxation that William Glasser, M.D., described in his book *Positive Addiction*, and identified as the main reason why runners get hooked on running.

But Dr. Morgan suggests that these benefits, which are real and scientifically documentable, may not be intrinisic to the running act. You do not need to run to "spin free." He describes a research project involving three groups, which was done by a doctoral candidate under his direction when he was at the University of Wisconsin. The first group exercised, the second group merely learned to meditate (from Benson's book *The Relaxation Response*), and a third "control" group did nothing but sit in comfortable chairs in a sound-filtered room. The exercise group showed definite reductions in anxiety, but so did the meditators and those who did nothing. This caused Dr. Morgan to speculate, "It may not be as important to meditate or exercise as it is merely to take time out."

Others have postulated different reasons for the benefits of running and other exercise. At a conference on physical fitness several years ago, Dr. Robert L. Arnstein noted that athletes generally use psychiatric services less than nonathletes. He concluded that exercise may burn up energy that otherwise might produce anxiety. Wes Sime, Ph.D., director of the stress and fitness research laboratory at the University of Nebraska-Lincoln, recently reported evidence suggesting that exercise reduces muscle tension and anxiety as much as meditative relaxation procedures. "The common element shared by exercise and relaxation," offered Dr. Sime, "may be the total diversion from anxious cognitions."

When questioned about the link between jogging and mental health, Pike C. Nelson, a sports psychologist at Chicago State University, speculated: "It sounds a lot like the striking-of-a-punching-bag techniques used by some therapists to help reduce anxiety in their patients."

Dr. Thaddeus Kostrubala, however, vigorously denies the assertion that running is therapeutic only because of its expenditure of energy. "That's not true," he counters. "The person who learns to strike a paper bag may just as easily strike someone else, because that's what he's trained to do."

As for Dr. Morgan's contention that exercise, meditation, and taking time out proved equally successful in curing depression, Dr. Kostrubala scoffs: "That's peanuts! If you're only curing mild forms of anxiety, you're not getting at the roots of true mental illness. Besides, there's a funny value system in our society that says anxiety is bad, and that's not true. Some anxiety is absolutely essential for survival in our society. And some depression is necessary too. If you go around with an absolutist notion saying that all anxiety is bad, all paranoia is bad, and all these symptoms are pathological conditions, you're missing the boat. There are many more serious mental conditions prevalent in society today, and in many cases long-distance running can provide some stunning cures, much more than most traditional psychiatrists today are willing to admit." Should Dr. Kostrubala be proven correct, he may be the prophet of a new era in psychiatric thinking, a therapeutic messiah who will lead those mentally disturbed out of the desert, and onto the tracks, into the woods, and along the roads.

Dr. Kostrubala also comments about the related work of two giants of the psychiatric profession: Sigmund Freud and Carl Jung. In his book *The Joy of Running*, Dr. Kostrubala writes: "There were friends and analysands of Freud who would take walks with him in the Vienna woods. They would have chats about the unconscious, and it was considered analysis. But that seems to be the extent of the therapeutic physical activity on the part of Freud. Jung practiced yoga. He felt he had to do it to counterbalance the extreme preoccupation with the psychic side of life."

When Karl Menninger founded his famous psychiatric clinic in Topeka, Kansas, he recognized that exercise might benefit his patients—that they should be given activities such as bowling, baseball, golf, and even dancing to occupy their minds. At the Nebraska seminar, Edward Greenwood, M.D., of the Menninger Foundation, commented: "The body and mind do not operate on different levels independently of each other. When one breaks down, the other suffers. Every change in the physiological state is accompanied by a change in the mental state; and every change in the mental state is accompanied by a change in the physiological state." If such is the case, it would follow that if you could strengthen one of those states, say the body, the mind might improve, too. Although the Menninger Clinic was founded on a belief in physical activity, it somehow drifted away in other directions, particularly after it expanded into many units. "We once had a fellow who liked to jog," Dr. Green-wood recalled. "The problem was he didn't always want to come back."

Jogging as a form of therapy is by no means new. Carlyle H. Folkins, Ph.D., of the University of California in Davis, recalls that as far back as the 1940s, certain veterans' hospitals used running as a means of calming their patients and keeping them out of trouble. "But we went backwards," claims Dr. Folkins. "Along came tranquilizers and other forms of drugs. All the psychiatrists got out their chemistry sets and forgot about the potential benefits of exercise. It was like the old DuPont slogan: 'Better Things From Chemistry.'"

Recently, however, a small group of researchers—psychiatrists, psychologists, and exercise physiologists—have begun to demonstrate that various forms of exercise may prove superior to drug therapy in their effect. Herbert A. DeVries, director of the University of Southern California's exercise physiology laboratory, comments: "We found that exercise in single doses works better than tranquilizers as a muscle relaxant among elderly persons with symptoms of anxiety tension—and without miserable side effects."

Thomas K. Cureton at the University of Illinois followed 2,500 adults through a physical conditioning program, and determined that the program helped people make friends, relieved tension, and increased their energy levels. He found, however, that such psychological gains were more apparent in people who were either anxious or physically unfit before beginning the program. With subjects who were previously fit, further increases in their fitness did not necessarily produce psychological gains.

Dr. Carlyle Folkins, who summarized the results of studies by Dr. Cureton and others in a paper titled "Psychological Fitness as a Function of Physical Fitness," has recently encouraged some of the chronic psychotics under his care to join his lunchtime jogging group. He admits that he has not yet been able to assess whether or not this is helpful, since it has not been convenient for him to set up tests. He notes, however: "Schizophrenics usually are less physically fit than normal people. But no one yet has assumed that if we made them physically fit, we could cure their schizophrenia."

He did perform one controlled study involving golfers, archers, joggers, and a control group. He found the greatest improvement among the women joggers, but also noticed that those individuals had the lowest psychological ratings before beginning the program: "The women who chose to take the jogging, or body fitness, course were more 'down' psychologically than their counterparts who elected archery or golf."

This seemingly would provide ammunition for those sedentary individuals who, for years, have been convinced that "all joggers are nuts anyway." Indeed, Dr. Thaddeus Kostrubala claims he can name at least two world class marathon runners who are mentally ill and only approach accepted standards of "normalcy" because of their running.

"One of the problems that I get into most often is that of definitions," says Dr. Kostrubala. "What is the definition of mentally ill? Mental illness is culturally and historically bound. In one sense persons are mentally ill if they get caught. If you break the social barriers around you sufficiently enough so that the culture identifies you as mentally ill, that seems to be one of the prime criteria."

Physiologists are still seeking the reasons why running may contribute to improved mental health. Dr. DeVries measured a 25 percent decrease in muscular electrical activity among eleven middle-aged men following a running and weight lifting program. At Purdue University, A. H. Ismail, Ph.D., noted a parallel between decreased emotional depression and changing biomechanical levels in the serum catecholamine. In an interview in *The Physician and Sportsmedicine*, Carlos J. G. Perry, M.D., describes the increased respect that he got from a paranoid patient who played handball with him. But he speculates further that improvements in that patient's condition might be more than merely from camaraderie developed on the court. "I think some chemical mediator is involved," he suggested. "Some chain of biomechanical events is caused by the exercise."

But which exercise, and how much of it? Among the psychiatrists who have begun to explore that question is John H. Greist, M.D., of the University of Wisconsin, who directed what he described as "a very preliminary, pilot study." It involved patients who came to the University of Wisconsin outpatient clinic complaining of depression, or with difficulties functioning as students, workers, and family members. Dr. Greist chose eight patients at random to be treated with 10 weeks of walking, jogging, and running instead of with standard psychotherapy. At the same time, fourteen individuals with "comparable presenting problems" received standard psychiatric treatment.

The eight subjects spent one hour, three times a week with a running leader, Roger Eischens, owner of an athletic store in Madison, Movin' Shoes. Dr. Greist described Eischens as "a warm and sensitive person," though Eischens had no formal training or experience in psychotherapy. "He made certain the patients did not overstress themselves and, in fact, progressed more slowly than most of them might have wished. He gradually phased himself out of the treatment, since one of our goals was to help these patients become 'independent runners.'"

After 10 weeks of such "running therapy," Dr. Greist found six of the eight patients to be essentially symptom-free, about the same rate of improvement as those undergoing normal therapy. But on one measure—the patients' rating of the severity of the chief complaint—the running group showed greater improvement. Dr. Greist avoided making any absolute statements about the benefits of running. He admitted that he was not treating the most severe kinds of depression (for which medications, and even electroconvulsive therapy, might prove more effective). Running therapy was ineffective for two of the patients, one of whom never ran (though both recovered shortly afterward). Nevertheless, he said, "We think that the results for running are positive enough to warrant a larger and more systematically designed study. Only after such a study is done can we reach *any* conclusions about the benefit of running."

Dr. Greist cautions: "I think it is possible that an emphasis on running as a treatment for depression at this time, without proper understanding of its limitations as well as its benefits, could actually be dangerous to many depressed individuals. It seems highly probable that the most seriously depressed individuals will not respond to running. These individuals are often suicidal (80 percent of the approximately 50,000 suicides per year come from this group) and a failure to improve from a highly touted 'running therapy' might well be the sort of failure that would lead to a suicide attempt."

Dr. Thaddeus Kostrubala also admits that running offers no absolute panacea, and cites several failures among those he has attempted to help by increasing physical activity. One individual, who once had electrotherapy, suffered such a severe reversal that he had to be rehospitalized. Dr. Kostrubala speculated that the patient's previously damaged mind could not cope with the insights he brought to the surface.

In the meantime, in Dr. Greist's absence in England, Roger Eischens continues to run a small clinic that takes referrals from local psychiatrists and psychologists. He works with four or five patients a week, while continually trying to refine his techniques of helping people deal with their mental problems through physical exercise. "Although running can be a powerful therapy," he says, "the way is still foggy."

Another individual attempting to penetrate the fog is Robert S. Brown, M.D., of the University of Virginia. A former athlete, he began a conditioning program to get back in shape five years ago and experienced what he described as "tremendous euphoria." Then, when he looked at his patient population, he realized that he had never treated a physically fit depressed person. "I began wondering," comments Dr. Brown, "do they become physically unfit because they are depressed, or are they depressed because they are physically unfit?" He has since studied psychologically 2,000 subjects before and after exercise. "I've demonstrated to my satisfaction that not just exercise, but athletic-type training, will reduce both anxiety and depression at the highly significant level, statistically."

Dr. Brown has begun to explore the area of actual body chemistry, working in conjunction with Dr. Fred Goodwin at the National Institute of Mental Health (NIMH) in Bethesda, Maryland. The NIMH and Harvard are the only two laboratories in the United States that have facilities to measure neurotransmitter metabolites. Dr. Brown draws blood and takes urine specimens from subjects before exercise, and at one-, two-, and three-hour intervals after exercise to see what chemical changes take place in the body. He has already noticed that people who are depressed obtain an antidepressant factor about two hours after they complete their exercise. But he is still trying to determine why.

"When you jog a mile and feel better," speculates Dr. Brown, "is it a salt loss? Is it a neurotransmitter change? Is it hyperthermia? Is it all these things, or just what? Certainly to me, as a psychiatrist, it's certainly more than a psychological phenomenon. It's a biological phenomenon too."

Dr. Brown has radically changed his practice of medicine because of his clinical and laboratory discoveries. "In the past, where I would use anti-depressant pills the way a trainer might pass out salt tablets, now I hardly ever use them. I now take an in-depth exercise inventory of a patient with the same kind of interest that I once took a sexual history. I talk with my patients, and I jog with them. Until this point it has been mostly a subjective demonstration, but we hope to demonstrate it objectively soon."

Dr. Kostrubala has begun to ask similar questions to those proposed by Dr. Brown. While noticing improvements in the patients he runs with, he asks: "Is it the change in cerebral blood flow that engineers the improvments? Or is it the stimulus to the lower brain centers? How is it possible to identify clearly factors such as the enthusiasm of the therapists who believe in the procedure? We know that this is often the critical factor. Do the changes last over a period of years? If we compare it to other diseases, are we speaking of a five-year cure rate or an absolute cure? At any rate, it is clear to me that running is a distinct form of psychotherapy."

At the Nebraska seminar the one who most often played devil's advocate to those favoring running therapy was William P. Morgan of the University of Arizona. "How do you involve people who are not involved?" he asked. He pointed out that practically everyone studied in research exercise programs were volunteers who wanted to take part, or wanted to run. He noted that in one study his colleagues conducted among professors at the University of Wisconsin, the location of their offices and their proximity to the exercise facility made a significant difference in terms of participation. Among one group of nonvolunteers in a study program, fifteen worked near the gym, and fifteen worked further away. Among volunteers in the same program, twenty-five came from nearby and only five from far away. "You can't put a gym in one place and expect everyone to come to it," stated Dr. Morgan.

He also suggests that people who exercise regularly are like the junkies who go to the pusher to get a fix. They feel good, like the dope addict does, but the reduction in tension from exercise is only temporary and anxiety will build up again. "When they come back to exercise the next day, they're right back where they were. Also, as they continue to exercise, like junkies, they need increasingly larger doses." He concedes that the exercise prevents the buildup of tension to the breakdown point, but points again to the time-out factor.

Purdue's A. H. Ismail refuses to accept the time-out theory. In his research, he has noted (in scientific terms) "significant relationships" between plasma catecholamine levels and personality characteristics, particularly emotional stability. "You can label what you see as taking time out from the sensory stimula that we're bombarded with, but I don't accept that theory."

Perhaps the single moment of truth of the entire seminar came following a dinner speech by Menninger's Dr. Edward Greenwood, who described that clinic's exercise program as including calisthenics, dancing, and juggling Indian clubs, which he claimed increased coordination. The running radicals seemed unimpressed. One of those who considered the exercise described by Dr. Greenwood insufficient was Michael L. Pollock, Ph.D., an exercise physiologist, who worked with Kenneth Cooper, M.D., at the Aerobics Center in Dallas until recently moving to Milwaukee to establish a new physiological research program at Mount Sinai Medical Center. "None of these exercises you describe provide a training effect," commented Dr. Pollock (meaning they were not exercises that raised the heartbeat rate to 75 percent of its maximum capacity, the level at which cardiologists feel jogging, or any other exercise, produces its best results in training the human body).

Dr. Greenwood conceded Dr. Pollock's point, but Dr. Morgan countered with the comment: "You don't need a training effect to get a psychological effect."

The discussion moved into other areas, unfortunately leaving dangling the next most obvious question: If you did achieve a training effect, would you obtain a *better* psychological effect?

Thus far, most American psychiatrists—even those interested in exercise as a possible means of therapy—have not yet been willing to confront that question and the possibility that a generation spent tinkering with drug therapy may have been on the wrong path.

On the day following the exchange between Greenwood, Pollock, and Morgan, during a round-robin discussion that closed the Nebraska seminar, Dr. Thaddeus Kostrubala stated: "We've come up with the idea that this type of exercise [running] is good physically. Can we now come up with the statement that it is good mentally?"

The answer was immediate, and it came from Dr. Morgan: "The only qualification for me to sign your statement is to also say that you can achieve the same effect by sitting in an easy chair in a quiet room."

And so the conference ended on a note of indecision, with the experts in the fields of psychiatry and psychology agreeing that something may be happening to the minds of people who exercise, but unwilling to say what that something was. They would go back to their laboratories and apply for additional grants from the foundations, and they would run more psychological and scientific experiments to determine whether running has psychological benefits.

Only Dr. Kostrubala among the Nebraska seminar participants seemed ready to provide a definite and unqualified answer to that question. "Within the psychiatric community," he says, "there is not a lot of acceptance, although it seems to be growing. I know of at least three other psychiatrists in this country who also are running with their patients. Many among the medical community consider this as something bizarre, something amusing, something that hasn't engaged their serious attention. But we're right, and I'm sure that as time passes, more and more people will begin to realize that the benefits of running are much more than merely physical."

3

The Mental Changes of Running

by Peter Whitis, M.D.

I t's easy for me to slip into an altered state of consciousness. In my work with hypnosis as a psychiatrist, it is actually important to be able to do that. My "inner mind" works easily at the fringes of consciousness, providing me with dreams, fantasies, intuitive feelings, memories of "lost objects," post-hypnotic reminders, and sometimes "peak experiences." At one point, I lived happily with the assumption that everyone was like that. But as I grew older, I found out indirectly that this behavior was frowned upon, considered a bit weird, even ridiculed as "fantasy" or "faked," and worst of all "unscientific." So I learned to keep it to myself and to share it selectively.

Then I discovered that long-distance running provided the same type of experiences. I have learned that I can't seek the altered state while running. It was after being asked to write this article, and trying to observe more closely what was happening to me, that I began to experience it more rarely. The more I consciously tried to capture the unconscious, the more elusive it became. The old fears came back: the fear of reporting something "strange" and my listeners just going blank, retreating from me, and then going about their business thinking their private thoughts. But worse than that rejection was feeling again the loneliness with my experiences. But now I am reassured. It is getting fashionable to report mystical experiences, even rhapsodic joy. Running has attracted so many for its physical effects, there were bound to be others who slipped across the boundary to altered mental states.

When I am running, I start with the traditional aching and stiffness and a sense of "lumbering"—everything disjointed and out of whack. (Let me say at the outset that I am talking about a "conversational pace," about 7½- to 8-minute miles.) Then, after 1½ or 2 miles, I have warmed up, with my limbs flowing smoothly, sweating, breathing loose and easy, and my mind no longer protesting. I begin to enjoy the scenery, the weather, and the sense of my body in motion. Fragments of the day come into my mind and I go over them, resolving unfinished mental business. Sometimes I experiment a bit with my stride, lengthening it, up on the toes, a little faster downhill or uphill. By now I am "following" my body, responding to what it wants to do. I know the rhythm will carry me as far as I want to go, so I play and tinker within the limits of that rhythm. By that point I have gone 3 to 4 miles, and I am getting positive reinforcement, a sense of pleasure in just being out here striding along. I am alone with my thoughts, which have taken a more creative bend. Now I sense an integration of thinking; thoughts combine and new ideas come. I seem to be more clear in my thinking, sharper. Solutions come and I mentally note to do this or that. Mental energy feels released and the mental burdens disappear. The sense of relaxation—physical and mental—is delicious.

Somewhere about 6 to 8 miles, other things begin forming. I find that pursuing these mystical experiences is like chasing a rainbow; you lose the whole thing looking for the origin. It's better just to sit back and enjoy it.

This experience of "letting go" is confirmed by the teachings of various religious orders and spiritual guides. These range from Buddhism (*abhisheka*, the pouring into an open and receptive vessel), Christianity (Christ's "losing oneself"), and Carl Jung (who stressed that the creative aspect of the psyche can only come into play when the ego gets rid of all purposive and wishful aims and tries to reach a deeper, more basic, form of existence). A more pop cultural expression of this concept is reflected in a successful movie, *Star Wars*, where the hero is encouraged to turn off his plane's computer and trust in "the Force." William James, in *The Varieties of Religious Experience*, remarked that rational consciousness was separated from many other forms of consciousness "by the filmiest of screens" and that we may go through a lifetime without suspecting its existence.

Certain physical conditions can keep this mystical experience from occurring: if it's too hot or cold; if there are too many hills or dogs; or cars; or pain. When I began training for a marathon, the anxiety of not knowing if I could finish was with me every training mile, and effectively blocked any mystical experiences.

But when conditions are right I experience different perceptions. Sounds become muffled and seem distant, and the colors of the sky, the grass, and the dirt road are extraordinary. It's as if foggy lenses had dropped from my eyes and I "see" everything more brilliantly, achingly clearer. I feel time has stopped, that I am somehow suspended in time and could stay this way forever. I no longer feel my body; it's as if I am floating and my feet barely touch the ground. I feel I could go on indefinitely without effort. There is a profound sense of "oneness" with nature, with life, with the moment, an indescribable sense of beauty and peace. Then, just as it appeared, this state leaves. It may last a minute, perhaps thirty. The sense of time is so distorted it's hard to tell, so I measure by distance. As the altered state melts away, I feel exhilarated, exuberant, refreshed within, and sense my ego bounding. I feel I have been given a glimpse of heaven, of my spirit, of my potential as a human being.

4

Running and Depression

by Jean Colvin

Most runners know that running makes you feel good without really knowing why. A recent study, "Running as a Treatment for Depression," points out some of the reasons running helps people feel good, and offers some new ideas about psychotherapy.

John Greist, M.D., internist-psychiatrist and associate professor of psychiatry at the University of Wisconsin at Madison, conducted a pilot study of 13 men and 15 women, eighteen to thirty years old, who complained of being depressed. The patients were randomly divided into three groups: 10 to receive running treatment for 10 weeks, 6 to receive time-limited psychotherapy, and 12 to receive time-unlimited psychotherapy. Greist interviewed patients in the running group about symptoms of cardiopulmonary distress and past histories of cardiovascular illness. They all received a resting electrocardiogram and a maximal stress exercise treadmill test.

Running therapy consisted of meeting three or four times a week for one hour with Roger Eischens, M.S., an avid runner, writer, teacher of hatha yoga classes for runners, and community organizer. Some patients ran in groups if they formed spontaneously during runs.

"The whole idea was to get these people to run on their own," said Eischens in an interview after the study was completed. "I taught them skills. I'm not a therapist."

It was hoped that the patients would become independent runners, and would continue their own treatment after the study ended.

Eischens emphasized comfortable running and avoidance of pain, injury, and fatigue. He taught patients to use the "talk test"—the ability to talk to each other as they ran—and to mix running with walking to be sure that the pace is comfortable.

Patients were encouraged to avoid talking about depression during or after the runs.

"I encouraged them to concentrate on rhythm, flow and movement; to feel it," said Eischens.

According to the study, focusing on the physical aspects of running, such as breathing, the sound of footfalls, and the position of arms, was successful in preventing depressive thoughts while running.

Greist and Eischens suggest that running is incompatible with depression. "In my mind I never worked with anyone who was depressed [during the study] because when they were with me, they weren't [depressed]," said Eischens.

Two patients dropped out of the running group: one moved away before beginning running therapy and another dropped out after three weeks. Eight patients remained in running treatment. Of the two who showed little improvement, one didn't participate actively in the program and the other said she didn't believe running was an effective treatment for her depression.

In comparing running therapy with time-unlimited and time-limited psychotherapy, it was found that running treatment was as effective in relieving depression as the other therapies.

Greist does admit to some problems with the pilot study that make it difficult to draw firm conclusions on running as a treatment for depression. The problems cited by the study included: (1) rather inexperienced psychotherapists; (2) the psychotherapists may not have been committed to the kinds of psychotherapy they were using; (3) knowing their patients were in a "research study" may have prevented the psychotherapists from feeling responsible for the patients; (4) runners had more contact with their therapists than the patients did with their psychotherapists; (5) the running leader may have been an effective "psychotherapist"; (6) the effects of group interaction may have been more important than running; and (7) running patients may not have been as sick as other patients. These problems, combined with some procedural problems, convinced Greist that there should be more studies of running as a treatment for depression.

Despite the problems, the study did advance a number of reasons why running makes people feel good, and why it may be an effective treatment for depression.

A sense of success. Running gave patients feelings of accomplishment and a sense of succeeding at something. According to Greist, this is important, since "much of depression is related to feelings of failure."

Patience. Because runners were encouraged to build up their physical activity slowly to avoid injury, pain, and fatigue, they learned that it takes patience to become a runner.

Ability to change. Runners found that their health, appearance, and body image improved, as well as their self-acceptance.

Generalization. Because they began to succeed at running, patients said that they felt they could succeed in other areas, as well.

Distraction. Patients reported that running distracted them from their physical symptoms of depression.

Positive addiction. Patients began to substitute the more positive habit of running for neurotic habits.

Relief of symptoms. All the patients who ran said they felt good during the run. "It feels good to function," said Greist. That seemed to be reason enough for the patients to continue running, the study said.

Consciousness alteration. Experienced runners who run longer than 15 to 30 minutes often describe a positive, creative, "high" feeling that is so pleasant they never want to miss a day's run.

Biochemical changes. The study didn't attempt to analyze this factor, but acknowledged that other studies suggest a relationship between biochemical changes and depression. The effect of running on this relationship is the subject of other studies.

The study also suggested some reasons for considering running as a form of therapy. Moderate depression is a common problem in our society. While there are medications to help people manage anxiety, there's nothing suitable for moderate depression. According to the study, running could be the "medication" for the many people who suffer from minor or moderate depression.

Running is natural. "We all knew how to run at one time in our lives," said Greist. "Some of us have to re-learn, but basically it's a natural skill." The study suggests that people can derive pleasure from having their bodies work in natural, rhythmic activities, such as running and walking.

Running is relatively easy to practice. "You can do it alone or with others, in any weather," said Greist, "and it doesn't cost anything other than a good pair of shoes."

Cost is an important factor in considering running as a possible treatment for depression. According to the study, the salary paid to the running leader was $850 per month. Treadmill tests cost $30 or $300 for ten patients. Assuming ten sessions of psychotherapy would cost about $500, based on a $50 per hour figure, then the cost of treating a running patient is $115, compared to $500 for psychotherapy.

Another factor to consider is that running has beneficial side effects, as opposed to the harmful side effects of some drug treatments.

The study also pointed out that running may help prevent a recurrence of depression in a patient.

Greist plans to do another "similar but better controlled" study on running as a treatment for depression.

"I believe, as a runner and individual, that running is good for a person," said Greist, a former competitive swimmer. "But we haven't shown that this is true in the scientific sense. It's still experimental."

Perhaps in the future, Greist's new study or another one will show scientifically what most runners already know and what depressed people need to learn: running feels good.

5

The Running Mind

by Jim Lilliefors

A line from Blake's *The Marriage of Heaven and Hell*—"If the fool would persist in his folly, he would become wise"—sums up what has happened to running in the 1970s.

Not long ago, runners were thought of as "odd birds" (as Joe Henderson put it). But today running is used as rehabilitation for mental patients, alcoholics, and drug addicts. Runners are now common birds. They are even considered by some to own some hint of the future, perhaps even of salvation. (George Sheehan calls all runners "secular saints.") The area of study that has been most responsible for this change in perception has been the effects of running on the mind.

First, a distinction should be made between the mind and the brain. The brain is a portion of the central nervous system, located in the vertebrae cranium. The mind is human consciousness, manifested in thought, perception, feeling, will, memory, and imagination. Mind is the greater mystery.

There is relatively little in the brain itself to distinguish individual motive, thought, and perception. There isn't much physical difference between the brains of different humans. In fact, scientists have been unable to find in the human brain any additional group of cells to distinguish it from the brain of a monkey. Yet certainly the workings of the mind—emotion and thought—vary greatly between individuals.

It is widely accepted that the abilities of the human mind evolved steadily over centuries of existence. It probably took millions of years, for instance, before the cortex of the brain was of a size sufficient enough to allow the mind the ability to *learn to learn*. We are now able to program ourselves to learn, to consciously expand our knowledge. Once, man didn't even know reason resided in the brain. Once, it was thought to exist in the heart; the brain was nothing but a gland. Now, we not only know about the function of

171

the brain; we also know something of the character of reason—how it might be formed and cultivated.

The recent interest in transcendental meditation, est, and so on is an indication of an increased interest in the mind. Along with these movements, psychiatrists have begun prescribing running—and millions have prescribed it for themselves. Running has become a tool toward understanding the mind.

One runner, responding to a survey I took of the effects of running on the mind, described running as a "problem-solving activity." Others, both competitive runners and newly converted joggers, spoke of it similarly. In this way, running has become accepted by some as an important avenue toward expanding and understanding the mind.

The use of running as therapy is consistent with the evolution in understanding of the mind and its abilities. We have become aware of the means by which our thinking is affected on a run; we have deemed it desirable. We are able to report in detail the emotional sensations of a run, and theorize about their causes. This ability is at the root of the interest in self-knowledge and is one reason behind the new interest in running.

Steven Rose described this type of thinking in his book *The Human Consciousness*.*   "Not only can one think, but one can think about oneself thinking about.... The infinite regress of the hall of mirrors that this makes possible seems closely related to the search for the meaning of an individual's identity, which permeates much of contemporary cinema and literature. What is the 'I' that does the thinking? How is it possible for one's mind to be *in one's* brain if at the same time it can think *about* one's brain?"

This paradox is plainly evident in running. Running doesn't fit easily into a societal context. It allows a person to step out, to free his mind from the grips of habit, perhaps to sense life as it was during childhood.

If running can provide a single clue to the greatest mystery on earth—the mystery of the mind—then it has a useful purpose. The recent interest in running by psychiatry testifies to the connection between running and the mind. Fifteen years ago, this connection wasn't even considered.

Peter Whitis, an Iowa psychiatrist, says that when running his "inner mind works easily right at the fringes of consciousness."

---

* Steven Rose, *The Human Consciousness* (New York: Random House, 1971).

Though some runners claim running solves the mysteries of their own minds, it probably isn't a final key. But it is clearly an advancement. Some psychiatrists, led by Thaddeus Kostrubala, believe that running might even advance the field of psychiatry.

Hughlings Jackson, the British scientist and researcher, considered by some the "Columbus of the mind," knew the vastness of the mystery: "I know that even today, we have conquered just one small corner of the vast unexplored territory of man's mind. What I accomplished is an infinitesimal part of what remains to be done."

We are hindered because we have too few tools of exploration. We have too many theories, many of which are contradictory. Psychiatry insists that body and mind are one, and examines the mind as a manifestation of matter. It has reached relatively few conclusions.

Yet the alternatives to psychiatry for exploration of the mind are only vague concepts—often-scoffed-at ideas such as ESP, clairvoyancy and spiritualism. Still, we have learned of the mind's tremendous power to imagine and, by imagining, to create. Placebos have shown us this. Placebos are drugs with no actual physical effect that are often used in testing new drugs. Recently, in a major study of mental depression patients who were being administered sophisticated drugs, they were taken off the drugs and put on placebos. The majority showed the same improvement on the placebos as they had on drugs.

If we believe we are depression-oriented, then we are depression-oriented. It isn't known whether this is the cause of depression-oriented thinking. But depression is often a sign of some inability, and running works against this (if for no other reason than the fact that running, itself, is an ability).

The studies conducted by people such as Dr. John Greist, have shown that running can relieve depression.

"Since the way we feel in our minds can make us feel bad physically, it can work the other way too," said Dr. Marjorie Kalum, associate professor of psychiatry at the University of Wisconsin. "In addition, depression is usually accompanied by feelings of not being able to accomplish anything. By running, patients are accomplishing something—running a certain distance and improving their health."

Darwin said, back in 1861, "What we want to know is what mind is."

If our many sets of muscles are coordinated by the mind and the brain is coordinated to mind, what coordinates mind? After studying brains—thousands of them—for 25 years, measuring and comparing them, Cornell professor James Papez still has more questions than answers.

"What in this," he asked, looking at a human brain, "accounts for the campaigns of Napoleon, for the theories of Copernicus, for a Beethoven sonata, for the propositions of Euclid, for a poem by Keats?" It is a question that science cannot answer. But it is not a question that the running mind ignores. The running mind differs from the nonrunning mind in the way in which it is actively engaged in exploration.

The brain of the runner doesn't differ much from that of the nonrunner. It is still two hemispheres, joined by a commissure, containing a cerebellum, cerebral cortex, parietal cortex, hypothalamus, optic tectrum, and dorsal thalamus. But the brain's structure is not what we have been concerned with here.

6

Going Beyond Jogging

by Mike Spino

T housands of people have taken up jogging as a way to maintain their health, but few have any idea how to incorporate general principles for improving their physiology. Yet in order for physical conditioning to improve substantially, you must vary your way of breathing and moving.

In other words, when you are running at maximum effort, there are a variety of breathing levels through which you pass. You need to practice these levels if you are to shift to them when you need them. In addition, you can move most easily if your action is appropriate for the speed and distance you want to run.

If you have been jogging around your block and have shown little improvement, I suggest a new approach to the activity.

First, time yourself over a mile. Then, after trying these tenets for a month or so, time yourself again. The types of breathing required in these workouts will vary between aerobic and anaerobic metabolism, since running a mile involves about 50 percent aerobic and 50 percent anaerobic breathing.

To explain metabolic variety, let me give an example. Suppose a person stands between two destinations 100 yards apart and plans to cover the distance from one point to the other in several ways. If he runs the 100 yards at 50 percent effort and walks back to the start, his breathing will totally recover. If he runs the 100 yards a second time at 50 percent effort and jogs or shuffles back to the start, his breathing will not recover as completely and the pulse will not return to its normal, resting rate. If a person runs the 100 yards at 50 percent effort, rests just a few seconds, and immediately heads back to the starting position at the halfway point, he will begin running out of breath.

The body has shifted from aerobic to anaerobic metabolism, the same shift it must make to run a mile at maximum effort. The most easily understood definition of this function I have found is in a textbook, *The Physiology of Exercise*, by Laurence E. Morehouse, the man who later coauthored the best-seller *Total Fitness*. Dr. Morehouse says:

> If a person engages in mild exercise, there is no oxygen deficit during the exercise. That is, a steady state exists, and there is no excess oxygen consumption during recovery. If the exercise is somewhat more strenuous, the oxygen consumption during recovery is above the resting level, indicating an oxygen deficit during the exercise.
> The lactic acid concentration (which is a cause of fatigue) is not increased, however, indicating that no extra lactic acid was formed during the exercise. It is obvious, in this case, that lactic acid has nothing to do with the extra oxygen consumption during recovery. If the exercise is made even more strenuous, the excess oxygen consumption during recovery is greater and the blood lactic acid concentration is elevated. During the recovery period, the rate of oxygen consumption and the blood lactic acid concentration gradually return to normal.

This somewhat technical explanation of the process of metabolic change is helpful in explaining the use of a training system involving varied gaits and tempos. Jogging or sprinting at a constant rhythm does not allow one to experience the changes to which Morehouse is referring. It is the fine tuning, accomplished by changing styles of movement and various paces, that enables a person to improve his performance.

If you want to improve your mile time, you need to practice the effort your body will be called upon to duplicate. Otherwise, when you come up against it, it will be a foreign experience. In other words, if someone only jogs or sprints, he does not prepare the body for the delicate levels of metabolic function that come into play in a fit person's running. The body can only accomplish what it has already practiced and experienced.

The risk of using jogging or a high-ratio anaerobic exercise (like sprinting) all the time is pointed out in Morehouse's book *Total Fitness*. He says that after the initial aerobic improvement, your condition will worsen. This is because your body has ceased working at the edge of your potential. Further improvement after the original endurance buildup from long, slow running requires variety of effort.

In my book *Running Home* I present workouts based on a 50 percent aerobic and 50 percent anaerobic ratio. The 30-day program is similar to the training that has worked for thousands of participants in my workshops and long-term programs at Esalen Sports Center and elsewhere. These exercises not only aid you physically; they create the possibilities, I believe, to use running for psychological and spiritual reasons.

I present five different methods of running, each with a primary purpose. The interchange among these elements can satisfy almost any requirement for improving fitness. The terms most used in the context of the workouts are *tempo* and *gait*. Tempo can be defined as the amount of effort applied during a specific run. Gait is the style of movement used to accomplish the particular segment.

TRAINING VARIATIONS

Intervals. The most complex form of training is interval running. Such running is usually preplanned and has a stable form. *Interval* refers to the specific distance you run—for example, 100 yards up the middle of a football field.

The kinds of running and the emphasis for the particular plan will change. At first, we will use simple gaits and easy tempos with longish rest periods. The intervals run will become increasingly complex and the rest periods will be varied, so that the changing metabolic functions can be accomplished. Often workouts will be done in a number of sets—a series of intervals at a given tempo and gait aimed at accomplishing a particular objective. Most sets have different purposes and will be separated by resting or slow shuffling (a tempo to be presented later). Once you experience varying tempo and gait, you will find it hard to return to mere sprinting and jogging.

Fartlek. This is a Swedish word meaning "speed play." The main difference between interval and fartlek running is that fartlek is done on a forest path or open road with greater spontaneity, while an interval workout is usually done on a track or grass section inside or around a stadium. The segments of distance in fartlek running can be either yards or time. Both interval and fartlek running should be done at less than 80 percent effort.

Speed. If you run at more than 80 percent effort, you are sprinting, using speed training. This form of running is highly anaerobic and involves practicing moving your legs at their quickest tempo. Speed running need not be all-out sprinting, but is always strenuous effort, usually over short distances. This kind of running improves your "carry," or the ability to maintain moderate efforts over longish distances.

Resistance. Using your body against a physical resistance builds strength. There are a number of ways to use resistance techniques. The first is the gradual hill. Find a 30-degree slope that will take about a minute and a half to run up. Break the distance into three segments so that you have options. Start with segments at 50 percent effort and work up to 80 percent. Keep the arms relatively low, and don't mince the stride.

A second type of resistance running involves short hills or sand dunes, which needn't be longer than 60-70 yards. The by-products of this kind of training are high-ratio anaerobic metabolism, and the kind of muscle work in which your legs quiver. Run the dunes at 50-80 percent effort and immediately return down the hill. You don't have to allow complete return to resting breathing or pulse before plunging back up the hill.

A third form of resistance training is *power running*. This combines muscle/skeletal exercise with spiritual development. The object in this exercise is not linear movement, but a striving, lifting-up motion that builds overall power. It is not a gait to be done in competition, but an auxiliary tool that prepares muscle groups for tasks to be accomplished in aerobic and speed running. It also teaches energy transfer, as you move from stationary to explosive movement in a split-second.

Begin the power run in a meditative state by half-closing the eyes so reality takes on a mystical blur. The thrust is with the opposite hand and foot, reaching skyward rather than forward.

Continuous running. *LSD* means long, slow distance running—simply another term for jogging, or moving slower than a 7-8-minute pace.

Specific body movements can aid in jogging-type running. At the slowest pace, I find it helpful to land as far back on the heel as possible, and to push out from the knees, while being aware of the lower leg. This is used in warming up or moving slowly for long distances. I call this the "shuffle." The arm action that can aid this shuffling involves carrying one arm across the body in front of the belly and directing a counter-movement somewhat more forward with the opposite arm.

If you want to increase this tempo, you can lift the knee slightly, step out in a cyclical action, and try to get a rolling feeling from the outside of the foot inward. This faster motion is called *fresh-swing tempo*, and is used for light efforts.

For more advanced runners, fast continuous running is done at half to two-thirds the distance covered in LSD running, but at a faster pace. Also, as a special supplement to racing practice, repetition running at specific times can help toward final conditioning. For instance, seeing how far you can run in 12 minutes or timing yourself at distances ranging from 100 yards to three-quarters of a mile is helpful if you are working toward a mile run.

ADDITIONAL GAITS

Besides the shuffle and fresh-swing tempo, other gaits aid in conditioning. The additional gaits are in a sense auxiliary to the main two. But for certain runners or joggers becoming runners the other gaits can add variety and heighten body awareness.

Shake-ups. These can help warm the body. They are done by letting all the muscles hang on the skeleton like a rag doll while moving along on a soft surface.

Tidal breathing. This is a technique that allows you to experiment with finding your full lung capacity and ways of releasing tension. Instead of using the arms in a forward motion, allow the palms to face upward and to rise up from the abdomen to the chest while the body inhales. Let the upper body act like an elevator. When the air is stored in the body, release it by turning the palms downward, pushing the air out, and propelling yourself forward.

Good speed. Varying the foot plant can be a useful way of giving overworked muscles a quick rest. In natural running, the foot usually hits on the outside edge and rolls toward the middle. This is common in swing-tempo running. But if you can change the foot plant, even for 20 or 30 yards, all the body muscles will change.

I refer to this as *good-speed running*. The way to practice this technique is to take a few steps on the ball of the foot, and use the arms as a balancer and rhythm-maker, rather than as a puller or fulcrum. Picture as if you were playing a drum with your hands as you move forward about 20 or 30 yards.

The surge. This can be used in competitive situations to pass someone. For improving general fitness, it is also used to focus power and to use the upper body as a tool for acceleration. To learn the surge, stand in place and picture yourself running at fresh swing. Then open your hands and stretch them out by your sides. Cup the hands and press the thumb to the first finger between the front of the finger and knuckle. Press as if you were pushing on the accelerator of a car, make a sound in your throat, and surge forward.

The judicious use of these gaits and tempos will aid the improvement of your physical condition. But equally important, it may change the activity from boring jogging into a variety of mental, physiological, and perhaps even spiritual experiences.

7

Running and Zen

by James Marlin

Regardless of how much we try to deny it, there is only one true freedom in life: the freedom of inner peace. Followers of Zen, like many runners, are actively seeking that freedom.

Running allows a positive view of something often considered frightening: aloneness. Many never accept it during their lives and are often depressed because of it. Such people surround themselves with other people and activities so they don't have to acknowledge their aloneness. If they are constantly surrounded, they can deceive themselves into believing they are not alone. This is the cause of their almost inevitable depression. No one is free until he has erased all self-deception from his mind. Perhaps the self-deception we tend to cling to most is the idea that we are not alone.

But it is true: we are born alone and we will die alone. Sure, along the way there are people to help us through individual situations and problems, to bring us joy and understanding, and to pull us along emotionally. But psychically, we are still alone, and in our decisions we are alone.

In his book *The Experience of Insight*, Joseph Goldstein wrote, "We are each going to die alone. It is necessary to come to terms with our basic aloneness, to become comfortable with it. The mind can become strong and peaceful in that understanding, making possible a beautiful communion with others. When we understand ourselves, then relationships become easy and meaningful."*

Interactions with others take on an entirely different meaning once we have accepted our inherent aloneness. Then, when we relate to others, we are communing with, accepting, their aloneness. If we can't accept this, relationships are a guise, a means to reinforce the false idea that we are not alone.

There is nothing wrong with being alone. It is not a unique position to be in. But, ironically, it is the lonely people who are not

* Joseph Goldstein, *The Experience of Insight* (Santa Cruz, Calif.: Unity Press, 1976).

able to accept their aloneness. Nothing is complicated about aloneness. One only has to ask oneself: "Am I afraid of being alone, left out?" If you suffer from frequent depression, your answer is probably yes.

One solution is Zen meditation, in which a person strives to begin to know himself. He can begin to accept his fears, to realize there is nothing abnormal about them. Fears are only abnormal when a person refuses to admit them to himself.

Running is similar to Zen in that it can act as a form of meditation to quell these fears. The runner is alone; and this fact becomes clearer as he continues in the activity. He is alone while running, because his mind has no immediate problem on which to focus its attention. Therefore, it must occupy itself. The runner must accept aloneness.

In a recent article in *Psychology Today*, Dr. William Morgan wrote of runners who entered trances while running by repeating mantras—the same principle as during meditation.

Fear of aloneness breeds a false caution that makes us hesitate unnecessarily, and rehearse simple tasks over and over again instead of doing them. Fear of aloneness leads to hastiness, to frightened, uncertain actions. Millions suffer this fear in varying degrees.

To stop it, the first step is to slow down. Often this happens naturally, when other alternatives run out. Once a person has slowed down, he can begin to realize what he was moving toward and why. He can ask if his goals are true desires, or merely involve carrying out obligations. The constant carrying out of obligation is a harmful, numbing process. The person is surrounded with deadlines, people, expectations, and fears. His actions are carried out in fear.

Through Zen, or through running, a person may begin to realize, and disperse, his fears. He may begin to act, not out of fear, but with the pleasure of assurance.

"The Zen way of doing things is to do them," wrote Christmas Humphreys in his book *Zen Buddhism.** He continued:

> Just like that. I stood at the foot of a high dive, waiting for the courage to climb the steps and dive. I measured the height from the water, worked out how to place my hands and how to fall, considered the temperature of the water, the people in the way and the chances of breaking my neck. All this took time, but I still remained where I was. I had not dived. Finally, I tried the Zen way of diving. I just walked up, took a breath and dived. The same applies to getting up in the morning, writing that letter, or doing those exercises. Just do them, before the vast array of emotions can interfere.

---

* Christmas Humphreys, *Zen Buddhism* (New York: Macmillan Publishing Co., Inc., 1971).

When this process takes place, a cleansing results; the waste that is removed is confusion, doubt, and fear. The whole process is a gradual transformation, with peaks of enlightenment, as barriers are surmounted.

The person will find, like myself and millions of others, that he is alone. And it will be a joyous discovery, filled with the strength of the person's possibilities, never before realized. It will not be a sinking sensation, as of loneliness. It will be a realization that the person isn't as closely tied to his responsibility, his work, as he perhaps supposed. He will realize that he doesn't have to accept his life as limited in any way. He will reconstruct the way in which his consciousness acts.

This was explained by Katsuki Sekida in the book, *Zen Training, Methods and Philosophy*:

> In ordinary life, our consciousness works ceaselessly to protect and maintain our interests. It has acquired the habit of utilitarian thinking, looking upon the things in the world as so many tools—in Heidegger's phrase, it treats them "in the context of equipment." It looks at objects in the light of how they can be made use of. We call this attitude the habitual way of consciousness. This way of looking at things is the origin of man's distorted view of the world. And he comes to look upon himself, too, in the context of equipment, and fails to see into his own true nature. This way of treating oneself and the world leads to a mechanical way of thinking, which is the cause of so much of the suffering of modern man, and which can, under some conditions, lead to the development of mental illnesses. Zen aims at overthrowing this distorted view of the world.*

It is this restructuring that many experience through running. Though there are similarities, running and Zen are subtly very different, since the Zen philosophy is that stillness of body leads to stillness of mind. Ideally, a person should practice both Zen meditation and running. But running can reorder thinking in a similar way. It separates a person from his day-to-day world, and forces his aloneness on him. Together with Zen, it can help the person reach a new perception. He will see the same things, but differently. Running can transform what once seemed drudgery into a clearer peace of mind.

Philip Kapleau wrote, in the book *Zen Keys*:

> Yet we live in a society where the object for so many is to do as little work as possible, where the work place, whether office or home, is looked upon as a place of drudgery and boredom, where work, rather than being a creative and fulfilling aspect of one's life is seen as oppressive and unsatisfying. How different is this from Zen! In Zen, everything one does becomes a vehicle for

---

* Katsuki Sekida, *Zen Training, Methods and Philosophy* (Rutland, Vt.: John Weatherhill, Inc., 1975).

self-realization, every act, every movement is done wholeheartedly, with nothing left over. In Zen parlance, everything we do this way is an "expression of Buddha," and the greater the simple-mindedness and unself-consciousness of the doing, then, the closer we are to realization.*

I've realized this state of mind, as have millions of other runners, not through fear and paranoia, but with a great joy and clear-headedness.

---

* Philip Kapleau, *Zen Keys* (New York: Doubleday & Co., Inc., 1974).

PART FIVE

COMPETITION

1

Beginning Racing

by the editors of Runner's World

There were 12,000 entrants in the Bay-to-Breakers race in San Francisco, 6,000 at the Atlanta Peachtree race, and 5,000 in both the New York City Marathon and Chicago's First Distance Classic. Amateur Athletic Union and Road Runners Club races are sprouting up like mushrooms on a warm night. There are more than 130 fun-run sites, with more being added each month.

The bulk of the record entry fields at San Francisco, Atlanta, New York, and Chicago included novice racers—people who've seemingly come out of nowhere, gone into training, and entered major racing events. The spectacular influx of new faces at the established races has prompted a huge demand for new local events.

The jogging and running explosion that is evident along every quiet street and busy highway very obviously has a racing counterpart. Running and racing are having a dual boom, thanks in large part to the refreshing attitude toward racing that new runners have brought to the sport. Racing is no longer considered the exclusive preserve of the elite. The average runner has suddenly realized that he is part of a huge mass of runners, and that races are as much open to him as they are to anyone else.

Everyone who's running seriously seems to be considering racing, if not doing it in one form or another already. The overwhelming interest in major races poses the following question: Is there room at races for every runner? Should every runner want to be a racer?

The first question is the easier of the two to answer. Yes, there is room for everyone who wants to race. Some organizational and logistical changes will be made in major races in order to accommodate the vast numbers of racers and their varying degrees of skill and preparation. At the same time new races are being established to keep the racer within the runner satisfied.

As for the second question, that's not as easy to answer. Racing is not something to fear. It is a logical progression in a body that is suddenly more willing and able to run faster. Racing is a sort of acid test that can be applied to all the miles that have been run as a solitary avocation to test if they were run properly. Has my training put me in good shape considering what I had to start with? Is my pace reaching competitive standards? Can I handle the tension and anticipation of pitting myself against other runners? All of these questions can be answered by racing. Or can they?

Is racing for everyone who runs? Isn't racing giving up the solitary inducements of running that drew you toward it in the first place? Isn't racing getting you back into the very rat race you have been running to escape? No matter what the veterans may say, racing is not necessarily for everyone. For those who run to escape the arena of competition they face everyday on the freeways, on the job, or at home, racing could very easily be one more tension situation. Running, for those people, is an escape and a rejuvenation ritual that would be violated by racing.

But many runners find themselves becoming more and more serious about guarding their time on the back roads and the byways in order to commune with their own bodies and minds through running. They are finding that running is a necessity for their psychological well-being. Racing, too, may hold some unexpected peaks of heightened sensations in the overall running experience.

Racing, for most runners, is also a good measure of their accomplishments—a measuring stick that makes the weekday training sessions more meaningful. Racing is also an opportunity to give in to the urge that is present to at least some degree in every person—the urge to compete.

For those entering their first race, let's mention up front that the material rewards of racing are pretty damned meager compared to other fields of competition. There are trophies and sometimes plaques for the best racers, often there are T-shirts and ribbons, and almost always there are certificates for everyone who can make it back to the finish line before the supply is exhausted.

The rewards, however, are often intangible and can't be displayed on the den wall or placed on a bookshelf like the neighbor's bowling team trophy. The rewards more often come like the rewards of daily running—in subtle and pleasantly insidious ways: in the feeling of having placed one's training and preparation on the line, and in having tested oneself against the clock and against other runners.

Racing is the vaulted roof that tops the foundations of training. Racing is the test of the daily training. But racing has even more valuable rewards. Begun in a logical manner, properly prepared for, and entered as a learning experience, the first races can become tremendous motivators to personal running programs, as well as providing a balancing factor to the daily training diet. For many runners, competition is the special edge that makes the whole running experience worthwhile.

The beginning racer, like the beginning runner, should be cautious not to overdo it at first. Just as you wouldn't jump into a bathtub of ice water and then calmly stay submerged, we must caution you to ease into racing. Don't start with anything that's too difficult, complicated, or overpopulated. The word *marathon* is not magic, and you shouldn't gear yourself to break into racing by trying to suffer through a marathon.

Enter a convenient race, a race close to home. Enter a race where the psychological rewards will outweigh what the race calls on your body to endure. For your own psychological safety and for the sake of your body, pick a race that you know you can finish in a respectable manner. Start, then, at either an organized fun-run, or at a run that will be fun; the more casual the race the better.

Racing can help the serious runner develop a new level of psychological involvement in the sport, it can provide a mental and physical climax to all the training and work that has led up to it, and it can provide good, playful fun if entered as a learning experience.

Racing is readily available to any runner on almost every weekend of the year within comfortable driving (and sometimes biking) distance. Each issue of *Runner's World* carries a directory of fun-run locations, and the Amateur Athletic Union provides a comprehensive listing of races that run the entire spectrum from fun-run-type contests to races featuring world-class competitors.

THE FIRST BIG STEP

Besides being a very euphonious phrase, a fun-run is a very euphoric experience. Perhaps you'll excuse me if I digress a bit to describe a typical fun-run. Picture, if you will, the peace and serenity of a Sunday morning. The streets and roads are only sparsely populated with automobiles and there are hardly any trucks. Nestled in the foothills just off the interstate is a well-manicured and well-maintained two-year college. Since it is Sunday, the parking lots are deserted and there is a distinct pastoral feeling about the setting. From our observation point atop a nearby hill, where the warming sun is beginning to spread a pleasant nectar through our veins, we can see several cars pulling into the parking lot. Several bicycle riders are converging on one corner of the previously deserted lot.

The people arriving are dressed casually, several of them wearing warm-up outfits. Some of the people converge into a group and begin talking, while others begin taking loose jogs around the parking lot, obviously doing limbering-up exercises.

More cars arrive, as do some people on motorbikes. The sun is becoming warmer and the assemblage below is becoming the size of a small crowd—but still looks casual and unhurried. A man is setting up a card table and placing various colored papers, books, and magazines on it. The crowd is a typical cross-section of the community: young children, old people, males and females, an occasional dog, trim people and medium-built people, with a few overweight people sprinkled in. The unifying characteristics are their running shoes and the fact that they are all moving and milling about, if only a few steps at a time, as though the entire crowd is waiting for the arrival of someone important.

An elderly man of trim build walks casually to the road fronting the parking lot. Most—but not all—of the crowd follows him. We're too far away to hear his words, but he's speaking to them for a moment. He raises his hand with a stopwatch in his free hand, and says a few words. Some of the people in the crowd are crouched down, ready to run, while others stand casually in the group as though there isn't a stopwatch within a thousand miles. He drops his hand, and the crowd breaks into a run along the road.

There are a lot of stragglers, and many of the children seem to be running along just to be running in a group. Some of the hardier runners race each other up front, but most of the people seem to be running just to run and be with others. Many of them are talking as they run. It takes a long time to get the race finished, as most of these people would be called stragglers in a sanctioned race; but they don't really seem to care.

Some of them move to the table, where they are handed colored certificates, while the elderly man beckons the crowd to join him at another starting point. No one seems to be hurrying and there's no pushing or shoving. The warm sun and the fun encourages any observer to wander down and join them. There doesn't seem to be any registration table, and it looks as though no one would mind if there was one more runner in the starting field for the next "race."

This, of course, is typical of fun-runs—nationwide gatherings of local runners at predetermined times and places to run predetermined distances, but with seemingly no expectations. Fun-runs are socialized versions of running alone—the middle ground, as it were, between pleasure running and sanctioned racing.

There are, of course, people at fun-runs who are as dead-serious about their running as they are about everything they do in life—people for whom walking across a crowded intersection is a competition to see who gets to the other side first. In a sanctioned race it is difficult to ignore a runner who is out to win no matter what the cost. But at a fun-run it's very easy to ignore the occasional runner who feels every move must be made in earnest. A runner can race at his own pace, with his own goals in mind, and let the life-or-death competitor race against his fondest dreams.

There are times, of course, when a runner should avoid even a fun-run. Those times are as important to recognize as knowing when you are ready to run competitively. Consider not running if it's too hot or cold, or if the distance or terrain is either too hard or long for your present state of conditioning.

Don't race if you are sick or injured, such that a race would further aggravate the ailment. Don't arbitrarily enter a race just because it seems like a good idea. Before racing, you need to put in a proper amount of time in training. We would not encourage a beginning *runner* to become a beginning *racer* until he is confident that the training phase has been passed. Entering a race unprepared will most often turn a runner off because of his inadequacies.

COVERING THE ESSENTIALS

Our emphasis is on aspects of the first race that are usually taken for granted. The easiest way to find out what is involved in racing is either to ask someone who has raced or to join a local club where there is a free and frequent interchange of information.

Do not attempt to run your first fun-run or sanctioned race as an all-out campaign on the world record. Plan on running your first race at a cautious pace so that you will enjoy it and so that you will be the master. Do not allow the race to dictate an unrealistic pace or unrealistic ambitions. You may ultimately be bound for glory, but you needn't set fire to the roadside grass by the friction of your passing at breakneck speed. Do not trust your instincts in your first race; trust your caution and work only to enjoy the experience.

As the first step in preparing for the race, stop at the doctor's office or a hospital for a thorough checkup. There are a lot of pros and cons to this advice. The detractors say that a nonsympathetic doctor can read your body analysis in such a way that his advice will have you sitting on your butt for the rest of your life. On the other hand, it is better to have a good idea of what kind of shape your body is in before putting it to the chore of racing. So have a checkup, but be prepared to get a second opinion on the findings. Ideally, have the tests administered (and interpreted) by a doctor familiar with the unique profiles of a runner.

CLOTHES AND FASHION

Since society judges people too often by the clothes they wear, clothing may be a good place to begin. A good rule of thumb is not to wear anything in a race that has not been previously tested in training. *Comfort* and *practicality* are the key words. Ignore the top-shelf warm-up outfits; plain old gray sweatsuits are just fine. Don't get sucked into buying the fancy Pierre Cardin-type running uniforms for your first race; a T-shirt and a comfortable pair of shorts will do. You'll probably run better the less concerned you are about the clothes you are wearing.

Bear in mind, however, that shorts that are comfortable for training may begin to chafe during a race because they will undergo more strenuous use. The material may begin to irritate the inside of the legs because the legs will be moving faster and longer than usual. Use a soft pair of shorts (usually nylon) or apply a thin layer of petroleum jelly to the inside of the legs to prevent the chafing that can result from running longer distances than you are used to.

Remember that your body heat will build up as you move farther into the race. Therefore, wear a combination of clothes that can be shed in layers as your body becomes warmer. In most fun-runs it is not improper for a male to remove his shirt entirely if it becomes hot. Female runners often run with a tank-top shirt that is either cut or torn off at the midriff.

The use of an athletic supporter for males or a bra for females is completely optional. Some men feel more comfortable running in a simple pair of jockey shorts under their running shorts. Small-breasted women may feel comfortable running without a bra (whereas big-breasted women may prefer a bra in order to avoid discomfort and soreness after the race). Women should keep in mind that if they go braless, they may want to wear a dark-colored shirt because perspiration is likely to make a light-colored shirt comparable to a second skin midway through the race. This, again, depends on the woman's individual attention to old-fashioned modesty as opposed to modern concern with comfort. Bear in mind that dark-colored clothing, although providing more modesty, also absorbs rather than reflects the heat of the sun's rays.

For cold-weather competition, a racer needn't overdress, since the running body works like a furnace, generating tremendous amounts of heat. But make sure that the ears and hands are warm. A stocking cap and mittens (which allow a runner to bunch up the fingers) or sweat socks over the hands should pretty well take care of the sensitive body parts. It is also permissible to wear long johns, tights, or panty hose if temperatures are extremely low. Stay comfortable and loose. A turtleneck sweater of light material is a good cold-weather garment.

For female runners who want to look good at a race, go lightly on the makeup. Your exertion will add color to your face and applying too much makeup may cause it to run once you begin perspiring.

The matter of whether or not to wear socks is something of an individual preference. Again, experiment in training sessions, not in actual races. Some runners find a pair of socks confining and refuse to run in anything but bare feet, while other runners would feel naked and unprotected without a pair of socks. As though to emphasize the individuality, some runners find that they get blisters from running without socks, while others find they suffer the pains and discomfort of blisters from wearing socks. Novice runners who are suffering from blisters might try switching their preference in wearing or not wearing socks. Sometimes such a simple matter can completely eradicate the blister problem. Never try to solve a blister problem by wearing more than one pair of socks. Socks do help cushion the foot, although many runners find that modern training or racing flats are so well constructed that they make use of socks superfluous.

DEVELOPING SHOE SENSE

The most important piece of running hardware, of course, is the shoe. It's the runner's biggest investment and his dearest friend—or direst enemy. Avoid buying cheap shoes or bargain imitations of running shoes. Buy one good pair of training flats; it will be your single best investment. The training flats can be used for racing at this point in your running career. In fact, for the beginner, it's best to use the training flats you've been doing your roadwork in. That way your feet will already be comfortable in them and will not be in for a shock on race day, when you force them into a new pair of shoes that are not already broken in.

RITUALS OF THE RACE

Prerace rituals are merely routines that will soon become very familiar to you. But they may be confusing at first. The following are some cautions and some information that will seem obvious tomorrow, but that may not seem so today.

Once you have training shoes on your feet and are ready for a race, take care to do two things with your laces: (1) tie your car key to one of your shoelaces near the top so you won't have to carry a whole chain of keys along with you; and (2) double-knot your laces, so that you do not lose your key if they become untied and so you do not have to stop along the route to retie your shoes.

One of the most important aspects of prerace preparation involves jettisoning waste material. Even if you feel you don't have to, take the precaution of using a rest room. Take the simple precaution of stashing a handful of tissues inside the elastic band of your running shorts in case a little spot of woods has to become your rest room.

A race is a form of competition, but it is also a social event. Some racers are extremely nervous before a race and become incredibly gregarious, while others become close-mouthed and antisocial. As a new racer, it is usually advisable to play the social aspect of a race by ear. Don't interrupt anyone who looks as though he doesn't want to be interrupted; conversely, don't be afraid to walk calmly away from another runner who wants to talk your ear off if you want a moment of quiet repose. After the race is over, it can become a social event. Use the time before a race to run down a mental checklist of little things that you may have overlooked in the excitement.

Whether it's your first race or your 500th, there will be some degree of apprehension before the race. You will undoubtedly have some physical aches because a race goes beyond the usual limits of your training.

As for the physical aches, disregard what people may have told you: Do not always run through physical pain like some wild-eyed monk. Run through aches, but don't run through severe pains. Analyze aches and pains through your training sessions to learn how serious they are. An ache is a dull pain that arrives because you are exerting your body beyond its normal capacities. A pain is something sharp and shocking like the passing of a kidney stone. Do not run through severe pain because that could put you out of running for a while. Listen to your body and learn to understand the signals that differentiate an ache from a downright pain. Be assured that you are not the only person who started the race suffering from aches. The aches are a necessary part of racing. Be prepared to put up with some degree of ache, braced with the knowledge that as you race more your aches will become less common.

Psychological pains are something else entirely. They are harder to deal with and they should be run through. Everyone who's lined up for the race is worrying about embarrassing him- or herself. This is natural and it is nothing to fear. Take a deep breath before the gun and push the fears of embarrassing yourself down into your legs, where they can be wrung out as you run.

The milling masses of runners at the start of a race can present a logistical problem for the new racer. Where should you place yourself? The best advice for a novice is at the back of the pack. First, if something goes wrong at the front of the pack (i.e., someone trips at the start), you will not end up being stepped on. Secondly, if you begin at the back of the pack you'll likely pass more people at different portions of the course. That will give you more of a needed psychological lift than if you start more toward the front and spend most of the race being passed by people coming up from behind. If you are somehow maneuvered into the front line, simply get out of line and walk to the back. If you find yourself in the middle of the pack, try to ease your way over to one side so that you have an escape route if something in front of you or around you begins to go wrong.

Before you get anywhere near the starting line, get information on the course and the race site. Allow yourself plenty of time to reach the site on race day. Take a walk around at least part of the course in order to see just what kind of terrain you'll have to traverse.

Your best companion at your first race meet might well be a stopwatch. It offers split-second reliability for the anxious new racer who needs unbiased pacing. From practice runs with the watch, it will be easy for the new racer to establish a pace that will guarantee success in completing the race, instead of allowing pace to be set by things as capricious as the frontrunner's pace or by the midrace panics. The stopwatch will let you know whether you are overexerting yourself or whether you can afford to pick up the pace.

Make sure to keep a record of your training pace for several days in advance of your first race. Then set yourself up with the stopwatch to slightly out-perform your training pace. For instance, if you run a 7:30 mile in training, attempt to set your race pace at 7:15. The extra adrenalin pumped into your system during a race situation can usually be milked for an extra 15 seconds of speed per mile.

As far as the prerace butterflies are concerned, be assured that many people who race have them. The butterflies are an indication that there's activity going on in the mind and the body to prepare you for the race. Experience as a racer contributes to decreasing the butterfly sensation. The butterflies will soon be replaced by that old hornet, the competitive urge, which your stopwatch will keep under control.

INTO THE RACE

Once the race has begun and you've cleared the starting line, stay flexible and watch what's happening around you. Arthur Lydiard's advice on pacing is simple: Treat the race as two separate events. Divide it right down the middle, staying fresh and relaxed in the first half, with the feeling that you're holding something in reserve. Be confident, strong, and in control of yourself when you reach mid-point. Then begin to push. This modifies the natural tendency to start too fast. (There's little danger of starting too slowly.) This system helps produce an evenly paced race.

Pacing should be on your mind during the entire race. You've done everything that's necessary before the race; now all that's left is the race itself. Keep your pace steady; do not make any sudden spurts or slow-downs. Make every change in your pace gradual and smooth. Run from one competitor to the next; key on the competitor in front of you.

When you do pass, pass on the outside (i.e., on the open side, farthest away from any obstructions on the roadway). Be careful of traffic if you are passing on a road. Avoid making contact with the other runner. If you are being passed by a faster runner, give him plenty of space to get around you; anticipate the runner by listening for the sound of breathing or footsteps.

At about the midpoint of the race, even if you have closely followed your stopwatch and the race is going as you've planned, take a reading of your body's instrument panel. Is your breathing regular? If it's becoming ragged and labored, a momentary drop to a slightly slower pace might be called for in order to help you finish in good shape. Are you feeling fatigue? You should be feeling some signs of fatigue, especially in your legs. If your legs aren't sending any signals to your brain indicating that they are working diligently, and that they are tiring a mite, you'd do well to pick up your pace. Your second wind should have come either during your warm-up or during the early portion of the race. If there is no second wind, you may have started the race too fast and gone right past it, like missing a shift in an automobile. This will be evident if you find your breathing at this point ragged and uneven.

If you're experiencing ragged breathing and fatigue, slow your pace a bit and try to get your breathing into rhythm. You can battle fatigue by relaxing and concentrating on other aspects of the race.

You can sometimes do it by slowing your pace, and sometimes by picking up the pace until your body finds a more comfortable niche.

Some aches and discomfort at the midpoint of the race can be expected, even for the experienced racer. It is merely an indication that there is exertion over and above training exertion. Body fuel is being used and the engine is being run at a higher r.p.m. than usual. At this point the body should begin to exhibit a few aches that you didn't know you had. Be careful to keep your stride smooth, or the fatigue that's creeping into it will begin taking its toll on ankles, knees, legs, and shoulders that will be running out of sync.

AN END IN SIGHT

As the finish line comes into sight on the far horizon, your body should be hurting pleasantly from the strain. It's time to grit the teeth and see if you can dredge up any more energy that's been hidden in remote crannies of your body. Dig down into the guts and into the sinews and come up with as much loose energy as you can find to put into an increased stride for the last half-mile. Do not sprint, just make a slight increase in your stride. The hurt will increase a bit, but you can grit your teeth and run through that kind of ache. Finishing with a speed greater than the speed you had at midpoint will leave you with a better feeling for the race.

With more races under your belt, you'll enter that delicious territory of the racer. Then, it becomes a pleasure to increase your stride so that you feel on top of your position in the race. This sensation often occurs for a veteran racer during the last stretch of a race, and for some as early as the midpoint of the race. There are very few sensations that can compare to driving toward the finish line at a racing pace.

A good finish will help to carry you psychologically to a good start in your next race. You can later draw on that reserve energy.

If you've literally used up every ounce of energy you had left in every pocket of your body, stand in one spot (but out of the way of oncoming runners). Place your hands on your knees and fill your lungs with air. Walk as soon as possible, so that you don't tighten up. If there's water available, take a sip and pour a few handfuls over your head. Take some deep breaths. Observe that other runners are in the same state as you are.

You've joined the growing fraternity of runners who race. If you heard your time as you crossed the line, savor it for a moment and then forget it. If you were too centered on your efforts to push yourself across the line and didn't hear your time, you needn't worry about it. Your time for the race isn't as important as the fact that you've successfully finished it.

If it's available slowly drink your fill of Body Punch or some other fluid replacement solution. (You might want to get in the habit of carrying it in your car.) There are direct beneficial effects from using replacement liquids, the most apparent being the ability to head off drowsiness later in the day and to prevent some of the aches the day following a race.

Get your sweats on so you don't get a chill, and then go into a warmdown routine. This moment—while parts of your body still hurt and before your breathing returns to normal—is the best time to evaluate your race and to pick out points that need improving. That's because later in the day, once all the heavy breathing and sore muscles have dulled, you'll see the race in a completely different light.

Ask yourself some of the following questions. How adequate was your preparation for this race? Did you stick to your strategy of pacing? Is there anything on your prerace checklist you forgot to include in your preparations? Did you control your breathing or did your body's need for air take over? Did you pass other runners smoothly? Did you allow faster runners to pass you without it becoming either a big chore or an obstacle for the other runner? Do you feel elated or depressed? Did you have strength left for a kick at the end? Does that mean you didn't expend your available energy evenly throughout the race?

TAKING STOCK

How long should you walk off the stiffness in your legs? Walk around until you can walk without fearing that you'll fall down if you don't keep your arms out to balance yourself.

How do I get rid of this overall lousy feeling? It'll go away on its own as your body comes back down from racing fitness to its normal state of affairs.

How come, with all the miles I've put in during the last two weeks, I'm being beaten by people older than I am? This is a good time to assure yourself that you are not a superman and that a bit more training or a different approach may be called for. It is also a good juncture at which to realize that there are some people racing who have been running ten or twenty years and who therefore have quite a head start on you. It's also a good time to realize that you have two paths to choose from. You can either give up and go back into your shell, thereby staying away from races. Or else you can reevaluate your training program and keep at your workouts, using the faster people as examples on which to key.

If I did better than I expected, why do I feel let down? Once the race is over, the levels of adrenalin you've managed to push through your body begin to drop, and a natural depression sets in as the body goes back into its normal mode. Don't worry, you'll see the race in a positive light again once you get home, take a refreshing shower, and get some of the stiffness out of yourself.

When you are properly recovered, where do I collect my time, place, and award (if any)? In a sanctioned meet, the officials will direct you to the proper table. Give them a chance to tally the results before bugging them for information. If the race was a fun-run, your time was probably shouted to you as you crossed the line, and in the excitement you probably forgot what it was. That's actually good. This first race should not count for much of anything other than to acquaint you with the process of racing.

Accept your first race as a learning experience, not as something that will go down in the annals of racing. Remember, you were supposed to be running against yourself and your stopwatch more than against your fellow competitors. (If you did hear your time or if you remembered to click the time on your stopwatch as you crossed the finish line, give the fun-run coordinator your time and your age, and he'll fill in the time on a color-coded certificate.) After this experience, you are now better able to approach your next fun-run or sanctioned race as a veteran. You now know what it's all about, how it feels, and whether or not it fits your own personal program.

Now all you have to do is figure out how to transmit the excitement of the race—and of completing it—to your friends and family without sounding like some barroom braggart. Is it normal, now that you're in your car, in your sweats, cooled down from the excitement, to feel a little cocky about having run a race and lived to tell about it—if there's anyone willing to listen? Why shouldn't you feel a little bit of exhilaration and accomplishment? This is a big moment in your life. You've done your last training session as a mere runner. From this moment on, you're officially a racer. At the moment— except for the advancing charleyhorse in your right calf—that's a stride in the right direction.

2

Racing Can Still Be Fun

by Bob Anderson

With the increased number of runners plying the highways and byways of America, there is an increased interest in fun-runs, those happy social races where everybody wins. For many runners fun-runs have become an integral part of their running—and their life. For those runners who are new to the sport, let me explain the fun-run concept.

A *Runner's World* fun-run consists of three races, held at a regularly scheduled time, at a predetermined site, usually weekly, but sometimes as seldom as monthly. The distances run are normally a quarter- or half-mile, a mile, and one longer race of from 2 to 6 miles. There are no runs longer than 6 miles because fun-runs were originally formulated to encourage beginning racers—and the fun-run concept has not changed. Additionally, we have found that it takes a minimum of time to recover from races less than 6 miles.

At a fun-run, there is no registration and no entry fee. The road courses are accurately measured, easy to follow, and not too difficult for the beginner. Brief instructions are given at the start—and the group is off. At the finish, times are called out, but not recorded. Everyone who finishes is entitled to receive a certificate, which is color-coded and awarded, according to time standards for the distance, based on age and sex.

The principle behind the fun-run is to have races that are fun and as hassle-free as possible. There is no need to arrive an hour early to stand around in line; a runner doesn't have to have an AAU card in order to run. You arrive and you run at whatever speed you want to for that particular day. If you don't want to run fast on a particular day, that's fine; we'll be there the following week in case you want to run fast then.

The fun-run program is not designed to compete with the AAU, but rather to supplement it. Fun-runs are places to get started in racing. It is a more relaxed setting for beginners and for runners who want to compete painlessly.

AAU races are special affairs. They are more official. Some runners, naturally, don't experience the same sense of satisfaction at a fun-run as they do at an AAU race. For them, a fun-run may be too low-key. That's fine; the fun-run program is for everyone. But if AAU races are too competitive for you, don't drop out of racing—try a fun-run.

I used to run many AAU races. I enjoyed them, but there were two things about them that I didn't like. One was spending half the day getting to and from the race site. The other was that people felt compelled to apologize to others when they ran poorly. People asked each other: "What happened? Haven't you been training? What place did you take today?" I found that I wasn't racing for myself—I was racing for others. While the actual racing was fun, the rest of the program often negated my enjoyment. A bad race bothered me and I found that too much emphasis was being placed on that one race. After traveling for an hour to get there, paying three dollars to run, and then waiting for the results, the race became overemphasized. If we remove those factors, racing once more becomes a joy rather than a pressure-cooker. For regular fun-run participants, prerace butterflies usually disappear after two or three races.

I'm making all these observations, though, without explaining why I think racing is important in the first place. I feel that there are three reasons why runners should race.

First, racing is a measure of your fitness level. It is an indicator that tells you if you are running too much or too little. It isn't necessary to set a personal record with each race to determine your fitness level at race time. You know how you feel at the finish. If you ran all-out and posted a relatively bad time it might indicate that there is a problem. The problem might be the 10 pounds you've gained in the past six weeks, the pressure at work, or maybe you are running too much and are too fatigued to race well. The race can tell you almost immediately how you stand.

Second, racing offers a climax—the same type of climax a writer gets when his book is published. The writing of the book is like the work done before the race. By climax, I am not referring to the reward. In the case of the writer, the reward is the money; in the case of the runner, the reward is a good time. But the climax is holding the finished book in your hands or running the race at a 6-minute pace and feeling great. The work you have put into preparation for the race has allowed you to climax. Racing fast when you are out of shape does not produce this climax.

Third, racing gives you a time—an official time that is measured accurately. The race provides you with a measure of your performance. Your time may be a world record, an age-group record, or a personal record. The time is very tangible and can be dwelled on as little or as much as you want. It is more than just a feeling of being able to run a set number of miles in a certain number of minutes.

Those are the main things racing offers. There is also a valuable by-product: racing brings together people with a similar interest. At a fun-run it is easy to make friends with other runners. There are comrades there who can share your feelings. Runners appreciate the problems and successes of other runners. Nonrunners seldom do.

I am addicted to racing. I like it. Fun-runs offer me all three of the ingredients in racing that I've mentioned—and I've made many friends at fun-runs.

Many people who've been involved in racing for a length of time are now stepping back from it. They are becoming tired of it. Many of them became disenchanted with racing because of the AAU structure of racing. If you are at that point, or if you are a new runner contemplating racing, try a fun-run. I found the program to be a very real answer for me. Perhaps you will, too.

3

Marathoning for Beginners

by Jay Dirksen

The increased interest among American distance runners in the marathon can readily be noted in both the increased participation and number of marathon races. More men and women are attempting this exciting, grueling, and challenging 26-mile 385-yard event than ever before.

Beginning runners have a multitude of questions concerning the marathon. Some have no idea how to prepare for such a race, while others have been scared by stories of the pain and agony suffered by runners who attempted a marathon without proper training or race tactics. The following discussion is designed to acquaint the beginning marathon runner with this race. The information is taken from personal experience and discussions with leading marathon runners in the United States.

Certain prerequisites should be possessed by a marathon runner. The most basic prerequisite is a love for running. Those who do not enjoy running solely for the sake of the run itself will seldom be attracted to the marathon.

In training for the marathon, the beginning marathoner should possess patience and determination. You should establish both short- and long-range goals. But realize that the top marathoners seldom arrive instantly at the top. Most top marathoners have trained patiently, often for years, to reach their present positions. At first, improvements are rapid, as the body adapts to running of longer distances. Often, beginning marathoners are discouraged and disappointed by their first marathon attempts and quit. However, the beginner must be aware that experience is important in the marathon. And the first marathon is generally the toughest.

Every marathoner must voluntarily be willing to put in hard work in training. A marathon runner can go further on hard work and less native ability than in any other event. There is little room in marathon running for a quitter or a loafer. This type of person will have little success if, indeed, he is ever drawn into attempting a marathon.

Marathon running requires little equipment. The basic uniform is a shirt, supporter, pants, socks, and shoes. A white or light-colored shirt that will reflect the sun's rays is usually worn on warm or hot, clear days. In cooler weather, you should wear a heavier shirt with long sleeves. The colder it gets, the more clothes should be worn. Usually running pants are sufficient, though, in extremely cold weather sweat pants or long underwear is worn. Socks are optional, but they are essential in cold weather, particularly if there is snow on the ground. When running in the snow, plastic bags or cut-off nylon women's hose can be worn over or between socks to keep the heat in and the cold out. Supporters can cause rubbing, chafing, and rash. This problem can be reduced or eliminated by wearing regular briefs, nylon swimming suits, or specially produced supporters for distance runners. In hot weather, sweat bands and caps can effectively reduce the amount of perspiration that runs down onto the face, particularly into the eyes.

The most important possession of all, except for those few marathoners who can run marathons barefooted, are the shoes. Regardless of the type worn, the shoes should afford the feet the comfort they deserve. A poor pair of shoes can make the marathon race or training most unenjoyable. All shoes should fit the runner perfectly. Good shoes for training will provide protection against stone bruises. Often marathoners race in shoes with thinner soles than are worn in training. The main point is to take good care of your feet at all times. Once the feet are injured or abused it becomes impossible or difficult to run. It should also be noted that tied shoelaces should be knotted or taped down so they do not come untied during the race. Valuable seconds will be lost if shoelaces come untied during a marathon.

Diet is an often-debated subject among marathoners and runners in general. Without a doubt, a well-balanced diet is essential. Food supplements and vitamins need to be taken only if the runner gets insufficient amounts of the needed body requirements from his normal diet. When in doubt, a doctor should be consulted. Fatty and greasy food consumption should be held to a minimum. Foods high in carbohydrates should be eaten at meals before long runs, because they break down into the needed glucose more rapidly and with less energy expenditure than either fats or proteins. Foods high in protein are needed following runs. Protein is broken down in the *catabolic* process of body metabolism and is used in rebuilding body cells broken down during marathon training and racing.*

Plenty of liquids should be consumed by marathoners. On hot days, it is essential to replenish the body liquids lost, or dehydration will occur. Many marathoners have been forced to slow down or drop out of races because they did not replenish lost liquids. Although some outstanding marathoners do not drink liquids during races, beginners are encouraged to replenish their liquids, especially during hot or humid conditions. Salt should also be replenished. Salt losses can cause soreness and cramping. Because salt is not stored in the body, it should be replenished after training or racing, either in the food or by taking salt tablets. Several commercial drinks are currently available that contain salt, glucose, and other substances that are lost.

Many marathoners have trouble drinking liquids during the race. This problem is easily solved by using a plastic squeeze bottle. This method makes it unnecessary to slow down to drink, and alleviates the problem of spilling into the eyes or on the body. Usually, these bottles can be used at official aid stations. However, local race officials must be consulted first for approval before the race.

Rest is vital for any marathon runner. Ideally, 8 to 10 hours of sleep is desired. If extra sleep is needed before a marathon, it is best to get it two nights before the race. Normal hours should be kept the night before a marathon, thus eliminating several sleepless hours of rolling around thinking about the race. Such things as going to a movie or watching television can be effective in taking the mind off the race before going to bed.

Alcohol, tobacco, and drugs have little or no known benefits to the runner. Any beneficial effects that they could provide can best be gained from less controversial products and methods.

Although there are several training methods currently used by marathon runners, consistency is necessary. Weather conditions should rarely be a reason to miss a workout. Even snowstorms, blizzards, thunderstorms, sleet, and other weather conditions short of a hurricane or tornado should be no barrier. Runners in the upper Midwest have run in windy, 20 below zero temperatures with no adverse effects. The psychological effects are highly favorable on completion of these bad-weather workouts. It should be noted that the amount and type of clothing worn is determined by the weather.

---

* *Catabolic* processes involve the release of energy, and the resulting breakdown of complex materials within the body.

But there is seldom reason to miss a workout solely because of the weather. If the weather is too severe outside, indoor facilities can be utilized. One can also run in place if there is nowhere to run. Zatopek was known to train by running in place continuously as long as several hours.

Regardless of the training method used by the top American marathoners, they generally run approximately 100 miles per week and include one run of 20 to 30 miles once per week. Lydiard-trained runners basically follow this type of program. Ron Clarke has stated that the 20-mile run once a week is essential.

Although not all marathoners keep a daily running diary, this simple procedure helps remove much of the guesswork from training. Daily information recorded in this diary can be used effectively to determine workouts, race tactics, pace, and other necessary facts.

Many marathoners have experienced blister problems. Several measures can be taken to help prevent blisters. Commercial insoles placed in the shoes help absorb shock in both the lateral and vertical directions. Areas that usually blister can be covered with moleskin, felt, or tape. Many runners lubricate their entire feet before running to reduce friction. Preventive treatment should also be given to the nipples, underarms, and groin, if necessary. Lubricants and coverings are effective in preventing or reducing rash, blistering, or irritation to these areas.

Although many pages can be written on race tactics, the most important advice to the beginning marathoner is to refrain from starting too fast. The result of this is that the marathoner begins to fade about 18 or 20 miles from the starting line. He may experience such pain and fatigue that he is forced to walk. The steady runner who runs an even pace well within his ability for the first half of the race will usually be rewarded by passing many of those who begin too fast. Once a runner is forced to reduce his pace in the marathon, it is difficult to increase the pace later.

Weather and course conditions will determine many race plans. In high altitude or in hot and humid weather, the pace will be slower. Hills will also result in a slower pace. It is desirable to drive or run over the course before the race. Hills, mile marks, and other pertinent information should be noted mentally and sound race plans should then be formulated.

Knowing the strengths and weaknesses of competitors is very necessary. Tactics and plans should be formulated somewhat on the basis of this information. But worrying about opponents is futile.

The best advice is to be physically ready for race day. This readiness makes the runner more confident of himself. Many races are won and lost during the months of training before the actual race.

Lastly, and very importantly, a marathoner must have a good mental attitude toward the race. He must be ready physically and mentally.

4

The Perfect Marathon

by George Sheehan, M.D.

I learned how much the body can stand," said Dr. Fred Blanton, a forty-year-old Florida ophthalmologist, after running the Boston Marathon. "You don't know what pain is until you get up around 21 or 22 miles. You just hurt like hell. You'd give anything in the world to quit, but you just keep going. The people who run these all the time must be masochists."

Others, besides Blanton, have taken this position. Olympian George Young, who qualified for the Mexico City Marathon as insurance for making the team, experienced the same pain. When asked later whether he expected to better his time when he ran the marathon again, he answered, "Anyone who would run more than one of these is nuts."

Why would anyone run more than one? It's a good question, especially if the marathon is in Atlantic City. In terms of weather, crowds, course, and coverage, the Atlantic City Road Runners Club Marathon is strictly "class D" compared to Boston. At Atlantic City in 1970, the 142 competitors outnumbered the crowd. The temperature is usually beyond good running range and the humidity excessive. But the course is the main hazard.

To the first-timer at Atlantic City, this appears to be the ideal place to run your best marathon. I doubt if there is a grade of more than one foot on the entire route. It's a loop course: you go out and back three times, which gives you three chances to stop right where the sweatsuits, blankets and hot showers are located. On an out-and-back course, when you hit the turn at a little over 13 miles, you feel at least relieved that you're heading home. And at Boston every step takes you closer to the finish. But leaving friends, warmth, and comfort at the 17-mile mark and starting out again is often more than a nonmasochist can stand.

Atlantic City may look easy, but it never is. Those who came to break 3, 3½, or 4 hours all find that the course is no breeze. The pain and agony are built into the 26 miles, not the terrain.

207

This pain and agony is sometimes expected and accepted. The world's finest marathoner, Ron Hill, says, "The fear of running a long race can come from the fact that you know it's going to be physically painful. And unless you are a masochist, nobody likes pain. And if you dwell on this, it can make you nervous." According to Hill, he can talk about where the pain is going to come and how distressing it's going to be without actually "thinking that it's the guy who's speaking who will be in that position."

But it also is a pain that is sometimes forgotten, like the pains of childbirth. So a runner moving surely and confidently in those final miles reaches that 21-mile mark, and suddenly the pain is there. And for the first time he remembers how terrible it was the last time, and how terrible it's going to be now and in the forever that is this race.

But sooner or later he will think about running the marathon again. Not, perhaps, slumped in the locker room, or on his hands and knees taking a shower, or even on the long painful ride home— but sooner or later, because the perfect marathon is like the perfect wave. And every marathoner keeps looking for it. On the day he runs that marathon, he will run his best pace all the way. When he comes to the 21-mile mark he will feel as if he just started, and that what he has gone through was just a warmup. Then he will float through those last 6 miles, strong and full of running. Even when he finishes, he will feel like running and running and running. This is why people run their second and third and even twentieth marathons— even at Atlantic City.

5

Racing Tactics

by Hal Higdon

Of all the runners I've seen race, one stands out as the premiere tactician of all: Herb Elliott. Most track fans remember Herb as a world record-holder and an Olympic gold medalist, but I remember him because of his superb use of tactics. He could lead from the gun; he could kick at the tape; and he could burst in the middle. He finished a career unbeaten in the 1,500 meters and mile by effectively employing all those tactics. Probably his most astonishing race came in the Rome Olympics of 1960, when he stunned his competitors by starting his sprint with roughly two laps to go. They gained on him near the end, but Elliott still had the victory.

A knowledge of tactics is essential if you intend to race successfully, but too many runners give little thought to this aspect of running.

Tactics is a military expression, usually coupled with the term *strategy*. Strategy, by a dictionary definition, is the science of planning and directing large-scale military operations and maneuvering your forces into the most advantageous position prior to actual engagement with the enemy. Tactics is the science of arranging and maneuvering military and naval forces in action, or before the enemy.

Translated into running terms, strategy involves training yourself to race. Tactics is the act of racing itself, particularly how you maneuver in crowded fields of two or more runners.

Tactics are least important in the shortest and longest events. In races up to and including 440 yards, runners generally go full speed all the way, separated in lanes. Little contact and no decisions are made concerning pace. In the longest races, beyond 10,000 meters, runners compete on wide, straight courses where, again, little contact occurs. Pace becomes an important tactic, but less important than at medium distances.

In the medium distances (road runs less than 10 miles, cross-country events from 2 to 6 miles, and track races from 800 to 10,000 meters) tactics become critical. Tactics increase in importance when runners move onto tight, narrow indoor tracks, where straightaways are short and hairpin turns make running widely difficult.

USING A KICK

There are two styles of running: from the front and from the rear (with numerous variations on both). Those who lead presumably do so because they possess superior endurance and like to break their opponent before sighting the finish line. Those who follow presumably do so because they have superior finishing speed and know they can beat their opponent as long as they stay with him. A handful of extremely gifted athletes possess both superior endurance and superior speed. When these occur simultaneously in one athlete, you have a racer.

Several excellent front-runners come to mind: Filbert Bayi, Ron Clarke, and Kip Keino. A letter that was written to *Runner's World* in September 1976 disparaged Keino's 1,500-meter victory over Jim Ryun at Mexico City as a "trick tactic," because teammate Ben Jipcho set a fast pace, theoretically allowing Keino to pull away from Ryun. Nothing was tricky about the tactic. It was simply a matter of strength over speed.

More often, speed prevails. This was particularly true during the reign of New Zealand's Peter Snell, Olympic gold medalist at 800 meters in 1960 and 1964 and at 1,500 meters in 1964. *Snell*, in German, means *fast*, and Peter was that. His typical tactic was to burst into a frantic sprint at the end of the back straightaway with 200 meters to go. His kick was superb. He did not merely beat opponents, he demolished them. It was almost as though Snell were sitting in the blocks at the 200 meters start, waiting for the others to go 3½ laps so he could race with them.

But kickers succeed partly for psychological reasons. Not only do they have unbeatably fast kicks, but others *expect* them to have unbeatably fast kicks. Snell toured North America during the spring of 1965 and began the tour as his usual invincible self by overwhelming rivals (including a young Jim Ryun) with his finishing burst. Then, one weekend he traveled to Toronto, Canada, to race Bill Crothers, the 800-meter Olympic silver medalist. Snell had a touch of flu and was beaten. This was hardly a disgrace, but word spread like a brushfire among middle distance runners of the world: "Crothers outkicked Snell!" The superb New Zealander's psychological edge vanished overnight, and he never won another race. One of those who defeated Snell that summer was Ryun, who reigned as "boss kicker" for three years until defeat by Keino reduced his psychological edge.

Kickers may not necessarily win more races than front-runners, but their victories seem more spectacular and so may be remembered longer. As a result, too many runners assume that kicking is the only tactic to employ for guaranteed victory. Sometimes this is true, but remember that Lasse Viren, a renowned kicker, won the 5,000 meters at Montreal by leading the last 6 laps. Viren understood a very important tactical rule: A runner who automatically assumes a back position lets others dictate his race.

FOLLOWING THE LEADER

There are times when discretion becomes the better part of valor, and a runner who desires victory should be a follower rather than a leader. The following are four instances when it is best to follow.

On windy days. If you run into a wind, it takes additional energy to battle it. A tactical runner may choose to tuck in behind an opponent and use him as a windshield. In NASCAR parlance this is known as "drafting." When a runner "drafts" on a windy day during a track race, he not only uses his opponent to block the wind going down one straightaway, but also blocks the wind pushing the opponent from behind on the other straightaway. This tactic works best when the wind blows parallel to the straightaway, and is of less value in cross-winds, which blow across the turns. A runner who employs this tactic must have a strong tolerance for disfavor, since his popularity among other runners (and fans) will eventually wane.

As a psychological weapon. Some runners have a low tolerance for tension and wilt under the psychological pressure of having another runner dogging their footsteps. Simply by trailing a runner (wind or no wind) you may cause him to worry about your presence and thus break his concentration. Although running seems an automatic function, it is not. You cannot run efficiently unless you concentrate fully on the act, and runners who worry more about those behind them than the track before them lose efficiency. Many runners will give up if passed forceably near the finish line. So, where and when you decide to pass is often more important in the psychological battle for supremacy than how fast you pass.

If you're faster. A runner who can run his last quarter in 59 seconds, all things being equal, will defeat a runner only capable of running his last quarter in 60 seconds. If you are the latter, you do not want to be behind the former going into the last lap. If you are the former, you need only stick on the latter's shoulder to defeat him. Of course, sooner or later somebody will come along who is capable of a last lap in 58 seconds.

If the pace is too fast. Any speed faster than what you consider an ideal pace may be too fast. If you plan to lead a mile race in 62 seconds and someone pulls you through the first lap in 58, you are better off staying behind and allowing the fast pace to lag before taking command. Sometimes, of course, the pace may not lag and you will find yourself permanently behind. But then that's racing.

LEADERS OF THE PACK

Even if you consider yourself a kicker, there are occasions when it is unwise to follow another's pace. The following are four such instances.

On indoor tracks. Following may be a poor tactic on short, 11-lap-to-the-mile board tracks used in most major meets. A stretching-out effect occurs on indoor tracks. As the lead runner slows going through the turn, others behind him slow progressively, depending on their position behind him. The sixth runner in a six-man field will find himself slowing while still on the straightaway and still going through the turn. The leader, meanwhile, has speeded up on the next straightaway. Since indoor straightaways are short, passing becomes a more difficult task—particularly on the last lap. The same stretching-out effect occurs in the 3,000-meter steeplechase, at each barrier where the lagging runners find themselves blocked by runners in the front (who lose momentum while in the air).

On rough cross-country courses. There are two particular instances when you do not want to follow a runner in cross-country. One is when the footing is hazardous, because running behind someone is a bit like running in the dark. The other is when the course narrows. If you get caught behind a slower runner in the middle of the pack, the rest of the field will draw away from you. In crowded fields, you can get stomped on if you hit a sharp turn.

If you're slower. If you are racing a runner with superior speed, you want to break him before the last straightaway. If the pace is too slow for any reason, you may want to get out front and keep it honest.

On hot days in road races. Probably one of the most frustrating experiences for a marathoner is to arrive at a water point during a warm race and be unable to obtain water. This is likely to happen if you are behind a group of runners who take all the immediately available cups before you get there. If the water is being handed out only on one side and your opponent unintentionally blocks you, you may also experience trouble. Speeding up or slowing down to get the water may cost energy, but on some days it may be necessary. The runner who runs alone may suffer loneliness, but he avoids these problems.

Another tactical reason for leading in the closing stages of a race is that if you are 2 yards ahead of your opponent with 100 yards to go, he has to run 2 percent faster down that final straightaway to beat you. Rick Wohlhuter understood this when he said, "One strategy is to say, 'to hell with everybody else,' and just keep them behind. If they work their way to your shoulder coming down that last straightaway, just hope they will have fought so hard to get there they don't have the speed or strength to go by." It was almost as though Rick had a premonition of the tactic Alberto Juantoreno would later utilize to wrest the gold medal from him.

Some runners (who are pace-setters) find it very disturbing when other runners (who are kickers) trail them for an entire race waiting for the precise moment to storm by. Unless they are very experienced and cool, this exerts excessive psychological pressure on the lead runner. The trail runner knows this, and this is one reason he stays behind.

Various methods are used to disengage a trailing runner, probably the simplest one being simply to run off and leave him. This works, obviously, only if the lead runner is clearly superior. For runners of near-equal ability, however, the lead runner must employ other tactics.

One method is to vary your pace, alternately slowing down and speeding up. Begin your fast spurts (particularly in cross-country runs) after you have passed some natural obstacle or crested a hill, so you can catch your opponent off guard and open a slight lead before he recovers. Since you pick and choose the places for pace changes, you expend less energy than your opponent. You control the tempo. Of course, if your opponent is experienced he will know enough to hold back and not try to match your every twitch. A confident kicker may trail almost to the point of losing contact, and only move into striking position when it comes time to strike.

In road races, while running into the wind, you can sometimes limit the benefit to an opponent by *weaving*, moving back and forth sideways. In order to keep you as a shield, he must constantly change position.

Sometimes while battling an opponent in a road race, I spurt when we reach a water point. As my opponent reaches for a cup of water, I start to move. He will lose distance, both while grabbing the water and while swallowing it. It's difficult to race hard those first few hundred yards after a good drink of water. This is not a wise tactic to employ on very hot days.

On one occasion I ran a two-mile track race against an opponent who had been instructed by his coach to follow my pace. Since I was doubling back after the mile, I was not eager to push hard. He was fresh, yet allowed the pace to get slower and slower, particularly after I sensed what was happening and decided to test how slow he was willing to go to remain in second. Finally, after one incredibly slow quarter, I actually started walking. The other runner, much to his coach's consternation, began walking, too. Eventually I won with a blistering kick. I think our time was around 11:30.

THE ART OF PASSING

There is a time and place to run from behind, and a time and place to run from the front. If you run from behind, and want to win, sooner or later you must pass the runner in front of you. Passing is a tactical art in itself. Passing on a road course usually poses no problem, because your straightaway may be 26 miles 385 yards long. But on a track you have considerably less distance to get by another runner. Let us consider three possibilities for passing moves.

Coming out of the turn. This is the most obvious place to begin your pass. You have the maximum distance to run after moving wide and before sliding back into the inside lane. If your opponent offers no resistance, you need to shift your pace relatively little to get around him. If he does offer resistance, you have more time to overcome it.

If I intend to pass somebody coming out of a turn (and I am not trying to disguise my move for the element of surprise) I will begin the pass at the apex (or midpoint) of the turn. As I pass the apex, I begin easing my way out toward the second lane so that when we reach the straightaway I am beside the runner rather than behind him. This is more efficient than making a sudden move to the side when you hit the straightaway, since anything done suddenly in a race wastes energy.

But since everybody knows that coming out of the turn is theoretically the best place to pass, many runners float through the turns and then increase their pace down the straightaway to keep their opponent from passing them. This is a good tactic if you want to maintain your lead.

Going into the turn. The last 10 yards of the straightaway is where most inexperienced runners, trying to hold the lead, tend to relax. They figure they have beaten their opponent going into the turn, and want to ease off as soon as possible. This is the best time to get a jump on such runners. Sometimes I make a false move coming down the straightaway, moving outside the lead runner's shoulder, but not seriously challenging him. Then, the moment he relaxes at the end of the straightaway, I charge past. Before he realizes it, I'm in front.

Sometimes I am the one being passed. If a runner challenges me down the straightaway and fails, I wait until the moment I see him abandon his move and tuck in behind me going around the turn. At that moment I slow down too, forcing him to stay in the outside lane while negotiating the turn. This psychological ploy defeats many inexperienced runners who fear that in running wide around the turn they cover too much extra distance, which will inevitably cause their defeat.

On the turn. A lot of coaches will read this and begin nervously foaming at the mouth. Last spring I attended a junior high track meet where two runners had a stirring shoulder-to-shoulder battle the entire race. The winner did around 12:03, and I overheard the coach of the loser inform the runner he added at least 100 yards to his distance by running wide.

If he had run in the third or fourth lane, he might have covered that much more distance. Actually, I thought the loser ran a relatively good tactical race considering his inexperience. He ran wide on the straightaways, but moved behind or at least in tight on the turns. But his coach implanted in this young runner's mind that he should never pass on the turns. I pass on a turn when I feel like it. You are much better off running a few inches farther than waiting until the straightaway to go around and risking a break in your tempo. This is a question of inches rather than feet or yards.

I recall some years ago watching Frank Shorter and Jack Bacheler running a race that appeared on television. Jack ran most of the way off Frank's shoulder, and the television commentator kept babbling about all the extra distance he was covering. He actually ran very little extra distance. Since Jack's legs are longer than Frank's, he probably could stride much more comfortably running to the side rather than directly behind.

That junior high coach and the television commentator failed to understand that when you run wide in a distance race, you rarely run a full lane wide, as a quarter-miler would when running in staggered lanes. You run a fraction of that. When I run second behind another runner I normally run slightly wide anyway, so I can see the track ahead over his shoulder and avoid being boxed. I often like to run half-wide, meaning that my inside (left) leg is behind his outside (right) leg.

It is easier to pass from half behind than from directly behind. Unless he holds you off, you can sometimes snake around a runner on the turn while still in half-wide position. It is a bit like the way a high jumper clears the bar without ever seeming to be completely over it. You dip your shoulder in front of the passed runner. You have moved the required one stride ahead before cutting in, but you do not cut in. You have moved from a half-wide position behind to a position half-wide ahead. From there you can gradually draw away to a lead sufficient to take the inside lane—if the lead runner permits you to do so.

If you do not wish to be passed in this manner, you must be willing to defend your position. You should not permit runners to cut in front of you unless they have the necessary one-stride lead. Since most runners who do cut in, do so unintentionally, a slight push or soft tap on the arm will usually warn them you intend to hold your ground. If they keep coming, it is an act of aggression, and I have found a sharp blow against the elbow will deter them. If worse comes to worst, the beleaguered runner can raise his arms and stagger into the infield, hoping to draw the attention of the judges to his plight.

In long-distance races run on a track, fast runners often face the problem of passing runners as they lap them. Although it is easier to pass a slow-moving runner, the hazards of collision increase because of the great variations in speed. For this reason I always object when officials order slower runners to move to an outside lane, either while being lapped or for the remainder of the race. Officials who make such rules often have never raced themselves.

I have two reasons for wanting lapped runners to stay inside. First, I see no reason why slower runners should be further penalized for their slowness by being made to run in the second or third lane. I am usually quite willing to move wide and run the slight extra distance. I don't need an extra advantage. But second, and most important, if the slow runner is told to stay on the inside, I know where he is going to be. Then I do not need to worry about him suddenly moving out into my path.

This happened in the Masters Championships at White Plains, New York, two summers ago in the 5,000-meter run. A lapped runner looked over his shoulder and saw me approaching. He remembered that the officials warned everybody to run wide and get out of the way when about to be lapped. But I was closing so fast that, by the time he got the message to his tired feet and moved out, I was on his outside. He only succeeded in bumping me. He apologized after the race, but it was the officials who owed both of us an apology.

Yet, I feel slower runners should not obstruct fast runners. The boom in jogging has enriched our sport, but conversations are best carried on in the infield, or in road races, rather than during track events.

Sometimes a fast runner treading his way through lapped runners can use them to his tactical advantage. By artfully dodging inside or out, a runner in the lead can break contact with those behind him. I recall one particular race two winters ago when a blizzard caused cancellation of the North Central Marathon and forced more than 200 runners of varying ability to run a 10-mile substitute race on a snowy track. I broke fast from the starting line, despite treacherous footing, because I knew we would start lapping trail runners within a mile. Anyone more than 10 yards behind at that point would get hopelessly enmeshed in the crowd. That is exactly what happened.

Soon only Barney Hance, of the College of St. Francis, and myself remained in contention. On a dry road course, Barney would have chewed me up and spat me out, but on that icy track with runners curb to curb, neither of us could gain on the other. I had fun psychologically playing with him because when he had the lead and moved wide to pass a group, I often found a gap on the inside and moved ahead of him. Eventually the organizers threw sand on the icy curves (improving traction), which allowed Barney to demolish me in the last few miles.

USING AND AVOIDING BOXES

Nevertheless, tactical knowledge often can tip the scales when two runners of equal ability meet. This is particularly true when it comes to boxes. Experienced runners get boxed less often than novices, or if they do get caught, know how to work their way free more easily.

A box occurs when a runner in position behind the leader suddenly finds another runner on his shoulder, boxing him in and preventing him from passing. If the box occurs on the last lap, it may result in defeat. If it is a moving box, one in which there is not one wide runner but a stream of runners passing, the one on the inside may find himself going from second to last with little control over his destiny.

If the box occurs in the middle of the race, many runners simply relax and wait for the wide runner to move either forward or back. But there are several ways in which a runner can disengage himself from a box.

Slow down. If you slow your pace, the runner boxing you in on the outside will probably move into your position, thus freeing you. But in doing so, you will have surrendered position. If you do this on the last lap, you may surrender too much ground to the leader.

Ask to get out. Most boxes occur unintentionally, and if you ask the runner on your shoulder to give you room, more often than not he will do so. In tactical racing, you want to take advantage of other runners, but you do not want to take unfair advantage.

Shove your way out. This is risky business if the judges are watching. This tactic should be employed only in desperation, and probably only if the wide runner is a teammate of the leader and is deliberately holding you in. (This is an illegal tactic and may result in the disqualification of both boxing runners.) However, you can push your way out of a box more subtly by exerting gentle pressure while going around the turn and forcing the outside runner wider. This should open a gap by the time you hit the straightaway.

Move inside. This is a desperation tactic, and one that usually only works on the final straightaway. If you find yourself boxed in at this point in the race, your only hope may be to wait for an inside opening. Often, the lead runner, in his closing sprint with another outside runner on his shoulder, often moves wide, forcing that runner farther out or, because of centrifugal force, begins sliding toward lane two. This sometimes opens the door for another runner to come up on the inside, but that door can close as soon as it opens.

The best defense against boxes is not to get caught in them. The way to avoid boxes is to run off the shoulder of the runner in front of you, in the same outside/inside overlap stride mentioned earlier. Thus positioned, you cannot be easily boxed; by moving slightly wide you can stay free of the runner in front of you. By thinking ahead you can avoid most boxes.

The same is true in the rush for position at the start. A runner who starts in the middle often gets caught, as others on the outside sprint to reach the pole, and then slow down once they get there. If I have a choice, I usually start in an outside lane, rather than an inside one—unless it is the innermost one. When in the middle, I try to edge outward to avoid being hemmed in.

TACTICAL SENSE

Some purists may object to the use of tactical devices to defeat other runners of equal ability. They consider tactics unfair. But to remove tactics from racing would also remove a lot of fun from the sport. I enjoy getting out on a wide-open road course and running solo, with only the clock to beat. But on occasion, I like to get on a tight track for a tussle with other runners. To each his own.

These maneuvers, as well as the other tactics described in this article, do not come easily and cannot be learned by reading a book. Many runners actually use these maneuvers and tactics without giving much thought to the fact they are using them. The best teacher, in the long run, is experience.

6

Racing Advice from the Experts

by Jim Lilliefors

Although every runner has his own theories about racing, there are some common themes. The following are collections of ideas from a survey of some of the top runners.

Don Kardong, Olympic marathoner. "I have a theory on marathon running, where a rational approach is so important. During the first ten miles of a race, I try to disassociate myself from what I'm doing. I talk, joke and daydream in ways that remove me from the race. But after ten miles, my consciousness re-enters the picture, and concentration begins. From that point on, the problem is concentration, and the feeling is one of acute association with the task at hand. I switch from auto-pilot to manual control, and through the last part of the race I pick off those people who have overassociated, i.e., who have tried to concentrate from the start."

Bob Hensely, 2:18 marathoner. "Planning and training are important, but it also has to 'happen,' which is something you can't really plan. You have to have a 'good' day. My best races are never a *complete* surprise. I know when I *might* be able to run a PR, and when there is a chance of running a PR."

Bill Rodgers, American record-holder in the marathon (2:09:55). "A racer should run his race according to his condition *prior* to and *during* the race and according to his competition and whatever moves they are making. If you know your competition and your condition, you can then judge how you should run your race.

"No two runners are alike in ability on a given day and that is a major factor in determining who's to win the race. If two runners are in equally good condition and of 'equal ability,' perhaps psychological factors or environmental factors (heat, wind) or one runner's kick at the finish will determine the winner. Effective, even pacing is the best way to win a race. But I do think the runner is at an advantage who can 'surge' or do a pick-up during a race.

"I generally run the first half of a marathon faster than the last half. I suppose this is because I'm a front runner and try to stay with the leaders. It may be worth the gamble to slow down the first half by 30 seconds to a minute and a half and then try to push extra hard the last 10 miles."

Dan Cloeter, winner of the 1977 Mayor Daley Marathon. "I set up goals for myself. When it comes to racing, I feel my mental preparation is more important."

Bill Haviland, 2:19 marathoner. "I just always try to run my best in a race. What happens, happens."

Chuck Smead, 2:14 marathoner. "I feel one can become a great runner without knowing too much about pace. I think the course and conditions will dictate pace. A person who is a master pacer could easily get screwed up by hills and/or wind.

"A racer should have firm goals. If he wants to run a specific time, he should run pace. If he is trying to beat somebody, he would probably be better keying on the person."

Jon Anderson, winner of the 1973 Boston Marathon. "Anyone who races seriously should concentrate on running his own pace (read: race) but he must be prepared to deal with changes in pace when strategy dictates those changes. Most strategic tactics involve pace."

Jeff Galloway, 1972 Olympian. "Your body develops its own clock. A runner should run his own race—use the tools he has, when he can, to his best advantage. The one who has conserved the most at the end is able to use it when it counts most. Even pacing is the best means of running any race, except in unusual tactical situations."

Bob Varsha, 2:15 marathoner. "Consistency of pace will lead to the best races. I believe there can be little question that the best races will not simply 'happen' no matter how you prepare. I say this despite the fact that some of my best races have come off a week of poor workouts, because I believe those two circumstances are not inconsistent.

"On the other hand, I won't deny that there is a large chunk of good fortune that works for a great performance. Let's just say we plan as much as we think we should and then hope for the best, but we must plan to *some* degree."

Amby Burfoot, winner of the 1968 Boston Marathon. "Everything

I know about racing, I learned by racing....Generally, I think that the runner who controls the race pace (and may make the pace very erratic) has the best chance of winning."

Brian Maxwell, 2:13 marathoner. "It's important to be able to pick up strategies. Running one's own race is best, but this takes great confidence. Sometimes, it is better to have someone to break wind and help with pace."

Tony Sandoval, 2:14 marathoner. "Sometimes, when I run a 5,000-meter race, for instance, it feels good to go out at a fairly slow pace and then fire home the last half-mile or so. In this case, even though I may have the same overall time, psychologically I'm better off.

"In the marathon, though, if you go out and time my first half and compare it with my final time, I can assure you it will be quicker than half of the overall time. Yet, when I consider racing a marathon and decide on a time I feel I'm ready for, I will first consider what I can run the *last* six miles in. Then I subtract that from the overall time I'm shooting for, and then I divide what's left over into an even-paced 20 miles."

7

Ultramarathoning

by Ted Corbitt

The standard marathon is 26 miles, 385 yards long. A race of greater length is called an *ultramarathon*: it's beyond the regular distance. The most often run ultramarathons are 30, 40, and 50 miles long. The 100-mile and 24-hour runs are also run, but less frequently. Five-, 6-, and 24-hour runs are usually conducted on tracks, making it easy to get an accurate check on the distance covered. Races up to 100 miles are conducted on roads and on tracks.

Historically, the running of these races has tended to occur in cycles. Interest rises and falls, only to rise again. Such running would seem to fall into the esoteric category. But the annual 54-mile Comrades marathon in South Africa, run since 1921, draws an annual field of 500 or so, and the annual London-to-Brighton 52½-miler has starting fields of 45 to 70. This compares with the starting fields of the average road races and marathons throughout the world.

People are astonished to learn that men, and occasionally women, run as much as 50 to 100 miles—a challenge that appeals to some athletes. There are even those who like to watch such races. For example, Doug Alexander, author of *The Comrades Marathon Story,* says, "I saw my first Comrades marathon when I was a boy of eight, back in 1931, and became a fan from the very first moment."

Men who run these distances fast usually have had some running experience and have in addition put in some special training. Ultramarathoners are graduates of marathons and shorter races. Ultramarathons are conducted on a formal, organized basis in English-speaking countries and only occasionally in other countries. There is also a revival of interest, with races in the United States and Australia, following the leads of South Africa and England. The latter two countries have an annual series of ultramarathons. Several women have unofficially but successfully run the 54-mile Comrades marathon, and at least one woman has run 100 miles.

223

Except for solo efforts, these long races are conducted under amateur rules. Some countries have age restrictions, especially at the beginning level. England restricts runners to 10 miles and less until age twenty-one. Japan permits teenagers to run the marathon. Czechoslovakia allows persons to run marathons at age twenty-three. In the United States, a runner under age sixteen may now run a marathon with parental consent and medical approval.

Many run ultramarathons because the challenge appeals to them. To South Africa's Don Shepherd, who ran across the United States from the West coast to New York City in 1964, long solo runs provide a sense of achievement. There are other runners who are interested, but who allow fear to keep them from trying the long runs. Others do not attempt ultramarathons for lack of formal opportunities.

In the United States at this time, a full program of ultramarathons exists in the Metropolitan AAU area (greater New York City) under the sponsorship of the Road Runners Club, New York Association. Races range from 30 to 50 miles. The New York City area has been a focal point of interest for ultramarathon running in past generations, during past cycles of heightened interest and activity. For example, the professionals did much of their ultramarathon running in the New York area. The current interest in New York City began in late 1957 when a half-dozen local marathoners started training to run a 50-mile track race. AAU sanction was unobtainable at the time and the program was delayed until 1962, following my trip to the 52½-mile London-Brighton race, with the assistance of the Road Runner's Club. AAU sanctions are obtainable now and a half-dozen ultramarathons are held annually in the area.

In preparing for races 30 to 50 miles long, there are several approaches, and all have produced successful results.

In one approach the runner gets into top form for the marathon and just makes up his mind to run the ultramarathon race. He just goes out and does it!

The second is essentially the same approach as the first, but involves doing some special training—specifically a few training runs of up to 30, 35 or 40 miles—before the event.

Finally, the runner can become an ultramarathon specialist. These men run all kinds of races—cross-country, track, and road—and all distances. But their main interest is the ultramarathon, other runs being more or less secondary to them. These men usually run the full distance or more in practice at least once before the race. Otherwise training is the same as for the marathon. The specialists average about 5,000 miles or more a year.

England's Ron Hopcroft set a world 100-mile road record while never training beyond 26 miles except for a few training runs around 31 miles just before the record attempt. However, he had run the 52½-mile London to Brighton race several times. With this background, he ran 100 miles in a record 12:18:16 in 1958 (he was under 6 hours at 50 miles). When asked recently how he had run 100 miles that fast, he said, "I just kept picking my feet up and putting them down until it was over."

It's as simple as that if you really want to do it. Other things to consider in planning to run an ultramarathon include getting a pair of roomy shoes, well broken in, and a handler to help out with sponges and drinks between refreshment stations set up by the race sponsor. The handler may be on a bicycle or in an automobile. If the race is on a track, the feeding station is on the infield at trackside. Here the sponsor will provide sponges and a variety of drinks—fruit juice, lemonade, tea, water, etc.—and if the runner has something special he may bring it along and give it to the feeding station attendants.

Running an ultramarathon is similar to running a standard marathon except that the runner parcels out his energy over a longer period. If the race is 30 miles it should be run at regular marathon pace. If the race is over 30 miles it will be run at a pace slower than regular marathon speed. If he runs hard, the ultramarathoner can expect to suffer from fatigue symptoms over a longer period of time than a marathoner. The runner's fitness level and his determination will dictate the pace at which he races.

There is no answer as to how frequently one should or can run an ultramarathon. In 1966 the Road Runner's Club of England felt that 3 weeks was the minimum time between the 52½-mile London-Brighton race and the "Balfe" Cup 50-mile track race. Both races were won in fast times. Nat Cirulnick, compiler of the *Marathon Guide*, ran 17 standard marathons and ultramarathons in 1964. Others have run almost as often, with no unusual problems.

The after-effects of running an ultramarathon parallel those of the standard marathon. The runner's first attempt, if hard, is likely to produce more profound after-effects than any subsequent effort, assuming that he is fit in all instances. Some runners have recovered rapidly enough to run a fast, short race a week later. Special aids to recovery include taking a walk of up to 30 minutes as soon after finishing as is convenient, and soaking in a tub of hot water for about 10 minutes.

Anyone with the urge to run 30, 40, or 50 miles should prepare and give it a try. An unforgettable experience may be your reward.

PART SIX

DIET

1

Diet and Athletic Performance

by Jim Lilliefors

As running has become more widespread and divergent, interest in the relation between diet and athletic performance has also gone in many different directions. Diet philosophies vary greatly. Some believe that marathon runners, because of their high energy expenditure, have a license to eat almost anything they please. Indeed, most world-class American marathoners do not eat a diet significantly different than that of the average American. Frank Shorter says he regularly consumes Schlitz beer and Ding Dongs.

At the other extreme is the athlete who meticulously chooses his daily diet based on nutritional content and need. Los Angeles Ram Jack Youngblood seemed to support this idea when he recently said, "The body is a test tube. You have to put in exactly the right ingredients to get the best reaction out of it. Nutrition is an essential element for any athlete."

Runners of equal ability frequently have very incongruous diets. Some top marathoners subsist essentially on junk food. Others are strict vegetarians.

Arguments can be made for virtually every diet philosophy. Amby Burfoot attributes his profound improvement in the marathon during the late sixties, which included a 2:14 and victory in the 1968 Boston Marathon, to a vegetarian diet. On the other hand, the Detroit Tigers pitcher Denny McClain, the only man in several decades to win 30 games, drank up to 10 soft drinks a day during his prime. Neither of these athletes is still of world-class caliber. Did their diets have anything to do with their success? This is a question that can only be answered with conjecture.

Success has been found with a myriad of ways. There are no formulas. Some top runners drink so heavily they border on alcoholics, while others abstain completely. Which runners have the "secret" if they perform equally well?

Interest in vitamins, vegetarianism, and carbohydrate-loading (all covered extensively in the following articles) has flourished in recent years. Yet for every diet that is endorsed by a popular athlete, there are inevitably detractors.

Much of the reason is the as-yet-misunderstood nature of diet. For instance, vitamin E, which is prominent in wheat germ, has been termed by some a "wonder supplement," capable of prolonging life. Others call it worthless. Some runners advocate high protein intake; recent medical research has found a potential harm in excessive protein intake. Many runners stuff themselves with pancakes and sweet rolls for days before a race; others abstain totally, fasting for two days before competition.

If all of these diet ideas work, even though contradictory in nature, there seems nothing wrong with them. Diet should be, in simplest terms, a personal matter. As George Sheehan said, "There are only two things I demand of a diet: (1) that it allows me to have a good bowel movement before I run and (2) that it causes me no distress while running." These should be the main criteria. As with training programs, no runner should imitate the diet of another. Instead, each should follow Dr. Sheehan's philosophy that we are all an experiment of one.

Illinois nutritionist Tab Forgac pointed out, "Most athletes seek the key to better performance. For some, the key may be improved diet. Everyone looks for the secret trick, the hot tip, the extra edge that will enable them to defeat their opponents, or at least maximize their own abilities. But there are few tricks or secrets in sport, and like the television commercial says, 'You can't fool Mother Nature.'"

Rather than emulate the latest fad, the athlete is probably better off getting a balance of the basic foods. This has been shown to be the best way to promote longevity, and no one has proven yet that it detracts from athletic performance.

There are approximately 50 nutrients known to man. Since no foods contain all of them, it is necessary to eat a variety of foods from each of the four basic food groups: meat, fruits and vegetables, breads and cereals, and dairy products.

The meat group includes poultry, fish, eggs, peas, and nuts. This group is the main source of protein, as well as B-complex vitamins and the mineral iron.

The fruit and vegetable group is the major source of vitamins A and C, and several necessary minerals.

Bread and cereals give the necessary carbohydrate content, as well as iron, thiamin, riboflavin, niacin, and protein.

The dairy group is the prime supplier of calcium, as well as several A and D vitamins.

If a runner gets a sufficient amount of each group, he is nutritionally well-off. Frederick J. Stare, founder of the Department of Nutrition at Harvard University, has offered this basic rule: "The average adult can very simply meet his recommended dietary allowance by consuming daily two servings from the milk group, five ounces from the meat group, four servings from the bread group and four servings from the vegetable-fruit group."

These simple guidelines apply to everyone, not just athletes. As long as the athlete is getting the proper nutrients, the rest of his diet is up to personal preference. Research has shown some correlation between diet and performance, but nothing has been proven conclusively. Following Dr. Stare's rule is probably as sound a practice as any of the fad diets that are popular today, both in terms of athletic performance and longevity.

As Dr. Sheehan said, "I think that on the day of judgement, the vegetarians and macrobiotic people will be similarly embarrassed because of the diets they've been subjecting themselves to in the belief that they will improve their health. If they do it because they enjoy it, that's fine. But if they do it because of a desire for longevity, they are like runners who figure the activity will prevent a heart attack, and then are struck by a truck. They wasted all that time when they could have been playing a harp or cello."

2

Diet—"More" Not "Different"

Twentieth-century science has taken the field against some 3,000 years of tradition in the diet of athletes, and athletes have lost the argument for a special dietary category. In the assault were two slim young nutritionists from the Harvard University School of Public Health, Jean Mayer and Frederick Stare. Both are nutritionists. The doctors have punctured some myths about the feeding (and not feeding) of athletes, and soundly attacked the concept of the training table.

Athletes, Dr. Mayer said, have switched from one food fad to another almost as long as fad diets have been in existence. As early as 500 B.C., he said, all sorts of recipes were proposed among Athenian athletes for keeping themselves in condition. In 400 B.C., red meat for athletes was the accepted thing. Both before and after that, athletes shunned meats and lived on grains.

"The bulk of the evidence," Mayer said, "is that none of the special foods seems to have any special value. We know of nothing to put the nutrition of the athlete on a different footing from that of any other healthy individual."

Science today, Dr. Stare said, can tell us the requirements of a balanced diet—one that should satisfy the needs of any healthy citizen, gladiator or not. The diet, he said, should include a large variety of foods, including a reasonable distribution of fats, carbohydrates, proteins, vitamins, minerals, and water. Each of these food values can be produced chemically, he said, so that a bottled synthetic diet can be prepared to maintain the individual's health. He doubted that synthetics would ever replace food because, in addition to its other values, eating is fun.

Food faddism, Dr. Stare said, not only can be dangerous, but it is

This article originally appeared without a by-line in the June 1959 issue of *Long Distance Log.*

231

good business. He said the specialized foods offered by the fads supply nothing nutritionally beyond a normal, balanced diet. As an example, he observed that honey is virtually nutritionally identical to sugar, and that wheat germ, while an excellent source of vegetable protein, is not nearly as good a protein source as meat.

Beer, he noted, provides more calories per gram than proteins, but fewer than carbohydrates. According to Stare, beer contains about eight times the niacin of milk. But he noted that this was the only area in which beer is nutritionally superior to milk.

The scientists agreed that food supplements, such as vitamin compounds, should be unnecessary to the healthy individual on an adequate diet. In some cases, these could even be harmful.

"Of the $250 million spent on vitamins each year," Dr. Warren Guild of the Harvard health staff added, "some $240 million probably is wasted." The popularity of vitamins, he explained, apparently is based on the belief that if a little is good, a lot must be better. The body can use certain amounts of all vitamins, Dr. Guild said. Excess quantities of water-soluble vitamins, such as vitamin C, are excreted, he explained. Excesses of A and D remain in the body and can contribute to the formation of kidney stones.

Dr. Stare did make one concession to the athletic appetite. He said that while athletes should eat the same food as others, they burn more energy than sedentary people and should be entitled to two or even three portions.

The nutritionists agreed that after age twenty-five, less active persons should cut down their food intake. An ideal body weight, it was suggested, was the average weight for the individual's sex and build at age twenty-five. But they agreed that maintaining that weight in the years after twenty-five would require a degree of perseverance.

3

Put Your Diet in Reverse

by Don Monkerud

T he two-inch steak, the bowl of ice cream, and the hamburger you eat every day could shorten your life. Although you may be running to maintain a healthy heart, eating habits may be closing your arteries. It is known that degenerative disease in the United States is caused to a large extent by the kinds of food we eat. Heart disease, atherosclerosis, strokes, diabetes, and hypertension are all associated with high intake of fat and cholesterol.

Runners often assume that because running strengthens their hearts, they are protected against heart attacks and are guaranteed long, healthy lives. Actually, artery closure plays the major role in degenerative disease, and is currently the greatest cause of death in the U.S., accounting for more than one million deaths a year. Examinations of persons who die from artery closure reveal that most had strong hearts. Their arteries may have become damaged because the average American diet contains 42 percent fat, accompanied by high cholesterol levels.

"If you eat more than 10% fat in your diet, you are going to close your arteries even if you are running," warns Nathan Pritikin of the Longevity Research Institute (LRI) in Santa Barbara, California. "Running doesn't burn up cholesterol because it's not metabolized with running or exercise. People think running somehow lowers cholesterol, but running only has an indirect effect on cholesterol levels. If you lower the fat level, it will eventually lower the cholesterol level."

Pritikin's experience at the LRI comes from spending the past decade cooperating with physicians handling the most difficult cases. Out of his research, Pritikin developed two basic diets. The *prevention diet* is a long-range maintenance diet for the average person. This diet will also reverse mild cases of hypertension, diabetes and other degenerative diseases. The *reversal diet* is a stricter diet intended for people on drug therapy or with advanced symptoms of cardiovascular disease.

Both diets utilize running and walking in conjunction with the diet. Although many of the patients coming to Pritikin couldn't walk 100 feet without pain at first, the average walking distance was increased to several miles. About one-fourth of the LRI candidates graduated to daily running. The reversal diet has worked well for runners with irregular EKGs caused by clogged arteries. One fifty-five-year-old attorney who followed the reversal diet rather than having a coronary by-pass operation is currently running 7 miles a day.

The reversal diet works on accumulations of fat and cholesterol that clog the arteries. These accumulations, called *plaque*, are an underlying factor in heart disease. By withholding fat and cholesterol from the diet, the body uses the plaque to fulfill its requirements for fat.

Both of these diets consist of 10 percent protein, 10 percent fat, and 80 percent complex carbohydrates. The reversal diet allows no cholesterol intake, but the maintenance diet allows 100 milligrams of cholesterol per day. No refined or simple carbohydrates are allowed on the reversal diet, although some are allowed on the maintenance diet.

If your cholesterol level, for example, is 150 or lower, it is below normal. Your chances of having a heart attack are one-tenth of what they would be if your level was at 220, that of the average American.

Runners with high cholesterol levels, who believe the massive evidence that high fat-high cholesterol levels are correlated with clogged arteries, might seriously consider the maintenance diet. USDA studies show, "The average daily intake for Americans of all ages is 3300 calories with 100 grams of protein, 157 grams of fat and 380 grams of carbohydrates." Keep in mind this is only the average; some diets contain even higher percentages of fat.

A runner who gets 3 or more hours of endurance running a week should have a maintenance diet that reduces fat and cholesterol, as well as sugar, salt, and caffeine. On the maintenance diet, fat makes up 5-10 percent of daily calories—one-eighth to one-fourth of average. Sugar and honey in pure form, and other simple carbohydrate-containing foods would be eliminated, compared to the average of 100 grams per day. Salt intake would be cut to 1-2 grams per day or about one-tenth of average. Caffeine would be restricted to 5-10 milligrams per day, compared with the 400 milligram average. Finally, cholesterol would be cut to less than 100 milligrams per day, or about one-eighth the American average.

The following are specific suggestions for achieving these levels, based on Pritikin's diet. Fats and oils can be eliminated by cutting intake of feedlot beef, cooking and salad oils, and all dairy products, except nonfat products. Olives and avocados also contain large amounts of fat, and nuts contain almost 60 percent fat. These should be eliminated. All sugar should, of course, be eliminated, including molasses and honey. Avoid adding salt to your food when eating or cooking. Sodium, the essential ingredient of salt, can be obtained from natural salts in vegetables. Coffee and tea should be eliminated or consumed sparingly. Meat should be cut to one-fourth pound of lean meat a day. Avoid organ meats, shellfish, and eggs, which contain large amounts of cholesterol.

Many runners may be perplexed by this diet. What about protein needs; or iron? What about oil the body needs? How much is 100 milligrams of cholesterol? Of course, things like iron and protein are necessary for proper body functioning. But they can be obtained from many different foods. To follow the diet, one may want to obtain an excellent handbook entitled *Composition of Foods* by B. K. Watt and A. L. Merrill. This 190-page book contains the vital vitamin, mineral, caloric, fat, protein, and carbohydrate content of thousands of everyday foods. (The book can be obtained from the USDA.)

The LRI encourages people to follow the basic diet of 10 percent protein, 10 percent fat, and 80 percent complex carbohydrates. The institute also emphasizes unprocessed foods and elimination of caffeine, salt, and sugar. The LRI contends this diet will provide all the necessary amino acids (proteins), vitamins, and essential minerals and trace elements necessary for a healthy life.

To get an idea of where your health stands in relationship to other Americans, the LRI has devised a brief test for men in their forties and fifties, showing overall trends for longevity. (If you are younger, project yourself 10-20 years ahead to see where you might stand.) If your diet contains large amounts of steak, sausage, bacon, eggs, shellfish, cheeses, milk, organ meats, sugary foods and beverages, caffeine, and salt, your chances for a heart attack in the next 6 years are 3 in 10. On the other hand, if you follow the maintenance diet your chances of a heart attack in the next 6 years are reduced to less than 1 in 100, according to Pritikin's research.

Pritikin, who runs daily himself, contends the diet can alleviate fatigue for runners by cutting down fats. Typically, a person feels drowsy after a meal. The reason for this is the fat that enters the bloodstream lowers the oxygen-carrying capacity of the blood, dulling the mind and senses. On the standard American diet, the blood is loaded with fat all the time. The LRI keeps fat and nerve-jangling free fatty acids at low levels in the blood, thereby reducing fatigue.

Based on the LRI list, the following foods would make up a recommended sample shopping list: breakfast foods like Wheatena, regular Cream of Wheat, Roman Meal, Grape Nuts, and Shredded Wheat. Stay away from all the other packaged cereals that contain added sugar. Also, avoid granola, for most brands have added sweeteners. Whole-grain breads should be sought out. Nonfat milk and 100 percent skim milk cheese, which is sold under the names hoop, pot, baker's, or farmer's cheese, contain little fat and plenty of protein. Chicken and turkey, as well as lean fish like halibut and snapper, provide ample animal protein. The LRI diet is essentially similar to a vegetarian diet, and encourages lots of fresh vegetables and fruits. Avoid canned fruits and frozen fruits and vegetables, since they contain sugar. Meals that do not feature meat dishes on center stage will also help lower food bills.

According to Pritikin:

> Our recommendation for a marathoner would be three meals a day plus three light snacks so you always have some food in your stomach. The basic maintenance diet with the modification of 1-2 pounds of fish or fowl protein a week would be excellent. You can arrange it so you can get a good variety. We have recipes where you can get one or two ounces of meat in a meat loaf or chop suey and have meat every day, or you can eat it all in one day or stretch it out—have three seven-ounce portions three days a week and go meatless the other four days.

In such a program, a sample menu for a day would feature oranges, apples, or strawberries, whole rolled oatmeal with banana and skim milk, tomato juice, and sourdough toast for breakfast. (Add decaffeinated coffee with skim milk if you can't kick the habit.) A salad with buttermilk dressing (strained to remove butterfat), rice and beans, and a tomato and hoop cheese sandwich on rye rounds out lunch. Mixed green salad, salmon loaf, brown rice, split pea soup, sourdough bread, baked potato with mock sour cream, and skim milk provides a filling but nutritious dinner. Fruit, bread slices, and unsalted crackers are good between-meal snacks. This diet offers plenty of variety. With imaginative substitutions in favorite recipes, there's no danger of losing your taste for food.

Nathan Pritikin has no doubt that a high fat/high cholesterol diet will shorten even the most devoted runner's life. But the diet isn't designed to be a crash program, except in life-and-death situations. The LRI recognizes that pressures from family, friends, business associates, and a busy life-style all can interfere with developing healthy eating habits. Cooking maintenance foods can be a big step toward converting your family to a healthier diet. Preparing food in advance or eating from grocery stores may be necessary on a trip. If you're at a restaurant, you can occasionally go off the diet or else find an innovative way to keep on the diet, like asking the cook to fix you something special. By all means, solve these problems in a way that is comfortable and free from pressure.

In the beginning, it's not necessary to adhere strictly to the diet. Gradual adoption is appropriate and convenient, and is much better than abruptly changing your whole eating style. The important point is to eventually establish a low fat/low cholesterol diet as the normal way of eating most of the time. Coupled with a sensible running program, you may indeed shorten the time of your runs and keep running until you're eighty or ninety years old.

4

To Drink
or Not to Drink

by David Costill, Ph.D.

Most marathon and ultramarathon runners strongly support the practice of drinking fluids during competitive races and long training runs. However, in my laboratory at Ball State University, we have observed little consistency with regard to the quantity and composition of the fluids ingested. Some distance runners prefer to compete in races as long as the marathon without taking fluids, while many athletes ingest large volumes of various sugar solutions. In either case, since performance seems unrelated to fluid intake, the benefits of this practice are in question.

In recent years, we have conducted extensive research on the effects of fluid loss and fluid replacement during marathon competition. A group of national and international class marathoners were examined at a Boston Marathon, at a U.S. Olympic marathon trial, and in our laboratory. The intent of this article is to present the findings of our research and to help you decide whether drinking fluids during competition and training will substantially improve your performance.

Large fluid losses may only temporarily impair a runner's performance (*acute dehydration*), provided that adequate water replacement is made. On the other hand, failure to replace the fluids lost during consecutive days of heavy training may produce an accumulated fluid loss (*chronic dehydration*).

ACUTE DEHYDRATION

In the laboratory, we conducted a series of three 2-hour runs at 6 minutes per mile, for a total of 20 miles. During the runs, the subjects (Higdon, Burfoot, Winrow, and Sparks) were fed a total of 4.5 pounds of water or Gatorade, a solution containing sodium,

238

chloride, potassium, phosphorus, and glucose. One of the runs was performed without fluid replacement. As you might expect, running on a treadmill for 2 hours at a 2:37 marathon pace is a real ordeal when you have to do it three times in one week. Higdon was able to perform his runs on three successive days. To add to the pain of the situation, the runners' stomachs were aspirated (pumped) immediately after each test to determine how much fluid remained in the stomach.

We found that drinking fluids during a 2-hour run significantly benefits a runner. Rectal temperatures were 2 degrees F. lower when the runners drank fluids than when they did not. Burfoot's internal temperature reached 105.5 degrees F. when he ran without fluids, but leveled off at 103.6 degrees when he drank either of the two fluids. Since a body temperature above 104.5 can cause extreme distress and possible collapse, this cooling quality of ingested fluids could be of paramount value on a warm day.

Drinking Gatorade, or any electrolyte replacement solution, has several advantages. It provides the active muscles with greater amounts of sugar for muscular energy. With the exception of Burfoot, the runners seemed to recover more rapidly when they received Gatorade during the run. In addition, we noted that the runners' blood sodium and chloride values were maintained closer to the preexercise level after the Gatorade feedings than in either of the other two conditions.

Generally speaking, when a man loses 2 percent or more of his body weight by sweating, his ability to perform prolonged exhaustive exercise is drastically impaired. During the laboratory test, we recorded weight losses of nearly 7 percent of the runners' body weights. A large proportion of such large water losses are normally derived from the fluids of the blood, thereby reducing the volume of blood available to meet the requirements of muscular exertion. To our surprise, however, we found that the large fluid losses incurred by our subjects during the runs were not being drawn from the blood. Despite weight losses as great as 9.5 pounds, the runners' blood volumes decreased very little. Perhaps this explains why many runners can successfully complete a marathon, drink little or no fluids, and suffer no circulatory problems.

When we pumped the runners' stomachs after the runs, we found that only about 81 percent of the 0.54 gallons ingested had actually been absorbed from the stomach. We have estimated that a runner will lose about 3.7 pounds per hour, but he can only remove about 1.8 pounds of water from his stomach in the same period. That means that regardless of how much a runner drinks, it will be impossible for him to keep up with the weight being lost by sweating.

Despite the large volume of fluids consumed throughout the treadmill runs, none of the men developed stomach cramps or nausea. However, all of the runners became extremely full during the final five or six feedings of the runs. Runners may develop severe stomach distress when they drink large volumes in the middle of a race. Our subjects were given about 3.5 ounces every five minutes for the first hour and 40 minutes of the run.

At the 1968 U.S. Olympic marathon trial, we recorded weight losses as large as 13.5 pounds (for Doug Weibe, the eighth-place finisher). The average weight loss for the top 10 finishers was 9.3 pounds. During the race we were able to measure accurately the amount of fluid ingested by such runners as Bob Deines, Jim McDonagh, Bob Scharf, Ed Winrow, Lou Castagnola, Hal Higdon, Amby Burfoot, and Eamon O'Reilly. We were amazed at the small amount of fluid drunk in the course of 2½ to 3 hours of running. The average volume of fluid taken at each of the feeding stations was 1.5 ounces. That means that these men were only replacing about 0.5 of the 9.3 pounds that they were losing.

CHRONIC DEHYDRATION

Large body water losses incurred on consecutive days may cause an accumulated weight and fluid loss. Man generally relies on his thirst to control body fluid balance. Unfortunately, this mechanism is far from accurate. In laboratory tests that required about 8 pounds of sweat loss, we found that thirst was temporarily satisfied by drinking as little as 1 pound of water. Total replacement of body weight may take several days, unless the runner forces himself to drink more than is desired.

Chronic dehydration can drastically damage a runner's endurance by lowering his tolerance to fatigue, reducing his ability to sweat, elevating his rectal temperature, and increasing the stress on his circulatory system. Probably the best way to guard against chronic dehydration is to check your weight every morning before breakfast. If you note a 2- to 3-pound decrease in body weight from one morning to another, efforts should be made to increase fluid intake. You need not worry about drinking too much fluid, because your kidneys will unload the excess water in a matter of a few hours.

Attempts should be made to drink fluids that will be retained by the body. After acute dehydration, drinking water will only produce a partial rehydration. The ingredient needed to improve the retention of water is sodium chloride (salt). We found that after a 4 percent body weight loss by sweating, men were able to regain and maintain their preexercise weight more rapidly with a sodium chloride solution (such as Gatorade) than with water. Despite the fact that the men consumed a volume of water equal to the weight that they lost while running, their urine production was very large and the men had great difficulty in maintaining a normal body weight.

CONCLUSIONS

I have reached the following conclusions regarding the replacement of fluid losses during and after prolonged exhaustive running:

- Drinking fluids during a run can help lower the runner's internal temperature.
- Drinking sugar solutions not only elevates the blood sugar level, but it appears to increase the metabolism of carbohydrates by the muscles.
- Drinking isotonic solutions containing sodium and chloride facilitates the replacement of body weight lost through sweating.
- Runners should keep a close check on their early morning body weight to prevent chronic dehydration.

Despite the positive contribution of drinking fluids during a race, certain problems impair the value of this practice in marathon competition. Runners lose body fluids, in sweat and respiration, at a rate that is nearly double the rate at which fluids can be removed from the stomach. That means that regardless of the runner's efforts to drink fluids during the race, he will still be markedly dehydrated at the finish.

International and national rules committees and race sponsors should become aware of the necessity for frequent feedings throughout marathons and ultramarathons. But most important, runners should understand the risk to their health and performance if they abstain from drinking cold fluids during a long run.

5

Carbohydrate-Loading

by Jim Lilliefors

Carbohydrate-loading was born from 1970s research that showed a prerace diet rich in carbohydrates can prolong endurance capacity. The basis of carbohydrate-loading is that over the course of a marathon, the average runner naturally depletes his glycogen (carbohydrate) stores to the working muscles. This is one reason for "hitting the wall," in the closing miles of a race.

Peter Van Handel is a researcher at the Human Performance Laboratory in Muncie, Indiana, which has conducted studies on carbohydrate-loading. According to him, "There seems to be no doubt that increasing the body's carbohydrate stores will enhance endurance performance. The question is, how does one go about carbohydrate packing?"

Several specific theories have been advanced regarding this. The basic idea is that on the week of competition, the runner should eat a diet high in protein and fat for the first three days, do a hard workout on the fourth day, and begin a high-carbohydrate diet from day four through race day. It is important that normal caloric intake is maintained during the carbohydrate depletion (high protein) phase. If not, there is a tendency toward weight loss that could nullify the rest of the week-long preparation.

Since fuel for nervous and mental energy is supplied by blood sugar, physiologists have suggested that there is some danger in the depletion phase. The runner may experience disorientation and weariness during this phase.

As Tom Martin wrote, in an August 1977 article in *Runner's World*: "There is little doubt that the 'carbohydrate loading' process can improve the performance during endurance work. But we are less clear regarding the average side-effects...that are inherent in the depletion stage of this process."

Because of the possible dangers, carbohydrate-loading is probably best used only once or twice in a competitive season. Despite its positive value, which can be considerable, it has also been linked to

242

stress and hypoglycemia. There are no absolutes here. The athlete is better off to experiment, especially during the high-protein phase.

Once the runner has learned how carbohydrate-loading best applies to him, he should still be concerned about race-pacing. The benefits of carbohydrate-loading can be offset by setting too fast an early pace. Dr. David Costill has found that the rate of glycogen use in a race is greatest in the early stages. Peter Van Handel said, "If you've packed, you are *not* going to be able to go out faster. You should, however, be able to hold your best pace longer, which then results in a faster running time."

Although it may take time to perfect, carbohydrate-loading has been shown to improve dramatically marathon performance.

6

The Case Against Loading

by George Sheehan, M.D.

Life is the great experiment. Each of us is an experiment of one. We are both observer and subject. We make choices, live with them, and record the effects.

"Living," said Ortega, "is nothing more than doing one thing instead of another." But that must be total. We must live on the alert and perform at capacity. "From my point of view," Ortega declared, "it is immoral for a being not to make the most intense effort every instant of his life."

When these conditions of conscious choice and maximum effort apply, we find that nature has set up the best of experiments. We need to study ourselves in motion, under stress, trying to be all we can be. Only then will our deficiencies become apparent in unmistakable ways.

The endurance athlete is the researcher's dream. When my mind and body turned to the marathon, my body could do nothing but follow. I became willing to accept any schedule, any training, any diet in the promise of better times, in the hope of breaking the three-hour barrier. And so I became, in time, one of the observers and subjects in the great carbohydrate-loading experiment.

The program is simple. One week prior to the marathon, you take a long run, preferably about 90 minutes. The following three days, you limit your diet to meat, fish, cheese, and eggs, staying away from carbohydrates. During this time, eat mainly carbohydrates, cereals, fruit, baked goods, spaghetti, potatoes, or my favorite, blueberry pancakes with blueberry jam and maple syrup.

This dietary sleight of hand first depletes the muscle sugar, or glycogen. It then supersaturates the muscles with glycogen, the major source of energy in marathons. Original experiments in Sweden showed that work capacity could be increased anywhere from 100-300 percent, and that running time in an 18-mile race could be improved by as much as 15 minutes. No wonder marathoners all over the world became carbohydrate-loaders.

You can now see the great carbohydrate-loading experiment taking shape. Given the large numbers of runners training maximally and eating much the same diet, the variables are reduced to those inherent in each runner's muscular system. We must look at those variables in the runner's intricate metabolic and biochemical and enzymatic reactions. It is here that nature conducts the most instructive of experiments. Here the lack of just one of thousands of enzymes can be shown to cause serious difficulty in body function.

So it is with carbohydrate-loading. For most of us, the results were marvelous. The last quarter of the run became less of a nightmare. If, perhaps, the three-hour barrier remained unbreached, at least the times were much faster. Paul Slovic's studies at the Trail's End Marathon of 50 "loaders" showed an average improvement of 8½ minutes, which translates to 20 seconds or 100 yards a mile.

However, nature had more to tell us. One of Slovic's "loaders" met disaster and ran one hour *slower* than his predicted time. Here and there, we heard of other runners who had developed leg cramps or fatigue. Some had been forced to drop out early in marathons. Recently, I corresponded with a Canadian doctor who was hospitalized for a week after the Boston Marathon, and another "loader" who had the same experience after the Penn Relays Marathon. The thing these unfortunates had in common was muscle breakdown. In addition, they both had an increase in myoglobin in the blood, sufficient in some instances to clog the kidneys and cause renal shutdown. These events are most likely set in motion by the first three days of low carbohydrate intake and continued training, rather than the three-day binge of carbohydrates that follows. Slovic's observation favors this thesis. Partial "loaders" (those who used the loading phase only) had no reported difficulties.

And so it goes, the marathoner who cannot load has discovered—as do all of us in some fashion—that life is unfair. But he also has learned what everyone performing this great experiment of life must know: that nature, as T. H. Huxley has told us, never overlooks a mistake or makes the smallest allowance for ignorance.

7

Vegetarianism

by Amby Burfoot

The first question most runners ask about vegetarianism is: "How will it affect my training and racing?" Some hope that the diet will prove to be a magic elixir, that it will change them overnight from slow, ragged runners to speedy, graceful runners. Others are more concerned with possible negative effects. They would be content to know that the vegetarian diet is a safe and healthy diet, one that will enable them to continue living and running as they have been.

MY EXPERIENCE WITH VEGETARIANISM

Whatever the case, the question these runners ask is exactly the same question I asked myself about a thousand times before becoming a vegetarian in 1966. At that time, I already knew and believed in the many ethical, environmental, and economic arguments for vegetarianism. I knew that I liked vegetarian foods and that the range of grains, nuts, seeds, beans, dairy products, fruits, and vegetables was more than enough to satisfy my needs for a varied and interesting diet. I was pretty sure that I wouldn't have any trouble giving up meats, gravies, fish, and poultry. True, I did like such foods, and probably ate as much of them as anyone else, but I didn't have an overwhelming desire for them. I had no craving to down a meat course at every meal, and I didn't feel cheated or unsatisfied when I left the kitchen table after a meatless meal.

Still, none of these arguments were enough to convince me to switch to vegetarianism. But there was one item on my agenda that ranked far above all the others—running. I had an intense personal investment in my running, and it was an investment I wasn't about to risk. I wanted to be able to run a lot—up to and over 100 miles a week—and I wanted to run those miles hard and to race successfully in cross country and marathon competitions. This involvement with running led me to question whether a vegetarian diet would provide the kind of superior nutrition to enable me to attain my training and racing goals? After all, the only vegetarians I had ever heard of or read about were Indian yogis or members of other aesthetic clans, who looked as if they'd have trouble getting out of the lotus position, never mind getting to the finish line of a marathon. Though they had a certain calm and healthy look about them, I wanted more; I wanted energy, strength, and endurance. If a vegetarian diet could provide these, I was interested.

My central question formulated, I probably still wouldn't have done anything to search out the answer if it hadn't been for an injury. In February 1966, I began to feel a sharp pain in my left foot the day after a 25-mile training run. Figuring that it would take care of itself somehow, I continued training through the next week, though at reduced distances and speeds. At the end of the week, I competed in an indoor 2-mile race, taping my entire foot beforehand. Enough race-induced adrenalin coursed through my body to get me around the track 16 times without discomfort, but the moment I crossed the finish line and relaxed, my foot exploded in pain. By the time I limped back to the locker room and unwrapped the tape, my entire foot had swelled to twice its normal size and turned an ugly blue-black color.

Resigned to the fact that I had a serious foot problem, I went to a doctor. The X rays told it all—a fractured metatarsal; standard cure: six weeks off from running. It was a bitter pill to swallow. I took up swimming, the recommended cardiovascular conditioner, and began to think more seriously about becoming a vegetarian.

With two free hours a day (the ones I had been setting aside for training runs), I started to dig up research on vegetarianism. It wasn't easy because the literature available in 1966 was nothing compared to what has been published since. I looked through lots of J. I. Rodale's publications on natural foods, and occasionally found a piece that dealt specifically with vegetarianism. Outside of these, I found little information that came from sources I was sure were reputable. The more I looked, the more I came to realize that I wouldn't find the answers I wanted in books.

In one respect I was incredibly lucky: I had a human example to follow. My high school coach and longtime adviser, John J. Kelley, had been a near-vegetarian for years. That is, he eschewed red meats, though he did eat fish and fowl on occasion. And the evidence that he was strong and healthy was overwhelming. He had won the National AAU Marathon Championship eight years in a row and the Boston Marathon in 1957. Twice (in 1956 and 1960) he was the first American finisher in the Olympic marathon. He finished second in the 1956 Boston Marathon with a time of 2:14:21, only 7 seconds behind the winner. These times so amazed Boston officials that they remeasured the course and found it to be 1,000 yards short. Still, Kelley's 1956 Boston time is the equivalent of a 2:17:30, making him the first American under 2:20.

Having living proof was reassuring, of course, but I was still tormented by doubts. Kelley did eat fish and fowl, after all, and I knew these were healthy foods. Perhaps they made the difference. Since I was planning a strict milk, egg, and vegetable diet, I still wondered what would happen.

Finally I accepted the fact that there was only one way to find out about vegetarianism and distance running: by doing it myself. An experiment of one.

I began after the end of my spring semester at college. Back at home for the summer, I was able to buy and prepare foods for myself in the family kitchen. I gathered together what little information I had been able to find on preparing healthy vegetarian meals, and cleared off a space on the kitchen bookshelf. At the same time I began running again. (The original six-week layoff had stretched out to nearly three months, when I attempted to "come back" on the metatarsal too soon, and refractured it.) Thus, returning home had a double significance for me: I was going to become a vegetarian for the first time and a runner for the second time.

The diet went well. I can't say that I selected and cooked the healthiest of vegetarian foods, since at first I relied heavily on packaged breakfast cereals, dairy products, rice, pasta, and canned and frozen vegetables. I know now that my food selection and combination was severely limited, but I didn't know it then. I only knew that I was feeling fine.

It was my running that truly amazed me. I had gotten home on May 31st, and immediately began running 2-10 miles a day. This was my first regular running in three months, the original metatarsal fracture having occurred on February 16. On June 12, I entered the Holyoke Marathon and easily ran 2:50 for sixth place on a hot day. After recovering from Holyoke, I increased my training to 12-15 miles a day and prepared for the July 4th National 20-Kilometer Championship in Needham, Massachusetts. This was a course I had run before, so it would provide me with my first direct test of the effect of my vegetarian diet. On one month of training after a three-month layoff, I had little reason to expect much. Yet I ran two minutes faster than the previous year, under much hotter conditions.

A month later I had a chance to run another comparison race over a local 12-mile course that I had been running since my high school days. This time I ran 3:45 faster than the previous year. After only two months on a vegetarian diet, I was now running almost 20 seconds faster per mile over a full 12 miles.

From then on, I showed dramatic improvement over previous performances in every race. For the next two years, I continued running 90-120 miles a week in training, much of it at a slow, relaxed pace, as well as racing frequently in college meets and summer road-racing events. During that time, I twice won the New England and IC4A Cross-Country Championships and, in the spring of my senior year at college, the Boston Marathon. Eight months after Boston I ran a 2:14:28 marathon in Japan.

This poses the question of whether it was my vegetarian diet or other factors that were responsible for my running improvement. I honestly can't say, but I think the diet had a role in it. For one thing, my improvement in race performances was dramatic, happening within two months of my diet change. Even though I was returning from three months with no training, my times immediately began to improve dramatically.

It wasn't that I began training harder after switching diets. The year before I had averaged 95 miles per week—about the same training I did after becoming a vegetarian. My race results, however, were strikingly different after going on the diet. In fact, the previous year had been a disaster. During cross-country season, I finished far back in races I should have won or at least placed in. I ran lousy and looked so crummy that people were constantly commenting on my pale, tired countenance. Many speculated that I had "mono." I had no idea what was wrong, but it was the most frustrating period of my 15 years of running. Though I had no obvious injuries, I was running like a sick man. During the winter, when I thought I was beginning to recover, I fractured the metatarsal.

My body seemed to be telling me something. Several coaches, skeptical of the amount of training I was doing at that time, also tried to tell me something. They said I needed more rest days or low mileage days. They claimed the accumulation of high daily mileages was the cause of my problems. While I certainly didn't dispute the fact that my body was rebelling, I didn't believe my training regimen was the source of my difficulties. I thought then—and I think now—that diet was the major factor. And the vegetarian diet proved me right. After switching, I never again encountered the kinds of problems I had in 1966-67. Sure, I occasionally ran poorly again, but never for long periods of time. And there was always an obvious explanation for these lapses, like lack of proper training.

For whatever reasons, my experiment of one was a huge success, and has continued to be a success for the dozen years I've been a vegetarian. Fortunately, as the years have passed I've learned much more about nutrition—especially about aspects of nutrition that are critically important for the vegetarian. I've also discovered a lot about myself and my own personal reactions to certain foods. For example, the two foods that make me feel and run the best are rice and bananas. I don't know why these foods work, but it's reassuring to be able to call on one or the other of them at times when I'm a little down.

OTHER VEGETARIAN ATHLETES

I've also learned that many other endurance athletes have enjoyed remarkable success on the vegetarian diet. One is Eric Ostbye, the Swedish marathoner, who now competes in the 55- to 59-year old class. But you'd never know it from his times. Last year he ran 2:26:35 in the marathon, and in the World Masters' Meet he finished first in his class for the marathon and the 10,000 meters, and second in the 5,000 meters. Ostbye, who has been a practicing vegetarian for over thirty years now, credits his amazing performances to his diet. He is getting somewhat slower, but not much. If Ostbye's times are any indication, vegetarian distance runners may be able to stay at their peak performance plateaus longer than other runners and decline more gradually.

Two of the best-known swimmers, Johnny Weismuller and Murray Rose, have relied on vegetarian diets. Weismuller's reign over the swimmers of his time was supreme. In all, he established 56 new world records before his powers began to wane. But for a period of five years, he was unable to set any new records. Then he went on a vegetarian diet for several weeks, and almost immediately stroked his way to five additional world bests.

Rose's vegetarian ways began in the cradle. His parents were firm believers in vegetarianism, and brought up their son on a diet of vegetables and fruits (for vitamins and minerals) and dairy products, whole grains, beans, nuts, and seeds (for protein). This wholesome diet fueled workouts of a duration and intensity virtually unknown before Rose. He eventually became the youngest triple gold-medal winner in the history of the Olympic Games.

There have always been bicyclists who are vegetarians. In fact, the members of the Vegetarian Cycling and Athletics Club once held 40 percent of the British national cycling records. In the all-around athletic prowess, few can match Alan Jones. Jones occasionally ate fish in 1973-74, before switching to a totally nonflesh diet in 1975. During this time, he set dozens of world records in events ranging from skipping rope and doing sit-ups to swimming prodigious distances under adverse conditions. And Jones accomplished all this after being nearly crippled by polio when he was five years old.

The contribution of the vegetarian diet to these athletic accomplishments isn't mystery or magic. On the contrary, the strength of the vegetarian diet rests solidly on basic nutritional principles. In the simplest possible terms, the vegetarian diet provides more of what's good for you and less of what's bad.

The following summary shows how the vegetarian diet rates in the most important nutritional categories.

Protein. The best vegetarian protein foods are eggs, dairy products, soybeans, nuts and seeds. Any vegetarian who eats liberal amounts of these foods will get plenty of protein. In addition, there are many other vegetarian foods that contain partial proteins. That is, they have large amounts of certain key amino acids, but only small amounts of others. When eating these foods, it is important to combine in such a way that you get all the necessary amino acids. Amino acid combining isn't difficult. You're probably doing it already, since many of the best combinations have evolved through different cultures. In this country we eat peanut butter sandwiches with wheat bread and milk: a great combination. The Chinese eat rice and various soybean products. Latins eat corn and beans. In the Middle Eastern countries, *hummus* (a combination of chick peas and sesame seed) is extremely popular. T.ie list also includes common dishes like macaroni and cheese, and whole-wheat breakfast cereals with milk, as well as less well known dishes like barley-millet loaf and spinach-mushroom casserole. (For more information on combining amino acids see *Diet for a Small Planet*.*)

The beauty of vegetarian proteins is that they contain so many bonus vitamins and minerals. Vegetables have much higher concentrations of these than meats. In addition, vegetarian proteins tend to be low-fat proteins. (See the section on fats below.)

Carbohydrates. Carbohydrates give you get up and go. They are the body's fuel—the food component that is burned most efficiently

---

* Frances Moore Lappé, *Diet for a Small Planet* (New York: Ballantine Books, 1971).

to produce energy. There are many carbohydrate sources, some good and some bad. Carbohydrates are found in wholesome, natural foods that also provide protein, fats, vitamins, and minerals. They are also found in white flour, white sugar, and other processed foods that supply plenty of calories. Most of these have little nutritional value beyond supplying carbohydrates.

The vegetarian diet excels in providing carbohydrates. There are many high-carbohydrate vegetarian foods, which contain numerous other nutrients. Vegetarian foods give people an energy boost, plus help meet other nutritional needs.

Vitamins and Minerals. The vegetarian diet will provide all of your vitamin and mineral needs. Despite the fact that the body needs a bewildering number of these substances, vegetarians don't have to worry about getting them. Vegetarians don't need to buy huge purple pills or to consume bowl after bowl of processed breakfast cereals, fortified with extra vitamins (and inflated in price). They need only eat a varied, balanced supply of vegetables, fruits, and other vegetarian foods to ensure themselves a bountiful stock of vitamins and minerals.

Fiber. Once considered "crude waste," fit only for the garbage can, the fiber content of foods is now known to play an important role in the digestive tract. Meats and highly processed foods pass slowly through the intestines, allowing harmful bacteria and toxins to grow and multiply. Eventually, this can cause *diverticulitis*, a rupturing of the muscular walls of the intestines that strikes one out of three Westerners over the age of forty-five. In less well developed countries, where fiber consumption is often eight times that of the West, diverticulitis is virtually unknown. In addition, one well-known group of American vegetarians, the Seventh-Day Adventists, have been shown to have a much lower incidence of cancer of the colon, breast, and ovaries than meat-eaters. Their diet, like that of most vegetarians, includes whole grains and seeds, vegetables, and fruits. Whenever possible leave the outer coverings or skins intact, since they are rich in fiber.

Fats. Fats per se aren't bad for you. On the contrary, they're a necessary part of any diet. Many Americans get 40-50 percent of their calories from fats, including those found in meats, fried foods, and shortenings. Nutritionists agree that half of this amount (20-25 percent) would be much healthier.

There is an additional complication with fats in that there seem to be "good" fats and "bad" fats. Much evidence indicates that saturated fats, such as those found in meats, eggs, dairy products, margarines, and shortenings can cause heart diseases when they are consumed at the 40-50 percent level. The polyunsaturated fats found in grains, seeds, vegetables, and fruits cause no such problems. Vegetarians, merely by avoiding meats, assure themselves of a healthy ratio of polyunsaturated to saturated fats. Cautious vegetarians can cut their saturated fat consumption even more by switching to skim milk products and eliminating egg yolks.

Additives. Additives constitute one of the lesser understood areas of nutritional science. The U.S. Food and Drug Administration would have us believe that all substances added to foods are completely harmless. But more and more critics and researchers are finding otherwise. There is simply no long-term proof of the safety of chemical additives that have been introduced in foods only in recent years. Unless you relish the idea of being a human guinea pig, common sense suggests staying away from foods that have been chemically adulterated. Stick with the natural foods that have been consumed for thousands of years, as straight from the harvest as possible.

Many vegetarians have developed this concept into an art form. Without question, the raw salad (vegetable or fruit) is their highest accomplishment. The raw salad offers a mixture of brilliant colors, different shapes and textures, and tingling tastes. At the same time it is fresh, untreated, and nutrition-packed. Other vegetarian foods, such as grains and beans, require cooking, and perhaps some spicing, but nothing more.

Pesticides. Pesticides are not an unknown quantity; they are known killers. Many have been banned in recent years, while others are used in extremely low concentrations because they are so powerful. Common sense, again, suggests avoiding pesticides as much as possible. For vegetarians this is easy. Root vegetables, grains, legumes, fruits, and leafy vegetables have about one-tenth the pesticide levels of meat, fish, and poultry. This is because pesticide levels increase dramatically on the higher rungs of the food-chain ladder.

DOING SOMETHING ABOUT YOUR DIET

As I've talked with athletes about vegetarianism, I've found that great numbers of them are interested. But far fewer are actually doing anything about it. The reason, I suspect, is that a change in diet is nothing less than a major change in life-style. For most people, diet is established in infancy and continues unchanged through a lifetime. It becomes a habit. The thought of changing one's diet is threatening, even scary. Conscious effort and willpower are necessary every step of the way. But taking that first step can be difficult. Nevertheless, as more people inform themselves on food issues, the number taking the vegetarian path is increasing dramatically.

For those willing to make the effort, the following suggestions will provide some encouragement and support.

1. Get yourself some natural food cookbooks and other good books on nutrition. The written word will ease some of your fears.

2. Expect your efforts to take time at first. Relax and give yourself a chance to get acquainted with new foods and new food preparations. Don't assume you can rush headlong into vegetarianism, preparing meals at the last second or stopping off at a fast-food joint when you're tired. It won't work. But take heart: the things that now take planning and concentration will soon be second nature.

3. Move into vegetarianism slowly. Eliminate red meats first, and then move on to fish and fowl if you like the way things are going.

4. Start with one meal at a time. Breakfast and lunch are easy; just about anyone can eliminate meats from these meals. Dinner is much more difficult, as that's when you're accustomed to a big meat meal, your reward after a long, hard day. Expect to have some trouble with dinner, but don't get discouraged.

5. Take delight in more than just eating your vegetarian meals. Cook with a flourish instead of just heating to a boil. Start to appreciate the colors of fresh vegetables, fruits, grains, and beans. If you steam or stir-fry vegetables, they will retain much more natural color than boiled ones.

6. Expand your use of spices and herbs. Try different combinations in different dishes.

7. Look to various ethnic foods for new and exciting tastes. At first you'll probably wrinkle your nose like a baby tasting new food for the first time. A second or third try, however, will usually win you over. As a special bonus, many of these ethnic food combinations have proven protein value.

8. Keep plenty of healthy snack foods on hand. Nuts and seeds are great during the afternoon, while raw vegetable sticks (carrots, celery, peppers, etc.) will keep you busy before dinner. After dinner you can't beat fruit.

9. Invite friends over to eat with you. They'll be impressed seeing

you in action, and they'll absolutely flip when they taste what you've prepared. Meanwhile, you'll enjoy their compliments.

10. Most importantly, enjoy it. More than eating healthily, vegetarians eat enthusiastically. Nonbelievers imply that a vegetarian diet must be limiting and boring. "I can't imagine what I'd eat," they whine, "if I didn't eat meat." They are the ones whose choice is limited. Vegetarians, on the other hand, eliminate one unnecessary item from their diet, and then pile their plates full of a world of wondrous foods. They constantly discover new foods and combinations of foods, and enjoy every minute of their eating.

8

The Physiology of Fasting

by Thomas J. Bassler, M.D.

Nature designed us to grow fat when food is abundant and grow thin when food is scarce. But fat or lean, primitive man had to remain active to stay alive—running after mates or game and running away from predators. Modern man should also remain active. When I review autopsies of athletes, I think I can tell long-distance runners from other sportsmen by the microscopic appearance of the fat in their arteries. This appearance is related to the ability to cover great distances on foot while fasting. This fat has a "friendly" appearance—unlikely to cause disease. This indicates either a marathon runner or a potential marathon runner.

The "unfriendly fat" is fat that gets into the arteries and causes obstruction or blockage with blood clots, cholesterol, and fragments of vessel wall. Many sportsmen have accumulated this "unfriendly fat" in their arteries even though they were very active in their sports—usually games requiring great speed or strength. Athletes with this "unfriendly fat" cannot fast, and they cannot cover great distances on foot. If such an athlete were to train for the marathon, he would first have to accumulate "friendly fat." One index of this change is a growing ability to fast for long periods.

HUNGER

Before we discuss the science of fasting, we must understand hunger. We desire to eat for several reasons. Some are important, others are not.

The need to chew dates back to our remote ancestors. We grow restless or irritable if we do not grind our teeth into something for about an hour each day. Crunching into hard seeds and nuts vibrates the "brain pan"—the bones at the base of the skull. Crunching on food has a soothing effect. (Note the growth of the snack food industry, based on selling foods that go "crunch"—breakfast cereals, chips, candies, and even fried chicken.) This could also explain the soothing effect of chanting a mantra. (The vocal vibrations of this Hindu invocation also vibrate the brain pan.)

This need to go "crunch" is probably unrelated to actual caloric intake. However, *hypoglycemia* (low blood sugar) is related to caloric intake. If we eat refined sugar (fruit juice, honey, table sugar, brown sugar, etc.) it is absorbed quickly. The blood sugar goes up and *insulin* is stimulated to bring it down. When the sugar level in our blood drops we feel weak and hungry again. This rapid cycle lasts only a couple hours. However, if we take in the same number of calories in the form of unrefined starch (rice, potatoes, beans, bread, etc.), the calories are absorbed later and more slowly. The blood sugar doesn't go up as high and it doesn't drop so low, since insulin isn't stimulated in this instance. Successful fasting, then, includes a lot of "crunch" and very little refined sugar.

But hunger is many things. Children who are low in body iron often eat dirt, plaster, and such things. Cravings can be important signals that the body is low in some vital nutrient. Pregnancy in humans is associated with a variety of cravings, probably dating back beyond the Stone Age. Many studies have shown that children will self-select a diet that fills most of their nutritional needs, simply by obeying basic flavor preferences. Salty food, for instance, tastes better when the body is low in salt. The need for a vitamin will turn us toward fresh fruit; the need for an amino acid calls for beans, peas, meat, or an egg. If the need is not met, a full stomach will not satisfy the craving, so we overeat.

Thus, we see that there are three types of hunger: crunch hunger, energy hunger, and nutrient hunger. If you ignore crunch hunger you can't sleep; ignore energy hunger and you can't work; ignore nutrient hunger and you might die. (As a pathologist for the coroner, I occasionally heard of cases of sudden deaths during various types of strict, monotonous fasts.)

HAZARDS OF THE FAST

What can go wrong during a fast? Dehydration can lead to kidney stones. Constipation can upset your gut and bring on an attack of hemorrhoids, diverticulitis, and other "low residue" problems. Irregular heart rhythms can cause death if the body salts are upset too much. In a poorly prepared individual, excessive fasting can cause faulty fat-burning with *acidosis* (altered body pH). This effectively disables you, making you literally sick and weak.

WHY FAST?

Marathon runners often say that they fast to train their bodies to burn fat. A more correct observation would be that they fast to see whether the body can burn fat. No amount of willpower can help your body burn fat that has a biologically unfavorable mix. You need *essential fatty acids* (EFAs) to burn fat efficiently. These EFAs are polyunsaturated fats; that is, they have two or more unsaturated double bonds. However, the food industry has produced other polyunsaturates that are not EFAs.

Industrial processes that stabilize vegetable oils destroy the double bonds of EFAs by *hydrogenation*, thus filling up the unsaturated bonds with hydrogen. However, at the same time, some of the polyunsaturates rotate part of the molecule. They are still unsaturated, but they are now biologically different—new to humans—and we do not have enzyme systems to handle them as well as the natural molecules.

So, the marathoner fasts to see *if* he can fast, as a check on his diet. If his fast goes smoothly, he knows he is eating right. (Of course he could run a marathon to check his fat-burning ability, but a quick fast is much easier on his joints than another marathon run!)

A number of human studies have shown that high tissue levels of EFAs are associated with fewer heart attacks and strokes and better health in old age. High levels of EFAs are probably "natural," in the sense that primitive man had no other food source except those high in EFAs. However, modern man is being fed a large number of items containing "unfriendly fat." Therefore he should practice fasting as a check on his diet.

HOW TO FAST

No one should go on a strict, water-only fast, even under a doctor's orders. This type of fast means that you ignore your cravings for crunch, energy, and nutrients. There are no laboratory tests that can rule out all the possible complications of a prolonged strict, or total, fast. In addition, there is no need for such a fast. A total fast produces a calorie deficit of only 1,800 kcals per day, while a correct, partial fast, combined with running, can produce a 2,300-kcal deficit and satisfy your cravings at the same time.

A correct fast must do the following:

1. protect your kidneys with fluids (herb teas)
2. protect your gut with food fiber (bran)
3. supply crunch (raw, whole fruits, vegetables, and grains)

4. supply energy (EFAs and starch)

5. supply nutrients (raw, whole seeds, nuts, yeast, and eggs)

When you mix the above items properly, and eat them whole and raw, you can take in about 500 to 600 kcals per day, with a diet weighing 3 or 4 pounds a day. Then, if you jog twice a day—10 or 12 miles a day—you can produce a caloric deficit approaching a half-pound of body fat per day.

HOW LONG CAN YOU FAST?

A 2:15 marathoner burns fat more efficiently than an 8-hour marathoner. If you have a high ability to burn fat, you can fast longer. A simple rule is that if your daily mileage goes well, you can continue your fast. If you lose your sense of humor, stop the fast for a week; then do it again.

Since your speed during the last hour of the marathon reflects your ability to burn fat, a one-day fast is appropriate for anyone who runs a marathon slower than 4 hours. Add a day of fasting for each half-hour by which you can lower your marathon time: two days for the 3:30 marathoner; three days for a 3:00; four days for a 2:30; and five days for anyone faster than a 2:30.

SAMPLE DIET

The 4:15 marathoner can eat a normal breakfast on Monday and a supper on Tuesday. The 36 hours in between will be his "one-day fast," during which he will eat 500 kcals of food and run 10 miles. He puts on his herb tea pot with alfalfa tea and sets out his alfalfa and yeast tablets. He gets out his calorie chart for raw food and counts out 500 kcals of uncooked potato, apples, rolled oats, bran, seeds, nuts, and other fruits and vegetables. The egg and yogurt are reserved for breakfast and supper after the one-day fast.

The 3:15 marathoner eats breakfast on Monday and supper on Thursday. This "three-day fast" includes a total of 1,500 kcals of food and 30 miles of jogging—divided into six, slow 5-mile runs. Each evening, a cup of dry, rolled oats is eaten with a spoon to vibrate the brain pan. Four ounces of beer can be consumed for each hour of running. An egg is scrambled lightly and eaten out of the pan with a fork. A cup of plain yogurt is eaten over a two-day interval. Quarts of herb tea are drunk. Bran and yeast are sprinkled on raw fruit slices. Seeds and whole grains are ground to a fine powder in a coffee mill and eaten raw. Each mile and each calorie is recorded. The weight loss comes to 0.6 pound per day.

Supplements include a gram of vitamin C for each hour of running; bran and alfalfa leaves for silicon; and seeds and nuts for linoleic acid. Heavy yeast intake, about 4 tablespoons a day, will help keep the mood elevated. Heavy vegetable intake, equivalent to a head of lettuce each day, will supply plenty of crunch and bulk. The rolled oats at bedtime give the gut a supply of starch to work on while you sleep.

RESULTS

Successful fasting documents your ability to burn fat—an index of the levels of essential fatty acids (EFAs) in the tissues. The faster marathoners can fast for longer periods because they have larger energy pathways for fatty fuel. Other athletes, middle-distance runners, and the track and field champions may be able to fast, as well. If they can fast, they can probably walk a marathon. Those who cannot fast, cannot finish a marathon. They will probably grow fat quickly, as soon as they hang up their spikes and stop training. There are reports of Olympic middle-distance champions who doubled their body weight after they stopped competing. They had a very high risk of heart attack or stroke. They had trained using intervals of high-speed workouts designed to improve their ability to burn glycogen, not fat. If one of these middle-distance runners had gone on a fast, you can bet that he would have become sick and weak. Since he couldn't burn fat, he would lose his ability to train after only 14 hours of fasting. Our 3:45 marathoner, on the other hand, could continue to run after 40 hours of fasting.

At autopsy, the middle-distance runner who could not fast would have "unfriendly fat" in his arteries. Anyone who can fast and run always has "friendly fat." That is the importance of fasting.

Fasting

by Jim Lilliefors

Man is the only animal who remains almost constantly drugged by unnatural and unneeded food. To other animals, fasting is a normal process. Many stop eating during the mating season; some refrain during the nursing period, and some after birth. Most don't eat when they enter a new environment. Wild animals almost always fast after being taken into captivity. But, regardless of what man is doing or where he is, his concern for food seldom diminishes.

To see how life looks when divorced from this unending food cycle, I stopped eating on three separate occasions, for 4-day periods. My first fast was a valuable lesson in what *not* to do. For four days, I consumed nothing but a half-gallon of water, two beers, and a half-pound of organically grown cashew nuts. I ran 30 miles during the first 36 hours. I quickly discovered this was not wise and stopped running, but dizziness and exhaustion hounded me for the rest of the fast. On the fourth day, 5 pounds lighter, I raced a quarter-mile. Although I did well, several minutes afterward I began to see spots, then everything turned yellow and I fainted.

Obviously, my interest outweighed my understanding. When I later took time to balance the two, and fasted a couple of times properly, I experienced physical and mental benefits I'd never expected, many of which aided my running. This time I consumed only three glasses of pure fruit juice a day, and did not overstrain.

The most profound effect was the isolation from food and the simple realization that I didn't *need* to eat. Just as withdrawal from drugs or drink forces a person to see the extent of his addiction, it isn't until you are deprived of food that you realize the extent of your cravings.

A new perception takes over once the withdrawal passes. In *Journal of a Fast*, Frederick W. Smith writes of reaching this state.*

---

* Frederick W. Smith, *Journal of a Fast* (New York: Schocken Books, 1976).

"For the most part, food is a stimulant or a depressant," he said. "It is different in degree but not in kind from the other drugs people use. And its purpose for the most part is to hide...the incredible depths and the profound meanings of existence. This is the purpose of most eating."

You only realize this after you stop, which few people ever do. Food is such a universal addiction, it is taken for granted. When not tied down by a dependence on food, I found I actually had a greater desire to run. There was simply less reason not to.

Comedian-activist Dick Gregory spoke of a similar feeling. He's been on one fast after another since the turn of the decade, when he stopped eating in protest of the Vietnam War. As his fast grew, so did his interest in running. "After I decided that I wouldn't eat," he said, "I decided that I would get down to some serious running and raised it to about 5 miles a day, and now I've done a couple of 10-mile races and some fives. I love jogging, but I haven't been jogging lately; I've been running."

During my three fasts, I became aware of how eating disrupts the day, how events are planned around it, and how productivity is lost to it. (Each day at work, people begin looking out the window 15 minutes before the catering truck arrives, unanimously wondering "Where's that truck?") Overeating calorie-wise and undereating nutrition-wise are both common. Athletes are even more susceptible because they often use their daily exercise to rationalize a huge consumption of junk food.

Olympic phenomenon Paavo Nurmi said in 1925, "All people eat too much and are therefore incapable of good performances." Percy Cerutty, coach of several world record-breakers and Olympic champions, including Herb Elliott, concurred with this view after lengthy study and experimentation. He stressed the distinction between appetite and hunger, believing the athlete should eat only when his body demands food. Usually, this is not the reason we eat. Most eating is done simply to stimulate the taste buds. Nutrition expert Herbert M. Shelton writes in his book *Fasting Can Save Your Life* (Natural Hygiene), "In the absence of hunger, there is no natural or normal reason why food should be taken.... Hungry or not, we eat as a matter of routine, as social activity, because we have nothing else to do or because eating seems to relieve some of our worries."

Many top athletes fast before competitions as a means of conserving energy. The popular practice of devouring plenty of carbohydrates is just a waste of energy. Ultramarathon champion Park Barner fasts for 24 hours before his races. Erik Ostbye, a Swedish senior marathoner who has run close to 2:20, often fasts during the days prior to a race. Ken Swenson fasted on juice for 7 days before making the 1972 Olympic 800-meter team.

There is always some desire for food during a fast (particularly when the aroma of broiled sirloin wafts out of a restaurant you're running past, or a television screen teases you with plump, butter-soaked blueberry pancakes drenched in hot steaming syrup). But fasting creates resentment toward and sympathy for the masses who blindly gobble away food their bodies can't use.

From a health standpoint, there are four reasons why the body needs to fast. The first is obvious: *weight loss*. Most people, runners included, have excess body fat. Another reason is *physiological compensation*. Blood flows to the digestive organs when food is consumed. The energy expenditure causes a general sluggishness, particularly immediately after eating. Fasting conserves the body's energy regularly employed in digestion, and channels it elsewhere. A third reason is *physiological rest*. This is the natural process man has managed to avoid. If you allow the body to rest, this rejuvenates the cellular structures. The final reason is *elimination*. Fasting provides a rare and much needed opportunity to remove waste products from the blood and tissues.

Although these reasons have all been well documented, the thought of abstaining from eating rarely enters most people's minds. They avoid it, shielded by misconceptions, the most common of which is that fasting is harmful. This has long since been proven false. In 1964, a group of 19 Swedes walked from Kalmar to Stockholm without eating anything along the way. They covered the 300 miles in 10 days. Dr. Ralph Bircher, a Swiss physician, said after the walk, "The happy, natural appearance and obvious liveliness of the walkers at the finish, and a one-minute examination both showed that they were all in the best of health."

Four days into my third fast, I raced again, this time in a 3-miler. I had lost nearly 7 pounds but felt fine. After starting out cautiously, I ran strongly over the last half and improved my best time by 10 seconds.

Ian Jackson, a 2:33 marathoner, found that long-distance running is easier and much more enjoyable during a fast. In the midst of a 7-day abstinence from food, he went 20 miles at sub-2:30 marathon pace. He later said (in *The Runner's Diet*), "I felt I could have picked up the pace over another six miles if I had been in a race." Jackson cites two reasons for this: (1) when you lose weight, your ratio of power to weight improves, and you can maintain a faster average pace; (2) fasting reduces internal friction. When fasting the body consumes its own tissues for energy. Fat tissues, tumors, and residual wastes, all of which interfere with running, are the first to go.

There is no guarantee that fasting will make you faster. At times, I felt much weaker than usual while running. But runners who fast invariably report that their running becomes more enjoyable.

After spending the first day of the second fast indoors, my next morning's run was remarkable. I became acutely aware of the trees, the grass, the sky, the warmth of the pavement, the occasional breeze, and the persistent smell of honeysuckle. My senses were bombarded.

A juice fast involves consuming three glasses of fruit juice a day. These should be squeezed from the fruit with a juicer (available at many health food, hardware, and department stores). Juice should never be squeezed and then stored in a refrigerator. If it is not drunk within 15 minutes, it loses its nutritional properties. Daily enemas should be done throughout the fast. But to achieve the mental rewards of fasting you don't have to follow this religiously. I found it more valuable to experiment.

Since fasting is never permanent, there are always thoughts (which quickly grow to fantasies) about what your first solid food will be and how good it will taste. During my first fast, it was a cherry yogurt; during my second, a grilled cheese sandwich. Although these foods often took on tremendous proportions in my mind, they were disappointing when I finally ate them. The first bites were satisfying, but quickly led to the familiar dullness that told me I was once again a food addict.

10

Feel-Good Foods

by Frances Sheridan Goulart

Now that sports medicine is with us, can preventive sports medicine be far behind? Such a science would let us know that super foods do exist in nature's pharmacopoeia. By definition, a super food should pack some seemingly miraculous punch, improve recovery and consistency, soup up endurance and strength, as well as enhance one's overall performance and feeling of well-being.

These are a few of the top-seeded feel-good foods:

Wheat germ and wheat germ oil (raw). In a remarkable series of studies in 1956 at the University of Illinois, T. K. Cureton increased the stamina of a group of Olympic swimmers by 51.5 percent simply by adding wheat germ and its oil to their daily fare for a period of 3 months. The wheat-germ-fed swimmers outranked the competition in all events.

Because of the large amounts of naturally occurring vitamins B and E it contains, wheat germ keeps the capillaries and muscles of the heart tissues open, increasing the flow of blood in the arteries. Note that wheat germ oil provides more vitamin E than the germ itself, but less protein. One-half cup of wheat germ contains 24 grams of protein, eight times as much as you'll find in a slice of white bread.

Liver. Any athlete trying to push up his oxygen intake cannot afford even a mild case of iron deficiency anemia. Fortunately, it can be prevented or remedied by adding iron-rich liver to the diet.

In tests conducted by Dr. B. H. Ershoff of the Thurston Laboratories in Los Angeles, rats were divided into three groups. Only one group received dried liver as a portion of their daily diet. At the end of 3 months, the rats were pitted against one another in a swimming endurance test. Both of the groups that were not fed liver expired after 13 minutes.

Liver is a blood builder and a superior source of iron and all other major minerals. Like yeast, it is a superior source of all the B vitamins you need.

Brewer's yeast. This is also known as "food yeast," "nutritional yeast," or "easting yeast," but never "baker's yeast." This is available in tablets, capsules, flakes, and powders of varying strengths and flavors at drugstores and natural food stores. This yellowish powder, with a faint peanut flavor, is a rapid energizer. Yeast contains all the elements of the B-vitamin complex in perfect harmony. In its natural form, it is a first-rate source of iron, as well as 18 other minerals and micronutrients. It is also low in calories and carbohydrates.

Nuts, seeds, oils, and others. Studies by Dr. Kenneth Cooper at the Aerobic Institute indicate that, contrary to the old myth about salt depletion, the main minerals lost on playing fields are electrolytes such as potassium and magnesium, not sodium. Nuts and seeds are a good source of both and should be liberally sprinkled raw (since cooking destroys 30 percent of the nutrients) by sportspersons on everything from mustard greens to ice cream. These little packages of power have the richest potassium count and the highest magnesium rating of all foods surveyed by U.S. Department of Agriculture.

Another important seed is sesame (packed with calcium, another mineral female athletes often need). Combine it with raw salad oil, cold-pressed from unprocessed sesame seeds, or with nuts or sprouted soybeans. According to Lars Carlson, a Stockholm exercise physiologist, these nut oils, rich in the super-nutrient linoleic acid, have a turnover rate of 40 times that of glycogen. Taken in conjunction with exercise, these seeds stimulate the production of muscle glycogen, a prime energy source.

Further muscle power is provided by fruits and vegetables like the avocado, which provides more energy per pound than almost any food known. It is as digestible as raw milk, and contains 17 unsaturated oils and vitamins A, B, D, E, and K.

Almost all of these foods can be combined into a food I call "wonder fudge." The recipe is:

½ cup powdered milk	1 cup shredded coconut
¼ cup soy or wheat germ oil	½ cup nuts
¼ cup ground sunflower seeds	¼ cup water
½ cup chopped or ground dried fruit	2 tablespoons brewers yeast
(or a mixture of these)	½ cup sesame seeds
¼ cup honey	¼ cup carob or cocoa powder

Combine everything in large bowl. When mixture sticks together, press into a buttered pan. Chill. Cut into squares, parcel in clear plastic wrap, and refrigerate for a quick pick-me-up. Yield: 1¼ pounds.

11

Vitamins

by Don Monkerud

The controversy over magic formulas to improve athletic performances has been going on for centuries. Runners have searched for potions that will help them run faster, longer, and further.

Running has become specialized, training programs have become intense, and often less than a minute separates the first- and second-place finishers in a marathon. With this high competitive level, the slightest edge makes a difference. Today's runners are wondering whether vitamins improve performance.

Competitive runners are not the only ones concerned with proper nutrition and the role of vitamins. The majority of runners run because they enjoy it. The physical activity gives them a heightened awareness of themselves and their surroundings, and they want to be in peak physical condition.

Running is one of the best forms of exercise. A 150-pound runner expends 570 calories per hour if he runs at a relatively relaxed 5.3-mph clip. This kind of bodily stress raises the requirements of food and nutrients. How does running affect the body's requirements for vitamins? Is it necessary to consume vitamins before and after meals?

According to David Costill, Director of the Human Performance Laboratory at Ball State University, "In the area of nutrition, the scientist is at a major disadvantage in the fight against quackery. The nutritionalist is armed only with fact, while food faddist and quacks have unlimited rules to govern their claims. It would be very easy to make wild claims to gain the attention of the press. After all, they are anxious to present readable material first and to educate last. Nutrition is a tough area to research and an easy one in which to gain attention."

The actual discovery of vitamins was tied to disease-causing deficiencies resulting from the industrial revolution, urbanization, and increased sea travel. Since that time, research has isolated a number of vitamins, and administered them to solve nutritional deficiencies such as beriberi, scurvy, and anemia.

Many vitamins have been discovered within the last 60 years, and several B vitamins weren't discovered until the early 1940s. Vitamins are necessary in minute quantities for certain metabolic functions and to prevent dietary-associated diseases. Since they cannot be manufactured by the body, they must be supplied by food.

Vitamins function as chemical regulators, or messengers, and are important for development and maintenance of the body. Vitamins aid in the hundreds of biochemical reactions governing organ function, growth, and energy metabolism. The runner should understand that vitamins are not a source of body energy and they do not supercharge the runner's food.

Many vitamins act as *coenzymes*, activating enzymes to produce their reactions. An *enzyme* is a complex organic substance that originates in living cells, and is capable of producing chemical changes in other organic substances by catalytic actions. Once activated by coenzymes, the enzyme then acts as a catalyst, enabling the body to function metabolically, producing the energy for running.

For some reason, the body lacks the gene responsible for the production of coenzymes and enzymes. The gene was probably lost in evolution, and as a result we cannot produce vitamins.

Since vitamins are not a source of energy themselves, the runner does not need any more vitamins than the average individual. But since the runner expends more energy, he will need more food calories. This increase of calories will be the only proportional increase of vitamins needed by the runner. Since vitamins are widely distributed in foods in a well-balanced diet, most researchers contend no supplements are necessary.

"Contrary to popular belief," stated Dr. Nathan Smith, author of *Food for Sport*, "the foods ordinarily consumed by active individuals from a varied diet contain a sufficient supply of vitamins to meet the body's needs. In fact, some of them are required in such small amounts (vitamin E, pantothenic acid, and biotin) that even the most irregular and poorly selected diets provide sufficient amounts."

No single super-food contains all the vitamins necessary to trigger the body's complex metabolic functions. Dr. Smith's statement is based upon the assumption that the athlete eats a well-balanced diet. A varied diet, with foods selected from all the food groups, is essential if the body is to have an adequate supply of nutrients. If a runner ignores certain foods or eats a limited diet, he may not receive adequate nutrients. Often symptoms of a lack of vitamins are difficult to detect.

Internal malfunctioning may prevent absorption of particular vitamins, and eating inadequate amounts of fresh fruits and vegetables, and poor cooking methods can lead to slight deficiencies. If the runner runs at night or early morning in a jogging suit, the long period without sunlight can lead to vitamin D deficiency. It takes special circumstances for the runner to have vitamin deficiencies, but it can happen.

Dr. Smith states that thiamine is needed in greater amounts when running. This is also true of the mineral, iron, as government researchers have found that a large proportion of the population is low in iron. Growing youngsters have increased needs for vitamins and other nutrients, as do nursing and lactating mothers. You should check vitamin tables in a health book for these special requirements.

If you take too many supplements it can be harmful. While small amounts of vitamins are vital, too much of certain vitamins can be dangerous. The toxic effects of a surplus of vitamins A and D is known as *hypervitaminosis*. While some excess vitamins are excreted, others accumulate in the body and can cause serious problems. This is why it's important for the runner to know both what vitamins can and cannot do for the body.

Vitamins are classified according to whether they are stored in the body or must be constantly replenished. Vitamins are grouped according to solubility. The fat soluble vitamins are stored in the body, usually in the liver, and the water soluble vitamins must be replenished by daily food intake. While this distinction is sometimes arbitrary, it is used for want of a better system. The fat-soluble group includes vitamins A, D, E, and K, while the water-soluble group includes vitamin C and the B-complex vitamins. Researchers feel new vitamins will be discovered in the future that will have a bearing on proper nutrition.

The only real advance in understanding the chemical workings of vitamins has been made in research with vitamin A. Even today, it is not fully understood how vitamins function chemically and how they perform in the body.

Runners want to know what is happening in their bodies and how the various nutrients function. Not only is this important for competition, but it can improve overall health. To give the runner a more in-depth understanding, the specific aspects of each vitamin will be discussed. The focus will be on how the body handles each vitamin, the role of the vitamin in bodily functions, the body's requirement for each vitamin, and how each is absorbed by the body.

FAT-SOLUBLE VITAMINS

Vitamin A

Vitamin A is essential to skeletal growth and the health of the skin and mucous membranes. Vitamin A plays an important role in visual adaptation to light and dark, and is important to endocrine function. It aids in the prevention of disease by helping form the epithelial tissues, the body's primary barrier to infections. The epithelial tissues include the skin and the mucous membranes of the body from the mouth to the gastrointestinal and respiratory tracts.

The presence of some fat in the intestine is apparently required for effective absorption of vitamin A, especially carotene. If the runner is taking mineral oil, a warning is in order. This oil isn't absorbed in the intestine. If it is present in the intestine along with fat-soluble vitamins such as A, it absorbs them and carries them out of the body. If practiced over a period of time, this could lead to a vitamin deficiency. Mineral oil should never be used immediately before or after eating.

Vitamin A is absorbed the same way as fat: it enters the lymphatic system and is stored and distributed to the body via the liver. The liver stores 90 percent of the total vitamin A in the body, an amount sufficient to meet the body's needs for 3 to 12 months without replenishment. Intestinal diseases or pneumonia can reduce absorption and utilization. With advancing age, elderly persons may experience increasing difficulties absorbing vitamin A.

Vitamin A, taken in large doses, can be toxic. *Hypervitaminosis* of vitamin A is characterized by joint pain, loss of hair, irritability, and jaundice. Several factors determine how much vitamin A is required by the body: how efficiently the liver stores it, the form in which it is consumed, the medium in which it is taken, and any gastrointestinal defects. The National Research Council determines recommended daily allowances based on international units (IU). The IU is determined in rats, based on their ability to forestall disease associated with vitamin deficiencies. Though the requirements for vitamin A have been difficult to establish precisely, the recommended daily allowance (RDA) for adults is 5,000 IU.

Few animal sources provide preformed vitamin A. They include liver, kidneys, cream, butter, and egg yolks. The major sources are yellow and green vegetables and fruits. Sources of carotene (associated with vitamin A) are carrots, sweet potatoes, squash, apricots, spinach, collards, broccoli, and cabbage. Many commercial products have been fortified with vitamin A. Margarine, for example, is fortified with 15,000 IU per pound.

Vitamin D

Vitamin D actually consists of several different vitamins. It is unique among the vitamins, as it is found in only a few common foods. It can be formed in the body after exposure to ultraviolet rays from the sun. A chemical supply of one of the vitamin D compounds exists in the human skin and is activated by sunrays. The synthesis occurs *on*, rather than *in*, the skin. Researchers have found that swimming or showering after exposure to sunlight washes vitamin D from the skin. The vitamin is formed on and absorbed through the skin, and then carried to the liver and other organs. Compared to vitamin A, a relatively small amount of vitamin D is stored in the liver. Excess vitamin D is excreted from the circulating blood via the bile.

Vitamin D facilitates the absorption of calcium from the small intestine. It is predominantly associated with the deposit of calcium and phosphorus in bone tissue. This demonstrates the vital interdependency among the nutrients in the body's overall functioning.

Most adults can acquire the necessary vitamin D through general exposure to sunlight. The requirements for vitamin D have been difficult to establish because of the limited food sources (yeast and fish liver oils) and the lack of knowledge of precise bodily needs. The RDA for children and pregnant and lactating mothers has been set at 400 IU daily. Milk that contains large amounts of calcium and phosphorus is commercially fortified with 400 IU per quart.

Too much vitamin D can cause nausea, loss of appetite, kidney damage, and deposits in the soft tissues of the lungs and kidney.

Vitamin E

The exact biochemical mechanism by which vitamin E functions in the body is still unknown. Vitamin E deficiency does not produce acute disease. In 1922, Evans and Scott, working at the University of California, withheld vitamin E from the diet of rats and found they became sterile. After reintroducing the vitamin, the rats began producing offspring. Although some proponents make claims for vitamin E, these have yet to be proven.

Some research suggests that vitamin E is a coenzyme in cell respiration, or in biosynthesis of cellular substances such as DNA. Several studies with animals suggest that vitamin E may help protect polyunsaturated fatty acids (such as linoleic acid)—the principal structural components in the *mitochondria,* the energy-production sites of the cell.

The aging process seems related to the role of lipids in cellular structure. The aging of the human body is affected by constant radiation bombardment from the atmosphere. Throughout life this radiation causes gradual deterioration of the cells. This radiation penetrates the entire body, striking the polyunsaturated lipids, the major structural components of the cell. Scientists conjecture that if vitamin E isn't present in large enough amounts, destruction of cells will proceed more rapidly. The energized rays strike the lipid molecules causing complete oxidation, which is believed to be the main cause of aging. However, the presence of vitamin E may retard this process.

The RDA for vitamin E was set for the first time in 1968. The RDA is 25 IU for women and 30 IU for men. Vegetable oils are the richest sources of vitamin E. These oils are also the richest sources of polyunsaturated fatty acids, which play a role in aging. Other sources of vitamin E include milk, muscle meats, fish, eggs, leafy vegetables, and cereals.

Vitamin K

There are three principal vitamin K compounds, involved in blood-clotting. They are absorbed with other fat-related foods and stored in small amounts. Intestinal bacteria constantly synthesize a supply and the body's needs are quite small. Since a deficiency of vitamin K is unlikely, no requirements have been drawn up. Sources of vitamin K include leafy green vegetables, cabbage, spinach, kale, and cauliflower.

WATER-SOLUBLE VITAMINS

Vitamin B-Complex

The crippling disease beriberi plagued the Orient for centuries and led to many scientific investigations. In 1882, a Japanese naval officer found that he could cure beriberi in sailors of the Japanese Navy by feeding them less rice and more vegetables, meat, barley, and canned milk.

In 1897, a Dutch doctor, Christian Eijkman, at a prison in the Netherlands East Indies, observed beriberi in prison inmates. Then he began experimenting with pigeons. He fed the pigeons scraps of prison food, mostly polished rice. (The rice was polished because the oil in the rice would spoil.) The pigeons developed the same paralysis. The prison director then refused Eijkman permission to continue using the prison food in his experiments. When Eijkman bought cheap natural (unmilled) rice to feed the birds, they miraculously recovered. Funk later isolated the compound in the rice hulls, which led to the name "vitamine."

The substance in the rice hulls was found to be not one, but about a dozen compounds, which today are called the B-complex vitamins. Additional research has shown that B-complex vitamins not only are important in preventing disease, but also play an important role in metabolic functions. They serve as vital partners in many reactions, and as coenzymes in energy metabolism.

Thiamine (B1)

According to Dr. Nathan Smith, excess vitamin supplement intake for athletic performance is a matter of concern. In *Food for Sport*, he says, "One B vitamin, thiamine, is an exception, since it is required in proportion to carbohydrate intake (and very active athletes as a group may be expected to eat more carbohydrate)."

Thiamine is a key coenzyme in carbohydrate metabolism. As a catalyst, it triggers the enzyme that not only speeds up reactions, but also makes possible turnover of compounds without which life could not exist. Since thiamine is not stored in large quantities in the tissues, it must be ingested in the diet. Carbohydrates increase the need for thiamine, while fat and protein spare thiamine. Excess thiamine is excreted in the urine.

Without thiamine, there could be no bodily energy. A thiamine deficiency hinders the production of energy and the proper functioning of nerves and muscles. The result is muscle weakness and nerve irritation involving the gastrointestinal tract, the cardiovascular system, and the central nervous system.

The requirements for thiamine relate to carbohydrate and energy metabolism, expressed in caloric intake. If calories are markedly curtailed, a thiamine deficiency is a distinct possibility. But if the runner is on a training program and eats enough calories to maintain body weight, this is unlikely. Good sources of thiamine are lean pork, beef, liver, whole or enriched grains, and legumes. Eggs, fish, and some vegetables are fair sources.

Riboflavin (B2)

Riboflavin forms coenzymes important in the metabolism of amino acids, glucose, and fatty acids. It is a vital factor in protein metabolism. The body's needs for riboflavin depend on body size, metabolic rate, and the rate of growth. The lower the protein intake, the more riboflavin is excreted and lost. Storage of riboflavin is limited, although traces are found in the liver and kidneys. Day to day needs must be supplied through the diet.

Cheap high-starch diets, limited in protein foods, milk, meat, and vegetables, increase riboflavin needs. Periods of normal body stress, such as growth and lactation, also increase the need.

The RDA for riboflavin is tied to protein needs. It is recommended that 1.3 milligram or more daily is necessary to maintain tissue reserves. The most important source of riboflavin is milk. Each quart of milk contains 2 milligrams of riboflavin—more than the daily requirement for all except lactating mothers. Other good sources of riboflavin are liver, kidney, heart, and vegetables. Because riboflavin is water-soluble and destroyed by light, considerable loss may occur in open cooking in excess water. Covered containers and use of limited water help keep the loss to a minimum.

Niacin

Niacin (nicotinic acid) is a coenzyme with riboflavin in the cellular system that converts proteins and fats to glucose. Glucose is oxidized to release controlled amounts of energy. Niacin and riboflavin operate together to generate bursts of energy. The total effect is similar to a generator. Energy is constantly produced and stored in "batteries." The body's cells may derive "current" when the energy is needed.

The body's need for niacin is determined by age, growth, illness, tissue trauma, body size, and physical activity. In addition, pregnancy and lactation increase the requirements for almost all nutrients, including vitamins. Check a chart in a health text if you have any questions concerning additional vitamin needs.*

The National Research Council recommends 6.6 milligrams of niacin per 1,000 calories. At least 13 niacin equivalents are required at intakes of less than 2,000 calories. In order to provide a safety margin to cover individual variances, these requirements are about 50 percent higher than minimum.

The major source of niacin is meat. Peanuts, beans, and peas are also good sources. For the most part, fruits and vegetables are poor sources. Unless enriched, since most grains lack *tryptophan*, a precursor of niacin, they are also poor sources of niacin.

---

* See Sue Rodwell Williams, *Nutrition and Diet Therapy* (St. Louis: C. V. Mosby Company, 1973).

Other B-Complex Vitamins

Other more recently discovered coenzyme factors include pyridoxine (B6), which plays a role in carbohydrate metabolism. The RDA, set for the first time in 1968, is 2 milligrams per day. Good sources are yeast, wheat, corn, liver, kidney, and other meats. Limited amounts are found in milk, eggs, and vegetables.

Intestinal bacteria synthesize considerable amounts of *pantothenic acid*, which is vital to body metabolism, carbohydrate metabolism in particular. Because deficiency is unlikely, requirements haven't been established. Studies of adults have shown that excretion rates range from 2.5 to 9.5 milligrams daily. Average American daily intake, with 2,500 to 3,000 calories, is about 10 to 20 milligrams. Pantothenic acid is readily found in many foods, including liver, kidney, and egg yolk. A fair amount is found in lean beef, milk, cheese, legumes, broccoli, kale, sweet potatoes, and yellow corn.

Vitamin B12 (cobalamin) is stored in active body tissues in minute amounts. These stores are slowly depleted, but they are vital to bodily functions. One cup of milk, one egg, or 4 ounces of meat provide over 90 percent of daily adult needs. (It is interesting to note what is meant when one refers to the small amounts of vitamins present in foods. In a ton of rice hulls, there are only about 5 grams, or less than one-fifth of an ounce, of vitamin B1.)

Vitamin C

Hippocrates, the Greek "father of medicine" described in 1500 B.C. the effects of *scurvy*, which is caused by a deficiency of vitamin C. Although sailors no longer suffer from this deficiency, a recent controversy has been raging about the effects of the vitamin.

Vitamin C is necessary to build supportive tissue. It builds and maintains bone matrix, cartilage, dentine, collagen, and connective tissue. Just how vitamin C functions in this process is unknown, but when vitamin C isn't present, *collagen* (a protein present in many tissues) doesn't form. The large concentration of vitamin C in adrenal gland tissue indicates that any body stress—shock, injury, fracture, or general illness—calls for vitamin C tissue stores. Lack of vitamin C can produce easy bruising, bone and joint hemorrhages, poor wound healing, and more easy bone fracture. Current research may reveal additional facts about the broader role of vitamin C in body metabolism.

Though it is not stored in single tissue deposits, vitamin C is generally distributed throughout body tissues. When body tissues become saturated with vitamin C, excessive amounts are excreted.

Infectious disease depletes tissue stores of vitamin C, necessitating additional intake. This is especially true of bacterial infection. While scientists maintain that optimum tissue stores of vitamin C help resist infection, the recommended dosages of therapeutic vitamin C are in controversy. At this time, there is insufficient evidence to support claims for consuming megadoses of vitamin C. Most nutritionalists recommend avoiding extravagant and wasteful dosages (which are excreted from the body in the urine).

The RDA for vitamin C is 60 milligrams, which was revised in 1968 to provide a "margin of safety" and allow for variations in tissue demands.

Handling, preparing, cooking, and processing can cause oxidation of vitamin C. This should be considered in choosing vitamin C sources. Citrus fruit and tomatoes are well-known sources. Other good sources include cabbage, sweet potatoes, white potatoes, and yellow and green vegetables. Such foods as berries, melons, chili peppers, green peppers, turnip greens, broccoli, asparagus, pineapples, and guavas are also recommended.

Any runner on a specific diet needs to check to make sure he or she is getting the proper amount of nutrients—vitamins, as well as the proper proportions of fats, carbohydrates, and protein. Generally speaking, vitamin supplements are not needed by any runner unless there is a specific disease-related health problem. The key to a good diet for the runner is one that is well balanced, and includes plenty of fresh fruits and vegetables. Foods that contain the highest concentration of vitamins are not very high in calories. No matter what type of diet is eaten, one vitamin-rich food can be added to a meal without adding fattening foods.

Future research may turn up additional dietary requirements that haven't yet been discovered. Most scientific and nutritional researchers, as well as exercise physiologists, tend strongly toward the view that it is unnecessary to supplement vitamins if the diet is adequate. They contend that if the runner gets an added boost from vitamins, it's a result of psychological factors.

At the same time, some trainers and runners recommend using supplements for specific injury-related problems. These proponents have yet to turn up any evidence to impress the medical community. The current view is that as long as runners have a well-rounded diet with foods selected from each dietary group, vitamins are not necessary for optimal performance.

12

One More for the Road

by Jim Lilliefors

The following two statements were made during 1976:

- "Because of the widespread social use of alcohol, athletes sometimes fail to see how destructive and debilitating this drug can be. The best advice is to eliminate the use of alcohol except on rare occasions."
- "I have spoken with an exercise physiologist who tells me that runners have actually tested better on his treadmill after a night of beer drinking."

The first statement, from a nutrition book, is typical of many made over the years by coaches, writers, and athletes. The second, by George Sheehan, M.D., represents something new.

According to Dr. Peter Wood of the Stanford Heart Disease Prevention Program, the longstanding idea that alcohol and athletes don't mix "is based more on the puritan ethic than on substantial medical evidence." Dr. Wood and four of his colleagues recently completed a study indicating that on a daily basis, runners outdrink nonrunners two to one, and in the case of wine drink three to four times as much. The survey was based on a sample of male and female adult runners whose average weekly mileage was 37 for men and 31 for women, compared with a random sampling of nonrunners from three California towns.

The widespread advice to avoid alcohol, whether substantiated or not, apparently has not been faithfully followed. According to Fred Wilt, in the book *Run, Run, Run*, published by Tafnews, "It is now known that even small amounts of beer will adversely affect the body's heat regulatory mechanism 24-48 hours." Even so, Frank Shorter didn't seem concerned when he drank 1½ to 2 liters of beer the night before winning a gold medal in the 1972 Olympic Games. "I don't mind getting half looped the night before a race," Shorter

277

said. "I worried about alcohol tests for about three seconds in the middle of my second beer."

Shorter had no cause to worry. Although alcohol was termed a doping agent by the International Olympic Committee, athletes were not tested for it at the 1972 Munich Games.

Alcohol has not only been consumed before races without adverse effect, it has been drunk during races with apparently positive results. In last year's Boston Marathon, one of the hottest ever, a runner reached the 20-mile mark in what he himself called a state of near collapse. After being given vodka and water, he passed 70 runners in the last 6 miles to finish in style.

Several months later, in the New York City Marathon, a runner competing in his second marathon in 8 days was in difficulty by the sixteenth mile. He drank a 12-ounce can of beer and blazed through the remaining miles rejuvenated.

Although its carbonation makes beer a questionable refreshment, Stanford's Dr. Wood claims that vodka and water "does make physiological sense. It would be absorbed very fast, would get used up by the peripheral muscles before it affected the liver or brain, and would satisfy a hunger for calories." This seems to refute the popular, though unproven, notion that "muscles cannot use alcohol as a direct source of energy."*   In fact, several books list alcohol among "ergogenic aids," which by definition increase energy or energy output.

Much of the controversy springs from the peculiar nature of alcohol. It is a food, yet is unlike any other food in the way it affects the brain. It has many stimulating effects, yet is a depressant. One explanation is that it affects the part of the body we understand the least. In their book, *Nutrition and the Athlete*, authors Morella and Turchetti deal with this idea.*   *   "In cases of excessive exertion, alcohol has been administered to athletes as a stimulant, to release inhibitions and decrease fatigue. Findings such as this indicate that the effects of alcohol are primarily on the mind."

This could explain the inconsistency in ideas about the effects of alcohol. The brain is not always stimulated in the same manner. "There are reports," the authors continue, "that described how anxiety may develop in the athlete as a result of excessive arousal of the cerebral cortex."

---

* Nathan Smith, *Food for Sport* (Palo Alto, Calif.: Bull Publishing, 1976).

* * Morella and Turchetti, *Nutrition and the Athlete* (New York: Mason/Charter, 1976).

Dr. Wood stresses that practically all claims for or against alcohol are "backed with extremely poor or non-existent evidence." One of the few adverse effects of alcohol that has been proven is that it increases a person's triglyceride (a blood fat) level. But it has been shown that running can counteract this increase. According to Dr. Wood, studies conducted with drinkers and nondrinkers have shown that when the nondrinkers are given alcohol, their triglyceride level goes up. But the extremely low triglyceride level in running subjects indicates that running can successfully counteract this adverse effect.

You may wonder about the long-term effects of drinking 6 to 9 beers a day? "You're not going to believe this," says Dr. Sheehan, "but the literature suggests there may not be any. If your intake of alcoholic calories is below 15-20% of your total caloric needs, you are presumably safe."

Sir William Roberts of Manchester, England, has even argued that alcohol is a necessary supplement to today's diet.* Modern man's diet contains such an array of rapidly digested foods, he believes, that digestion happens too quickly. Alcohol is needed to slow this process to a more normal rate.

Drinking oneself into delirium on a regular basis is a questionable activity for any athlete. But research has revealed practically nothing to disclaim the beneficial effects some athletes report when they use, not *abuse*, alcohol. Depressant effects have even been purposely used in athletic competition. *Nutrition and the Athlete* tells of racers in a 6-day bicycle race who, "at the beginning of a rest period would take drinks of brandy, beer or bourbon to make them sleepy."

The use of alcohol in athletics is nothing new. According to Dr. Max Novich (*Drugs in Sport*, 1970), European athletes used alcohol extensively at the turn of the century. There were reports of cyclists in 24-hour races drinking rum and champagne throughout the race, as well as marathon runners consuming considerable quantities of cognac or beer during competition.

Alcohol takes on a new value when competition is over. Frank Shorter has called his daily beer consumption a good way to relax. An Oregon doctor recently visited the Sierra Madre Occidental of northwestern Mexico, home of the legendary Tarahumara Indians. He found that they employed alcohol liberally as a relaxant. The Tarahumaras, noted for their all-day runs and 200-mile kickball games, spent most of their time while the doctor was present lying in the shade, drinking a homemade concoction.

---

* Herbert Shelton, *Health for the Millions* (Chicago: Natural Hygiene Press, 1968).

Not only has there been a severe lack of agreement about the effects of alcohol, there has been great difficulty in defining just what alcohol is. One author writes, "It is neither a food, thirst-quencher nor medicine. It is a poison pure and simple."*   Yet Dr. Sheehan says, "First we must understand that alcohol is not only a drug but also a food."

Though we are far from understanding alcohol, we are closer than we've ever been. The most important distinction would seem to be between use and abuse. It has been shown that, on occasion, abuse may have no adverse effects whatsoever.

"I recall a teammate in college," Dr. Sheehan relates, "who was carried home after a night-long beer blast and rose the next day to win the intercollegiate two-mile championship. I have heard much the same story of a well-known runner who was poured into bed the early morning of a national championship and later that day won going away."

But the memory of the late Steve Prefontaine stands as an illustration of how devastating abuse can be.

The distance between this extreme and that of the exhausted Boston runner who was revitalized by vodka is great, and represents the spectrum of effects of alcohol. A more common effect was experienced by Dr. Sheehan when he decided to test the merits of alcohol on himself. On a Saturday night he drank 6 beers, about Shorter's consumption on the eve of his Olympic victory. The next day he ran a good 6-mile race. "After a day off," Sheehan said, "I again drank six beers the following night. The next day I thought about running, but went home and took a three-hour nap instead."

---

* Herbert Shelton, *Health for the Millions* (Chicago: Natural Hygiene Press, 1968).

13

Running High-Calorie Workouts

by Joe Henderson

You down a Big Mac, fries, and a shake, gain a quick 1,000 calories. To work off those calories, you will have to run about 10 miles. Running uses up about 100 calories of energy per mile. 100 times 10 equals 1000. One hundred calories per mile is a round, easy-to-remember figure, but it is little more than an educated estimate that doesn't take into account several variables. One is the runner's pace, another is his size.

Three Air Force doctors reported earlier this year that a runner's weight has the greatest influence on his energy consumption. With an important qualification, pace has little to do with it.

Drs. Bruce C. Harger, James B. Miller, and James C. Thompson took much of the guesswork out of calorie-counting for runners.* "It seems logical," they wrote, "that careful accounting of calories for both input and output would be the most precise means of prescribing a weight control program."

"Many people run to lose weight," they said. "However, very often fitness books give caloric value for running that is based on a single weight for a period of one hour. We believe this is doubly erroneous since weight is such a large factor in determining cost, and because comparatively few people run for a full hour."

Their research centered around 1½-mile runs—a standard distance in the "Aerobics" program used in the Air Force. For 150-pound men, the caloric cost of running this distance in 8 minutes (5:20 mile pace) is only slightly higher than the caloric cost of a run twice that slow. The difference, 16 calories, is less than you'd get

---

* Bruce C. Harger M.D., James B. Miller, M.D., and James C. Thompson, M.D., "The Caloric Cost of Running," *Journal of the American Medical Association* 228 (1974):482-83.

from a cube of sugar or a few peanuts. It takes 3,500 calories eaten
or used to gain or lose one pound, respectively.

The doctors noted, "It can be readily seen that pace has very little
effect on the caloric cost of running, and thus individuals in low fitness categories can expend almost as much energy as a similarly
sized person for a given distance. However, the difference in energy
cost when comparing various weights is much more dramatic."

TABLE 6			CALORIES USED PER MILE OF RUNNING						
WEIGHT					PACE PER MILE				
(pounds)	5:20	6:00	6:40	7:20	8:00	8:40	9:20	10:00	10:40
120	83	83	81	80	79	78	77	76	75
130	90	89	88	87	85	84	83	82	81
140	97	95	94	93	92	91	89	88	87
150	103	102	101	99	98	97	95	94	93
160	110	109	107	106	104	103	101	100	99
170	117	115	113	112	111	109	107	106	105
180	123	121	120	119	117	115	114	112	111
190	130	128	127	125	123	121	120	118	117
200	137	135	133	131	129	128	126	124	123
210	143	141	139	137	136	134	132	130	129
220	150	148	146	144	142	140	138	136	135

Note: expenditure of 3,500 calories equals one-pound weight loss

They tested runners weighing from 120 to 220 pounds. The heavi-
est used up as many as 100 more calories than the lightest at a given
pace over the 1½-mile test distance.

Using the Air Force doctors' figures, Russ Akers, a runner from
Washington, adapted table 6. It lists the caloric costs of running in
per-mile terms. As mentioned, there is almost no difference between
running fast and slow.

This is where the important qualification comes in—one the doctors didn't spell out in the previously mentioned article, other than
mentioning "for a given distance." You may be thinking, "They're
saying it takes about the same energy to run at 5:20 mile pace as
10:40? They've got to be kidding. One's a hard run; the other's
almost a walk."

The doctors are as correct as you are. It is harder to run fast, but
the slower you go, the longer it takes to run a given distance. At a
slower pace, you burn fewer calories per minute, but for a longer
period of time.

Dr. David Costill explained this: "Total energy expenditure per kilometer distance is constant and independent of velocity."*

Costill gave the example of two marathoners—one running at 6-minute pace (2:37) and the other at 8 minutes a mile (3:30). The faster runner had an estimated caloric expenditure only about 4 percent higher than the slower one. But running at 6-minute pace cost significantly more per minute—about 40 percent more.

TABLE 7	CALORIES USED PER MINUTE								
WEIGHT				PACE PER MILE					
(pounds)	5:20	6:00	6:40	7:20	8:00	8:40	9:20	10:00	10:40
120	15.6	13.8	12.1	10.9	9.9	9.0	8.3	7.6	7.0
130	16.9	14.8	13.2	11.8	10.7	9.7	8.9	8.2	7.6
140	18.1	15.9	14.1	12.6	11.5	10.5	9.6	8.8	8.1
150	19.4	17.0	15.1	13.5	12.3	11.2	10.2	9.4	8.7
160	20.6	18.1	16.1	14.5	13.0	11.8	10.9	10.0	9.3
170	21.9	19.2	17.0	15.3	13.8	12.7	11.5	10.6	9.8
180	23.1	20.2	18.0	16.2	14.6	13.3	12.2	11.2	10.4
190	24.4	21.3	19.0	17.0	15.4	14.0	12.9	11.8	10.9
200	25.6	22.4	19.9	17.9	16.2	14.8	13.5	12.4	11.5
210	26.9	23.6	20.9	18.7	17.0	15.5	14.1	13.0	12.1
220	28.1	24.7	21.9	19.6	17.8	16.2	14.8	13.6	12.6

Let's switch things around now and assume the runners are competing for the same length of time. It involves an hour run on the track. They go the same paces as before, 6- and 8-minute miles. They cover 10 and 7½ miles, respectively. The caloric costs are about 950 and 675. So pace does make a difference. Your fast miles may not be worth much more than my slow ones. But minute-for-minute, your running is considerably more productive in caloric terms.

Table 7 extrapolates calories-per-minute from the Air Force doctors' research. And since many runners run by the hour, hourly totals are in table 8.

If you want to run off that 1,000 calories quickly, run hard for a set period of time. If you aren't in such a hurry, run a set distance at any pace you like. Both ways work.

---

* David Costill, Ph.D., "Physiology of Marathon Running," *Journal of the American Medical Association* 221(1973):1024-29.

Francie Larrieu, winner of the mile at the AAU Nationals in 1973, burns up the calories. (Photo by M. J. Baum)

TABLE 8	CALORIES USED PER HOUR								
WEIGHT	PACE PER MILE								
(pounds)	5:20	6:00	6:40	7:20	8:00	8:40	9:20	10:00	10:40
120	936	828	726	654	594	540	498	456	420
130	1014	888	792	708	642	582	534	492	456
140	1086	954	846	756	690	630	576	528	486
150	1164	1020	906	810	738	672	612	564	522
160	1236	1086	966	870	780	708	654	600	558
170	1314	1152	1020	918	828	762	690	636	588
180	1386	1212	1080	972	876	798	732	672	624
190	1464	1278	1140	1020	924	840	774	708	654
200	1536	1344	1194	1074	972	888	810	744	690
210	1614	1416	1230	1122	1020	930	846	780	726
220	1686	1482	1314	1176	1068	972	888	816	756

PART SEVEN

THE PEOPLE

1

Running for Life

by John A. Kelley

In my early boyhood, I can recall active games such as "relievo" and "duck on the rock." How we used to chase around! Occasionally, a sporting goods salesman would take two new American League baseballs, line us up, and throw those new baseballs as far as possible down the street. Then, we would chase after them. My younger brother Jim was the fastest kid in the neighborhood and almost always got one of those baseballs. I was not so lucky.

From about age 11 to 15, Jim and I spent summers as caddies at the Maplewood and Bethlehem golf courses in the White Mountains of New Hampshire. We walked miles, which, though we didn't know it at the time, was probably a good foundation for the future.

Then, for a while we played baseball. We had a good team, the West Medford Baseball Club, with uniforms and all. At Medford High School I ran the 600- and 1,000-yard runs in indoor track. Shortly, we transferred to Arlington High School, across the river, because our family was growing (there were 10 of us kids) and we needed a larger house. "Doc" McCarthy was our track coach at Arlington High, and we competed against the Dartmouth College freshmen and ran in the Yale Interscholastics. I was glad to be on these track teams, even though they were nothing outstanding.

One day in July 1927, after graduation, I decided to run a 5-mile handicap road race in Norwell, Massachusetts. I finished second, and from then on I was hooked. This was really the beginning of my fifty-year love affair with running.

The following year, 1928, I decided to run the Boston Marathon. It turned out to be much tougher than I thought, and I dropped out at about 21 miles. I decided to stay with the 10-milers and other shorter races for a few years, and had a fair amount of success. But again in 1932 I ran Boston, and for the second time dropped out—in Wellesley, with blisters. Nowadays, I don't run fast enough to get blisters!

I recall the days when California had only one marathon, sponsored by the *Los Angeles Times*. In the first one, an Indian named Chauca won, and Clarence DeMar, of Boston fame, was second. Clarence was the winner the following year. In 1932, this race was the final American Olympic Team marathon tryout, because the Games were to be held that year in Los Angeles. My friend "Whitey" Michelson was the winner.

My parents told me in later years that they used to go to watch the Boston Marathon when they were courting. They saw Timmy Ford win, when he was a post entry, 18 years old, and 113½ pounds. Mother used to say she never dreamed she would have a son who would run in the marathon.

In 1933, I had been ill with the flu, but managed to finish thirty-seventh. The following year, I was a surprise second, behind Dave Komonen, a Finn from Canada. I was twenty-six years old and seemed to be getting stronger. The next year, 1935, was my first Boston victory. What a thrill, and such a happy time for family and friends. From then on, it was serious running, including my win in the first revival of the Yonkers Marathon on Thanksgiving Day, 1935. In 1936, I qualified for the American Olympic Marathon Team to compete in the Olympic Games in Berlin, Germany. I was the only American to finish the Marathon—eighteenth.

But one needs a steady job, too. Finally, after several different jobs, in 1937 I went to work for the Boston Edison Company, and stayed with them for thirty-six years. The company was good enough to allow me the necessary time to travel by boat to the Olympics with the teams. But except for my two weeks' vacation pay and a small donation from management, it was at my own expense, and I lost my wages.

Years ago, we did not have a tartan track, only cinders. It sure would have been great to have had one. We did our *ins and outs*—now called *intervals*—on these cinder tracks. Today's runners do what they call their "quality work" and "quantity work." We did a mixture of everything, but we worked hard.

In 1940, I again qualified for the U.S. Olympic Team in the marathon, along with my friends Les Pawson and Don Heincke. The Games were supposed to be held in Helsinki, Finland, but Germany invaded Norway in June and the Games were canceled.

In the 1940s, the Boston Marathon was dominated by Gerard Cote, Les Pawson, Tarzan Brown, and yours truly. I won it again in 1945.

There were no Olympic Games in 1944. I will not venture a guess about how I would have fared in trying for a place on it, because

Now in his seventies, Johnny Kelley is a legend at Boston, where he has run the Marathon all but one year since 1932, winning it twice. (Photo by Jeff Johnson)

only three men are selected in each event on the track and field program. There were many good marathoners around.

However, I continued running, and in 1948 qualified, at age forty-two, for the Olympic marathon team to compete in London, England. I finished twenty-first—the second American.

Every athlete knows how it feels to put one's heart and soul into a contest and lose. It's not a very pleasant feeling, but it is one that must be endured.

My dear wife, Laura, has been a tremendous help to me in all this business. She has maintained interest in my running for many years, helps me with the driving to and from the races, and really enjoys them. And I'm not too hard to cook for. As for diet, I'm not fussy, except the day before a race, when I require three heavy, well-balanced meals. I have never emphasized carbohydrate intake, though I know that today's runners consider that an important factor the day before a race.

Throughout the year I try to watch my weight by avoiding fried foods and overeating. The only supplement I use is wheat germ. And I have trained in moderation. Years ago, we used to train only on Tuesday, Thursday, and Saturday. Don't overtrain, we were told. How did we do as well as we did under those circumstances?

I have been lucky over the years as far as injuries go—the usual stiff muscles, but nothing serious (although in 1968 I had surgery for a hernia). That year I saw the Boston Marathon from the window of a bus. It was thrilling to watch Amby Burfoot win.

My training program is one of common sense—hard one day, easy the next, playing it by ear. It involves steady, all-year-round training, with an occasional day off now and then. I have always trained myself. I don't need a coach or anyone else to yell at me "run faster, run faster," which I find infuriating. Clarence DeMar used to say, "Self-directed work is play." He was right.

Over the years, I have seen the running game grow rapidly, so that now it is the "in" thing. There was a time when people would say, "What's he doing?" if they saw me training.

So, if a runner wants to excel and be a top-notch runner, he should pay attention to the "3 D's": desire, dedication, and determination.

My fifty years of running have been hard work and a labor of love and sacrifice—a rewarding experience. I have had more thrills than the average man, and at my "advanced athletic age" I can still shake a leg. I am most fortunate, and I would do it all over again—well over 1,300 races, including 103 marathons. Quite a life.

2

Making Miki a Marathoner

by Jonathan Brower

It was late-summer 1976, and Miki Gorman was on a 20-mile Sunday morning run atop the Hollywood Hills along Mulholland Drive. We were speaking with her about her goals and hopes for upcoming marathons. Miki's immediate objective was to run the marathon under 2:45, barely a minute better than her personal record set in 1974 (then a world's best for women). Yet she seemed doubtful that improvement would come. She was in her forty-first year, after all, and her first child was not yet two years old.

New Zealander Jack Foster and Miki Gorman have running careers with striking similarities. Both of these over-forty phenomena, the best at their sport for their sex and age, began running relatively late in life. Miki took up light jogging nine years ago, with absolutely no expectation of being a competitive runner, let alone a world-class marathoner. But like her male counterpart, Foster, her late and unheralded start bloomed into extraordinary talent.

After one of our runs, while stretching and cooling down, I mentioned to Miki that she was, like most great athletes, a physiological freak. Not knowing what I meant, but hearing the term *freak*, she wrinkled her nose and furrowed her brow. I tried to explain.

Miki looks like a woman in her late twenties, with her thin frame, smooth skin, buoyant demeanor, and friendly charm. But there is no denying she is a woman approaching middle age, who can explode in a race and run with tenacious and fierce competitiveness. Yet looking at her in nonrunning contexts, one would not guess that she is a top athlete. Rather, she gives the appearance of being a dainty and fragile Oriental woman.

In late September, Miki ran 34:50 in a 10-kilometer road race, and appeared little taxed by the effort. She stepped up her training,

292

In her forties, Miki Gorman ran several of the fastest marathons ever run by a woman. In 1977, she won the Boston Marathon. Here, she is warming up for the Fukuoka Marathon. (Photo by Duomo)

progressing to a 120-mile week before the New York Bicentennial Marathon.

On October 24, 1976, Miki outdid the expectations of both her running cronies and herself. On a hilly course with poor footing in places, her 2:39:11 was the fastest-ever for a Master, her second fastest marathon, and 7 seconds under her previous best effort. She's convinced her time could have been substantially under 2:39 had there not been iron-gratings on surfaces of the four bridges, cobblestone streets, several sharp turns, and occasional potholes.

Some of the dynamics of running a marathon closely and subtly mirror the navigation of one's life. Just as Miki's successful New York Marathon was dotted with some annoying obstacles and unwanted inconveniences, her life in general has been crammed with delights and sorrows. Miki's marathon successes and her approach to running parallel her orientation toward living.

GROWING UP

Michiko "Miki" Suwa, a Japanese born in China on August 9, 1935, moved to Tokyo at age nine with her mother and younger twin brothers. Her father, a stern and autocratic parent, was a surgeon, who remained in China for the duration of World War II. Michiko and her family moved to a rural area a week before Tokyo was decimated by American bombs. Her most vivid memories of World War II include numerous, incessant air-raid sirens and quick trips to bomb shelters. She never saw a bomb drop, but her mind was crowded with vivid images of brutal Americans.

Michiko's father was little more than an ambulatory skeleton when he returned to the family after the war. For years, he had been saving enormous amounts of nonperishable foods for his family, in the process denying himself an ample diet.

Michiko's childhood was far from idyllic. Her devoted but strict father required regular displays of obedience from his children. He screened his only daughter's boyfriends, and chased away more than one active suitor.

But her father was not the only fact that prevented a carefree childhood. Her own physiological and cultural roots proved troublesome. Michiko's reed-thin physique, dark skin, and reddish tinted hair were antithetical to Oriental beauty standards. As a girl from cosmopolitan Tokyo, she wore clothes and spoke in ways different from her schoolmates in the simple rural setting of Yamanashi. To top off her maverick style, she was one of the best at physical games, a fact that displeased her male chauvinist schoolmates.

In retaliation for her nonconformist ways, boys often attempted to intimidate and even physically hurt her as she walked home from school. Many of those walks turned into runs as Michiko fended off the bullies with sticks and outran them. Much of her stamina for dealing with those harrowing situations, Miki reflects, came from her parents' concern for proper diet and exercise. All of the Suwa children were encouraged to eat healthful foods and walk instead of ride buses.

At nineteen, Michiko had to adjust to abrupt changes and hard times. Her father died and she needed to work, day and night. For several years, her social and recreational life was nonexistent. Later, she encountered more frustration with a stifling, dead-end secretarial job and her first broken love affair.

Always a dreamer by her own account, she had been scheming for ten years to make a trip to the United States. She took English lessons and baby-sat for the child of an American army family stationed in Japan. Since she was too self-conscious to expose her English to anyone else, she'd spend hours talking with the American child.

At twenty-eight, Michiko finally came to the United States. The army family sponsored her adventure. She needed a sponsor since she came to the shores of America with only $10 and a few belongings.

Living in Pennsylvania, Michiko Americanized her name to Miki. She moved to Los Angeles, which put her abilities to survive to a severe challenge. She lived at a Salvation Army dormitory and worked as a secretary for a Japanese trading company, living on $130 per month and sending $100 to her mother in Japan. Though poor and leading a frugal existence, her spirit for good times was bountiful.

At a dance, she met Mike Gorman. Their attraction to each other was spontaneous and combustible—the proverbial love at first sight. A mere four months later, Mike proposed marriage. But Miki, being more prudent and level-headed, opted for a longer engagement, if for no other reason than shaky finances. Two months later, they became husband and wife.

There still was no hint of the enormous distance running ability that lay dormant within Miki's petite body. At thirty-three, she had adjusted to the sedentary American way of life. Stomach aches and other disorders nagged at her.

Mike, an active handball player and occasional jogger, urged his wife to join him as a member of the Los Angeles Athletic Club.

There, she took an exercise class that began each session with mild jogging as a warm-up. She jogged a half-mile every other day for six months.

Then, in September 1969, she stepped up her mileage to about 40 per week to prepare for the annual Los Angeles Athletic Club October Run Festival, in which members compete in amassing prodigious, but slow, mileage. Miki compiled a staggering 589 miles, 85 of which she ran in the last 24 hours. In the later stages of her big-mileage month, and in successive weeks, she was in pain, walking with a limp and tossing and turning through many nights.

In 1970, after the negative memories of her October "mileagefest" had faded, Miki ran 100 miles in 21 hours on the Los Angeles Athletic Club's tight indoor track. The next three years for Miki held no big running challenges or goals, just consistent low-key recreational jogging, 40 to 50 miles a week.

Then Peter Daland, then the club's swim coach and now the head of the University of Southern California swim team, told Miki she was a good runner who should try competition. Such encouragement from a well-known and respected coach so inspired Miki that she decided to give racing a go.

She did not complete her first official marathon, the June 1973 Seniors Olympics in Culver City, California. Lack of conditioning and ability were not the causes of her failure. Rather, it was that ever-present nemesis of running novices—too much enthusiasm and lack of experience.

The week before, she had decided to run as an unofficial entrant in the Palos Verdes Marathon. She planned to go only 10 miles. But once she started the race, her urges and instincts took over. Before the 10-mile mark, other runners and spectators were encouraging her, since she was the leading woman. This was enough to keep her going, but by 15 miles she began to have some doubts. At the 20-mile mark, exhaustion had set in. She could barely walk without sitting frequently to rest. But knowing that only 6 miles remained was a powerful incentive to finish.

A glimpse of the battling competitor, who would later emerge, was shining through her lackluster struggle. She finished with a time of 3:25. Seven days later, she still was too wiped out to make her first official entrance in a marathon.

In December 1973, at the Western Hemisphere Marathon, with many 100-mile-plus weeks of running and even a couple of 140-mile weeks, with more running sophistication and prerace carbohydrate loading, Miki exploded to running prominence with a woman's world best of 2:46:36. She proved her time was no fluke four and a half months later, winning the women's division of the 1974 Boston Marathon in 2:47:11.

For trivia buffs, her Boston time may be a world first of sorts. Miki may have crossed the finish line pregnant. (The conception of her first child was within days, if not hours, of the race.)

Fear of miscarriage prevented her from running for the next three months. Seven years of wanting to be pregnant could not easily be overshadowed by her running pursuits. Her new sedentary life-style proved uncomfortable for her.

"I felt as though my body was clogged with old sewer water," Miki recalls with a trace of a grimace. "I needed to get out and be active. After the first three months of pregnancy, when the possibility of miscarriage was very small, I began easy jogging. I got up to five miles a session."

She continued running up to a week before Danielle's birth on January 9, 1975. When Danielle reached her second month, Miki resumed jogging, but encountered unexpected difficulties. Her Caesarian wound opened because of the strain of jogging, necessitating another month layoff. She began again by jogging slowly, gradually building up speed and mileage. After two months of good running, she raced in the 1975 New York Marathon and recorded a respectable 2:53.

The San Fernando Valley Track Club has two of the top women marathoners in the world—Miki Gorman and Jacqueline Hansen. Laszlo Tabori, the great Hungarian middle-distance runner who coaches Miki, Jacqueline, and many other club members, senses the differing styles and temperaments of his two star runners. Many Tuesday and Thursday evenings, Miki and Jacqueline join the hordes of club members on the Los Angeles Valley College track, but the two women never run together. Coach Tabori is emphatic that they run in separate groups. "They have different needs," he says. "Jacki has more natural speed and Miki more endurance. For psychological reasons, too, I don't want them together. They might get too competitive and race and ruin what they're working towards."

As it is, Tabori runs Miki to fatigue on most interval days. Two weeks before her 2:39:11, Miki was worn out and feeling flat. She attributed this to the interval training with Tabori and her high-mileage weeks.

"Mr. Tabori gives me very hard workouts on the track Tuesdays and Thursdays," she says. "He tells me to stop only when he sees that I'm very tired and can't move well. He didn't give me easier workouts two weeks before the marathon."

Though the coach is a hard taskmaster, many of his runners, including Miki, are exceedingly fond of him. On occasion, Miki and some of the other runners have postworkout beers with their coach. Yet Miki cannot bring herself to call him anything other than "Mr. Tabori," a clear example of her strong Japanese socialization.

As a married woman with a child, Miki's running is facilitated by family cooperation. Her mother, who now lives nearby, watches granddaughter Danielle during most of Miki's runs. Miki says that her mother understands her running desires and feels that her daughter should have the opportunity to perfect her special skill.

Mike plays a significant role in his wife's success, too. While some men merely talk about enabling their wives to express and fulfill themselves, Mike's deeds and actions speak for themselves. Since Miki is a wife who works out and races, and has lots of good friends who are male runners, a trusting and understanding husband is a necessity.

Two other people are important to Miki's running. Dr. Myron Shepero, a general practitioner, and Luan Dosti, an aerospace engineer, often run with and counsel her. Myron could be characterized as Miki's medical and spiritual advisor; Luan, who has run 126.7 miles in 22½ hours, helps Miki plan her long-distance running.

While Tabori recognizes Miki's enormous ability, he says that none of her success would be possible if her life was not as oriented toward running as it is. "Not too many women, with a child and husband have as relaxed an atmosphere and as much support from others as Miki has," Tabori says.

Miki approached the 1976 New York Bicentennial Marathon with realistic goals and a relaxed mind. She was hoping to go under 2:46 or to win the women's division. Waiting for the start of the race with more than 2,000 other entrants, Miki was relieved to know the weather would be ideal—high forties with a heavy cloud cover. Miki's one fear at the starting line and in the early stages of the race was of Doris Brown-Heritage, former women's American record holder in the mile and now a 2:47 marathoner.

Doris dropped off Miki's pace before the first quarter of the race. That's not surprising, since Miki was sailing along at a fast and strong clip, reaching the 10-mile mark in 59:12. As she passed the 15-mile mark in less than 90 minutes, Miki knew she was headed for a fast time. As so often happens with good, fast races when everything is clicking, Miki found the effort unusually easy. Because of the ease and fast times, Miki wondered if the course was short and the splits inaccurate. Nevertheless, with about 5 miles remaining Miki entertained the idea of a sub-2:38 performance. Entering Central Park and going over the last 4 miles of rolling hills, she found it a bit too much. "I would have made it [sub-2:38] if there were no hills," she says.

She was extremely tired after the race—much more than usual. As spectators and officials at the finish excitedly approached her with the good news of a fast race, this helped revive her. Minutes later, she found out her time, but her celebration was completely internal. She had no energy for excited, animated movements.

One of the high points of Miki's 2:39:11 experience—and something that tells much about her as a feeling, compassionate human being—came from Doris Brown. The second woman finisher, at 2:53, Doris was delighted for Miki and gave her warm congratulations in the form of kind words and loving hugs. For Miki, who calls Doris a "wonderful sportswoman," the delight of a competitor savoring her opponent's outstanding performance was a precious part of the athletic experience.

As a forty-one-year-old, Miki knows that her potential for improving in distance running is decreasing. When the peak of her competitive career is clearly passed, she plans to run merely for fun and health. In her words: "... less mileage and *no intervals* [her emphasis] when I stop competing. I'll run just like I feel. I'll stop to take in pretty scenery."

This is not to say that she finds her current training routine to be drudgery. She seems to enjoy it genuinely most of the time. But the training grind the 2 months before a big race sometimes becomes heavy and intense. The serious business of running deprives her of some of the joy and spontaneity of her prized activity.

Vanity in modest amounts and some concern about appropriate displays of cleanliness and orderliness creep into Miki's life at times. Corrective lenses would help her vision, but contacts are a worry and glasses, she feels, would detract from her appearance. So she doesn't see as much at a distance as she might.

A small amount of dust on her bookshelves was cause for an apology, as she showed me around her attractive and comfortable apartment. She didn't want me to see her running diary because it was "too messy."

Yet she doesn't succumb to the comments from many women racked with envy who tell her that she's too thin and needs to put on more weight. In her shy and polite way, she skirts the issue for fear of making an uncomfortable scene. What a pity if she gained weight and lost her ability to run gracefully mile after mile. Not only are her times impressively fast, but her grace and rhythm are balletlike in efficiency and beauty when she runs. Most beautiful of all is the freshness, simplicity, and vitality she brings to distance running.

3

The New Women Runners

by Nell Weaver

In 1967, the year Kathy Switzer ran as an official entrant in the Boston Marathon, my father told me I had "runner's legs" which would be useful in track "if you were a boy." So instead I became a high school pom-pom girl, and watched as the boys ran each afternoon after school. In those days in the American provinces, the only women who ran were a few black women—lean, sinewy athletes who sprinted across our television screens on Sunday afternoons. In 1969, *Fact Finder*'s list of "Sports Immortals" included 19 runners—18 men and Wilma Rudolph.

My father's lack of faith in women runners was supported by the tone of the titles of sports articles written about them in the early seventies: "They're Sweet 16 and Deserve a Kiss" (*Sports Illustrated,* 1972), "Thank Heaven for This Little Girl" (*Sports Illustrated,* 1973), "It's No Go for the New Go-go Girl" (*Sports Illustrated,* 1973), "Mary, Mary, Not Contrary" (*Sports Illustrated,* 1974), and "Nice Girls Finish First" (*Newsweek,* 1974). In 1972, *Harper's Bazaar* featured an article emphasizing the genuine camaraderie with men that running offered to Beth Bonner and Nina Kuscsik.

The last few years have at last brought candor to the reality of women and sports. Aided by publications like *WomenSports* and *Runner's World,* urban America has begun to recognize women are running. The reality is that: (1) women run because running makes them feel very good (the same reason that men run), and (2) women can compete effectively and continue competing, just as their male counterparts have been doing for centuries. Beth Bonner and Nina Kuscsik were substantiating both of these facts when they became the first females to run sub-three hour marathons. Today, the sport abounds with well-known females like Madeline Jackson, Francie

Larrieu, Patty Johnson, Doris Brown-Heritage, Sara Mae Berman, Miki Gorman, Jackie Hansen, Ruth Anderson, and Joan Ullyot.

But what about the runners we haven't heard about? There are women all over America, in small towns and larger suburbs who are running. Their schedules vary from a regular morning jog around the block to 70-mile weeks. What makes them run? They get little or no public recognition; sometimes they suffer from personal criticism or even from bodily threats. Running has developed into an acceptable activity for women in cities like Los Angeles, San Francisco, and New York. But in rural America, the woman runner is still a novelty. Perhaps nowhere does she run more anonymously than in Little Rock, Arkansas, population 250,000, a rural community that has grown into a rural city. It's a friendly down-home sort of place, with steak restaurants, predominantly male beer taverns, and Southern Baptist churches. The local media feature the University of Arkansas Razorback football and basketball teams. (The official state pastime is "calling the hogs.") Though the local media occasionally offer brief statements about running sports, I have never seen coverage of any local AAU races. Little Rock expects its women to be grownup Razorback pom-pom girls—period.

Three women in Little Rock run competitively, and there are numerous other female runners in the city, just as there are in other parts of rural America. All of them are the victims of traditional myths about women and sports. Competitors and noncompetitors, alike, go unrecognized by their communities as serious runners, largely due to sexist myths, like "ladies don't sweat." (My high school grammar teacher in my rural school had a favorite expression to help with verb usage: "Boys sweat, girls perspire.") The women runners I've talked with are constantly fighting the anonymity given them by their community. They fight it each time they set out for a run, and the three competitors in Little Rock fight it each time they cross the finish line.

I've interviewed women who run 7 miles, those who do 35-45 miles, and the competitors, who log 70 miles or more each week. All of the women noted similar changes in their life-styles, which they attribute directly to running: (1) alterations in diet and new attitudes toward nutrition, (2) immediate and sustained weight loss, (3) new feelings of strength and confidence in their bodies, (4) increased sense of self-esteem, and (5) the initial motivation to get in shape soon gives way to a joyous satisfaction gained from the running experience alone.

Lou Peyton, the first Arkansas woman to qualify for the Boston

Once a sport dominated by men, running became much more integrated in the seventies as women's races attracted thousands. (Photo by Jeff Johnson)

Marathon, began running nine years ago after the birth of her first child. She says, "People have been staring at me for a long time." Although Peyton now averages 70 miles a week, she still remembers the first day she ventured outside. "I ran a quarter of a mile and thought I was going to die. But I had loved that quarter—I got a free feeling that very first time. During the first few months, I began to feel more positive about myself, and of course the weight loss came immediately."

One senses a serenity, an equilibrium about Lou Peyton—a strength from within. She radiates the same inner calm I have observed before in people who have practiced yoga for many years— a "centering," a quiet acceptance of life's challenges, joys, and its inevitable frustrations. She shows this acceptance in her voice as she describes her years growing up in Vicksburg, Mississippi, where she tried out for the ninth grade track team but didn't make the cut. "There was no proper or adequate teaching for the girls, and I didn't know anything about sprinting. I was on the girls basketball team, but here again, you either learned on your own, or you didn't.... There was little encouragement to excel."

Although she qualified for Boston in October, 1977 at Crowley,

Louisiana, with a time of 3:27, a subsequent femoral artery injury and corrective surgery interrupted her running for four months. So Peyton will have to wait for another chance at Boston. During her four-month hiatus, she walked her 70-mile week, but now she's ecstatic about getting back to running. "After losing the ability to run, and then getting it back, I love and appreciate it so much more. I will do a 3:13 marathon this year, I know I will."

Pat Wyatt, a part-time teacher and occasional actress in musicals, is Arkansas' only entrant in this year's Boston meet. I talked with her briefly before she went on her weekly 20-mile run. Wyatt, thirty-one, runs 80 miles each week, and hopes to improve on her White Rock (Dallas) qualifying time of 3:28 in the Boston classic by concentrating now on intervals and hill work.

Wyatt is a self-confessed "Tulsa tom-boy," who was encouraged by her parents to compete "in anything." Though she originally chose the tough world of the theater, she now sees running as the perfect equalizer. "No one says you aren't pretty enough; no one is able to use any other silly criteria traditionally used on women; you just *run*."

Although Lou Peyton and Pat Wyatt are the first Arkansas women to qualify for the Boston Marathon, no local paper has written a word about their achievements. Wyatt admits that one time she tried to publicize a local race by writing the story copy herself. "They didn't print it. There were some good times that day in unbelievable heat, and they didn't print anything."

Wyatt was the only woman I interviewed who prefers to run accompanied by others, especially in distances over 6 miles. The danger inherent in running alone, particularly on isolated country roads, was mentioned by all the women with whom I talked. But this element was usually dismissed with a shrug, or "I'm usually up too early and moving too fast for the weirdos...."

Beth Walker, twenty-six, after running for one year, ran a 3:39 marathon at White Rock. Walker certainly must be destined to be Arkansas' answer to Gayle Barron, with her tall, graceful body, long blonde hair, and luminous, glowing eyes. Beth says she does get bothered by truck drivers during her 60-mile weeks, and frequently receives hoots of derision and bothersome language from passing drivers, "especially from men in pick-up trucks; they've got to be the very worst!" Walker refuses to be daunted by any of this, and is committed to qualifying for Boston, 1979. "Running has given me a tremendous amount of self-confidence," she says. "My diet is also so much better—steak or red meat sounds terrible; fresh fruits and vegetables, bread, and milk have become vital."

I asked her if she has had any difficulties adjusting her part-time physical therapy work and her family obligations with her running. She answered, "Running comes first—everything else fits in."

Since Walker and Peyton work on a part-time basis in a local running store, they have had an opportunity to observe new women runners as they come in to try on shoes, get warm-ups, and look through the running literature. According to them, "They're eager to get started. If they're ready to pay $25.00 for shoes, they're ready to commit themselves to running."

One of these new customers is a veteran neighborhood walker, recently converted to running. She says that after two months of running, she senses that her body is "working harder and the post-running time is definitely more relaxing than the period immediately following my walking."

Another new runner of five months, now up to 7 miles a week, told me that her problems vanished—or at least became much smaller—after a run. She confided that although she loves running, she doesn't want "running to run me." Another runner, after running 3 miles a day for over a year, suddenly stopped for a similar reason. "I felt that I had become quite crazy about this thing, quite fanatical, so I wanted to stop for awhile. I went back to it after six months. I've gained a lot of strength from the recent literature about other women who run. Now I know I'm not so crazy."

For all of these women, running has been something they've discovered on their own, perhaps encouraged by a husband or another male runner, but without any formal training or coaching. The gradual realization of Title IX's goals of nondiscrimination by sex will change this training vacuum, as more girls in rural America are allowed into their school's athletic structure. Eventually it will no longer be necessary for a girl to be only a sports groupie—a pom-pom girl, a cheerleader, or a majorette. Eventually, women runners of all colors will be able to profit by proper coaching, and enjoy the support of their community's population and its media. At least today there are more well known women runners than the lone Wilma Rudolph of the sixties. Today, there are many women outside the big cities who are running anonymously. But they're running hard.

4

The Prefontaine Legend

by Tom Jordan

S omeday, as those who saw him run grow old, the memories and
emotions will surely fade, and the name Steve Prefontaine will
become a distant drum, beating softly against the consciousness of
the living. Then, the distance prodigies of that time will read of his
records, his causes, his life—and shrug. It is the way of things, but
those people will be the losers.

Steve Roland "Pre" Prefontaine was born January 25, 1951, and
died in a one-car crash on May 30, 1975, in Eugene, Oregon. In the
twenty-four years between, he became the best and most famous
distance runner in American history. Early on, as a ninth grader in
coastal Coos Bay, Oregon, he discovered that the longer the distance
the better he liked it. From that time to the day he was killed ten
years later, Pre held every American record from 2,000 to 10,000
meters, except for the 1,500/mile.

Were that the sum of the man, his story could be told between the
ellipses of a University of Oregon pressbook:

> STEVE PREFONTAINE: 5-9/145...Hometown, Coos Bay, Ore....Major,
> Communications...Prep 2-mile record-holder (8:41.5 in 1969)...4th in the
> 1972 Olympic Games, Munich, W.G....Only 4-time NCAA track and field
> champion in one event, 3-mile...Never lost at his home track at a distance
> over a mile...American record-holder at 2,000, 3,000, 5,000, & 10,000 meters
> ...Oregon team captain, 1973....

Pre was a personality unique in running history. He was fired with
an enormous energy that lasted long after he had left the training
track. He was possessed with a great confidence that many, at times
correctly in the early years, termed arrogance.

While going to Marshfield High School, Pre found time to hold
down three part-time jobs in between his wins in the state meet 2-
mile his junior and senior years. He did not endear himself to his
opponents during those years, once taking a swing at a rival during a
cross-country race, another time turning around and running back-
ward, so great was his lead.

In his senior year, he set the national 2-mile high school record and chose Oregon over dozens of other colleges. By this time, the self-styled "hick" from the tough town of Coos Bay was brash enough to think he could do anything he put his mind to, on the track or off.

"He was just pretty naive as a freshman," reflects Bill Dellinger, the Oregon coach. "He was someone who didn't know any better and went out and did whatever he said he was going to do. We nick-named him 'The Rube.'"

Pre showed that his talent was of the sticking kind by winning the NCAA 3-mile in his freshman year in 13:22.0. The next year, he raced 19 times, set an American record in the 5,000 meters, and lost only once, taking second in a mile race in 3:57.4.

Fame was coming to him, and the fans, especially in Eugene, flocked to watch him as he would grind his opponents into the track. That done, he would drive himself on—alone—to the finish. The spectators loved the fact that he gave 100 percent every time, as well as his brashness in predicting the victories that always came at Eugene. But what attracted the legions of fans was something more than a string of wins on the track. Ralph Mann would become Pre's friend and European touring partner in the summers after the Munich Olympic Games. He comments on the charisma that surrounded the well-publicized figure of Steve Prefontaine. "He had this magnetism that just drew people toward him. He had the per-sonality that people would just take to. It was strange, because many times we discussed it, and he said it was just the way he acted, nothing unnatural. He didn't know what it was, and I couldn't figure it out just by watching it...."

By 1971, the year before the Olympics, Steve was a "personality," known for his running, and defined by it.

> I hate the image of being a super jock, an untouchable. When I'm on campus, I'll walk by a group of people and they'll whisper, "Guess who just walked by." These are things I know I have to live with, but still they can get me down once in a while. That's one of the reasons I'm living in the trailer.

To escape the limelight, Pre bought a trailer in Springfield, down the road from Eugene, and settled in for two years. His roommate during that time was Pat Tyson, who gives a glimpse of what the off-track personality of a maturing Steve Prefontaine was like during those college years.

> It was a small place—not much privacy. But he was very kind, considerate. I lived there a year-and-a-half, and we never had a fight, never argued. The

Steven Prefontaine, running here with his hero Gerry Lindgren (#485) and indoor mile record-holder Dick Buerkle (#222), completely dominated middle- and long-distance running in the U.S. in the early seventies. He was killed in an auto crash at age twenty-four. (Photo by Rober Kasper)

phone would ring a lot. I almost felt that I was Prefontaine's Answering Service, but I didn't *really* feel that way.

I began to settle down a little bit for the first time, seeing him so hyperactive. I thought my day was filled up, and I saw him doubling that. He'd often do two things at once. Instead of just writing a letter, he'd be writing a letter and eating at the same time.

After a meet, we might go out for dinner and have a couple of beers. Steve wasn't one to sit back and think—he'd go from table to table and visit. He liked to move about and talk to people.

Pre was what you would call a "toucher." He wasn't scared to come up and look you in the eye and touch you. He was a very warm person. He'd hug you, and in this society the way it is, you don't hug other males. But Pre was never ashamed to do that, ever.

In 1972, Pre drove himself as never before, preparing for the Olympic 5,000 meters in September. Under the guidance of Oregon coaches Bill Bowerman and Bill Dellinger, Pre went from one victory to the next. But in that spring and summer of 1972, perhaps no race held the drama, or revealed as much about the man, as the Olympic Trials 5,000 meter final. Here for the first time, the twenty-one-year-old Prefontaine competed against the only American thought to be in his class in the 5,000, thirty-four-year-old George Young. Young was a major figure in the 5,000, having held the American record before Pre. But the two men had never raced until now. The people filling the stands at Hayward Field in Eugene—Pre's home track— had the feeling that if Pre were going to suffer his first defeat at his distance in Eugene, George would be the man to do it. Young had experience, speed, and extraordinary toughness.

On Sunday, July 9, twelve men toed the line for the final on a warm evening. For the first few circuits of the 12½-lap race, they jockeyed for position. Then, as Pre pushed from the third lap on, the twelve dropped one by one from the lead group. By the ninth lap, only two remained with Prefontaine: Leonard Hilton and George Young. Famed track writer Cordner Nelson called the race:

> Now Pre began the task of breaking Young, one of the guttiest runners in track history. Pre ran a lap in 63.4, which dropped Hilton 25 yards behind, but the veteran Young held on grimly. With the crowd roaring, Prefontaine began a remarkable drive. A lap in 61.5 weakened Young and left Hilton 75 yards back, but Pre was only beginning. He increased the pace and opened an 8-yard lead with a lap to go. Young had to surrender, and Pre completed the lap in 58.7.

Marty Liquori was there at the finish. "The thing I remember about it was that coming off the last turn, Pre was completely dead—just wobbling up the straightaway. He hit the inside rail and almost stumbled, and the fans were loving it, because he was completely spent when he hit the line."

Later, as he signed autographs for the multitudes, he explained to Blaine Newnham of the *Eugene Register-Guard* what it meant to run in front of the people in his hometown:

> I'll tell you one thing, I love every one of them. I've thought about the Olympic Games every day of my life since 1968, but there is a breaking point in each race when you wonder if all the sacrifice is really worth it.
> You think "why should I do this? I don't have to run this hard." But that's when I think about them. They keep me going.

The Olympic Games themselves were a disappointment for Steve. He had envisioned them as a meeting of the world's best athletes; what he found were politics and murder. The killing of the Israeli athletes affected Pre greatly, and from that moment his enthusiasm for the upcoming competition waned. Earlier, he had said of the Olympic Final, still months away, "I want a race where it comes down to who's toughest. . . ."

But as the pace dragged through an 8:56.4 2-mile, he was running fourth. Suddenly, he took the lead and ran 2:03.7 for the next 800 meters. Many in the thirteen-man field dropped, but Lasse Viren, who was still there, assumed the lead with two laps to go. Pre waited for the last backstretch to make his bid for Olympic gold. Twice he tried to go by Viren, and twice he was cut off by Mohammed Gamoudi of Tunisia. Chastened, he gathered for the final home-straight, but his answering power was not there. Pre slowed, stumbling in exhaustion, was passed by Ian Stewart of Great Britain, and attained the bronze.

Pre recognized that he was, in Bill Bowerman's words, "a kid running among men," and that time was ahead of him. But the defeat was nonetheless terribly depressing. Under different circumstances, he felt, the race could have been his. He was encouraged, though, by the support he received when he returned to the United States. "If anything will keep me running," he said, "it's the fantastic response. Complete strangers write wishing me well. The local people are so great. I would have to move away from Oregon. I couldn't retire here."

After Munich, Pre did not compete in the fall. But he did keep running, an activity as necessary to him as eating or sleeping. In the indoor season of 1973, he ran well, even running a 57.6 last quarter in a 3:59.2 race of a mile, to beat, among others, Marty Liquori. His two-mile wins were all the more impressive.

"He would come to these indoor races and just kill the fields," recalls Liquori, "and win by half a lap or so, running 8:25. I think the biggest thing in Pre's mind was to please the fans. He would respond to the crowd and pick up the pace before it should have been picked up, doing things that take a lot of mental and physical energy. I think it took a lot out of him. . . ."

This expenditure of energy may have ultimately hurt Steve when the important international races in Europe began in July. For all of Pre's success in the United States, he took his share of defeats when he traveled to Europe. "He wasn't prepared to go over to Europe to lose," recalls Oregon teammate Lars Kaupang of Norway. "I think as soon as he lost once, he had problems. He started to think he was out of shape, or that he was injured. It really got him down."

One race, against Harald Norpoth of West Germany, typified the frustration he encountered in Europe. Despite a sciatic nerve flare-up, Pre pushed the pace through an 8:02 3,000 meters, and then tried to bear down. Instead, the wraithlike Norpoth sprinted away for a 3.2-second win over the last 200 meters. "Anybody but him," declared Pre, who had lost to Norpoth before. "I'll be back."

Pre cut short his tour and returned to Eugene, later training with some members of the Oregon team. One day, shortly after his galling defeat by Norpoth, a group of Oregon runners were out on a road run. One of them, Dave Taylor, is a runner of slender physique. According to him:

> Guys on the team used to give me hard time about how I'm built, so I had this T-shirt made up with *Norpoth* on the back. About halfway through the run, I whipped off my sweatshirt and took off sprinting in front of Pre. He went into a rage, and came up and grabbed me and started choking me, and said, "If that skinny sonuvabitch, if he ever does that to me again, here's what I'll do to him," and here he was beating me up on the run. It was in fun, and he was smiling, but he let us know that he didn't really appreciate what the guy had done.

It was on these road runs that Steve relaxed a bit, and became less competitive. "That's where I really got to know him," reflects his friend Mark Feig, "on the roads, where we could talk. That's where I first learned of his warmth, and where he was headed."

The question of his future was one that stayed close and was worrisome to Steve. He was disillusioned with the Olympics, and 1976 was a long way off. He was tired of being poor, and he teemed with ideas to make his mark. One was to quit amateur track, and run for the International Track Association. His friend Laura Hollister remembers a conversation she had with Steve in 1974.

> Once I asked, was he going to do it, turn pro? No, probably not, he said. Sometimes he was really thinking about quitting. He had spent so much of his time running. He didn't want to be "like an old football player who could never die," he said. He wanted more than a good track record out of his life.

He wanted people to know there was more to him than that, that he was intelligent and hardworking and creative. Not that he drank lots of beer and was on an ego trip. He wanted to give the people of Eugene—"My People"—more. When he thought about quitting track or turning pro, he thought about his people and how much support they had given him and he didn't want to let them down, ever. So he would keep running, until the Olympics at least. That was his decision. No pro track.

That decision made, close friends noticed a renewed enthusiasm for running in Pre that had been missing to some extent since Munich. He trained hard, preparing for a "year of Europe" in 1974. His first big test was a 3-mile race against Frank Shorter in Eugene. As they warmed up together, Pre and Shorter exchanged thoughts about racing goals. "There was an understanding between us that we would go together, sharing the lead until a half-mile to go, and then whoever won, won," says Frank. "But the object was to run under 13 minutes."

The agreement to share laps worked through nine laps, and then Pre led for three straight. They had entered that stage of fast races where the protests of the body overrule the willingness of the mind. With a quarter-mile remaining, Frank poised himself beside Pre and suddenly shot into the lead. The din, already awesome, increased in volume. Don Kardong, running alone in third, had never heard anything like it. "I almost stopped," he says, "because it was *really* loud, and they weren't even watching me." Pre and Shorter approached the last bend with the outcome still in doubt. Then Steve started one of his fastest homestretch drives, winning by six-tenths in a new American record of 12:51.4. It was perhaps his greatest race ever.

As Frank and Pre warmed down together, the Eugene fans applauded both runners. One friend down on the crowded infield asked Pre, "What happened out there? I thought you slowed down."

"Yeah, I almost let him win," said Pre. "I was just thinking it wasn't that big a deal. Then, I don't know, something inside of me just said, 'Hey, wait a minute—I want to beat him,' and I just took off!"

Later, when the reporters asked how he had pulled it out, Pre's answer encapsulated the strength he received from racing in Eugene. "The idea of losing the three at Hayward Field and the idea of losing my specialty to someone who wasn't running his specialty. Mostly the idea of losing in front of my people.

"They haven't forgotten about me."

That summer, Pre ran faster races than any American before at 2,000 meters, 2 miles, and 5,000 meters. By the standard of the clock, Pre's month in Europe was a smashing success. Yet by the toughest standards—his own—Prefontaine's summer in Europe was unsatisfactory. He had not defeated the top men in the world in his event. More typically, he finished second, or third, often leading until the last home-straight. It was especially dissatisfying, since some were beginning to stereotype him as capable of winning in Eugene, but not in Europe. "Just how tough is Steve Prefontaine?" asked Jon Hendershott of *Track & Field News.*

"When he's ready, very tough," said Pre. "When he's not ready, not very. Well, tougher than average anytime. It's just a matter of priorities, how tough you want to be. The toughness comes from my training and with the proper training I'm very tough, at home or away from home. My toughness is in my ability, when I want to win, to go out and do it."

His last season, 1975, looked to be his best ever. His indoor season was a strong one, and outdoors during April and May Pre seemed to be rounding into shape. A planned series of races with Olympic champion Lasse Viren fell through—some say because Viren feared Pre's good form, as evidenced by a 28:09.4 in the 10,000 meters. After initial feelings of frustration caused by Viren's cancellation, Steve was understanding. "There were meets in Europe when I didn't show up to run against him," he shrugged.

He went ahead with the tour around Oregon—to small towns like Madras, Burnaby, and his home of Coos Bay. Pre set a 2,000-meter American record at Coos Bay, solo, on the same track where the people of Coos Bay saw him run some of his best high school races.

Finally, there was the last race, over 5,000 meters in Eugene, against Frank Shorter, filling in for the missing Viren. For much of the race, the drive and aggressiveness the fans were used to seeing in Pre were oddly lacking. When he accelerated to 63-second pace with three laps to go, the 7,000 spectators in the stands reacted vocally. There was relief that Pre still had that spark at Hayward Field in Eugene. He finished in 13:23.8, just 1.9 off his own American record, in his first serious 5,000 of 1975. His winning string at distances over a mile in Eugene was extended to 25 straight. He never lost.

The next morning, the people of Eugene awoke to the mind-numbing news that Pre's car had gone out of control and overturned on the way back from a postmeet party, and that Steve was dead. Parents groped vainly for a way to tell the news to children who had run after Pre for autographs the day before. How could they explain that they could no longer shout "Pre! Pre!" as he surged away from all opposition, seeming to give everything, and then giving even more.

The records will be surpassed and the times beaten, but the rapport with "his people," and his ability to draw energy from them, will not be forgotten. Those who ever saw Pre rounding the last bend and driving himself on to the finish will long remember that picture of power and grace.

"Some people create with words, or with music, or with a brush and paints," Pre once said. "I like to make something beautiful when I run."

Perhaps that is the lasting legacy of Steve Prefontaine.

5

A Decade of Marty Liquori

by Jim Lilliefors

The Marty Liquori story—among the more interesting sagas in sport, filled with drama and pathos—continues to unfold. More than ten years ago Liquori, then a high school student from Essex Catholic in Newark, New Jersey, ran a 3:59.8 mile. He then became the third, and to date the final, high-schooler to break the 4-minute mile barrier. Jim Ryun set his world-record 3:51.1 in that same race. A year later, the 19-year-old Liquori earned a place on the Olympic team and went to Mexico City to compete in the 1,500 meters, along with Ryun. He made it through the preliminary heats and qualified for the final. But, in the process, he experienced the first of a succession of Olympic-year heartbreaks, when he injured his foot. Diagnosed as a stress fracture, the injury slowed him considerably in the final; he was forced to watch from across the track as Kip Keino won the gold medal.

He knew then that, more than anything else, he wanted to return in 1972. "I planned my whole life around it," Liquori recalls. "Everything I did between 1968 and 1972 was designed to help me at Munich. I never made that kind of commitment before and haven't since."

Liquori's philosophy at the time, as opposed to his current view, was that record-setting is less important than victories and medals, because no one can ever take the latter two away.

"Running a fast time is really no monument to your greatness," Liquori said in 1970. "We know that within 20 years the athletes are going to be surpassing anything we can do anyway. So the way you have to judge a person is how he did against his competition."

Indeed, until the mid-seventies, Liquori was thought of as a "competitor," who ran to win, not to break records. When he raced Kip

315

Keino, and Keino gave up on the final stretch, Liquori slowed too
and yelled, "don't quit, dammit." Ryun, on the other hand, has been
considered more of a "time" runner.

In 1969 and again in 1971, Liquori was rated the top miler in the
nation by *Track and Field News*, beating such top athletes as Ryun,
Keino, and Bodo Tummler. His NCAA victory over Ryun in 1969
made him the first man in five years to beat the world record-holder
over a mile. A week later, at the AAU championships, Liquori again
prevailed. This time Ryun stepped off the track after just two laps
and entered an eighteen-month retirement.

When the two raced next, in May 1971, the event received as much
media attention as any mile race before or since. Many were skeptical of Liquori, whose best time for the mile was only 3:57.2
compared to Ryun's 3:51.1, and thought the only reason he had been
rated so well was because Ryun had been in retirement. But that
May, Liquori beat Ryun by inches in 3:54.6, improving his own best
time by nearly three seconds.

"That was so satisfying," he says, "after working so hard and
withstanding so much pressure."

Liquori was especially successful indoors, winning several NCAA
and AAU titles, and going unbeaten in races at Madison Square
Garden. Sometimes, though, he would attract boos for his occasionally demonstrative physical tactics, which won him the nickname
"the Man with the Golden Elbows."

Off the track, Liquori drank beer, wore bellbottoms, and bet
money on billiards; sports magazines called him controversial. "Just
because I'm a runner doesn't mean I have to spend my life as an
advertisement for clean living," he said at the time, rejecting a
stereotype that often seemed to fit long-distance runners.

Yet even amidst his success, Liquori was still profoundly worried
about the threat of further injury. "It constantly bothers me," he
said in a 1970 *Runner's World* interview. "It hangs over my head
like a dark cloud. I think it's going to be my biggest problem in the
future—these feet."

His problem returned the following year, with miserable timing. A
torn foot muscle, incurred during cross-country running in the fall of
1971, failed to heal, and in fact worsened, during the Olympic year.
After consulting several podiatrists and orthopedists, and valiantly
trying to pursue his dream in spite of the problem, he finally
resigned himself to another waiting period. The one blessing was
that ABC signed him as an announcer for the Olympics, greatly

hastening a career he had expected would take considerably longer to develop.

Between 1972 and 1976, competition in the mile and 1,500 meters became increasingly tenacious, with Filbert Bayi of Tanzania and John Walker of New Zealand dominating. Liquori found himself finishing behind these relative newcomers, even though he was improving his times, to a 3:52 mile. He started to concentrate on longer events, notably the 5,000.

By the next Olympic year, 1976, he was the American 2-mile record-holder, and one of the fastest runners in the world at 5,000 meters. It was the 5,000 that he planned to run at Montreal.

But in June, he suffered a slight muscle tear, and at the AAU championships, he pulled a hamstring muscle. When he was not healed by the Olympic Trials, he was forced to drop out. He went to the Olympics, again as an announcer with ABC.

Although the disappointment of a third Olympic-year injury was obviously great, it was not enough to discourage him from continuing running. "I'll stick with it a while longer," he said after the Olympics. "I'm so close to the world record in the 5000."

Liquori recommenced training late that summer, competing in several road and cross-country races, though with only moderate success. He was slowly building, once again, into top competitive form.

By the summer of 1977, he was running as well as he ever had. In August, at Zurich, Switzerland, he beat many of the top 5,000-meter runners in the world, setting an American record of 13:16.0. "That was maybe the most satisfying race of my career," Liquori says. "It felt so easy and there was a magical feeling running against the best runners in the world. I knew that night that I could get the world record."

Shortly afterward, he further lowered the American record at the World Cup, running 13:15.1, and finishing second only to Ethiopia's Miruts Yifter.

"I feel very good now," Liquori said after the World Cup race, "but I'm not in top shape. I will be next year, though."

Now Marty Liquori intends to make a total commitment to running, something he didn't do in 1977. His goal is to attain the 5,000-meter world record.

"Right now, there are a half-dozen people who are capable of breaking the world record, but I know that, on a given day, I can run with any of them."

Whether he continues running beyond 1978 is uncertain, and depends in part on whether or not he sets the world record. Because of his Olympic frustrations, Liquori's running is now based more on short-term, though still very intense, goals. It is no longer his style to dedicate himself to a single goal for four years. "I'll decide [soon] whether I'll continue running, whether it's worth it. I may not. The Olympics aren't driving me anymore the way they once did. I devoted my whole life to the 1972 Olympics and after that it hasn't meant as much. Nineteen-eighty is simply not that important to me now. I'm more concerned with what I can do next year."

He admits that another Marty Liquori is increasingly intruding on his running career: Marty Liquori the businessman. This man, who once said he wanted to be a millionaire by the time he was thirty, seems, at age twenty-eight, to be nearing his goal. His sporting goods chain, Athletic Attic, already has about 80 branches across the country.

"Jimmy Carnes and I planned to open 25 stores in the year after the Olympics and we ended up opening about 40. We've got a lot of good people working for us now across the country and we would like to be able to open four or five stores a month. We're really only just starting to grow."

Liquori also plans to continue his work with ABC, at least for another year.

Despite the plans, though, the Marty Liquori story, never typified by predictability, will probably contain more surprise in the future.

Marty Liquori was the world's top miler in the late sixties and early seventies. Now, he has one of the best 5,000-meter times in the world. In this race, the 1977 World Cup, Liquori finished second to Miruts Yifter. Liquori has a record of bad luck in Olympic years. (Photo by Mark Shearman)

6

An Interview with Cierpinski

by Brian Chapman

More than anything, Waldemar Cierpinski is a product of his environment. And since that environment is East Germany, the product has turned out to be the reigning Olympic marathoner champion. Not only was his victory at Montreal unexpected, but the ease with which he won has confounded so-called running experts who could not comprehend Cierpinski's lifetime of preparation.

Waldemar Cierpinski, twenty-seven, grew up in a small farming village near Halle, where he lives with his wife Marita and their three-year-old son Andre. When Waldemar was twelve years old, his running potential was spotted, and he joined Aufbau Nienburg, a factory sports club, where he received intensive coaching and training. Cierpinski showed enough talent and tenacity to be sent to a special boarding school in Halle, where he was groomed for the steeplechase.

By 1970, he had graduated from the boarding school and won his first major title—the 2,000-meter steeplechase at Spartakiad '70. The next couple of years were painful for Cierpinski because of frequent injuries suffered due to a risky hurdling technique. Though he was the national steeplechase champion in 1972, his injuries often prevented him from his true love—running long distances. So, in 1974, he switched his training to the marathon.

While vacationing in Czechoslovakia, Cierpinski ran his first marathon in the 1974 Kosice. His 2:20 in terrible conditions was good enough to place him third ahead of such notables as Ron Hill and Jack Foster. He returned to Kosice the next year; though he lowered his time by 3 minutes, Cierpinski finished seventh.

But the 5'7'', 128-pound runner remained an unknown commodity until his triumph at Montreal. In the following interview, arranged for Brian Chapman and *Runner's World* by Doug Gilbert of the *Montreal Gazette*, Cierpinski reveals for the first time the thoughts, motivations, and training techniques that led to the biggest victory of his life.

Runner's World: Despite your Olympic victory, why haven't there been any interviews with you published in any North American magazine?

Cierpinski: No western sportswriters have approached me since Montreal.

Runner's World: Let's talk about Montreal. What were your expectations for the marathon?

Cierpinski: Earlier in the year, I felt confident because I had won our Olympic trials with 2:12:21, which ranked me fifth in the world at that time. However, when the Montreal marathon arrived, I was facing 20 runners with faster times than mine. I was expecting no better than tenth, and yet I did have a secret wish to get a bronze medal.

Runner's World: What were your impressions of the race?

Cierpinski: I was emotionally impressed with the way we were received by the 70,000 spectators. Out on the course, there were so many enthusiastic onlookers even though it was raining. It stimulated me very much. Everyone was calling out "Shorter" and "Rodgers," so I felt like an unknown runner. Even the people at home watching on television did not know there was an East German runner among the leaders.

Runner's World: Was that because you wore a white singlet instead of the usual blue GDR colors?

Cierpinski: Yes. I had to wear a white shirt because it reflects the sun's rays. It wasn't until I took the lead that people called out my name and urged me on. This was very helpful.

Runner's World: Early in the race, Frank Shorter was running very strong. What were your thoughts at that stage?

Cierpinski: Shorter ran with surges, just as we expected. His first surge came at 23 kilometers. It was hard to catch up at that point because it was unexpected and Shorter did it with such great strength. In fact, it broke up the field. Since I had enjoyed good training with no injuries, I decided to catch up with him. I had been told to stick with the leaders, and I had this in mind since Shorter was the favorite. My only fear was that by catching him, I would ruin my own pace.

East Germany's Waldemar Cierpinski surprised everyone with his marathon victory
and record at the 1976 Olympics, beating favored Frank Shorter by nearly a minute.
(Photo by Mark Shearman)

Runner's World: Why didn't his surges ruin your pace?

Cierpinski: Because each successive surge had less distance and was done with less strength. They became easier to make up. As the race went on, I started to gain confidence.

Runner's World: When did you first think you could win it?

Cierpinski: Just after 30 kilometers. I decided to challenge for the lead because I felt Shorter was fading, and I had all the reserve I needed. So at about 32-33 kilometers, I went right past him after his final surge.

Runner's World: What were your thoughts as you took the lead?

Cierpinski: It was very emotional for me. Earlier, everything had been in Frank's favor, and then it became man-to-man.

Runner's World: What would you have done if the pace had been slower?

Cierpinski: Nothing. I never intended to make a move. I was expecting no better than tenth.

Runner's World: What were your thoughts as you ran into the stadium and you heard the GDR national anthem being played for your winning women's relay team?

Cierpinski: I couldn't hear the anthem because everyone was shouting as I approached the stadium. I was overcome by the event and I had an indescribable feeling that made me dizzy.

Runner's World: Why did you run an extra lap?

Cierpinski: I was mixed up at the finish because an official told me to stay in lane three. I saw the "one lap to go" sign, but it didn't register. Also 2 kilometers from the finish, I looked back and saw Shorter just behind, so I wanted to make certain of the win and sprint home with a fast final 100 meters if necessary. I was concentrating so hard that I didn't react to the one lap sign. Also, it was raining and I couldn't see it clearly. Then I came around and saw the "one lap to go" sign, so I went around again. When I finished, it still said I had one lap to go.

Runner's World: What thoughts did you have as you crossed the finish line?

Cierpinski: I was furious with myself because I could've done a faster time if I had known the sign meant just one lap to go on the track. I could've become the fourth fastest marathoner ever in the world.

Runner's World: How many marathons had you run before Montreal?

Cierpinski: In 1974 I was vacationing in Czechoslovakia and feeling in good humor, so I decided to try a marathon in Kosice. I came in third with a 2:20:20. In 1975, I ran Kosice again and came in seventh with 2:17:30. My first serious marathon was at Karl Marx-Stadt in 1976, which I won with 2:13:57. Six weeks later, I won our Olympic trials and nine weeks later was Montreal.

Runner's World: Your victory certainly surprised most marathon fans. To what do you credit your great performance?

Cierpinski: Our team spirit played a great part. I owe my victory, to a great extent, to the challenge of my teammates' successes.

Runner's World: Did you have a special diet?

Cierpinski: No, I maintained my general diet which is 60 percent carbohydrate and 20-25 percent protein and fat.

Runner's World: What about carbohydrate overload?

Cierpinski: I only heard about that after the race. When they interviewed me in Montreal, I knew nothing about it. Since then I have examined it, but I don't think it is good for everyone.

Runner's World: Where did you do most of your training?

Cierpinski: In and around Halle, where I live.

Runner's World: But we visited Halle a few days ago and the air seemed very polluted. It didn't seem like a good place to train.

Cierpinski: It is good enough to produce an Olympic champion. I usually run in a nearby forest area we call "the marshes."

Runner's World: Can you describe your training routine?

Cierpinski: It consists mainly of running, but I also play football [soccer] and cycle. I hate to swim. During my winter conditioning period, I just run long distances until I feel I've run enough. This is usually between 15 and 20 kilometers a day, though occasionally I'll go up to 60 kilometers. To help my leg speed, I often run 5,000-meter races on the track.

Runner's World: Yes, we noticed earlier this week you ran in the Spartakiad International Meet.

Cierpinski: (*embarrassed*) Oh, I was expecting a better performance, but I was only running because the people expected me to. Since my victory at Montreal, I have been under much stress. I have many things to do and so many friends and people are now interested in me. I have a busload of letters that all must be answered.

Runner's World: Does this surprise you?

Cierpinski: Yes it does. I was surprised to become a hero to the people and find that they had voted me GDR Sportsman of the Year. I've received letters from all strata of the population saying that seeing me push ahead on television was one of the biggest moments of their lives.

Runner's World: How did you start running?

Cierpinski: When I didn't fare badly at the regular cross-country runs and competitions at school, I began to develop an interest in athletics, and made up my mind to give running a try.

Runner's World: What role did your coaches have in your development?

Cierpinski: My former instructor, Manfred Bringezu, passed on to me his enthusiasm for sport, and gave me guidelines for the future. At the Chemie Sports Club, Jorg Ramlow coached me; he gave me an interest in the arts, discussed literature, went to the theater, and listened to classical music.

Runner's World: Did you ever compete in the Spartakiad?

Cierpinski: Yes, I took part in two Spartakiad finals in Berlin. For me, as for many other GDR athletes, the Spartakiad was the first highlight of my sporting career. At the time, a sporting event of such wide dimensions, with such an atmosphere, was unique for me. I was not only able to gather valuable experience in sports, but I also had many moving experiences I will never forget. I am thinking of the forums and discussions with leading representatives of mass organizations or government, as well as cultural events and sight-seeing tours.

Runner's World: How did you do?

Cierpinski: Although my first start was 11 years ago, I still remember the details. My coach had entered me in the 1,500-meter steeplechase final and the 7.5-kilometer road race for 15- and 16-year-olds. I was so overpowered by the overwhelming atmosphere of 10,000 boys and girls, and by the milling crowd that I erroneously went to the wrong stadium before the steeplechase. I hastened to the right stadium, arriving at the last moment, dripping with sweat. I quickly changed and rushed to the start. I clocked a new personal best in the heats and made up my mind to win a medal in the final. But inexperienced as I was, I fell at the start of the final. Though I got up quickly and continued, the fall had cost me too much strength. I finished fifth, and was disappointed because I knew I could've done better. From that, I learned to avoid rash and unsurveyable situations, and took home the silver medal in the road race.

Runner's World: Why didn't the steeplechase work out as your best event?

Cierpinski: Apart from all other reasons, the tempo over the 3,000-meter distance was simply too fast for me. Training for it certainly promoted the development of my basic speed, but the marathon distance was more my cup of tea.

Runner's World: What are your future racing plans?

Cierpinski: I've been concentrating on training for the 5,000 and 10,000 meters.

Runner's World: Some Canadians are hoping to organize a "Return of the Champions" marathon in Montreal next year. They want to invite five stars from the Olympic marathon and have maybe 3,000 other runners. Would you be interested?

Cierpinski: I cannot decide my future races by myself. They must fit into my program.

Runner's World: What about the 1980 Moscow marathon?

Cierpinski: I'm hoping.

7

Kings of the Marathon

by Jim Lilliefors

During the mid-seventies, American marathoning was dominated by two men—Frank Shorter and Bill Rodgers. Between them, they owned the five fastest marathon times in U.S. history.

FRANK SHORTER

Once, Frank Shorter was simply a good college runner at Yale, uncertain if he should pursue a vocation, run, or both. Whichever he chose, he would do well; it was just a matter of making the choice. In 1970, after trying medical school for eight weeks and dropping out, Frank chose running. Restless and working odd jobs, he moved across the country. Finally, he settled in Gainesville, Florida, where he soon enrolled at the University of Florida to run with Jack Bacheler "because I didn't have anywhere else to go."

Once committed to running, Shorter quickly tripled his mileage. In 1970, he won the AAU 6-mile.

"He surprised me a little," said Jack Bacheler, who in 1970 ranked as one of the nation's top 10,000-meter runners. "I didn't expect Frank to come quite that far."

Talking of his potential, Shorter then said, "It all depends on the importance you give to running. . . . [It involves] being able to sleep that much with being able to run that much—and wanting to run that much. . . . It's the compulsion to get out there and do it."

With his compulsion for greater mileage, Shorter was improving so fast he had no time to consider concrete goals. He wasn't yet striving for the Olympics; in fact, he spoke of the futility of aiming for a single long-term goal: "How long do you stand up there on that victory stand? It seems inconceivable to me to say it's got to be this or nothing."

Indeed, until the 1971 AAU championship, Frank Shorter had never run a marathon. His forte seemed to be the shorter distances. He was the American indoor record-holder in the 2-mile, and talked

327

of trying to break 4 minutes for the mile. In 1970, he had run several fast 10,000-meter races, including a victory at the AAU cross-country championship. But his style—fluid, buoyant, almost imponderable at times—seemed to favor longer races. After the 1971 indoor season, he finally decided to try a marathon. Preparing for that first marathon, his ambition was dizzying: "If I could run 2:15 my first time out, I wouldn't be disappointed."

He ran 2:17:44 at the AAU championship, second place behind Kenny Moore. "I have a feeling I'll do much better next time," he said shortly afterward. Later that summer, he began a string of marathon victories, winning the Pan American Games race at Cali, Colombia, with 2:22:40. There, he also took home a gold medal in the 10,000 meters. Between that race and the 1976 Olympics, Shorter won nearly all the marathons he entered.The only ones he did not win were the 1976 Honolulu race, which he "ran through" after Fukuoka, and a European race, which he was forced to drop out of with an injury while leading.

Late that year, Frank traveled to Japan with Kenny Moore to run the prestigious Fukuoka Marathon. "Whoever wins this will have to be a favorite at Munich," he told Moore before the race, showing an initial sign of crystallizing a goal. His victory in Japan, with 2:12:50.4, surprised many, and further fueled Shorter's drive.

John Parker, who shared a house with him in Gainesville during the fall and winter of 1971, witnessed the transformation. "It was during that time that I began to realize Frank Shorter was really serious," Parker said. "He had always been thoughtful (and occasionally downright "spacy"), but during that fall he seemed to shift gears. He became a mass of total concentration on an impossible goal. But I suppose that's how one accomplishes such goals."

His aim seemingly firm, Shorter worked hard all winter and spring, running 170-mile weeks at high altitude in Taos, New Mexico. At the Trials, he tied with Moore to lead the U.S. marathoners, at 2:15:57. He also won the 10,000 meters.

At Munich, the town in which he was born, Frank Shorter started with the leaders—imposing talents such as Ron Hill, Derek Clayton, and Karel Lismont—and ran with them until 15 kilometers, when he sped up. "It is a little scary to throw your cards on the table so early," he admitted afterward, "but if no one chases me I feel fine. . . . I ran a little harder and no one came with me. I pushed a little more and still no one. So I said okay. I guess this will be it." It was. "At 41 kilometers, I think I said to myself, 'My God, I've really done it.'"

In the mid-seventies, Frank Shorter (#244) was challenged by Boston runner Bill Rodgers (#228), who beat his   U.S.   record at the 1975 Boston Marathon. When they met in the 1976 Olympics Rodgers ran an inexplicably poor 2:25 for fortieth place, while Shorter placed second to Cierpinski. (Photo by Jeff Johnson)

Since no American had won the Olympic marathon since 1908, this event was never considered an American specialty. But this changed drastically after Shorter's victory. In 1971, Frank was the lone U.S. representative among the world's 15 fastest marathoners; by 1975, three of the five fastest were Americans. After Munich, there was a dramatic marathon boom in the United States. Although it's difficult to isolate any single contributing factor, Shorter's victory certainly had a part in it. In the years between the 1972 and 1976 Olympics, Shorter's name became a household word—a rare thing for a runner. He was a nationally recognized sports figure, featured on the cover of such magazines as *Life* and *Sports Illustrated*. Shorter was deluged with requests for interviews, training schedules, and advice. In 2 hours, 12 minutes, and 19.8 seconds, he had become the best-known American marathoner in history.

The intense concentration, developed a year earlier, finally let up. "I can do it now because I like it," he said.

To date, Frank Shorter's most effective year was 1972. Besides his marathon victory, he placed fifth in the 10,000 meters—behind such greats as Lasse Viren, Emiel Puttemans, and Miruts Yifter—setting an American record of 27:51.4. After Munich, he won the classy Springbank 11.6-mile race, and repeated as AAU cross-country champion. In December, he returned to Japan and ran the fastest marathon of his career, 2:10:30, an American record until 1975.

In the post-Olympic year, Frank still led the U.S. in marathoning, with 2:11:45, second best in the world. In 1974, he ran a U.S.-leading 2:11:31.

However, by 1975, Shorter's leadership in performance was threatened, even though his spirit and past accomplishments were still leading thousands into the sport. This change began late in 1974, when Shorter's four-year winning streak at the AAU cross-country meet was snapped by John Ngeno. Rather than finishing second or third, Shorter placed an oddly distant eleventh. In 1975, another streak was broken: it was the first year since 1970 that Shorter wasn't the U.S. leader in the marathon. Bill Rodgers ran his amazing 2:09:55 at Boston that year, beating Shorter's American record by more than half a minute. At that point, Shorter was far from the top of the U.S. list, with 2:16:29. Seven American runners ran faster than him. In shorter distances races, a close rivalry developed between Rodgers and Shorter, but Rodgers seemed to be gaining an edge.

Evidence of Shorter's faltering motivation was revealed in a March 1975 interview with *Track and Field News*. "If I decide that I want to go back and run another Olympics, then everything is going to have to be right and I'm really going to have to *want* to do it," he said. "Everyone says, 'Well, are you going back to another Olympics?' and the answer is a definite 'maybe.' Right now, it's probably 'no.'"

Yet by early 1976, Shorter's thinking and motivation had again turned to the Olympics. His previous victory had dimmed, and he seemed anxious once again. "I don't think about it anymore," he said of his 1972 victory, at the start of his 1976 quest. "It's something you do, then it's done, it's gone."

By the Olympic Trials, he was in top shape again, mentally and physically, and won in 2:11:51, 7 seconds ahead of Bill Rodgers. "It was just a good hard 20-mile run and then a nice jog home," was his description of the effort.

Unlike at Munich, attention was on him at Montreal. The pressure he spoke of in 1972 was much more profound in 1976; this time he was the favorite. Bill Rodgers, who had run faster, was still less known. Of course, few anticipated Waldemar Cierpinski's superb race—not even Cierpinski. "I expected to finish tenth," he said recently.

As in 1972, Shorter employed surging tactics, but this time he couldn't shake the field. He began his surges at 20 kilometers, but the lead group stuck. Gradually they began to drop behind — Rodgers, Viren, Lismont, and Drayton—but Cierpinski kept up. At 34 kilometers, Cierpinski broke away. Shorter never caught him. Besides the East German, the rain created problems for Shorter. "I don't run in the rain very well," he said. "I get tight." Shorter ended up with another medal, this time silver. Sportswriters immediately recorded the tale of his "defeat," but Shorter was hardly bitter. He had said, after all, back in 1971, "I don't consider coming in second losing. It's just not winning."

After the Games, Shorter's uncertainty returned. He was quoted in *People* magazine as saying he intended to return to cross-country skiing instead of running. He told a *Runner's World* interviewer, "I'm going to start practicing law pretty soon and not train very hard for about 2½ years." Meanwhile, he had opened a lucrative sporting goods store in his hometown of Boulder, Colorado, and was marketing a line of apparel bearing his name.

However, in the 1977 indoor season, Shorter ran an 8:27 2-mile, his best time in six years. In the final stretch of that race, he threw up his arms in obvious elation. Afterward, he told Bruce Jenner, "The marathon is still primary." Later that year, he discounted the rumors about skiing, claiming he'd been misinterpreted.

His great ambition seemed intact in 1977, though without the innocence that had characterized it six years earlier. He entered big money races across the country, sometimes even two races in different cities within a single weekend, and ended up injured. At the New York City Marathon, he dropped out at 17 miles.

With his various interests—business, law, running—still in conflict, Shorter's ambition seems as splintered as it's ever been. And though he expresses uncertainty over which direction he will take in the future, he has an uncanny ability to return, if sometimes inconsistently, to running.

BILL RODGERS

In 1975, at the Boston Marathon, little-known Bill Rodgers ran an American record 2:09:55, among the most unexpected sports records in history. "It was a combination of several factors that combined over a period of perhaps three years," was Bill's simple explanation. "These factors were training techniques, luck, emotion and several people who helped me."

His explanation contrasts starkly with Shorter's more analytical reasoning. Improving one's time nearly 10 minutes in twelve months invites a need for more analytic explanations; but it is not a matter Bill Rodgers has mulled over publicly. One explanation is simply the frame of mind Rodgers was able to assume on that day, for he is a runner whose intensity often wavers. He admitted he thought of quitting during that 1975 Boston race. "The noise was incredible. It kept me going when I felt like quitting."

The fact that Bill Rodgers is an emotional runner accounts for both his surprising successes and for the inconsistency that has sometimes bothered his success. He is a runner who sometimes puts too much pressure on himself—such as at the Montreal Olympics and at Boston 1977—and then wilts beneath it. It's a problem that has affected many great runners, most notably Ron Clarke. It can usually be traced back to a runner's earliest races. When Bill Rodgers was in high school, he ran a 9:36 2-mile. Yet at the New England Regional Championships, the most prestigious race of the season, he managed only 9:56.

At Wesleyan University in Connecticut, where he attended school and ran with Amby Burfoot, also a Boston winner, Rodgers developed his unique approach to marathoning. Perhaps influenced by Burfoot, he quit doing interval work entirely, and ran mostly long-distance workouts, at a 6:00-6:30 pace. Burfoot noticed something innovative in Rodgers' style: "It is his relaxation that most amazes me. He seems to be able to run with almost complete detachment from the mental and physical effort involved."

At Wesleyan he didn't have the chance to develop as a marathoner, even though his training was geared for long races. He competed in the 2-mile, an event in which his time improved slightly, from 9:32 as a freshman to 9:23 as a sophomore.

As in high school and in his later marathoning, surprise success and inconsistency characterized Rodgers's running in college. As a junior, he failed to improve at all on his 9:23. But then in his senior year, he ran an 8:58 indoors, and quit running entirely. "I was worried because of the draft situation," he said. "I wanted to apply myself to some school work, which had really piled up." He stopped running "for a long time," resuming only when his motorcycle was stolen and he was forced to run the 1½ miles to and from work. This rekindled his interest; he started running at the local YMCA track and found himself enjoying it again. Steadily, he decreased his smoking and increased his mileage. By October, 1972, he was doing 100 miles a week.

His first competition, after the hibernation, was a 20-miler in February 1973, in which he ran 1:44. When asked to explain how he was able to run so well after his long layoff, Bill replied, "Well, psychologically, I was really high to be racing again after such a long layoff."

In October 1973, he ran the Framingham Marathon in Massachusetts in 2:28, and set his sights on the following year's Boston race. His preparation involved running 100 to 140 miles each week, and racing in several class competitions. At the highly regarded Coamo, Puerto Rico, half-marathon, Rodgers took off in the lead, in front of a number of Olympic runners. He led for 4-5 miles, until a pack headed by Lasse Viren burst past. Still, he finished seventh.

At Boston, Bill started ambitiously—a 2:13 pace—but was destroyed by leg cramps at 18 miles. Despite having to stop several times to stretch and massage his leg muscles during the remaining miles, he improved his marathon best dramatically, to 2:19:34.

During the 12 months before the next Boston race, Rodgers's training became more varied and, at times, much more voluminous. One week he ran 201 miles.

At the International Cross-Country Championship in Morocco, he surprised many with his third-place finish, after having led for more than 2 miles.

Before Boston, in 1975, Rodgers said modestly, "I just want to improve upon my 2:19:34 of last year. If I have a good day, I may be able to hit 2:16 or something around there." It was a far cry from Frank Shorter saying he wanted to run 2:15 his first time out.

As the runners passed through Framingham, 6.8 miles into the run, Bill was with the leaders. Shortly afterward, Jerome Drayton and Mario Cuezas took a 20-yard lead. Rodgers pursued and caught them. By the town of Natick, the 10.5-mile mark, Rodgers and Drayton were running stride for stride, just 2 seconds behind Ron Hill's 1970 course record pace. At Wellesley, 3 miles later, Bill was alone, 11 seconds faster than the record pace. "I kept thinking, 'Too fast. I'll crack just like last year,'" Rodgers recalled. "I don't know what made me go to the front. Sometimes I think I have a suicidal instinct."

At Heartbreak Hill, he lost 20 seconds tying a shoelace. Before the finish, he stopped completely several times at the aid stations to drink fluids. But he was never challenged. His final time of 2:09:55 broke Frank Shorter's American record by 35 seconds.

Bill Rodgers is not a calculating runner. The suicidal instinct—that Rodgers credits with carrying him to the front and setting such a fast pace—obviously paid off at Boston. But if a runner takes that sort of chance, there will be days when it won't work as well.

Less than a year and a half later, Rodgers finished fortieth at the Olympics, having run with the leaders for much of the race. Bill admitted, "The pace I set for myself was suicidal."

Rodgers has always been a gambler, and bit of a rebel. He has said, "One hardly has to be in the Olympic Stadium as a competitor to run the race of his life." Many sportswriters picked Rodgers to win the Olympic race. He had, after all, the fastest time of anyone in the field.

The great irony of Montreal is that Waldemar Cierpinski's winning time was the identical time—2:09:55—that Rodgers had surprised so many with at Boston in 1975. He gave no excuses for his 2:25 showing, but a connection could clearly be drawn to that 9:56 2-mile race he had run in high school many years earlier. If Shorter's problem was the rain, Rodgers's was the pressure. Bill's explanation was basic, if a bit cryptic: "When one loses one's focus on aim, the results are understandable."

Still, time-wise at least, Rodgers was the greatest American marathoner in history, and the urge to redeem himself was great after Montreal. His chance came just eight weeks later, when he met most of the world's top marathoners, though not Cierpinski, at the New York City Marathon. This time, the pressure was different. Though he didn't have to prove himself, he wanted to. His victory at New

York, with 2:10:10, beat second-place Frank Shorter by more than 3 minutes. Bill's time was the number two time for an American, second only to himself.

It was clearly an emotional race. "I was psyched up just because I got nailed at Montreal," he said. Emotion very plainly drives Bill Rodgers. "Emotion as a stimulating factor is a quality scientists and researchers cannot analyze effectively," he said. "The physiological results induced by a highly charged emotional frame of mind can be devastating. A good example of a runner exceeding himself in a superlative effort is Billy Mills's tremendous 10,000-meter victory in the 1964 Olympics." (Or Bill Rodgers's 1975 victory in Boston and 1976 in New York.)

Jerome Drayton has said of Rodgers: "He has his moments, and then he has his downfalls, whereas a guy like Shorter is very consistent."

At Boston, in 1977, Rodgers was reportedly as hot as he'd ever been. Friends indicated he was planning a world-record attempt. But Jerome Drayton won, in 2:14:46, and Bill Rodgers dropped out.

Just as after Montreal, Rodgers came away from Boston in need of redemption, and found it. He turned the rest of 1977 into one of the best years of his career. He won the New York City Marathon, over Drayton, and ran even faster, 2:10:55, to win the Fukuoka race. He was virtually unbeaten in the last half of 1977, recording the world's two fastest marathon times of the year.

Also in 1977, following the trend of Frank Shorter, Gary Tuttle, and others, Bill Rodgers opened his own sporting goods store, the Bill Rodgers Running Center in Boston.

Rodgers said, after he rose to national prominence with his performance at the International Cross-Country Championships, "It was the race of my life. I'll probably never run that well again." This was before Boston, 1975. Then, after Boston, he said, "We have all had our perfect races or have come close to having them. Mine came at Boston."

Yet Rodgers's running has demonstrated that his predictions and analyses must be taken with a grain of salt. One senses his perfect race may not have come at all. He might not be able to predict it, but he will probably find it. As Marlon Brando once said, "It's the hardest thing in the world to accept a pinch of success and leave it that way."

8

Bob Campbell, Man Behind the Scenes

by Jim Lilliefors

Hundreds of people have been working behind the scenes to make road racing a simple matter of signing up and running. Of these people, one of the most deserving of attention is New England's Bob Campbell, cochairman of the AAU Long-Distance Running Committee. Certainly there are others as well: Will Cloney and Jock Semple, who annually put on the Boston Marathon; Fred Lebow, who works on the New York City Marathon; and Campbell himself lists AAU chairmen Vern Whiteside, John Brennand, and Stan Stafford, as well as Campbell's cochairman Vince Chiapetta. But few can claim the lengthy experience that Campbell has, both as runner and AAU worker, or the crusading ambition he has shown.

Campbell's experience in road racing began in 1929 when he launched a fourteen-year career as competitive runner. In that period, he won 15 New England road racing championships. During World War II, though, he lost his competitive zeal, and joined the AAU as a handicapper. His ambition quickly won him higher positions. "I saw there were things wrong and nobody was doing anything about them," he said.

Within a few years, he was New England AAU chairman, a position he held for twelve years. In 1956-57, he was national AAU chairman. Today Campbell remains active, as one of the most respected AAU workers in the country.

When Bob Campbell started with the AAU in New England, there were 50 races in that region. By 1977, there were 300. If you ask him why New England has grown so tremendously to become the center of U.S. road racing, you will get a blunt reply. "You want plain English? Because we're workers. We're not talkers and we're not beefers. It takes work. Prize-wise, I don't think there are any races in

336

the country that can match us. Sure, one or two may put on a big splurge, but on an overall basis, we have more."

New England races regularly award up to 150 merchandise prizes. At one recent race, they gave 15 CB radios as prizes. "Chuck Smead couldn't believe it when he won the AAU 20-K title at Gardner in 1976," Campbell said. "I took him downstairs to look at the prizes and he just couldn't believe it. They don't have anything like that out in California. You'd be surprised what some people will donate if you ask."

Campbell also attributes New England's road racing dominance to the fact that most races are run right through the towns, giving visiting runners a feel for the local town's flavor. "Take New York City," Campbell said. "They run most of their races in Central Park. We run ours right through cities and towns. We get people from the Midwest out here on their vacations. They run through, say, Salem, right through all the traffic, and they love it. They run through Harvard Square in Cambridge with all the students there yelling and shouting. They love it."

The AAU is far from trouble-free, and Bob Campbell acknowledges the fact. "The larger you grow and the more you do, you're going to be criticized, because if you don't do anything, you're never criticized."

One dispute involving the AAU concerns registration fees. Campbell stresses that race fees are set up by individual chairmen, not the national body, and points out that in New England, entry fees are as low as elsewhere. According to Campbell:

> Each association is responsible for itself. We have no effect on what happens in other parts of the country. This is what runners don't understand, and what the RRCA doesn't understand. Any district with five or more clubs has the right to elect its own chairman, but they don't do it, and then sometimes when they do, they appoint a deadhead. If the runners don't elect the right person, then that's their problem. Many chairmen just sit on their rear ends and charge $4 or $5 to belong to the club, which is more than they pay for their AAU dues, and then charge $4 a race. This is ridiculous. Let your sponsors pay for the prizes. This is what we do in New England.
>
> In New England, we charge $3 registration. It's the same for all sports. Of the $1.50 the LDR [Long Distance Running] Committee keeps, 50 cents goes right into a travel fund for the athletes. That gives us a dollar, which in part goes toward putting postage on all the mail we send out. Just today we got 150 letters.
>
> In New England, if a man wants a sanction from us, we charge $5 if he's not a member of the NEAAU [New England AAU]. If it's for a charitable cause, the sanction fee is waived. If you belong to the association, there is no fee. So the most we can get out of any race is $5.

Another controversial area is the AAU's relationship with the

RRCA. Recently, several AAU members have publicly quit, and have praised the RRCA as a better organization. Campbell realizes this, but feels the matter has been getting more ink than it deserves.

> I have some reservations about which way the RRCA is going. I am a charter member and one of the guys who started the RRCA. In the AAU Long Distance Running Committee, there are possibly some 30 members who belong to the RRCA who, over the years, have worked within the AAU, to get the benefits. I'm talking about people like Ted Corbitt and, more recently, Nina Kuscsik.
>
> We [AAU] are the ones who got autonomy for men in long-distance running. We got the right to set up traveling funds to send them to Europe for the international cross-country. We've fought for autonomy for women. The only way this is accomplished is you have to go to the voting booths. You have to be at the convention to get your ideas across. It's the RRCA people working within the AAU who have accomplished this. All the people who are yelling and shouting but not attending the convention aren't doing anything.
>
> There are workers and there are talkers. We who stay with the RRCA within the AAU are the ones who can accomplish things. I quote Browning Ross in 1958: "Wake up, gentlemen. We're on your side. We're here to help, not to hinder, the AAU cause." This man is the founder of the RRCA.
>
> But this year, the three people who were designated to represent the RRCA at the AAU convention didn't show up. So how can you make changes?

Campbell resents charges that the AAU is not doing all it should to help athletes:

> Aren't we trying when our long-distance international selection committee asked permission to have Craig Virgin, first American in the 1976 NCAA cross-country championship, go to Europe? We're trying our best to get along with everybody, but we need cooperation. Any organization is only as strong as its weakest link, so if you're going to have someone continuously wanting to take over everything, of course the AAU's going to buckle up.
>
> There's no doubt that the AAU has been very important in the promotion of long-distance running. We've had national championships since 1880. The RRCA didn't have its first championship until the mid-60s, even though they were organized in the 50s.

The AAU, he contends, is doing well as anyone in dealing with a monster. For most of his years within the AAU, Bob Campbell has dealt with a steadily growing sport. According to him: "The big fields come about because you have sponsors trying to outdo one another. We have three races on one day this year, all within 50 miles of each other. We have a 300-race program overall, and there are only 365 days in the year."

Campbell doesn't think it's possible to isolate one, or even a few, factors responsible for the growth of running. "I think a lot of things are responsible. The cities have grown, and that had an effect. But mostly, people are just more aware of it."

Campbell is skeptical of claims that the growth of running was caused by just one person, or organization, such as Ken Cooper's *Aerobics*, or *Runner's World*.

> I think Dr. Cooper may be a very brilliant man but I don't think too many of the average runners pay much attention to him unless they go to a clinic.
>
> I think there's no question that Bob Anderson [the publisher of *Runner's World*] has done an awful lot to create interest in road racing.
>
> But I think you have to give a great deal of credit to the local AAU chairmen who have gone out and done the work.

Campbell admits there are aspects of the growth he isn't enthusiastic about.

> They're giving more prizes today, which I'm not sure I approve of because then you have guys running just to get a certain prize.
>
> I ran a race many years ago where I broke the course record. I finished eleventh and I didn't get a prize. I was so happy I'd broken the record, I never thought of the prize. Yet today, people expect it.
>
> I do know that there are several runners today who are just interested in prizes and this is bad.

But despite all the problems and headaches, Campbell says, "The growth has been good, it has helped running."

Many runners and writers have made predictions about the future of running. What does a man, whose job is to make room for the crowds, think about the future?

> Who can say what'll happen? It's been steadily growing every year. Despite some of the criticisms, AAU registrations are still growing. In New England, we had thousands more registrations last year than ever before. So we must be doing something right.
>
> As it grows in the future, people are going to have to realize it takes organization and work. I think it will continue to grow. But I think that to have a successful program, you are going to have to have rules. For instance, this might sound old-fashioned, but in New England we don't let anyone under eighteen run a marathon. Most other places do.
>
> But look back at all your champion marathoners and tell me what age they were when they started running. Go back and look at all the kids picked to be champions five or ten years ago. How many of them are even still running? You've got to keep in mind the history of this sport.

9

A Triumph over Blindness

by Harry Cordellos

When I told people I planned to run a marathon (and later after I'd run and finished it), they reacted with shocked disbelief. You see, I'm blind. And no one quite believed I could run 26 miles of open road in total darkness without encountering disaster. Understandably, they bombarded me with questions: Isn't it scary to run on the open highway and not see where you are going? How can you keep from running into people or tripping? Have you ever approached this distance before? How could anybody ever run so long without scenery to take his mind off the pain of a marathon? What do you think about when you try such a thing?

Very few of these were answered until the Golden Gate Marathon in Marin County, California, was over.

I knew from the beginning of the year that this would take many more training miles than I'd ever run before. I also knew that the main part of the battle was not my physical strength, but the attitude I would take to the starting line. I had to keep above the situation. This was the key to my success or failure. I knew if I had any chance to make it I would have to be ready for the first sign of panic and then to ignore it. This worked for me in a deep swimming pool where control of the situation made the difference between drowning or being saved. But I did not know how it would operate when the alternatives were not this serious. All I had to do was run.

Quitting might hurt my pride. But after three hours or so of constant running up and down hills in the heat, one might place different values on which is better: quitting or suffering. I knew only that many thoughts would run through my mind once the gun sounded; I would try to discard the bad ones as soon as I could recognize them.

340

Two months before the May 30 race, I had still never run 100 miles in one month. My partner for over 18 months, Bill Welsh, ran with me rain or shine, but we both had one setback after another. One must realize that when two work as one there are twice as many things that can go wrong: four legs to gather shin splints, four ankles to sprain, and so on. The first obstacle came when a lower back injury prevented Bill from running long mileage with me. I soon had to accept the fact that he could not cross the finish line with me.

Then, one of our regular running companions, Jack Bettencourt, offered to train with me and go the full marathon distance as well. Our schedules did not allow for good regular training, but we both arrived to sign up on race day. Our confidence was high, but there were still more unknowns than we could count. As we left for the start, I wondered how long it would be before I finished. And if I did finish that day, how would I feel? This was the first bad thought that slipped into my mind, and it already had me nervous. Before we knew it, we were at the starting line and were off and moving along the winding roads of Tiburon. I thought of how smooth the pace was, and how tempting it was to blast off. But I knew that we were not trained to run the same pace as we do for 10 miles.

Then I thought, "A real marathon; it doesn't seem so bad after all." Just hearing the word *marathon* gave me a few butterflies. But the first few miles kept me above the situation and I never enjoyed a course more. Then came 5 miles, at a little slower than our 3½-hour goal. Ten miles came, and again I realized I was worrying about burning out; I struggled to get that thought out of my mind. "A real marathon," I thought again, and could not help getting more determined than ever.

Mill Valley came at last, but it was not the Mill Valley I expected or wanted. The road suddenly got rough and bumpy. The temperature seemed to soar into the nineties, and we found ourselves happy to maintain our pace, without trying to make up for lost time. After being doused with water a few times, my number got soggy and drooped until it no longer would stay on. Then, what seemed an awfully long time later, we reached the 15-mile mark. This was a shocker: how could it seem so long? Our pace slipped a few more minutes behind schedule, and I began to worry about how the last 10 miles would feel.

Somebody on the roadside shouted, "What's everybody running for?" "A marathon," I commented with a sudden burst of confidence. The spectator repeated, "A marathon!" in surprise, and whatever else he said faded behind us. Again I realized that Jack and I were still strong, and we had no reason to doubt our ability to finish with a respectable time, even if we missed our goal of 3½ hours.

Then came the section along the railroad tracks. I knew it meant an automatic sprained ankle, but ran as if nothing was going to happen. Jack somehow got me through without even a stagger. I never ran with fear in spite of what could have happened. We just kept going and soon hit the 20-mile mark, thinking about the big hill up to the bridge.

Having met and corresponded with Dr. Ken Cooper, author of *Aerobics*, I thought how great it would be to let him know that I finished the Golden Gate Marathon, instead of just saying I participated in it. This made me continue with more confidence. A little farther along, I still had no terrible pain, but I needed something powerful to give me the final push. Finally, it hit with full impact. On the night before the marathon I received a telegram from Bill Welsh, who would have given anything to be with me in my first marathon attempt. His message simply said, "Good luck, partner; the word is confidence." That did it.

We passed several more runners, went over the top of the hill, and headed toward the bridge. The road got rough and narrow, and then it happened. The noise of the freeway traffic got closer and louder, and I could not hear anything else. I felt a sharp metal object scrape my leg, and then I caught my right foot on a vertical object. I was not strong enough to keep my footing, and I knew I was going down. Jack pulled me away from the guardrail, but it was too late. I made a nosedive and bounced on the gravel road. I was not hurt, just skinned up a little.

We went on, probably without ever losing forward motion. I ran behind Jack, with my hand on his shoulder. In a split-second, we had invented a new technique of running—both untested and uncertain. I fishtailed a few times and hit the rail again. This time, I staggered, but did not fall. We had to finish now. The long-awaited Golden Gate Bridge seemed endless, but I had no real pain. But I realized that after almost losing it, I now wanted to get it over with before anything else happened.

Anyone who ever ran a marathon knows how we felt at the finish line. We could not believe that we had run that distance without even stopping for a drink. Three hours and fifty minutes plus a few seconds was not what we had hoped for. But we had conquered a marathon without walking a step. I even kept running while recovering from the fall. Even as the stiffness set in and I found it hard to walk around, I knew there would be another marathon for me. I had heard too much about this "never-again" attitude. I know I will want to run many more marathons. It was the most satisfying and thrilling experience I have had in thirty-two years.

But what about those questions? Every marathon runner could write a book about his first marathon. If this summary does not seem too different from most of them, maybe blindness is not the tragic handicap people often make it. As for the scenery, sure I enjoyed it. It truly was the most beautiful marathon course I could have run. Much of my outlook may be shaped by the fact that I finished. It is true that I had seen some of the area when I had partial vision fifteen years before. But I sensed every tree and scenic point along the way. The sounds of encouraging spectators along the route, shouting and yelling at us, kept me on top of the situation when I needed it most. Even above the roar of traffic on the bridge, I heard people in cars screaming at us.

And, of course, there were the smells. I never felt closer to nature nor appreciated it as much as I did on May 30. When a car went by and we inhaled the exhaust, I knew just what people meant by the pollution problem. Most enjoyable was the thought that I was running for almost 4 hours without smelling one miserable cigarette. In the stuffy, smoky world we work and live in, I wish I could run a marathon every week. Of course my body could not stand up to that. But it was truly the most beautiful course I could have run.

As for fear of running, that is no problem. Though I have been considered by my mobility instructors as skilled in the use of the white cane, and though I travel free and relaxed, I cannot describe accurately what it was like to run completely free on the open road for over 26 miles without worrying about accidents or other problems. I had faith and confidence in Jack Bettencourt's ability to direct me. As long as he kept going ahead, I figured I would just keep bumping his arm or wrist and stay with him. Even the fall did not shake my confidence except at the moment it happened. The thought of finishing a marathon, running all the way, was too much for me to forget. So I realized the fall could not have been helped and just forgot about it.

I can only say that runners are a tremendous group of people. So many of them have given me encouragement and help in accomplishing every runner's dream—to run a marathon.

PART EIGHT

THE POSSIBILITIES

1

The Future of Running

by Joe Henderson

In 1974, to end the first half of the decade, I wrote an article called "Reflections on a Golden Age." Those five years had such glitter to me, I said, that I doubted they'd ever be matched. I suggested that running had crossed a peak, and had started down the other side in the first half of the seventies. By now, I've softened my view of this as a post-Golden Age. I haven't been thrilled by everything that has happened in running since 1975. But on balance it is better to be a runner now than at any time before.

Undoubtedly, if I'm still here to write as the first half of the 1980s ends, I'll do another such review. I'll again run down what has happened for better or worse in running in those 5 years. And in the truest tradition of journalism, I'll probably once more devote most of the space to the negative side.

But there's no guarantee I'll still be writing then. And since I have things to say about running in the 1980s that should be said before that time comes, I'll jump ahead a little more than 5 years—to 1984. Nineteen eighty-four has come to symbolize a chilling future year, when science fiction comes true. Yet when George Orwell wrote his book by that title, the year had no more significance than a reversal of the numbers from the year when he did his writing—1948.

I don't want to make the year too significant either. Nineteen eighty-four just happens to be the year when the Olympics will probably return to the United States for the first time in a half-century. And this is as far ahead as I care to look. It's a time within reach of most of us who are now running. We'll soon be living the ways of 1984.

I'm not making actual predictions on what will happen. In part, I'm just extending by a few years the trends I already see at work. I'm discussing certain things here in hopes that writing about them now will keep them from happening later.

Looking ahead is both the easiest and hardest kind of writing to do. It's easiest because I can make up anything I want, and no one

346

can say I'm wrong until later. If I'm wrong, they will have forgotten it and I won't remind them. If I'm right, I can say, "See, I forecast this back in '78!"

This is a hard story to write, though, because changes in running are coming at a faster and faster pace. The sport has changed more in the last ten years than it had in the previous fifty. It will again change more by 1984 than it has in the seventies. It's as much a test to foresee changes yet to come as it will be to adapt to them when they come. With that introduction, open your mind and go with me into the near future. We're looking back now from the end of 1984.

NUMBERS

In the glory days of the 1970s, it looked as if everyone with two good legs would be running by now. If the sport's growth rate at the time had continued, almost all of them would have. Well, it hasn't happened—and it never will. Boom times are over, probably never to return. The growth peaked out in 1979, when a Gallup poll estimated that 30 million American adults were running (or "jogging," as the media still insisted on referring to it).

If we plot a stock-market-type chart for the ebb and flow of runners in the last twenty years, we see this: a gentle climb in numbers through the 1960s, growing abruptly steeper in the early seventies, and then shooting up almost vertically in 1977-78. Since then, however, the running population has gradually declined. It now appears to have leveled off at about 15-20 million. There aren't as many of us as there were a few years ago, but still more than there were before the boom. The sport is smaller and stronger now. *Sport* is the right word, because people have returned to viewing it the way it always should have been—as a sport or recreation.

The main reason for the decline in the number of runners was that the fad of "jogging" for exercise faded away. Millions of people tried it in the 1970s, and most found it wasn't the miracle-worker they expected. Great effort, time, and patience were needed to produce its promised results, and few Americans were willing to invest any of these commodities. So people either got less than promised, or more—in the form of injuries and even death.

The most serious blow to "jogging" came in 1980. A government agency, alarmed by reports of injury and death, issued a warning that "jogging may be hazardous to your health." This sent tens of thousands of exercisers looking for alternatives, and frightened many others out of ever trying this activity. Meanwhile, people who ran for sport just laughed off the warning. The risks, they said, were small and as much a part of their sport as the risks skiers or football players took in theirs.

GROUPS

Despite the overall drop in the running population, the number who race has held steady—perhaps even gone up a bit. Certainly, the proportion of racers among the runners has never been higher.

In recent years, runners of various levels have split apart. As more runners race, they increasingly give the appearance that they're in distinct groups. When the sport was small, it had a democratic ideal. "We're all in this together," the runners said. Men and women, young and old, fast and slow all raced as one body.

Above all the other groups is a super-group of professional athletes. In the 1970s, a few were pros in fact, but not in name. After the 1980 Olympics, the rulers of the sport faced up to the realities of modern competition and allowed these runners to earn their living with their feet. This has become an exclusive, almost closed, club, usually entered only by the most promising school athletes. One who must work for a living can't spend the time or find the coaching needed to become good enough to join. So the lines between professional and amateur are sharply drawn. The "class" and the "mass" rarely mix.

RULERS

Everyone complains about the AAU, but no one works to reform or replace it. Perhaps that's because most runners want neither to rule or to be ruled. There have been moves for more than twenty years to take control of running away from the AAU. But no other group seems able or willing to step in to replace the creaky old organization. So the AAU limps along, absorbing potshots from its own members and from opposing groups, trying to keep runners running as best it can.

The administrative load grew astronomically in the 1970s. Road running, in particular, added thousands of new members to the AAU rolls. (Since 1977, it has been the second-largest AAU sport, behind swimming.) But there wasn't a corresponding jump in the number of volunteer officials handling the new runners. This was the big problem then and still is: the sport has grown much faster than the machinery to control it.

Another crippler of AAU organization is that each part of the sport has its own kingdom. Men's long-distance running is distinct from women's (which now accounts for about 40 percent of the runners). Men's track and field is separate from women's, and neither is attached to long-distance ... except among veterans, where all athletes over age forty are under one committee—which, in turn, is separate from all others. Race walking comprises yet another group. Each ruling body makes its own rules, policies, and schedules, with little coordination among them.

Club running, the local arm of the AAU, remains as weak and uncoordinated as the parent body for many of the same reasons. There was hope a few years ago that corporations would sponsor well-organized running clubs. Several tried and appeared to be succeeding. Then, their interest waned, the economy tightened, and they had an excuse to withdraw support.

However, probably the most significant reason why running organizations aren't effective derives from the runners themselves. Many of them run to escape organizations, crowds, and rules—not to become part of new groups. Many have rebelled against the pressures of bigness in recent years.

One man wrote that "we have a new *group*—not a club. We call it OUR group—*O* for the state, *U*nderground *R*unners. We have races, we have members, we have awards, we have dedication, and we have smallness—all the things the old-timers want. And we have done it very simply. We just don't tell anyone. Members are obtained by word of mouth only. When a member joins, he or she is given a packet containing a race schedule with dates, times, and locations of races, and a detailed description of each course. The description is important, because the race courses are not marked. Each member is expected to know it." This sort of organization keeps the job of organizing from growing more important than the running. The group works on the sound principle that it's more fun to run than to hold a clipboard.

SCIENCE

Scientists take much of the blame for our current technological nightmares. But science itself is neutral; it simply turns out new products and techniques. They become good or bad by the ways in which they are utilized—constructively or destructively.

Scientific advances—and retreats—have touched everyone in the sport. Yesterday's dreams have become today's luxuries and will be tomorrow's necessities. I'll discuss later the items that have come into everyday use this way. But first, let me tell a story to illustrate how ambitious runners can become reliant on the tools of science.

American athletes hoped to shake loose East Germany's grip on world track and field supremacy, as they prepared for the 1984 Olympic Games in Los Angeles. The distance runners—running 800 meters and up—trained high in the Rockies near Colorado Springs. Little hard information is known about the methods employed there. But reports filtering down from the mountains are that the doctors there are developing runners who make the Six Million Dollar Man look like a physical retard.

The advances have come from several directions: (1) more careful identification and recruiting of prospective champions; (2) increased amounts of training, and (3) manipulation of the runners' bodies and minds. These were, after all, what the East Germans appeared to be doing.

Overseeing the work of the distance runners is a staff of coaches, exercise physiologists, physical therapists, psychologists, and dietitians. Although visitors are not permitted inside the center, and athletes and staff are sworn to secrecy, I have talked with an expelled marathoner. He said:

> We were linked 24 hours a day to computers that processed the raw data from telemetric devices measuring all body functions and reactions to exercise. Warning signals sounded in the control area at the first hints of overstress as well as understress.
>
> Based on this input, the computer spit out a perfectly tailored daily program for each athlete. This generally averaged about 300-400 kilometers a week for me, portioned out into 3-5 daily workouts.
>
> Back in the early seventies, a runner named Gerry Lindgren attempted a crude version of this training. But without expert coaching and computer monitoring, his experiment failed. Now, there are no mistakes.

I asked my source, "If there were no mistakes, why are you no longer at the center?"

He explained, "It was this needle business. The doctors were always wanting to shoot something into us or take something out without telling us what the effects were. I balked."

"You mean they kicked you out for that?" I asked.

"No, not exactly. But without whatever it was they were giving the runners, I couldn't keep up during races. I couldn't meet the performance standards set by the coaches, so here I am on the outside." He thought for a moment, and then added, "I only ran a 2:10 marathon. It isn't good enough any more. Now that I've washed out of the national center, I probably won't run anything fast again. I may not even break 2:12. But at least I'll be failing on my own instead of succeeding at the hands of my doctors and my computer programmer."

EQUIPMENT

It would seem that the things runners wear are so simple they couldn't be improved on. But never underestimate the combined skills of scientists and promoters. Take shoes, for instance, the main item a runner needs. The models of the 1970s now look like relics dug up from another age. No modern runner would wear these stiff, heavy, ill-fitting shoes. New materials have cut their weight in half, while improving the properties of flexibility, durability, and cushioning. The same shoes are worn for racing and training.

The biggest advance is in custom-fitted shoes. Runners now buy a shoe "shell" in the size and style they want. Then, a quick-hardening liquid rubber is molded to their own footprint inside the shoe. In effect, each runner then has an "orthotic" to correct his foot and leg problems.

Promising experiments are currently going on with a product that may partially replace shoes. Tough, transparent spray-on adhesives are being tested. These protect the feet on all-weather tracks and cross-country courses, while providing the lightness and freedom of running barefoot. These "artificial calluses" peel away as easily as tape after each run.

Space-age technology also has given runners cooling and warming systems in the form of clothing that maintains critical temperatures without interfering with movement. For instance, the winter suit fits like a second skin and weighs mere ounces.

Wristwatches now are much more than timepieces; they are coaches worn on the arm. These sophisticated micro-computers can give pulse rates, distances, and paces per kilometer, as well as telling time to the hundredth of a second. They can be used as a pacer that beeps at specified intervals, as a two-way radio to take instructions from the sidelines, or as a receiver for commercial radio broadcasts. You can't have all of these functions at once, of course, but you have the choice of several that interest you.

BUSINESSES

Running became big business in the late seventies. So, along with all businesses, it suffered during the "crash of '79." Actually, it was more a recession than the depression that had been forecast. But the dip in the economy was blamed for the collapse of many running-related enterprises. In fact, the economy was only partly to blame. Times had been too good, and the market had attracted too many shoe companies, too many retailers, and too many publishers of books and magazines. Then, too, the "running look" had been a fad.

The store shelves were glutted with running things, both to wear and to read. Then, tastes changed. The look that had previously been in style went out, as styles always do. This, coupled with a sharp drop in the number of people jogging for exercise, left merchandise unsold in the stores. Many stores soon closed, and producers soon followed.

The surviving businesses, like the runners who survived the boom times of the seventies, are stronger for it. There just aren't as many of them now—a few shoe and clothing companies, a retailer or two in each major city, and a single big magazine-book publisher, supplemented by several regional and specialized ones.

TRAINING

Dr. Ernst van Aaken predicted it almost forty years ago. He said the top runners of the future would not train any differently than at any other time. They would run by the same principles as fun-runners; only the champions would do more because they had to, and do it faster because they were able.

That future is here. After going to both extremes—first all fast interval training on the track and then all slow running on the roads—all runners now use a combination of fast and slow running. The most common proportions are 90 percent *base work* and 10 percent *sharpening*. This is what van Aaken and Lydiard had advised for decades.

Though there may seem to be a regimented uniformity to training now, the opposite is, in fact, the case. The general formula may be the same for everyone, but the specific applications of it will always be different because of variations in runners' abilities and needs. The applications were never more individual than they are now. Science has made it so. Surprisingly, the tool most responsible for this is the computer, which has been falsely labeled a destroyer of individualism. Cheap computer rental now allows almost any runner to hook himself up to a well-known coach who quickly analyzes great amounts of technical data fed in by the runner each day. The result is a personalized daily program that takes into account the latest running conditions, as well as the runner's own condition. Part of the information comes from actual training details, while the rest is the result of simple tests of saliva, hair, and blood that runners now can perform themselves.

The East Germans perfected computerized training and biochemical testing. In response to charges that this took the "sport" out of sports, a scientist said, "Is it sport to allow an athlete to run a hard distance race when his hemoglobin level is dangerously low and when the effort could set him back 6 months in his training schedule? Is it sport to have one of your young athletes go on a 30-kilometer run with no knowledge of his true physiological condition? Is it ethical to have an athlete train 120 to 150 kilometers per week without first giving him an electrocardiogram?"

If coaches err now, it is in the direction of being too cautious rather than taking chances with an athlete.

RACING

One good thing has come out of the severe fuel shortages of the last few years. They have made it easier to be a runner—especially a runner who races. Car-clogged roads were polluted and dangerous in the 1970s. Groups of runners found it hard to compete with traffic. But since gas rationing has come and apparently will stay, driving is a luxury. The streets are quieter and cleaner than they have been since World War II.

The gas shortage has had other side effects. Runners can't travel to races as easily now, so most events appeal only to local people. The corporations and service organizations that used to sponsor races have felt the money pinch, and thus withdrawn most of their support. This has resulted in a general improvement in the quality of race organizing, since fields are smaller and more manageable, and inexperienced promoters have pulled out.

Other significant racing trends include:

- Timing and scoring have been revolutionized as runners wear tiny sensors, programmed with information about themselves. They're automatically checked in and timed by computer as they cross the finish line.

- Each major city has a mass run like the Boston Marathon or the Bay to Breakers in San Francisco. But this is more an annual celebration of the sport than a true race.

- The marathon mania of the seventies has cooled, and more runners now are aiming their big efforts at the 10- to 25-kilometer events. This is simply because they can race these more often and with less effort.

- On the other hand, there has been a great surge of interest in ultramarathons—runs of 50 to 100 kilometers, or longer. However, most runners treat these not as races, but as leisurely long-distance "tours" combining running and walking.

OLYMPICS

Los Angeles of course hosted the 1984 Olympic Games. Aside from the usual politics and media hype, the topic running fans discussed most was the smog. Not since the altitude controversy of Mexico City has so much been said about the air runners breathe.

They called this the "unfair Olympics." A quick look at the five longest races—those affected most by the polluted atmosphere—seems to show that the appraisal is justified. Lasse Viren of Finland, trying for his fourth straight 10,000 meter title, ran like a zombie during the last three laps of his race, stumbled home sixth, and was unconscious for 10 minutes afterward. Meanwhile, a New York subway commuter won the race. An almost unknown coal miner from West Virginia stunned viewers with his steeplechase win. A Japanese taxi driver raced to an easy victory in the marathon.

An African, writing in a highly regarded sports weekly, assailed the selection of Los Angeles as the Olympic site. "It's grossly unfair," he said, "that athletes from my country and others that don't have the advantage of this type of air were forced to compete—against great odds—with those who've spent their lives in it. My heart cried for some of the greatest runners in the world when I saw them reduced to struggling, gasping also-rans."

The U.S. coach, on the other hand, defended the Olympic city and his three runners who'd run there. "I'm convinced," he said, "that our three boys would have won their races anywhere. They might have been closer, but they would have won. Too many people are using the smog as an excuse for poor performances."

Olympic committees worldwide and individual athletes began to make plans and preparations right after the last Olympics—some of them drastic. A few lucky countries had natural features that gave them immediate advantages. London, Los Angeles, New York, and Tokyo became highly prized training sites. But places like Kenya, Ethiopia, and Tunisia were far from these cities and had no comparable ones at home. Not surprisingly, their officials complained loudest about the site of the Games. They were about to move their athletes to industrial nations for special training when the International Olympic Committee ruled: "No nation can bring its team together for high-smog training more than 4 weeks before the Games."

Coaches and runners, in mild panic, still went to extremes in their preparations. Coaches quickly dropped their longstanding smoking taboo and recommended cigarettes as beneficial to Olympic training.

Runners supported themselves by working as parking garage attendants. Herds of marathoners darted through a maze of stalled cars while training downtown during rush hour. But in the end, the crash training accomplished little. High-smog natives had too big a head start. The winners of the five longest races came from dirty-air countries.

Olympic officials want no more cries of "unfairness," so they're searching long and hard for the perfect site for the next Games. Their search caused one observer of the sport to comment, "Imagine, an Olympic site that everyone likes, one that doesn't scare athletes into taking crash preparations, doesn't provide a ready-made excuse, and doesn't give the papers a ready-made controversy to fill their pages. It'll be the dullest Olympics ever."

TIMES

Despite the improved competition and recent scientific advances, records haven't improved as quickly as experts predicted. This is particularly true for the men, though women aren't improving as rapidly as they were in the 1970s. The main reason for this is that the emphasis in training is to aim for one major event every year or so. Lasse Viren made this practice popular with his long string of Olympic victories. This leads to long valleys between peaks. Then, when athletes peak, they either run tactically or conditions aren't quite right for records.

The barriers the men are scrambling hardest to cross now are 3½ minutes for 1500 meters, 13 minutes for the 5,000 meters, and 27 minutes for 10,000 meters. The 30-minute 10,000 is in sight for women, but it probably won't come until this is made an Olympic event—and there's no hint of that happening at least through 1992.

Even though the marathon was said to have gone through "revolutionary" development in the seventies, the men's record has improved only slightly. The record for the marathon is just a minute and a half faster than the time Derek Clayton ran fifteen years ago—before the "revolution."

While women did have an exhibition marathon in the Los Angeles Olympics, the race is still not standard enough to draw the fastest women. The marathon specialists have reached their limits and haven't yet broken the 2½-hour barrier.

RETURNING TO THE PRESENT

The trip to tomorrow is over. We're back to now. I'm sorry if the ride felt a little rocky to you or if it depressed you some. The fact that the story from 1984 has a "down" tone probably says as much about me as it does about running. It shows my age. I come from the distant past, in the way time is measured in this sport, and my values were set in that simpler era.

My Golden Age was the late sixties and early seventies, when running was starting to grow but still wasn't crowded. Long-distance running was new to me, and I liked its informality after years of more structured school track. I prefer to remember running as it was then—or maybe never was. Memories work that way. They are old pictures, retouched to blot out the bad and highlight the good. We view life through the wide, innocent eyes of a child experiencing things for the first time and see the promise of better things to come.

"The memory of a supposed Golden Age," says longtime runner Rollin Workman of Cincinnati, "is usually the memory of one's youth—when everything is new and exciting and seemingly filled with possibilities which everyone feels are unlimited. When people realize that the alternatives are limited, and that what one is familiar with is no longer new and unformed, the lost Golden Age begins to appear."

It appears, too, when the new way of running isn't the same as the old, familiar, comfortable one. Not better or worse, just different.

A runner who started in 1975 might feel that the present is his Golden Age, to be viewed from the perspective of 1984 with a mixture of sadness at lost innocence and disgust at new complications. I suspect that his discomfort, like mine, will have more to do with his length of time in the sport than with running's state of development. The newcomer of 1984 will someday call that year his Golden Age. It all depends on when we begin, and what we come to expect as normal and right.

2

Runners' Stake in the Environment

by Hal Higdon

O ne of the absurdities of life is that many track men, road runners, and walkers are moving to California to further their careers. If pressed, I could probably name dozens of young men who have followed Horace Greeley's classic advice to go west. At times, I have been tempted to do the same. The reasons seem obvious: plentiful competition, many active clubs, year-round outdoor training. Perhaps the latter reason has the most appeal. No more slogging through snow-drifts, slipping on ice, or failing to find a clear running surface; no frigid winds; no need to pile on double sweat suits, which make running at a 7:00-minute pace a Herculean achievement.

I enjoy cold weather; perhaps it is the masochist in me. Some of my most pleasurable running memories come from my most miserable experiences—20 miles in a pounding Chicago rain and pelted by hail while running on the beach; braving raw winds in the hills above Stuttgart, Germany, during one of Europe's coldest winters. On the other hand, I can understand why others might want to run in perpetual sunshine—but at what price?

Consider a few medical facts:

- One California study of heart attack patients suggested a definite increase in death rates among those exposed to "freeway levels" of carbon monoxide.
- A New York City heart patient study showed "straining" of the heart under high carbon monoxide conditions.
- Among the 22 men working toll booths at either end of the Brooklyn Battery Tunnel, more than half suffered dizzy spells during a typical month. Five of these men experienced blackouts.

357

• A University of California report warned that concentrations in the California atmosphere have reached "high toxic, if not lethal levels."

It occurs to me that while we may be prolonging our life by jogging, we may be shortening it by breathing polluted air. "We're flirting with something immeasurably worse than war or genocide," one of the organizers of Earth Day (the national pollution protest in April 1970) told an interviewer for the *New York Times* recently, "and that's specie-cide. The death of man is involved here, and time is running out."

"Specie-cide"; think about that for a moment.

I heard one report (which I've been unable to confirm) that on days of high smog in Los Angeles the physical education activity in the grade schools is curtailed under the theory that students won't be breathing so much polluted air. If children are endangering their health by doing push-ups, what does that do for a long-distance runner on a 100-mile-a-week workout schedule?

Let me toss some more statistics at you. The nation's 87 million cars account for 60 percent of pollution in the air, 90 million tons worth. The most toxic element of that is carbon monoxide (70 million tons a year), which remains in the air as long as five years before decomposing. Fresh air contains less than one-tenth of one part per million carbon monoxide. The average city's air contains 100 times that concentration. During business hours the air over Chicago, Denver, Philadelphia, and Washington contains 300 times as much. Every day 8.3 million pounds of carbon monoxide belches from exhaust pipes in New York. In Los Angeles, a normal day's driving produces 20 million pounds of carbon monoxide. It kills trees, plants, and lawns along the freeways, and causes $25 million in annual crop damage.

How do you feel now, all you track men who just moved to Los Angeles because you like sunshine? You're lucky if you see the sun at all. I don't mean to single out California. The entire world is on an environmental collision course. Anybody who has seen much children's art knows that kids like to draw bright, cheery suns, sometimes with smiling faces. Educators recently discovered that children living on the south side of Chicago have stopped drawing suns in their pictures in the last few years. They look up at the sky and see overcast skies: smoke from the factories, steel mills, and power plants. They assume this condition is natural.

When I lived in Chicago in the early sixties, I went for long-distance runs along the lakefront with my friends. These moments now provide pleasant memories. But frequently I would return home, blow my nose, and the mucus would be black.

I now live in the Indiana dunes where the air is relatively clear. But at about the time I moved they raped the dunes south of here (despite public protests) to construct two mammoth steel plants at Burns Ditch. The big steel executives said not to worry: the plants would contain the latest in antipollution devices. Ask some of the people living near those steel plants how effective the antipollution devices are. I've run from pollution, but it is pursuing me.

When I visited Cleveland last fall, John O'Neil, former Road Runners Club president, took me on a tour of the foundry where he works. The noise was ear-shattering. The heat was intense—and this was November. The smell of urea used in one process just about made me puke. But most objectionable was the dust and dirt in the air. Outside the foundry, the lawns were littered with beer cans and broken gin bottles.

The foundry management couldn't understand why it had trouble getting people to work overtime on weekends, and blamed it on the fact that the workers were lazy. "It's a company union," John explained. "It doesn't push any harder than it has to. The attitude of the boss is that if the union demands too much, they'll shut down the shop." A sign on one wall offered a $25 bonus for anyone responsible for hiring a new employee. They paid more than that for slaves before the Civil War. Smoke belched from overhead stacks, but not as much (according to John) as at the auto foundry outside town. After a half-hour's visit here, the mucus in my nose was black—ink black!

What's that got to do with long distance running? Plenty, because we run in the environment and the environment is declining rapidly. This will continue if we don't do something to change it. Cross-country courses will disappear. Smoke and acid will eat away the forests through which we run. Cars, trucks, and buses will blast us with their noxious fumes. As road runners, we cannot run through the countryside, assuming it will be there forever. We should raise our voices along with those of conservationists and concerned citizens to demand that the polluters be stopped in their tracks.

The establishment can be challenged. It can be defeated—and you don't have to burn down a bank to succeed. In Chicago, a group known as the Committee Against Pollution (CAP) took on Commonwealth Edison, the utility responsible for roughly 16 percent of the city's dirty air. Public pressure was brought to bear on this organization and its executives. The utility was previously pressured into switching to low-sulphur coal, but this is only one step. CAP is also gathering pledges from individuals and organizations willing to cease payment of their electric bills unless the utility shows good faith in developing more effective antipollution controls. If Commonwealth Edison fails to bend, it will be ripped off. If it does bend, then CAP can proceed against the other polluters: the big steel firms, the automotive companies, the oil refineries.

The Road Runners Club should be just as concerned about ecological survival as conservation organizations such as the Sierra Club and the Izaac Walton League. We can't jog in a vacuum. Each runner should become aware of efforts in his own community to halt the polluters, and should cooperate in every way possible. The inevitable result may be that even southern California distance runners will be able to breathe clean air once more.

3

The Running Religion

by Jim Lilliefors

Seldom has a nonreligious movement been so positive in its message and "healing" abilities as running in the seventies. To many, running has become, like religion, the pursuit of salvation. Runners have religiously borrowed religious terminology to describe the effects of running. New runners proclaim they have been "saved" and "born again." Some become more religious as they grow fitter; many report a complete change of life-style.

The connection is clear, and is responsible for much of the new interest in running. Dr. George Sheehan, best-known of the new breed of running writers, went through a transformation when he returned to the activity after several decades of sedentary living. Said Sheehan, "I can't remember what those years were like before I discovered running.... I was born again in my 45th year."

The reborn gather regularly at fun-runs and road races to celebrate their discovery, their pursuit of salvation, much as other people gather at church on Sunday morning. In a questionnaire of *Runner's World* readers, many indicated that running had actually become more important to them than religion. As one runner from Georgia put it, "I find a solitary run more meaningful than going to church."

The spiritual value of running has become its most profound benefit, perhaps the element that will give it a lasting impact on society, not just a temporary fad. As Bob Anderson, publisher of *Runner's World*, recently said, "Fads and crazes hit with the frequency of waves striking a shoreline.... But because of its spiritual nature, running is a movement, a religion.

"Someone once said, 'For humanity to survive, it will have to invent a new religion.'

"The religion has been invented. It is the religion of the runner."

PRAYER

For many runners today, their running has become their prayer. It is their time of aloneness, their wish for survival and betterment, perhaps their connection with God. For them, such terms as *addiction* and *running high* aren't satisfactory descriptions of their feelings. These terms carry implications of daily fixes and negative consequences. Running isn't a "high" to them, it's a connection.

"The word addiction has an objectionable connotation," wrote Clive Greene, a runner from Yakima, Washington. "Running isn't something I *must* do." The difference is similar to that of people who go to church out of a sense of obligation, perhaps even guilt, and those who go because of true belief.

It requires practice and patience to reach the point where running becomes a form of prayer. As in meditation, negative thoughts must first be dispelled. According to San Diego psychiatrist Thaddeus Kostrubala, this may take 45 minutes or more. Sometimes it doesn't happen at all. The runner's attitude going into the run will largely determine whether he reaches this state.

When the prayer state is attained, the effects may be profound. Joanne Dignazio, a thirty-one-year-old runner from Ardmore, Pennsylvania, said, "I feel that I have come to know God through nature. When I finish running, I often find that I'm a completely different person than when I started."

Bill Warford, a Syracuse, New York, runner, said, "I get a spiritual feeling, sort of a purist feeling through running."

The prayer, the communion, may either be subtle or obviously profound. It varies with the individual, and from run to run. But if the cleansing takes place, there will be occasional peaks when prayer seems to become direct spiritual communication.

Craig D. Wandke, a runner from Chula Vista, California, described this exceptional experience: "I suddenly found myself with tears streaming down my face and felt an unbelievable powerful force of the rightness of the world and optimism for my life. I was indeed a Child of the Universe. I glanced down at my legs, which pounded the ground methodically, and I felt the rich summer air fill my lungs. My feeling lasted maybe 30 seconds, after which the tears dried and I returned to the task of moving the physical me over the soil, immeasurably richer for the brief experience that had taken place."

The value of exercise as prayer is even supported in the Bible: "Glorify God in your body" (I Corinthians 6:20); and "Even the young shall be weary; in their prime, they may stumble and fall. But they that wait upon the Lord shall mount up with wings as eagles; they shall run and not be weary, and they shall walk and not faint" (Isaiah 40:30-31).

ENLIGHTENMENT

Belief in any religion produces moments of tranquility and of exciting religious enlightenment. The enlightenment is often rooted in simplicity. Dr. Thaddeus Kostrubala explained one such experience that he had while running, based on something as basic as a seagull: "What happened was a moment of aesthetic arrest. I had a glad, flying, delightful, deep inner penetration of my mind and soul that was triggered off by that seagull."

Moments of enlightenment are often experienced even by those who don't consciously consider running a religion. In a poll of *Runner's World* readers, 50 percent claimed they experienced euphorias while running, which they would describe as "spiritual."

William Duggan, a Brooklyn, New York, runner, wrote, "The feeling while running is of great joy and omnipotence. In training, I feel I can do anything."

If a runner finally accepts running as a religion, as many have, the enlightenment will become less profound. Instead he will accept a more serious uniformity of enlightenment. The peaks will be less unique, but the cumulative effect of his devotion will be considerably more profound. The enlightenment produced by running then becomes a steady spiritual state.

Ed Muzika, a Los Angeles Zen priest, has been practicing Zen for ten years, and running for three. He compares the spiritual enlightenment of running to that experienced by meditation:

> The spiritual effects of running are the same as those experienced in meditation. At first, for a beginner, meditation is different than anything else. But both become the same after awhile.
>
> Most beginning runners and Zen students achieve this spiritual state of enlightenment only rarely. But by and by, this state becomes more and more common, until it is the usual state of mind. But, as it becomes the usual state of mind, it no longer is recognizable as a special state. Thus, experienced runners and Zen priests, monks, etc., rarely talk of spiritual "highs," because they are high all of the time.

SACRIFICE AND SALVATION

Religious philosophies differ greatly on the question of sacrifice. There are men today who annually allow spikes to be driven through them; to be, in effect, crucified. Others go to confession to establish a spiritual connection. Many more feel this is a function of church attendance.

So it is with running. Some believe that the pain of running leads to pleasure afterward; increasingly, though, this is becoming an anachronism. The new breed of runner is more like a person going to confession. It is not the pain and suffering that redeems him, but rather the excitement of spiritual connection.

Author-runner Joe Henderson is one of the prime instigators of this philosophy as it relates to running. He believes that runners who derive a sense of redemption only through the pain of their running are only gaining artificial, temporary fulfillment, and will soon tire of their self-torture. He advocates running as a lifelong commitment.

> The people who keep running are normal individuals who treat their runs as normal parts of their day. Running, in other words, is their habit. These are not ascetics who take their pleasure in self-sacrifice. Their running is a plus, not a minus. They are not masochists who take delight in pain. Like any normal person, they do what gives pleasure and avoid the painful.
>
> Look at me. I've been running for all of my adolescent and adult life. I've been through my share of pain, but never because I liked suffering. I like what goes with it. That's all. And there has been a hundred times more of "what goes with it" than pain.

It was probably inevitable that this philosophy would infiltrate running. It has become a major cultural philosophy, which grew out of the various movements of the sixties. There is now a greater emphasis on pleasure than in past decades; parents are less strict; the family is less stable; alcoholism and drug use are at all-time highs; and magazine racks are filled with sex-related magazines.

In the sixties, John Lennon, most experimental of the Beatles, dealt with this question. He described it as the underlying theme of the two books he wrote. And, in song, he observed, "They said when you were young that pain would lead to pleasure."

"That was the Catholic-Christian concept," Lennon explained in 1971. "The idea that if you're tortured, then it'll be all right. I didn't believe that, that you had to be tortured to attain anything."

During the late-seventies, Lennon has retreated from rock music and reportedly fasts and exercises regularly, including jogging.

Even competitive athletes have replaced their "do or die" philosophies with a commitment to longevity. Sixties coaching slogans such as, "It has to hurt to do any good," became archaic in the seventies. The pain of struggle for the sake of victory is no longer stressed as it once was. Workouts are less grueling than previously.

Brian Mitchell wrote of the religious nature of competitive pain in *Today's Athlete*:

> It is doubtful whether a wish for pain, or even discomfort, characterizes the athlete; he does not look upon himself as a victim brought to the altar of the track to be sacrificed in the latter stages of a race. He distinguishes the pleasure in movement from the inevitable pain that has to be endured. The athlete will not like this pain; rather he will accept it. It is an athlete's nature to savor physical movement and he knows that if he is to achieve anything competitively, he must take himself through speeds or distances that will be

uncomfortable. This he is prepared to do, training and racing. But it does not constitute "immolation." If an athlete wished to cultivate pain, he would buy himself a bed of nails.

In one sense, the new attitude toward running may be hurting top-level competitive racing. Marty Liquori said recently that the reason no high-schooler has run a 4-minute mile since he did in 1967 is because of "the proliferation of fun-running." But still, competitive times in general have improved. Many of the younger runners, who perhaps would have grown tired of the sport had they subsisted on grueling interval workouts, are now enjoying it as a lifelong activity. There is less desperate sacrifice and more deep commitment.

Self-understanding is more consciously sought after today than ever before. There is a massive rush toward what has been described as "holism." "Holism, as it relates to endurance running," explained Kenneth Doherty, former University of Pennsylvania track coach, "seeks to understand and use all of the positive influences that help a man become a better runner and at the same time to eliminate all the negative factors that might detract from his ability or stop him from running. It is as simple—and as complex—as that."

Ten years ago, few would have imagined running would evolve so far. But as Bob Anderson wrote, "Recently I was asked what religion I am. The answer came without hesitation: 'I am a runner.' "

4

In Pursuit of a Fantasy

by Cris Cusack

It all begins in fantasy. He puts his glass on the bar, turns, and is out the door before he realizes his last beer is gone. He has resolved to stop drinking—but that is not the fantasy. The fantasy is believing he can run again as he ran before.

Picture the next day. Cold air constricts his lungs and sour spirals of fluid swirl in his throat. Uphill stretches pain his limbs and shave his breath. Small rises in the road loom as great barriers and are individually conquered. He stops, exhausted. He has run 2 miles. Last year he did 20.

He rests, with too little hope to plan or imagine a plan. He reflects on his first reward, a diminutive sense of good feeling balanced exactly with the merit of his effort. He has opened the door. The light has seeped in and is brighter than the shadow in the room in which he was trapped.

Morning runs, hazel dawns, amber dews. Sunrise dreams. Plans revolve in his mind: the first sparks of aspiration. Months ago he had a pride. It had a name, a place, a time. He did 20 miles. First a slight digression, and then a neglect took it from him. He made some half-expectant returns, but none with his spirit in it. But now he was beginning anew.

He begins again with a return to the roads and an inward return to the heart. He gains color; all sounds are musical; every touch is soft, smooth, or warm. He reaches a balanced pride: a dual respect for what he has done and what he has yet to do. At night his mind turns over the images of his recent efforts and those of his brighter past. Flashes of the new and the old dance before him, each finding the other an odd reflection.

He is a long way from his goal, a small figure. The ugly hills hover over him. Fatigue weighs on his shoulders; his limbs turn taut and tender. The whole of his effort rises before him, frightening. Not just pain, torment, worry, frustration—but fear. He devises a game, a

366

ritual for running, which involves a few days of rest, in hope, anticipation, freedom, and lethargy. It is all earned, to be repeated, and to be earned again. The ritual is a gift: he puts it away today, opens it tomorrow.

Tomorrow he returns and rotates the ritual. He runs for time, for speed, for hope, for the future. He runs miles of new wonder, miles of smooth flowing motion, all with an ease, all with a magical and persistent strength, all without need for explanation or logic. That day and night exuberance flows through him, lifting him with a lightness of feeling that holds him above the ground. There's a surging in his chest, a new freedom; barriers have given way. The air is a buoyant bubble of purity; the ground is a springboard of foam; lightness is everywhere. Power thrusts beneath him, contained and returned to itself after being unleashed. Pride is there under the skin like the muscle he has gained.

He rotates the ritual. Midway between hope and calculation, he plans. He plans and dreams and works. His hopes glimmer, shine, and dazzle his ego. His mind skirts the edge of rationality as it moves beyond reason. The intangibility of success—and failure—frightens him.

He dwells on the marathon, a myth in his life, a fantasy of the past, and a haunt of the future. There's the feeling that this is the last chance. Daylight sun and heat harass his sleep; he works at night. He enters the Ocean to Bay Marathon, discovering too late that it is one of the toughest in the country. But lucky for him, he arrives too late at the starting line. He drives a few miles up the winding road, at most 6 miles, to a mountainside fire trail. He watches the climbing runners, the also-rans now struggling with less than a quarter of the course behind them. He sees the unconditioned teenagers running with football jerseys hanging from their waists; the oldsters, bearded, white-haired, robust, sweat-soaked; the women and the children, all running on, the whole troupe passing him by. He decides to join in, to attempt the last 20 miles, to give it a go. He strips; wipes Vaseline on his thighs, his feet, and his face; ties his shoes; puts a sweatband to his head; and runs off, rambling into the shadow-enclosed, hushed and secret world of the marathon.

He ran 13 miles on that mountain, up and down, stopping toward the end to retch and then to quit. But he was proud to have climbed it all without pausing, proud to have passed so many runners. They cried, coughed, cursed, and wobbled, and walked. It was nearly 90 degrees in the shade, and only two runners broke 3 hours. He failed to finish—but that was the beginning.

Today, when he runs particularly well, or when the day has been particularly beautiful, his love for it all gets the best of him. He begins again to build fanciful dreams, visions of attainments far beyond him. His heart leaps and his body anticipates. In his delirium, he envisions a great and powerful run, paced to perfection, while confronting pain to the perfect end. But it all ends in fantasy.

5

Searching for Ourselves

by John Disley

By the time he is over the top, the successful middle-distance runner has worn a deep groove in his local track and altered his personality to some extent. Life, like running, has troughs and crests, bad times and good times.

We traditionally produce fine middle-distance runners. Our milers, 3- and 6-milers, marathon runners, and steeplechasers challenge the world's best with success. We are in a good position to discover what motivates these runners to drive past mere participation into the realm of top-class competition.

Middle-distance training is like a religion; it is all a matter of belief. Somewhere in his impressionable youth, the runner hears the message; perhaps he wins an innocuous interschool race. From then on, conversion sets in; the novitiate is strengthened by every race he wins. For the rest of his career, success at a higher level is imperative; his life depends on it.

The dreadful anomaly of this condition is that, to reduce the time spent racing, training time has to be increased. To take this phenomenon to its logical conclusion, there comes a time in an athlete's career when he can't afford time off from training to race!

In certain circles, it is believed that several British and American athletes have already reached this point of no return. This condition is known in the trade as "dedication."

Just as it is logical to worship at the altar of the god that first answers your prayers, it is equally natural to pay allegiance to the training system that wins you races. Just as there are many forms of religion, there are various types of training schedules. Each one of these methods demands its own dedication. The novice, searching for a method, selects the schedule currently in fashion with the top runners. He lives by this gospel for at least a season. Then, if he doesn't find the appropriate one, he moves on to an alternative form of torture.

This procedure continues for several seasons until the athlete finally hits form. His name appears in one-inch letters on the back pages of newspapers when he wins—two inches when he loses. Success arrives despite all the changes of systems; it comes as a direct result of four or five years of unremitting hard work. For the common factor of all the training methods is pain.

The athlete's head is filled with loud, undiminishing echoes of the words—*faster* and *more*. He cannot escape from the tendency to overload.

What is it that drives the middle-distance runner through the long hours of compulsive training? I suppose a good psychologist could pinpoint the phase when the athlete turns aside from pure recreation and natural enjoyment. The reasons why he chose the path he did could also be found.

To understand the motivations, here are a few observations on some of the more traditional reasons for wanting to run and race.

Run to be fit and healthy. This will raise a hollow laugh from the champion. Any international athlete worth his salt has a long medical case-history. He can easily hold his own with a neurotic in any other field. The fitter he gets, the more he feels the slightest wobble in his physical equilibrium. Health is a phase that one passes through on the way to athletic fitness. My own doctor told me that I looked fit and well on the very morning of my disastrous intercountry race earlier this year. I knew then that the afternoon was doomed.

An athlete, when racing fit, feels and looks ill—wan and drawn. He has heard the worst in his doctor's consulting room several times before the crux of the season even arrives. He has been convinced that he is the victim of such diseases as tuberculosis, Parkinson's, endemic migraine, or systolic valve enlargement.

The team spirit ideal makes the runner want to give his best. The athlete is so concerned with his personal compulsive adjustments that he hasn't time to worry about esprit de corps. I make a point of shaking hands with my opponents before races. I wish everyone luck with the unspoken proviso that I hope they won't beat me.

The top athlete is prepared to give his teammates encouragement during the race—first as he laps them and then later on from the side of the track after he has finished.

By his nature, the runner is a lonely individual. He doesn't want to be in a group; he wants to be ahead of the group. Coming in first is the basis of his life. He tries not to let anything pass him and stay in front. His whole life is an extension of his athletics.

It is this awareness that indicates the champion. Unfortunately, it often resembles selfishness. Coaches may try to correct this trend, and if they succeed another "natural" is spoiled.

Runners run because it is great recreation. Well, it could be, but not at the top. Training is an occupational obsession, akin to eating and sleeping. It must be part of every day for the day to be complete. Sooner or later, the runner finds that his life is becoming a withdrawal from all the things that interfere with training. This is no hobby; it is a way of life. Every day is so arranged that work, sleep, and meals revolve around this "hour or two of truth."

Most athletic-club social secretaries cry themselves to sleep at night. The dedicated athlete requires little from his club except entrance into the right races. It is this lack of gregariousness that makes the average club exist only on notepaper and in the title on a program. This is not an indictment of the athletic club, but rather the logical condition of any organization that serves such self-confident individuals.

Runners are trying to prove something. Here we could be on to something. It is fairly certain that the runner is trying to prove himself superior. He usually tries so hard that it is obvious he is driven on by a strong inferiority complex. It is significant that many champion athletes suffer from this disability. Handicaps other than physical are more difficult to observe, but are still very real.

Research into the early life of our top athletes will probably prove that they were all polio victims, unloved baby brothers, failures at eleven, or born on the wrong side of the tracks. Professor Soki has written a book dealing neurologically with three Olympic champions who were physically afflicted. It is debatable how much their physical handicaps induced exceptional mental determination. But there is a balancing of body and mind. It would appear that there is overcompensation in most cases.

Now to whom is the athlete trying to prove himself? In my own case, I found it difficult to find anyone who was enthusiastic about my best performance. Even my mountaineering friends—participants in one of the world's most unjustifiable sports—failed to see the logic in scrambling around one mile 1,426 yards of cinder dotted with road barriers and wedge-shaped ditches. In fact, only my fellow track nuts seemed to be interested.

This lack of impressionable material leads to the conclusion that the runner is running to prove something to himself. That should give the psychologists something to think about.

APPENDIX

Race Contacts

Organized running can be broken into five major classifications: AAU events, RRCA events, fun-runs, running clubs, and school events. Since the last category is exclusively for members of high school and college teams, we'll deal only with the other four. Each of them offers opportunities for the beginning racer. The first three are listed in descending order, from most competitive (and formal) to least competitive, although any runner can compete in any of these.

1. *Amateur Athletic Union.* The AAU sponsors frequent track events and a full series of national championships, from cross-country to the ultramarathons. Runners must secure an AAU card as a prerequisite for competing in an AAU event. These, however, can be obtained at any AAU-sponsored race. Major AAU events are featured each month in the "Coming Events" column in *Runner's World.*

It is, however, more practical to join before the race, since many events have entry deadlines, and some have age or time restrictions. Yearly AAU dues are generally $4, with an additional fee, usually less than $3, charged for individual competitions.

The following are major AAU contacts in the United States:

- New York Road Runner's Club of America, Box 881, FDR Station, New York, NY 10022; (212) 595-3389
- Pacific AAU Office, 942 Market St., Suite 201, San Francisco, CA 94102; (415) 986-6725
- AAU House, 3400 W. 86th St., Indianapolis, IN 46268; (317) 297-2900
- Southern Pacific AAU, 10911 Riverside Drive, North Hollywood, CA 91603; (213) 877-0256

2. *Road Runners Club of America.* The RRCA chapters sponsor a variety of distance runs on a regular basis (often weekly). These are less formal than AAU races, and generally less expensive to enter.

The RRCA charges an annual membership fee (for which the runner receives a regular club bulletin), and then a small fee of as little as a quarter at each event. Nonmembers are allowed to enter the events, but may be charged an entry fee closer to $2 (which automatically makes them members).

The national president of the RRCA is Jeff Darman, 2737 Devonshire Pl. NW, Washington, DC 20008.

3. *Fun-runs.* These are low-key, regularly scheduled running events, usually featuring three runs, ranging from 440 yards to 6 miles. No entry fee is charged, no official results are tabulated, and runners of all abilities participate. Times are given and certificates are available based on times. The sites are listed each month in *Runner's World.* Anyone is welcome to run in a fun-run. For information on starting or participating in the program, write *Runner's World* Fun-Run, Box 366, Mountain View, CA 94042.

4. *Clubs.* There are currently thousands of running clubs in the U.S., ranging from two- or three-person jogging groups to large organizations for world-class competitors. Clubs are often harder to locate than the previous three types of organized events, but can usually be found by contacting the sponsors of those three.

For all levels of running, there are books that can be of enormous help. These are the major ones, covering most aspects of running, training, and racing.

- *Beginner's Running Guide*, by Hal Higdon. Everything the beginner would want to know about running is covered in this book, from diet to training methods. 1978.
- *The Complete Marathoner*, edited by Joe Henderson. The only comprehensive book about marathoning, including training advice for beginners and advanced runners, profiles of the top marathoners, and a history of the event. 1978.
- *The Complete Runner*, by the editors of *Runner's World.* This book covers the full spectrum of running, including philosophy, medicine, training, diet, and racing. 1974.
- *George Sheehan's Medical Advice for Runners*, by George Sheehan, M.D. The most practical and complete medical reference text prepared exclusively for runners. 1978.
- *Jog, Run, Race*, by Joe Henderson. In 33 lessons, the author takes you from a beginner to a competitive racer, including day-by-day training problems. 1977.

- *Runner's Training Guide,* by the editors of *Runner's World.* All of the major training ideas are explained and discussed, including the physiological principles behind them. 1973.
- *Running the Lydiard Way,* by Arthur Lydiard with Garth Gilmour. The former New Zealand Olympic coach outlines his pioneering training program for all levels of runners. 1978.
- *Women's Running,* by Joan Ullyot, M.D. Complete training advice and practical suggestions covering all aspects of women's running from a marathoner and M.D. 1976.

Pacing Charts

Proper pacing is a vital part of distance racing. Here is a handy reference chart showing what the track distance times mean in terms of pace per quarter-mile. For instance, it not only tells what the average pace per quarter would be in a 30-minute 6-mile race (75 seconds, or 1:15), but also what even pacing would be for the miles en route.

1-6 MILE PACING CHART

440	1 Mile	2 Miles	3 Miles	4 Miles	5 Miles	6 Miles
:57	3:48					
:58	3:52					
:59	3:56					
1:00	4:00					
1:01	4:04					
1:02	4:08	8:16				
1:03	4:12	8:24				
1:04	4:16	8:32	12:48	17:04		
1:05	4:20	8:40	13:00	17:20		
1:06	4:24	8:48	13:12	17:36	22:00	26:24
1:07	4:28	8:56	13:24	17:52	22:20	26:48
1:08	4:32	9:04	13:36	18:08	22:40	27:12
1:09	4:36	9:12	13:48	18:24	23:00	27:36
1:10	4:40	9:20	14:00	18:40	23:20	28:00
1:11	4:44	9:28	14:12	18:56	23:40	28:24
1:12	4:48	9:36	14:24	19:12	24:00	28:48
1:13	4:52	9:44	14:36	19:28	24:20	29:12
1:14	4:56	9:52	14:48	19:44	24:40	29:36
1:15	5:00	10:00	15:00	20:00	25:00	30:00
1:16	5:04	10:08	15:12	20:16	25:20	30:24
1:17	5:08	10:16	15:24	20:32	25:40	30:48
1:18	5:12	10:24	15:36	20:48	26:00	31:12
1:19	5:16	10:32	15:48	21:04	26:20	31:36
1:20	5:20	10:40	16:00	21:20	26:40	32:00
1:21	5:24	10:48	16:12	21:36	27:00	32:24
1:22	5:28	10:56	16:24	21:52	27:20	32:48
1:23	5:32	11:04	16:36	22:08	27:40	33:12
1:24	5:36	11:12	16:48	22:24	28:00	33:36
1:25	5:40	11:20	17:00	22:40	28:20	34:00
1:26	5:44	11:28	17:12	22:56	28:40	34:24
1:27	5:48	11:36	17:24	23:12	29:00	34:48
1:28	5:52	11:44	17:36	23:28	29:20	35:12
1:29	5:56	11:52	17:48	23:44	29:40	35:36

1-6 MILE PACING CHART (continued)

440	1 Mile	2 Miles	3 Miles	4 Miles	5 Miles	6 Miles
1:30	6:00	12:00	18:00	24:00	30:00	36:00
1:31	6:04	12:08	18:12	24:16	30:20	36:24
1:32	6:08	12:16	18:24	24:32	30:40	36:48
1:33	6:12	12:24	18:36	24:48	31:00	37:12
1:34	6:16	12:32	18:48	25:04	31:20	37:36
1:35	6:20	12:40	19:00	25:20	31:40	38:00
1:36	6:24	12:48	19:12	25:36	32:00	38:24
1:37	6:28	12:56	19:24	25:52	32:20	38:48
1:38	6:32	13:04	19:36	26:08	32:40	39:12
1:39	6:36	13:12	19:48	26:24	33:00	39:36
1:40	6:40	13:20	20:00	26:40	33:20	40:00
1:41	6:44	13:28	20:12	26:56	33:40	40:24
1:42	6:48	13:36	20:24	27:12	34:00	40:48
1:43	6:52	13:44	20:36	27:28	34:20	41:12
1:44	6:56	13:52	20:48	27:44	34:40	41:36
1:45	7:00	14:00	21:00	28:00	35:00	42:00

The One-Hour Pacing Chart gives per-mile pace for the 1-hour run: if a runner covers 10 miles, he averages 6 minutes per mile.

ONE-HOUR PACING CHART

Distance	Per Mile	Distance	Per Mile	Distance	Per Mile
6 miles	10:00.00	8 miles	7:30.00	10 miles	6:00.00
6¼ miles	9:36:00	8¼ miles	7:16.32	10¼ miles	5:51.24
6½ miles	9:13.32	8½ miles	7:03.44	10½ miles	5:42.84
6¾ miles	8:53.28	8¾ miles	6:51.42	10¾ miles	5:34.80
7 miles	8:35:46	9 miles	6:40.00	11 miles	5:27.24
7¼ miles	8:16.50	9¼ miles	6:29.16	11¼ miles	5:20.00
7½ miles	8:00.00	9½ miles	6:19.02	11½ miles	5:13.08
7¾ miles	7:44.50	9¾ miles	6:09.24	11¾ miles	5:06.20

Distance	Per Mile
12 miles	5:00.00
12¼ miles	4:53.88
12½ miles	4:48.00
12¾ miles	4:42.36
13 miles	4:36.90

This chart is similar to the one on page 376, except that it concentrates on the most common long distances and is based on average pace per mile. For instance, a 3:03:33 marathon is run at a 7-minute mile pace.

5-50 MILE PACING CHARTS

1 Mile	5 Miles	10 Miles	15 Miles	20 Miles	Marathon	50 Miles
4:50	24:10	48:20	1:12:30	1:36:40	2:07:44	
5:00	25:00	50:00	1:15:00	1:40:00	2:11:06	
5:10	25:50	51:40	1:17:30	1:43:20	2:15:28	
5:20	26:40	53:20	1:20:00	1:46:50	2:19:50	
5:30	27:30	55:00	1:22:30	1:50:00	2:24:12	
5:40	28:20	56:40	1:25:00	1:53:20	2:28:34	
5:50	29:10	58:20	1:27:30	1:56:40	2:32:56	
6:00	30:00	1:00:00	1:30:00	2:00:00	2:37:19	5:00:00
6:10	30:50	1:01:40	1:32:30	2:03:20	2:41:41	5:08:20
6:20	31:40	1:03:20	1:35:00	2:06:40	2:46:03	5:16:40
6:30	32:30	1:05:00	1:37:30	2:10:00	2:50:25	5:25:00
6:40	33:20	1:06:40	1:40:00	2:13:20	2:54:47	5:33:20
6:50	34:10	1:08:20	1:42:30	2:16:40	2:59:09	5:41:40
7:00	35:00	1:10:00	1:45:00	2:20:00	3:03:33	5:50:00
7:10	35:00	1:11:40	1:47:30	2:23:20	3:07:55	5:58:20
7:20	36:40	1:13:20	1:50:00	2:26:40	3:12:17	6:06:40
7:30	37:30	1:15:00	1:52:30	2:30:00	3:16:39	6:15:00
7:40	38:20	1:16:40	1:55:00	2:33:20	3:21:01	6:23:20
7:50	39:10	1:18:20	1:57:30	2:36:40	3:25:23	6:31:40
8:00	40:00	1:20:00	2:00:00	2:40:00	3:29:45	6:40:00
8:10	40:50	1:21:40	2:02:30	2:43:20	3:34:07	6:48:20
8:20	41:40	1:23:20	2:05:00	2:46:40	3:38:29	6:56:40
8:30	42:30	1:25:00	2:07:30	2:50:00	3:42:51	7:05:00
8:40	43:20	1:26:40	2:10:00	2:53:20	3:47:13	7:13:20
8:50	44:10	1:28:20	2:12:30	2:56:40	3:51:35	7:21:40
9:00	45:00	1:30:00	2:15:00	3:00:00	3:56:00	7:30:00
9:10	45:50	1:31:40	2:17:30	3:03:20	4:00:22	7:38:20
9:20	46:40	1:33:20	2:20:00	3:06:40	4:04:44	7:46:40
9:30	47:39	1:35:00	2:22:30	3:10:00	4:09:06	7:55:00
9:40	48:20	1:36:40	2:25:00	3:13:20	4:13:28	8:03:20
9:50	49:10	1:38:20	2:27:30	3:16:40	4:17:50	8:11:40
10:00	50:00	1:40:00	2:30:00	3:20:00	4:22:13	8:20:00

Contributors

Bob Anderson is publisher of numerous books and magazines, including *Runner's World.*

Tom Bassler is a pathologist from Los Angeles. He's a frequent contributor to *Runner's World.*

Jonathan Brower is a runner and freelance writer.

Amby Burfoot, winner of the 1968 Boston Marathon, is East Coast editor of *Runner's World.*

Bob Carman is a veteran marathoner and ultramarathoner.

Brian Chapman is a runner, coach, and freelance writer.

Carolyn Clarke is a freelance writer and runner.

Ron Clarke, of Australia, held numerous world records during the 1960s.

Jean Colvin is a freelance writer and runner from Wisconsin.

Ted Corbitt is a former Olympic marathoner and veteran ultramarathoner.

Harry Cordellos, a blind runner from San Francisco, is a sub-three-hour marathoner.

David Costill, Ph.D., directs the Human Performance Laboratory at Ball State University, Muncie, Indiana. He's author of *What Research Tells the Coach About Distance Running.*

Cris Cusack is a runner and freelance writer.

John Disley, of England, is a former Olympic steeplechaser.

Jay Dirksen, a 2:21 marathoner, is track coach at South Dakota State University.

Jack Galub is a freelance writer from New York City, a runner, and a frequent contributor to running publications.

Frances Sheridan Goulart is author of four natural foods cookbooks and is founder of the nation's only year-round natural foods cooking school.

John Hamburger is senior book editor at World Publications. He was the compiling editor of the *Cross-Country Skiing Guide.*

Joe Henderson is the author of several running books including *Jog, Run, Race,* and is consulting editor of *Runner's World.*

Hal Higdon is the author of 18 books, many on running. He's also a gold medal winner at the World Masters' competition.

Ron Hill, a 2:09 marathoner, at age 40 is still among the best distance runners in the world.

Ray Hosler, a marathoner from Colorado, is currently on the editorial staff of *On the Run.*

Tom Jordan, assistant publisher of *Track and Field News*, is author of the book, *Pre!*

O. Karikosk is an Estonian coach and runner.

John Kelley won the Boston marathon twice, in 1935 and 1945, and has run it every year since 1932, except for 1968.

Paul Kiell, M.D., is a runner who has written several articles about running and medicine.

Arnd Kruger is a runner and freelance writer.

Jim Lilliefors is a freelance writer and runner. He is the author of *The Running Mind* and *Inner Running.*

James Marlin is a student of Zen, a runner, and a songwriter from Hollywood, California.

Paul Milvy, M.D., has done a number of studies on the physiology of running, and has reported the results in his frequent contributions to *Runner's World.*

Don Monkerud is a freelance writer from Watsonville, California. He frequently writes about running and diet.

Doug Rennie is a freelance writer and runner.

Lee Rodin, a freelance writer from Chicago, has written several articles for the *Chicago Tribune.*

George Sheehan, M.D., a cardiologist from Red Bank, New Jersey, is medical editor of *Runner's World* and author of three books, including *Running and Being.*

Mike Spino, a writer and runner, authored *Beyond Jogging* and *Running Home.*

Henry Uhrig, M.D., is a colonel in the U.S. Army medical corps and a runner.

Jane Underhill is a runner and freelance writer.

Nell Weaver is a runner and freelance writer from Arkansas.

Peter Whitis, M.D., is a runner and psychiatrist from Iowa.

Denis Wright is a leading British sports physiotherapist and a runner and writer.

RECOMMENDED READING